D1139746

The Canadian
Social Inheritance

Jack A. Blyth

The Copp Clark Publishing Company

Toronto   Montreal   Vancouver

cover design by Ted Michener

© The Copp Clark Publishing Company 1972.
Printed and bound in Canada.

All rights reserved. No part of the material covered by this
copyright may be reproduced in any form or by any means
(whether electronic, mechanical or photographic) for storage
in retrieval systems, tapes, discs or for making multiple copies
without the written permission of The Copp Clark Publishing
Company.

International Standard Book Number 0-7730-3117-0

*. . . it is always possible, in spite
of appearances, that the age we live in
is not worse than the other ages
that have preceded it,
nor perhaps even greatly different.*

George Orwell,
In Front of Your Nose

Contents

Illustrations

Preface

The writing of a survey work on social history inevitably requires the co-operation of many individuals, and I would like to record my sincere appreciation to them.

My thanks go to Dr. A.P. Thornton of the University of Toronto and Dr. T. Tanner of Algonquin College who read the initial manuscript and offered constructive advice. I want to express my appreciation to my colleagues at Sheridan College who assisted in many ways; in particular, I am grateful for the professional advice of Art Director Frank Miller and of Colonel Craig McFarlane (Ret'd), who commented on Chapter 8. Above all, I wish to thank my editor, Mrs. Ruth Russell of the Copp Clark Publishing Company, for her clear guidance, patient understanding and expert supervision.

The unfailing courtesy and help of numerous other people is acknowledged. I hope this collective thank you will let them know that their responses to my questions and requests are appreciated. Finally, on a personal level, my wife deserves honourable mention for great forbearance, and for effectively training our children to "leave Daddy alone while he writes his book."

This book was written as a part-time project over a two-year period and grew out of my conviction that a study of our social inheritance has intrinsic value. The theme of this study is limited to the development of certain aspects of Canada's social inheritance that are related to immigrants; that is, the contributions of Canada's native peoples, the Indian and Eskimo, are so important that they are worthy of discussion by another author who possesses more adequate knowledge of their social milieu and customs. The present volume concerns principally the development and export of British social ideas, and the changing forms of these ideas in the multicultural contexts of Canada and the United States.

Some readers may feel that the presentation in this book is apt to concentrate on seeing society from the bottom: from the point of view of the governed rather than the governors. If so, the perspective accords with an observation of Stephen Leacock that people who live in castles do not emigrate. The emphasis in this book is upon the problems faced by ordinary men and women rather than the difficulties of kings and statesmen.

On social issues there can be no definitive study. Like the writer of any historical study, I can only claim to have presented one interpretation of the events described. But if this book helps to shed some light on Canada's social inheritance, then the attempt to explore this subject will have been well worthwhile.

J.A. Blyth

Introduction

[Canadian history is largely] a trackless jungle of which Americans know nothing and which is incomprehensible to nearly every Englishman.

A.R.M. Lower, *Canada: Nation and Neighbour*

This study is an attempt to cut a few trails through the jungle of Canadian history in order to examine certain social issues that have vitally affected the collective development of Canada, the United States and Great Britain. This study is not, therefore, a constitutional history of these three nations. Canadian history has long suffered from a tendency to emphasize the memorizing of neat little Acts of Parliament and the like with the result that, as some students stated, "even the teachers seem to be as bored as we are."[1] This approach reflects the preoccupation of our historians with seeking or creating an elusive ideal called national unity. Comparatively little, however, has been written about the roots of our Canadian social inheritance.

Many generations have tried to grapple with such fundamental issues as poverty, slums, economic insecurity, religious and political apathy, and the need to update educational ideas. Social history is a continuous process, and a study of past attempts to resolve social problems provides a frame of reference for assessing our present situation. A

1

long-standing problem such as air and water pollution has undoubtedly intensified in recent years and may require a vigorous solution, yet we should first ask ourselves how earlier generations tackled pollution problems; for example, our modern sources of power are much cleaner than such relatively dirty fuels as coal. A student who familiarizes himself with the past record of social reform gains the opportunity to formulate his own social philosophy. Today's student is very much aware of social issues but, like the family doctor, he needs the history of the disease to aid him in drawing his own conclusions and deciding upon the necessary treatment.

This book focuses upon what has been termed the North Atlantic Triangle. Two expatriate Canadian scholars who moved from the Canadian to the American point of the triangle, J.B. Brebner and N.S.B. Gras, developed the metropolitan concept that the great cities of Britain and North America were linked by the economic exchange of goods and services as well as by the migration of people. In this setting, London and New York have historically exerted economic and cultural influences upon Montreal and Toronto; a further set of forces entered into the operation of this North Atlantic Triangle when Canada joined the other two nations as a modern urbanized community. Rapid technological advancement capable, for example, of producing atomic weapons, has made political maps sometimes obsolete, and the question of social issues seems more relevant today to many people than that of political nationalism. The growth of the multi-national corporation, employing people on both sides of the Atlantic, has helped to produce an awareness of our interdependence in such areas as jobs and social security. Executives involved in international finance may well endorse E.P. Taylor's view, "Canadian nationalism! How old-fashioned can you get?"[2] The onrush of industrial and urban development in Canada, Britain and the United States has created an international megalopolis which is a segment of an even larger industrialized world. For the first time the citizens of many of the western industrial nations are beginning to acknowledge their common humanity, as exhibited by the formation of the European Community, and devote their energies to common social problems.

Canada has experienced since the end of World War II a population explosion in her major cities similar to that of American and British cities. According to the 1941 Canadian Census, there were approximately 1.5 million people residing in the twin metropolises of Montreal and Toronto; in 1971 this total had tripled to approximately 4.5 million persons. And, furthermore, the end of this process of continuously expanding concentrations of industry and people is not yet in sight. Toronto itself is merely the core of a dense conurbation stretching from Oshawa to Hamilton, along the shore of Lake Ontario; British Columbia seems to be increasingly represented by the population of the Vancouver-Victoria region. The problems produced by such urban concentrations are similar to those in the Northeast United States or the Midlands of Britain; for example, Hamilton, Ontario has similar industrial problems to Sheffield, England, or Pittsburgh, U.S.A. Smoke tastes dirty to the inhabitants of all of these cities and a desire to have full employment is a common aspiration for the workers of all three countries.

There has, of course, always been an exchange of ideas within the North Atlantic community, although the degree to which social ideas have been transplanted and accepted has varied. After 1945, Britain committed herself to the formation of the welfare state. In the United States, the idea of a "socialist state" was energetically resisted by articulate spokesmen like William K. Buckley and Barry Goldwater, and apparently with some success: according to government statistics, in 1939 the Congressional fiscal budget allocated 44% of the revenue to labour and welfare programs; by 1963, the allocation for these items had dropped to 7%.[3] It would seem, therefore, a point of conjecture to determine whether the much-criticized monster of "creeping socialism" is advancing or retreating. A War on Poverty was declared by both Canada and the United States in the 1960's, but no victory parades have yet been scheduled.

Paradoxically, though, this generation is the first to live in a society that is generally described, with a large measure of truth, as affluent. Our position as members of this affluent society conditions our perspective on the specific social problems discussed in this book. Yet most of us today may be standing on a pinnacle from which we have nowhere to go but down—down to a future where we witness interplanetary flight while standing ankle-deep in garbage, or down to a past in which the following scene was recorded in Chicago less than 40 years ago: "We saw a crowd of some fifty men fighting over a barrel of garbage which had been set outside the back of a restaurant. American citizens fighting for scraps of food like animals."[4] If it is true that those who do not remember the past are compelled to relive it, a study of past solutions to vital social problems may be imperative.

The response of politicians to social problems is inevitably conditioned, often for the worse, by the electorate's resentment of the high taxation necessary to pay for programs of social welfare, and by that electorate's preference for private rather than public goods. Politicians do respond to social pressures, however, and their responses of the past provide interesting comparative studies in social history. A leading example is the spread of legislation passed by Parliament in England, the Poor Law of 1601 and the complementary Act of 1603. In the United States of 1972 the "general assistance provisions in the laws of many states retain much of the language of the law of 1603"[5] which had been carried across the Atlantic. Nova Scotia also adopted the Tudor Poor Law legislation, while Upper Canada specifically refused to adopt this particular social facet of British law. Seen from the point of view of social history, this example may indicate that the usual emphasis on revolutions and specific nationalistic loyalties has obscured the basic social inheritance common to all members of the North Atlantic Triangle.

The unsophisticated minds of children see our world quite clearly, and they can appreciate the directness of the story of Robin Hood. In this ageless story, Robin Hood sees poor people being exploited by rich people. Let us hope that educational television never depicts Robin taking a modern, adult and conceptual view of the "socially deprived" or "culturally underprivileged" and beginning by establishing a Labour Relations Committee to study the situation. Meanwhile another committee of Robin's merry men, under the chairmanship of Friar Tuck, would, in this updated version, investigate social mobility around Nottingham. A Sherwood Research project would be established, with suitable advisory experts to be contacted by Little John's co-ordinating committee. Other committee work would doubtless be needed before a meaningful dialogue could commence on establishing an agenda of items to be discussed before sending in a brief to the Sheriff of Nottingham. Much later the Hood Report could be taken under advisement. If this imaginary scene is enacted, it is likely that some child will ask "When is Robin going to do something?" Sadly some adult will have to explain that social action will have to be kept pending while the situation is kept under continuous study.

The point is not that reform comes slowly, but rather that the aspirations of youth do not usually coincide with the responsibility and power required to redress social problems. Yet the really interesting aspect of social history is that the problems are familiar ones, affecting daily life. The themes with which this book deals are vast areas for exploration. As an introductory survey, it inevitably neglects some aspects of certain areas; it should be considered as a general reconnaissance of the landscape which will, hopefully, encourage a student to pursue in depth an aspect of social history that appeals to him. The book is written for students to read, rather than to "play the all-too-common academic game of writing only for . . . peers and of pretending detachment and neutrality."[6] At the end of this book a suggested list of further readings is provided to encourage investigation: these sources are usually in addition to those mentioned in the footnotes.

1. A.B. Hodgetts, *What Culture? What Heritage?* (Toronto: Ontario Institute for Studies in Education, 1968), p. 108.
2. G.M. Grant, *Lament for a Nation* (Toronto: McClelland and Stewart, 1965), p. 42.
3. F. Krinsky and J. Boskin, *The Welfare State* (Toronto: Collier MacMillan Canada Ltd., 1968), p. 26.
4. Louise Armstrong, *We Too Are The People* (Boston: Little Brown and Co., 1938), p. 10.
5. Krinsky and Boskin, *The Welfare State,* p. 26.
6. K. Levitt, *Silent Surrender* (Toronto: MacMillan of Canada Ltd., 1970), p. ix. The statement is contained in the preface written by Professor Melville H. Watkins.

1

Poverty

O let us love our occupations,
Bless the squire and his relations,
Live upon our daily rations,
And always know our proper stations.

Charles Dickens

At the beginning of man's history, all men were poor, and spent their lives in a basic struggle to obtain the necessities of life; only when certain men came to possess more goods and power than others did poverty become a definable condition. Even then it was often accepted as an inevitable state, part of a large plan which included the rich and the poor in a necessary pattern; this point of view seemed to be sanctioned by many religions, including the early Christian Church. But seeing poverty as largely a result of economic factors is seeing it as a soluble problem, and it is in this light that politicians have been tackling it for over six hundred years.

IN FEUDAL TIMES

In medieval England, the concept of feudalism gave every class its rights and responsibilities, with each of the three estates (nobles, priests, and lower orders) playing its role as predetermined by God. The epidemic known as the Black

Death had wiped out one-third of the labouring force and a demand for increased wages was anticipated. Parliament decided that labourers had to accept employment in their own parish so that they could not bargain for higher wages elsewhere, and in 1351, Parliament passed the Statute of Labourers in an attempt to maintain the social status quo. Then, having exerted control over the labour market, Parliament apparently felt that wages would be stabilized. Now the burden of taxation could be shifted onto the backs of this economically static peasantry, with a poll tax to be collected from all men over fifteen years of age.

In 1381, Wat Tyler was sufficiently aroused by the hardships caused by the Statute to lead a Peasants' Revolt. After lynching some landlords—including the Archbishop of Canterbury—and burning farms and houses, Wat Tyler discovered, as did the American Negro in the 1960's, that men of wealth begin to take grievances seriously if they threaten property rights. Wat Tyler also employed this early commercial jingle to advertise his cause:

When Adam delved and Eve span
Who was then the gentleman?

Such a slogan has an ageless appeal to the propertyless and poverty-stricken. Yet Wat Tyler, while causing a temporary panic as he led a mob in a march on London, had not really allowed for the recuperative powers of the nobility. In the confusion, the wealthy recovered their wits and Wat Tyler was knifed by the Mayor of London.

At this time, the primary responsibility for alleviation of poverty rested with the Church. Religious foundations such as the monasteries and almshouses, founded by benefactors, supplemented the charity supplied by the local parish church. Generally speaking, although the attitude of the church was paternalistic towards the poor, it was an article of faith that the poor would receive their real reward in heaven, so that one needn't worry too much about rewarding them on earth. And, in the secular view, the poor were a nuisance, and treated accordingly.

The pattern of feudalism in France was generally similar

to that in Great Britain but it lasted much longer, and eventually travelled across the Atlantic to New France where it became diluted into the unique pattern of seigneurialism, a secure social mould. The poor of New France received official attention in 1688, when the Sovereign Council took action to help those who sought charity. In each town a Bureau des Pauvres (Office of the Poor) was established and presided over by the curé. Thus the priest became the first welfare officer in North America, making enquiries about the needs of the poor, and placing orphans into apprenticeship. In addition, nuns from the Hôpital-Général of Montreal helped to take care of invalids and old people.

THE REFORMATION

In England, after Henry VIII had finished his argument with the Pope, he found that he was forced to become an early proponent of the welfare state through providing public relief. Since dissolution of the monasteries in 1536 had caused the major source of charity virtually to disappear, Parliament enacted a Relief of the Poor Statute which made use of the Justices of the Peace as an administrative corps, to investigate the claims of the aged and paupers. This formation of an unpaid civil service implied that the state now accepted a responsibility for helping the poor.

In spite of this Statute, methods for helping the poor did not change very much. The traditional religious attitude, later reinforced by Calvinist ideas, held that God punished the poor for hidden sins, which in turn implied that it was wrong to go against God's will. The pauper, caught in a period of religious, social and economic upheaval, received little sympathy. Whipping of "sturdy beggars" was frequently carried out. In this brutal age, it was not felt unreasonable to identify a beggar by cutting off the gristle of the man's right ear.

Yet social legislation on behalf of the poor was a feature of the Tudor Age. In 1536, the "impotent poor" were relieved of making voluntary contributions to church collections. The parish of a single church was established as the smallest unit of administration, with each parish being responsible for its own poor. Under Elizabeth I, the voluntary giving for the relief of the poor in the parish was changed to direct compulsion. Each householder had to contribute to the church rates and the property of uncooperative householders was seized. Churchwardens and householders were appointed as overseers of the poor by Justices of the Peace. Parliamentary provision was made for almshouses to be erected for the old, blind and lame. The standard of care would vary according to the affluence and conscience of each parish.

All of this legislation was integrated in the famous Elizabethan Poor Law of 1601, which is the bedrock of the modern welfare state in both England and the United States. Under the Elizabethan Poor Law, different types of poor people were distinguished. "Sturdy beggars" were to be sent to the "houses of correction." The "impotent poor," such as the sick, blind and lame, were to go to almshouses, for this was felt to be more humane than haphazard boarding with individual householders. If they stayed in their own home, the impotent poor received "outdoor relief." Orphans were to be given to any citizen willing to support them. Accompanying all these provisions was a general desire to limit costs to a minimum. Keeping down the poor rate was regarded with the same type of evangelical fervour that, in our age, accompanies the silent prayers that income tax will not be increased.

EXPANSION TO NORTH AMERICA

The English legislation of the Parliament of 1601 assumed that the central government had authority to make binding rules with respect to social welfare. On the other side of the Atlantic, the colonial governments assumed this authority. The same broad principles were adopted in America, yet in the pioneering North American environment, the problem of poverty was seen mainly in terms of a "help thy neighbour" policy. Each community supplied outdoor relief in food, clothing, firewood and household necessities. Also following the traditions established in England, transients were often "warned-out," that is, ordered to leave the community.

Rogues or vagabonds were whipped or confined to the town jail. These practices were conducted in an effort to spare the citizens of the colony any taxes for poor relief. Alternatively, another method of taking care òf the "town poor" was to farm out the paupers to the lowest bidder. Most smaller towns auctioned off their poor to the residents who offered to take the lowest amount to cover food, clothing, and shelter. Contractors were apt to skimp on necessities, to take full advantage of this source of cheap labour.

When New Englanders moved into Nova Scotia, they took with them the concept of putting up the poor for public auction. In fact, the law was not amended until 1900 when the doctrine was established that, "The overseers shall not provide for the maintenance of the poor by putting up the same at public auction." This reference to overseers refers also to the fact that in 1763 Nova Scotia had copied the Elizabethan Poor Law, with its provision for poorhouses, although the unit of administration was the township, rather than the British parish, and the overseers were appointed at township meetings.

Life in the workhouse was far from pleasant. In the Halifax workhouse, or Bridewell,as it was termed, there were "for many years, whipping, shackling, starvation, and other necessary inducements which served to correct the behaviour of the idle, vagrant or incorrigible inmates."[1] New Brunswick, populated by the Loyalist migration which followed the American revolution, also adopted the general framework of the Elizabethan Poor Law. Only a few large cities in the Colonies established houses of correction or almshouses. Not until the nineteenth century did the almshouse become really common in the United States, when investigations in Massachusetts and New York in the 1820's revealed that more efficiency, at less cost, could be obtained by institutional care. Underlying this reluctance to build establishments for the poor lay the need to accumulate capital. England had a long lead in amassing social capital in the form of legacies, endowments and bequests that supported the poor in hospitals, asylums and orphanages. In North America, however, private charities played an insignificant role until the nineteenth century.

10

Although institutions were set up to provide for the poor, there was little encouragement for them to help themselves. The Restoration of Charles II had seen another basic piece of social legislation, the Law of Settlement of 1662 which, like the earlier Statute of Labourers, sought to restrict the movement of poor people, by in effect binding them to the situation which helped to cause their poverty. Especially important was the objective of preventing a poor person from entering another parish, where he might become a public charge. But where such low moral characters as "disorderly persons or unmarried pregnant women" could be clearly identified, they could be "expelled immediately" from a parish. Overseers had forty days to investigate any newcomer whose rent was under £10 yearly and who might become a public charge. Frequently overseers gave bribes to borderline cases to persuade them to move on to another parish.

Like the earlier Elizabethan Poor Law, this legislation concerning settlement was transmitted, with a minimum of changes,[2] to North America. The most recent example of the spirit of this law in Canada has been the action of the government of British Columbia in the 1960's. Despite the protests of the government of Ontario, poor people have been shipped back to their place of origin in Ontario on the premise that they might become public charges.[3] It is apparent that the official attitude of taxpayers towards helping poor strangers has not changed over the past three hundred years.

SOCIAL UPHEAVAL IN BRITAIN

Legislation concerning the poor of the United Kingdon was usually prompted by social unrest, such as that which arose during the Napoleonic Wars from 1793 to 1815. Disabled veterans objected to going into the poorhouse and added to the upheavals produced by the Industrial Revolution. In addition, for centuries the common land had provided the village poor with a place to graze a pig or cow, and these rights disappeared with the enclosure of over 3 million acres of land between 1760 and 1800. Bad harvests added a further element of distress. And as the costs of living rose, labourers sought wage increases.

Unfortunately the illiterate labourer could not understand the emerging "dismal science" of political economy. The first element in the new hard-hearted "classical economics" was indicated by Adam Smith in his pioneering *The Wealth of Nations* (1776). Wages paid to labourers had to be at a subsistence level to enable them to reproduce themselves. A further refinement was added by David Ricardo. The total amount of wealth available for labour was called a "wage fund" which represented a relatively fixed proportion of the resources available. A wage fund was divided among the total number of labourers to provide an average wage. If the population increased, the supply of labour would force down the average wage. It followed that this "iron law of wages" prescribing subsistence could not be changed by legislation. Buttressed by economic laws, parliamentary legislation set maximum rather than minimum wage standards. This wisdom of the time was not appreciated by the poor.

By 1795, a flood of requests for poor relief made local authorities abandon the idea of placing the poor in a workhouse, in favour of outdoor relief. By now the authorities were alarmed at the evident unrest. In Speenhamland, in Berkshire, a group of magistrates met in the Pelican Inn to discuss the situation. Their deliberations upon how to devise a guide for the relief of the poor were to have a far-reaching effect. Basically, this group decided to use the cost of a loaf of bread as a guide; this was the so-called "bread-scale." As the price of bread changed, a labourer's income was to be adjusted. Wages were to be supplemented from the poor law rates, and a scale was published that related the amount of assistance to the size of the family. As a warm-hearted attempt to solve the problems of the labourer, the Speenhamland system was commendable, and it was widely copied; but it failed. It did not allow for the reaction of employers who were, of course, also taxpayers. Employers reduced wages in the knowledge that a supplementary amount would be paid by the Poor Law, and hence by all local taxpayers whether they were employers or not. At the same time, the incentive of the labourer to work was reduced, now that a guaranteed income was assured.

The Napoleonic Wars were putting considerable strain on the economy, and the added burden of increasing Poor Rates was not welcomed by the taxpayers. People were reading Adam Smith's influential book *The Wealth of Nations,* (1776) which preached the idea that the forces of supply and demand would be brought into balance by market conditions, and by what Smith termed an invisible hand. The state was to stay out of a citizen's life, which to many of Smith's supporters implied the elimination of poor relief. Another influential book at this time was by Thomas Malthus, *Essay in Population* (1798). Malthus showed that the rate of population increase would outstrip food production. Only the three great checks of famine, war and pestilence ensured that a balance could be maintained; therefore paupers should not take valuable food needed by workers. Moreover, further evidence that the Poor Law could be eliminated came from Scotland after 1819. The prominent preacher Thomas Chalmers organized within his Glasgow parish an efficient system of helping the poor and his example was noted by Englishmen opposed to the Poor Law. One result of this agitation against the Poor Law was the establishment of a Royal Commission for enquiring into the Administration and Practical Operation of the Poor Laws.

A different type of approach was brought to the problem when Benthamites came to dominate the Commission investigating the poor laws. These followers of Jeremy Bentham believed in the doctrine of utilitarianism, which advocated a criterion of usefulness in judging all aspects of life, with the object of securing the greatest happiness of the greatest number. Edwin Chadwick, the former secretary of Jeremy Bentham, and Dr. Southwood Smith led the investigation, which lasted from 1832 to 1834. Thousands of witnesses were heard and the subsequent main report comprised a massive 13,000 pages of printed evidence. It argued, with considerable documentary support, that the Speenhamland approach had led to the Poor Law being used as a subsidy by farmers, landlords and manufacturers. And the Poor Law was being abused by the recipients of relief as well. The editors of the Report stated that:

> From the preceding evidence, it will be seen how zealous must be the agency, and how intense the vigilance, to prevent fraudulent claims crowding in under such a system of relief. But it would require still greater vigilance to prevent the bona fide claimants degenerating into imposters; and it is an aphorism among the active parish officers that "cases which are good today are bad tomorrow, unless they are incessantly watched." A person obtains relief on the ground of sickness; when he has become capable of returning to moderate work, he is tempted, by the enjoyment of subsistence without labour, to conceal his convalescence, and fraudulently extend the period of relief. When it really depends upon the receivers whether the relief shall cease with its occasion, it is too much to expect of their virtue that they shall, in any considerable number of instances, voluntarily forego the pension.[4]

The idea that recipients of welfare should be closely watched to prevent fraud still has its disciples. In 1834, the report sounded to the taxpayer like the answer to a prayer for relief from taxation. So did the recommendations concerning a new Poor Law. A new system was planned to produce more efficiency at less cost with a uniform policy for all of England, to be supervised by three permanent Commissioners. Advice was to be supplied by fifteen Assistant Commissioners who would act as inspectors as they toured the country. The smallest unit of administration was not to be the individual parish, but a Union to be created by amalgamating several parishes. Each Union was to build a workhouse to be staffed by employees paid from local taxation. Operation of the workhouse was to be systematically ruthless in providing moral uplift. The poor obviously were full of vice and were badly in need of the stern discipline of labour. As the high moral tone of the Union workhouse could be provided at less cost than the Speenhamland method of outdoor relief, it appealed to taxpayers on both moral and financial grounds. Furthermore, sloth and laziness were to be discouraged: the position of an able-bodied pauper in the workhouse was to be made so miserable that he would willingly try to secure any alternative work. In the words of the Act, "his situation on the whole shall not be made really or apparently so eligible as the situation of the independent labourer of the lowest class." Of course this assumed that a job always existed for a physically fit pauper. It was only a century later, in the 1930's, that it was finally recognized that a man might not be able to find a job, no matter how hard he tried.

The Reform Parliament of 1834 received the recommendation for a new Poor Law, and quickly legislated it into effect. In financial terms, success was immediate, for between 1834 and 1837 relief expenditures fell by one-third. Two hundred Union workhouses were constructed as 13,264 parishes were regrouped into 568 Unions. But what of the human cost? Impoverished workers rapidly learned to hate the Union workhouses which were popularly known as "Bastilles." In point of fact, however, the plan was only partially carried out. While southern England accepted the new Poor Law with resignation, fierce opposition was encountered in the north. Riots occurred in northern in-dustrial cities against the "heartless tyrants" in Parliament who had declared, in the words of a young novelist and future Prime Minister, Benjamin Disraeli, that "in England poverty is a crime." Another novelist, Charles Dickens, also made some scathing remarks in his classic work *A Christmas Carol.* When Mr. Scrooge is initially approached by two gentlemen collecting for charity, the following dialogue ensues:

> *Collector* At this festive season of the year, Mr. Scrooge, it is more than usually desirable that we should make some provision for the poor and destitute, who suffer greatly at the present time. Many thousands are in want of common necessities; hundreds of thousands are in want of common comforts, sir.

Scrooge [probing the matter in a series of pointed questions] Are there no prisons? . . . And the Union workhouses, are they still in operation? The treadmill and the Poor Law are still in full vigour then? If they [the poor] would rather die, they had better do it, and decrease the surplus population.[5]

Scrooge thus showed his familiarity with the views of Thomas Malthus on population, Adam Smith on the invisible hand, and the whole spirit of the 1834 Poor Law.

THE EARLY RESPONSE IN NORTH AMERICA

During his visit to New York in 1842 Dickens aroused interest among American writers in the problems of poverty. Public relief for the poor was in bad repute in the nineteenth-century United States and no attempt was made to copy the English Poor Law Act of 1834. Public indifference to the poor stemmed from the heavy emphasis upon individual self-help; public relief was viewed only as an attempt to prevent starvation and death as economically as possible. At least, though, the practice of auctioning off the "Town Poor" was condemned by a writer in 1960 as "private enterprise in human stock."[6] Private charity and voluntary organizations tended to reflect the same ethic. However, after investigations by the State governments of New York and Massachusetts in the 1820's, there was a burst of activity in building almshouses.

In general, the United States faced some problems relatively unknown in Great Britain. Immigrants flowed steadily into the East Coast ports and delivered waves of poor people. And an applicant for poor relief faced the view held by many native-born Americans that he had brought unnecessary hardship to them, by his ill-advised and uninvited arrival in the United States.

The story of how Upper Canada faced its problems concerning poverty makes revealing reading. For one thing, it helps to explain why Canadian history books tend to stick to constitutional development and do not generally discuss social issues. In the first place, there was no legislation for the

16

poor. While a great deal has been written about Upper Canada being founded upon a firm British legal basis in 1791, rarely has it been mentioned that there was a rider on this attachment to English law and traditions. The First Statute of Upper Canada in 1792 adopted English law, except that "nothing in this Act . . . shall . . . introduce any of the laws of England respecting the maintainance of the poor." Richard Splane, who wrote the definitive history of social welfare in Ontario, diagnosed the reason as a reluctance to pay taxes:

> The intensity of the prevailing antipathy towards taxation on property suggests that even if the English Poor Law had been nominally brought into the province by the act of 1792, it would have remained, for lack of local tax support, a dead letter for an indefinite period.[7]

As Britain had paid the expenses of the Loyalists, it was assumed that the mother country would continue to defray colonial expenses. The root of this attitude concerns an important issue that is also rarely mentioned in Canadian history books. In an attempt to stave off further revolution in the American colonies, the British Parliament had promised, in 1778, that it would never tax colonists again. It is doubtful that this measure was intended to provide colonists with a free ride on the back of the British taxpayer; when the colonists realized they would henceforth have to raise their own taxes, they were understandably reluctant to introduce any Poor Law to Upper Canada.

Until Confederation Upper Canada adopted only piecemeal measures for relief of its poor. The attitude of legislators reflected the nineteenth-century belief in the voluntary principle that the social needs of society were best met by individual citizens co-operating in a "voluntary" organization with a declared purpose. In 1836, public subscription by interested citizens provided the funds to start a poorhouse in Toronto, termed a House of Industry. The next year the Legislature was sufficiently motivated to pass an Act providing for the erection of additional Houses of Industry: this was never implemented. Again, in 1866, the Legislature made it mandatory for a well-populated county to build a poor-house; however, immediately after Confederation the Ontario Legislature deleted the element of compulsion.

The Ontario Legislature solved its welfare problems by handing them on to the municipalities. A succession of Municipal Acts starting in 1849 gave responsibility for the poor to local councils to solve as best they could. The usual municipal solution was to respond only to crisis by declaring a special local levy for relief of the poor in bad years. A feature of Ontario parsimony was to have town jails double as poorhouses. At the same time, the Legislature dribbled out small grants to the hospitals and orphanages established by private charity. In 1853, when there was a United Legislature of the Canadas, the Roman Catholic majority in Lower Canada forced the passing of an Ecclesiastical Corporations Act which permitted the Church to found charitable institutions as it saw the need. This action reflected the Catholic belief that Church and State were indivisible. Protestant politicians, led by George Brown, still insisted on tight control of charity by granting a charter and a limited annual subsidy to individual institutions, which were generally expected to sustain themselves by voluntary contributions.

Upper Canada's refusal to accept responsibility for social welfare matters was extended into the constitutional framework created by the British North America Act of 1867. Those provinces which joined the Dominion of Canada after 1867 had very little constitutional provision for handling widespread poverty. Unlike Nova Scotia and New Brunswick, the colony of British Columbia had never adopted the English Poor Law system. After the Province of British Columbia entered into Confederation in 1871, provincial support for welfare was virtually limited to providing small grants to charitable agencies. In turn, when Alberta and Saskatchewan became provinces, they were influenced by the basic model of Upper Canada.

Attitudes in Upper Canada were really a refinement of those in the United States where a number of men and women worked zealously to provide adequate care for the poor, but the tendency to regard relief as a local issue made effective reform difficult. In the 1850's, one determined woman, Dorothea Dix, sought to make the federal government intervene in matters of social welfare, but President Franklin Pierce vetoed the proposed legislation with an argument that was not challenged until the 1930's.

> The question presented . . . is upon the constitutionality and propriety of the Federal Government assuming to enter into a novel and vast field of Legislation . . . providing for the care and support of all those, among the people of the United States, who by any form of calamity, become fit objects of philanthropy. . . . I cannot find any authority in the Constitution for making the Federal Government the greatest almoner of public charity through the United States.[8]

In the absence of Federal effort the main instrument of relief was a State Board of Charities, an idea which was first introduced in Massachusetts in 1863, and which spread to 38 states by 1914.

But the idea of a Board handling public charity did not originate in the United States. Further north, the United Province of Canada had established in 1859 a Board of Prisons, Asylums and Public Charities, which anticipated by four years the development of the Massachusetts board of public charities. Much discussion of prisons and penitentiaries took place in the Legislature over the next thirty years, but there were few changes. An Ontario Royal Commission of 1890, investigating the prison and reformatory system, condemned the practice of using jails for locking up poor people. The recommendations that were made reveal a good deal about contemporary attitudes:

> It is urgently recommended that, in order to abolish completely the inhuman system of committing homeless and destitute men, women and children to common gaols . . . the establishment of a poor house be made compulsory (instead of permissive as at present) on every county in a Province . . . [and] that it shall be unlawful when a poor house is established in a county or group of counties, for a magistrate or justice to commit to a

common gaol as a vagrant any homeless and destitute person who seems to be physically incapable of working unless such person has committed some offence.[9]

The Legislature responded by passing the House of Refuge Act of 1890. This Act provided a provincial grant to assist in the construction of buildings, and was expected to cover a quarter of their cost, while not exceeding the sum of four thousand dollars for any one institution. By 1900 there were eighteen county "houses of refuge," analogous to the poor-houses of England; in 1903 the provision of county poor homes was made mandatory in Ontario by the Municipal Houses of Refuge Act, which produced another fourteen such institutions by 1918.

The kind of attitudes towards the poor which late nineteenth-century Acts attempted to remedy, reflected the prevailing doctrine of Social Darwinism. The biological theories of Darwin that nature progressed by eliminating the weakest members of the species found their social parallel in the writings of Herbert Spencer. In an age of economic expansion, it seemed obvious that men of any energy and ability could make their way, and that incompetence and poverty were clear signs of biological and social inferiority.

THE NEW SOCIAL CONSCIENCE

There was an awakening realization in the 1880's that the unsuccessful contestants in this age of Social Darwinism were not necessarily morally defective, lazy or incompetent but that social and economic conditions beyond the control of the individual might be the cause of their situation. Conscientious reformers tried to shake middle-class congregations out of complacency and make them aware of the existence of social injustice. A leading crusader was Washington Gladden, a religious editor and Congregational minister. Clergymen who sought to apply Christian teachings to society at large, preached what was to become known as the Social Gospel. Emphasis was laid upon the practice of Christian charity in commercial life, and in 1905 Washington Gladden was openly attacking "predatory wealth."

More direct help to the poor came through the students who took part in the University Settlements on both sides of the Atlantic. The first of these was established in the 1870's. A permanent residence was established in 1884 in the East End of London, named Toynbee Hall, where students from Oxford and Cambridge aided Canon Barnett of Whitechapel in bringing education and recreation to slum dwellers. Students lived in the slums in an effort to provide cultural assistance to the inhabitants. American visitors to the Hall were inspired to launch a similar venture in New York City in 1887. Hull House in Chicago followed in 1889, and helped many immigrants of European background to adapt to America. By 1902 over one hundred settlement houses were operating in American cities. The idea of a "drop in centre" was one response to the poverty of the 1880's that has enjoyed continued popularity down to the present day.

Possibly the most widespread attempt to help the poor was the voluntary charity work conducted under the auspices of the Charity Organization Society. This central organization was formed in London in 1869 in order to create some order out of the chaos provided by the overlapping activity of 640 charitable institutions. The ideals of the organization were to bring into co-operation the numerous local charities, who were expected to co-operate with the agents of the Poor Law, and to give aid to the deserving poor. The popularity of this voluntary form of organization stemmed basically from its cheapness and the relief it accorded to local taxpayers. Money could be saved if private charities used unpaid volunteers and members of religious orders.

THE CRUSADE TO HELP PAUPER CHILDREN

A byproduct of the activity of the Charity Organization Society was increased concern about the future of children in the slums. During the 1860's, a warm-hearted Irishman named Dr. Thomas J. Barnado discovered his life's work in helping to care for waifs and strays. The first Dr. Barnado home for destitute children opened its doors in the East End of London in 1870. Dr. Barnado extended his activities by arranging to ship children of twelve to fourteen years of age to Canada. It has been estimated that the various groups organizing emigration, such as the Church of England Incorporated Society for Providing for Waifs and Strays, sent approximately thirty thousand children to Canada over the next thirty years. The organizers of this child migration were motivated by the desire to create a better life for children who would otherwise languish in the poorhouse. The idea of a new start in the fresh air of Canada was also supported by the Charity Organization Society on the grounds that this worthy venture was less expensive than maintaining the children at home.

Unfortunately, the well-meaning ladies who despatched children to the docks at Liverpool were not usually aware of conditions in Ontario where most of the human cargo was destined. Ontario had her own poor children. Yet there was a steady demand for child labour by farmers who insisted that they had room for healthy children: it is true, of course, that a "healthy" child able to labour all day was less expensive than an adult male labourer. A farmer provided food, board and clothing in exchange for labour. Undoubtedly there were good employers but the reports that reached the ears of the authorities publicized complaints about abuse of child labour.

Surprisingly prominent among humanitarian organizations were the Societies for the Prevention of Cruelty to Animals, which have always enjoyed more ready sympathy than charities devoted to helping the human unfortunate. The Society for the Prevention of Cruelty to Animals, founded in England in 1824, was permanently established in Nova Scotia in 1876. The Nova Scotian branch helped not only animals but abused and neglected children and, in 1880, an Act was passed in Halifax officially enabling the S.P.C.A. to deal with wrongs against children under 16 years of age. By 1888, over two-thirds of all cases handled by the Society concerned children and families.[10]

Simultaneously with this development in the Maritimes, a young reporter for the Toronto *Globe,* John Joseph Kelso, was pressing for the curbing of cruelty to animals and children. Kelso's campaign was aided by the example of Britain's Act of 1889 for the Prevention of Cruelty to and Better

Protection for Children. By 1891, Kelso had mobilized public support for the founding of the Toronto Children's Aid Society, modelled after a similar organization in New York City, but adding a children's shelter and an appointed probation officer. Ontario went on to enact, in 1893, the Ontario Children's Protection Act, the first comprehensive Act of its kind on the North American continent. It authorized the formation of children's aid societies to assume legal guardianship of neglected and abused children, while creating the office of a supervising Superintendent, which Kelso occupied for the next thirty-nine years. The unique feature of this Ontario scheme was that it preferred foster-home placement for children to institutional care. Kelso also helped to inspire the campaign that stopped the unregulated abuse of orphans from Britain. In 1897 the Ontario Legislature passed "An Act to regulate the Immigration into Ontario of certain classes of children." Child agencies had to secure a Provincial charter and inspectors supervised the placement of wards. Other provinces adopted the Ontario system and the guiding genius of J.J. Kelso deserves to be well known for child crusades in Canada. Both Kelso and Barnado were Irishmen and the children in Canada and England owe a great deal to these emigrants.

URBAN POVERTY AT THE TURN OF THE CENTURY

Another prominent humanitarian of this time was Goldwin Smith, an Englishman residing in Toronto, who urged political action for relief of the poor, and particularly for the appointment of a full-time welfare officer by the city council. Ultimately the council yielded the principle but, being concerned over cost, they accepted the kind offer of Smith to pay the salary of this civic official for a two-year trial period, beginning in 1893.

By the beginning of the twentieth century a mass of information existed on the conditions of the poor. It was generally accepted in informed social welfare circles that in industrial cities approximately one-third of the inhabitants lived below the poverty line. In England, scientific studies described in Charles Booth's *Life and Labour of the People of London* (1903) established this pattern. Seebohm Rowntree in the city of York came to similar conclusions. In New York, Jacob Riis also estimated that about thirty per cent of the city's population lived in penury. In 1904, according to Philip Hunter's book *Poverty,* there were between ten and twenty million Americans living in conditions of squalor.

A more enlightened attitude towards poverty spread as the Social Gospel gained disciples. Slowly the new creed penetrated Protestant churches in Canada. Ministers such as J.S. Woodsworth (later, founder of the Co-operative Commonwealth Federation) felt that the problems of poverty could be solved by economic and social changes. The general belief persisted, however, that the issue was basically a moral one, and the biographer of J.S. Woodsworth summarizes this social attitude in this sentence:

> The rich were rich because they deserved to be so; the poor need only stop drinking, save their money and all will be well.[11]

As the twentieth century dawned in England, there was considerable argument over whether the workhouses should be abolished. One of the leaders of the movement against the Poor Law system was George Lansbury, a rising socialist politician who crusaded for more humane treatment of the poor, without the usual emphasis to keep down the taxes. In 1905, an opportunity occurred for Lansbury to apply his ideas to the nation as a whole when he was invited to serve on the Royal Commission investigating the Poor Law.

The Commission of 1905 was soon divided. On one side ranged the majority of fourteen members who believed that it was sufficient to modify the principles of 1834. The vociferous minority led by Beatrice Webb, the Fabian, felt that the problem was essentially one of re-education and that the Poor Law ought to be abolished. Through four years, from 1905 to 1909, a struggle raged inside the Commission. During this time the Commission conducted 159 hearings, and examined 452 witnesses who answered over 100,000 questions. Mrs. Webb claimed that the investigation showed that there were 928,621 recipients of poor relief in England, including

300,000 children. In addition to the public hearings of the Commission, a team of investigators conducted private enquiries. When it was all over, the mass of testimony and research provided forty-seven published volumes which detailed the relationship between poverty and unemployment. As it turned out, both the majority and minority reports stressed identical unanimous recommendations. Labour exchanges were proposed as an aid in helping the unemployed seek work, and a change to larger administrative areas was recommended for poor relief, or what was later termed "public assistance." Essentially the 1905 Commission provided a blueprint for social action, and a national approach for dealing with social issues.

THE LIBERAL REFORMS

The Commission's recommendations were received by the Liberal government elected in 1906. David Lloyd George and Winston Churchill were two outspoken champions of social reform. It was Churchill, at the Board of Trade, who quickly carried through the proposal to establish labour exchanges to aid the unemployed to obtain jobs. But the Liberals balked at the position of the Webbs, in their minority report of 1905, that it was a moral duty of the state to pay for support of the poor. The government was not prepared to replace the hated Poor Law with a national system of social insurance and an enforced minimum wage.

However, an important start in state-provided welfare was made with the provision of Old Age Pensions in 1908. It had been discovered that one in four of the aged sought poor relief during retirement, and this legislation was at least an attempt to provide some dignity in old age. While the pension provided only five shillings a week at the age of 65, this pittance enabled many labourers to avoid the workhouse. Nearly twenty years later, in 1927, Canada introduced a Federal Old Age Pensions scheme, after pressure had been exerted on Ottawa by Labour organizations who were aware of the British precedent.

By 1911, Lloyd George and Winston Churchill realized that an effort had to be made to head off the appeal of socialism, and David Lloyd George did not stop at introducing ways of paying for Old Age Pensions. Borrowing the idea from Bismarckian social legislation in Germany, Lloyd George introduced his justly famous National Insurance Act of 1911, a measure that established health and unemployment benefits for a large number of workers who suffered from seasonal unemployment. R.H. Tawney, scholar and socialist, voiced the new attitude to poverty when he pointed out that moral solutions to poverty were not the answer, for unemployment fell on the just and unjust. But British Liberals of 1911 were not very enthusiastic about abandoning laissez faire, particularly when state action might impede the freedom of the many manufacturers in the party. George Dangerfield in *The Strange Death of Liberal England,* stated that the Liberals "advanced on social reform with noisy mouths and mouse-like feet."

These Liberal reforms were, however, very significant in heralding a new attitude towards poverty on the part of the State. The middle class supported the idea of social insurance as it provided an alternative to the degrading means test, if one should fall on hard times. A barometer of Britain's social progress could well be the diminishing number of pauper children who were exported. After the Great War this flow of children virtually ceased. It should be pointed out that in half a century, Canada gained around 50,000 young citizens this way, of whom many later "made good."

THE IMPACT OF THE GREAT WAR

The cataclysm of 1914 to 1918 produced profound social changes. Men who had survived the bloodbath on the Western front were a different breed from the idealistic youths of 1914 who had responded to a call to arms. As discharged soldiers and sailors made their way home, they found, despite Lloyd George's promises, a land unfit for heroes to live in; in general, it was felt that if the government could finance a Great War, it could also find lesser sums to relieve distress. Adding to the unrest was the fear of Bolshevism which, in turn, led the government to make quick concessions to returned servicemen and former munitions workers.

At this time the financially sound plan of 1911 was abandoned. National funds were now used to provide 26 weeks of unemployment relief. The term "dole" became popular as a description of this weekly sum doled out; after the initial period, an unemployed worker could apply for poor relief. Variations in technique were introduced in the next two decades, but the basic principle remained: insurance payments as a matter of right for a limited time and then an appeal for poor relief. The motivation for supplying relief was not purely altruistic; rather, it was in part a realization that one aspect of social insurance was insurance against revolution by men trained in the use of arms.

North America also felt the impact of the returned serviceman. The United States had not become very heavily involved in the military struggle on the Western front, and consequently a return to "normalcy" or prewar condidions, as promised by President Warren Harding, was fairly readily accomplished. In Canada, whose war dead exceeded those of her neighbour, a more bitter mood existed. The Social Gospel flowered under Methodist auspices, with ideas drawn from European socialism and the earlier movement in the U.S.A. In 1918, a Methodist Committee condemned privilege and wartime profiteering in no uncertain terms: "we declare it to be unchristian to accept profits when labourers do not receive a living wage, or when capital receives disproportionate returns as compared to labour."[12] This statement accurately reflected the new understanding of poverty, that wages were the key to maintaining a decent standard of living. As total material wealth increased, employers should accept an increase in wages as the corollary to increased profits.

It seems, however, that in Canada during the 1920's the rich got richer and the workers remained almost as poor as ever. The average income of a family of five was only $1,900 which was, according to the government's own calculations, $300 below the minimum needed to keep a family in health and decency. In contrast, 416 extremely wealthy men and women paid 35% of all the income tax collected by the federal government. In 1920, Ontario adopted one major welfare measure, a Mother's Allowance Act. It was not the first in Canada, as Manitoba had already passed a similar Act in 1916. By the terms of the Ontario legislation widows or wives of completely disabled men could receive a maximum of $45 a month, with 50% to be paid by local municipalities. "Moral" scruples were not completely forgotten, however, for where a husband had deserted a family, the abandoned woman and children were not entitled to relief.

During the American Roaring Twenties a new attitude towards poverty influenced many of the professional social workers being trained by universities. Graduates had discovered psychoanalysis and began to treat "clients" through individual therapy. It is not surprising that social workers found that it was relatively easy to become rather detached in their attitude towards economic poverty. The scientific approach "subjected poverty to a casework analysis, transforming the poor from socially inadequate individuals to socially maladjusted individuals."[13]

Britain never recovered from the economic, social, military and psychological scars inflicted by the 1914-1918 struggle. Basic export industries such as textiles, steel, coal and shipbuilding went into permanent decline, and unemployment stayed high throughout the twenties. Casting around for some type of alleviating legislation, the cabinet backed the Minister of Health, Neville Chamberlain, in his administrative reform of the Poor Law in 1929 which belatedly followed some of the recommendations of the Poor Law Commission of 1909. The Local Government Act of 1929 created fewer but larger authorities to handle welfare relief by abolishing Boards of Guardians and transferring their powers to 145 local Councils. These Councils came under the direction of the Minister of Health and their duties included education, public assistance, public health, slum clearing and town planning. The Treasury under Winston Churchill made "block grants" calculated more or less on local needs. Although the Local Government Act did not abolish the Poor Law, it did reflect a change of attitude, since the Government now recognized that unemployment of able-bodied men rather than poverty was the real problem, and it was willing to spend money to alleviate the distress caused by unemployment.

THE DEPRESSION

However, during the 1930's Britain went backwards in terms of tackling the problems of the poor. Because relief payments to all members of an unemployed family could often amount to more than the man could earn in a job, the heads of such families were understandably slow in their search for employment. Also, a household means test was introduced, which assessed total family income and would reduce the amount paid through the dole, if a member of the family gained a raise in pay. The resentment caused by the means test helps to explain why, when an election was called in 1945, the Conservative Party was defeated at the polls. It was not dissatisfaction with Winston Churchill's wartime leadership so much as bottled-up resentment from the 1930's that led to the Labour party's victory.

On the other side of the Atlantic, President Franklin D. Roosevelt in his message to Congress of January 4, 1935 eloquently denounced the idea of the dole for Americans. Roosevelt declared that:

> The lessons of history, confirmed by the evidence immediately before me, show me conclusively that continued dependence upon relief induces a spiritual and moral disintegration fundamentally destructive to the national fiber. To dole out relief in this way is to administer a narcotic, a subtle destroyer of the human spirit.[14]

Work of any kind was seen as more desirable than handing out cash payments. Roosevelt's philosophy had widespread appeal for Americans who, unlike the British poor, had no bitter memories of labour in a poorhouse. The New Deal relief measures during the depression were generally aimed at providing jobs. Harry Hopkins, who had gained experience as a social worker in New York, took the lead in initiating action under the Federal Emergency Relief Act of 1933. Financial grants were made to state legislatures to stimulate employment. The Civil Works Administration employed the talents of skilled workers, artists, teachers; young people were employed in conservation measures to preserve national resources as members of the Civilian Conservation Corps. The keystone of this legislative edifice was the Social Security Act of 1935, which recognized the need for social and health insurance in the same way that David Lloyd George had recognized it in 1911.

Canada planned its own New Deal in 1935 under Prime Minister R.B. Bennett, but the legislation was subsequently vetoed on constitutional grounds. Relief measures in Canada tended to be patterned on American measures. One rarely noted exception to this trend was that the Canadian Unemployment Relief Camps predated the equivalent American plan by some five months, and drew Americans to study the Canadian scheme before implementing the Civilian Conservation Corps.[15] The need for help to the poor was evident in many ways. The Stevens Royal Commission that investigated price spreads in 1934, cited some remarkable figures on wages of the "employed." A shocking example was provided by this testimony: "one man of ten years' experience worked 70 hours per week in a Montreal contract shop, to earn $7 at 10 cents per hour." The Stevens Report continued that:

It is bad enough to pay such wages as these. It is adding insult to injury to hand them to the workers, as is often done, in pay envelopes which, thoughtfully provided by banks, bear such encouraging advice as:
Think of tomorrow,
Divide your pay in two,
Take what you need to live
Put the balance in safety.[16]

In 1934, over 120,000 people of a total Toronto population of 600,000 were living on relief. And this figure of one person in five does not include the poverty-stricken whose pride would not permit them to seek charity. Local relief committees doled out hand-me-down clothes, while soup kitchens helped the transients. By 1935 one-tenth of the population of Canada was in receipt of public relief. For Britain, Canada and the United States, the answer to their depression problems was provided by Adolf Hitler. Once war clouds began to appear over Europe after 1936, the need for rearmament tended to stimulate industrial activity. It was

World War II itself that really lifted the poor out of despondency.

THE FIGHT FOR A BETTER WORLD

The years between 1941 and 1944 isolated the British population and mingled its various strata in an unprecedented fashion, causing a new intensity in the discussion of social issues. An architect of the 1911 Insurance Act, William Beveridge, was asked to investigate the existing social services and make recommendations for a happier postwar Britain. When the resulting Beveridge Report was made public in 1942, it created a sensation: it proposed complete social coverage of every citizen from the cradle to the grave and placed the onus for security on the government. Five basic needs of man were listed: food, clothing, fuel, light, and rent. And the report attacked "five giants": want, disease, ignorance, squalor and idleness. The national press designated the document as the Magna Carta of Social Welfare and, as a state paper, it sold over 625,000 copies. This best-seller had one fundamental idea, that all citizens were entitled to a basic income to be paid out of general taxation. This underlying philosophy implied a universal right to a life of some dignity; poverty was not caused by individual moral defects and poor individuals should be helped in a spirit of consideration rather than condescension.

The Labour party embraced the Beveridge Report and thereby ensured its return to power in 1945. Beveridge's plan, in somewhat modified form, was followed in framing the National Insurance Act of 1946 and a supplementary National Assistance Act of 1948. These two complementary Acts of Parliament destroyed the vestiges of the Poor Law and the dole, although a humanized form of the means test was retained. Workhouses were legislated out of existence; the actual buildings, due to a shortage of accommodation, sometimes started a new life as "residential homes" for the aged, complete with gay coloured paint and window boxes.

By this time, the electoral appeal of welfare legislation had been felt in Canada as well. As a result of reading the Beveridge report, the Canadian government prepared a report on Social Security in Canada. This document, the Marsh report (named after its author) made recommendations which were implemented in the Federal Family Allowance Act of 1944. Popularly known as the "baby bonus," monthly payments were distributed to nearly three million children, in amounts ranging from five to eight dollars per child. In general, though, the federal structures of Canada and the United States made legislation on social issues more complicated than in England. Social action has generally been implemented in state or provincial action, which can allow for the specific needs of a particular region. In Canada, the constitutional framework of the British North America Act has been interpreted to put the main areas affecting a citizen's everyday life in the control of the provinces, under the elastic phrase "property and civil rights." However, the depression of the 1930's showed that the power of the federal government to control taxation tends to mitigate against the provincial legislative power.

It was World War I that initially drew the federal government of Canada into welfare measures of national importance. Incapacitated veterans were granted pensions for their military service, and from this grew a modest Old Age Pensions Act in 1927, whereby half the cost of pensions was to be borne by the federal government. In 1940 the federal government obtained the consent of all provinces to an amendment of the B.N.A. Act that gave exclusive jurisdiction over "unemployment insurance" to Ottawa. And an Unemployment Insurance Act of 1940 established a contributory plan for workers with certain levels of income, similar to the British scheme of 1911. Again following British legislation before 1914, Labour Exchanges were established.

In 1941 the national emergency of war permitted the federal government to override provincial authority; Ottawa collected income and corporation taxes and made adjustment grants to the provinces to compensate for the loss of "their" revenue. When the war was over, federal-provincial "tax rental" agreements continued the co-operation between Ottawa and the provinces, and by the Act of 1956 Ottawa took the responsibility for unemployment insurance, inviting provincial co-operation on a cost-sharing basis. The new era of federal-provincial co-operation reflected the determination of the federal government, in the age of the welfare state, to ensure equality of opportunity for all Canadians. Furthermore, it was quite consistent with Canadian history to have Ottawa cast itself in the role of fairy godmother, coaxing rich provinces like Ontario and British Columbia to help their poorer sister provinces in the Maritimes. In Nova Scotia, the Poor Law was repealed in 1958 and a Social Assistance Act adopted which, with federal subsidies, provided provincial responsibility for the needy. In the rapidly growing area of Toronto, there was need for a new form of federalism known as a metropolitan form of government. An authority formed from representatives of individual municipalities handled common problems such as welfare.

THE WAR ON POVERTY

A new burst of interest in poverty developed after the publication in 1955 of John Kenneth Galbraith's *The Affluent Society*. Galbraith saw poverty amid the affluence of America and distinguished between two types of poverty: "insular" poverty in depressed areas such as the Appalachians or Ozarks, and "case" poverty due to factors such as poor health, lack of education, alcoholism, drug addiction or racial or ethnic discrimination. A few years later, Michael Harrington substantiated this view of poverty amid affluence in *The Other America: Poverty in the United States*. A great deal of literature on poverty began to appear from 1963 onwards. Interest in the poor was heightened by several outbreaks of violence among Negroes. President John F. Kennedy launched a "fight to eliminate poverty" while, after his assassination, the new President, Lyndon B. Johnson, made anti-poverty efforts a major feature of the construction of his Great Society.

The statistics on poverty are rather surprising to anyone raised on the concept of a classless society where anyone can rise to affluence if he tries hard enough. Sargent Shriver, director of the Office of Economic Opportunity, suggested as a yardstick that a family of four in 1962 with an annual income under $3,130 could be classified as poor, or an individual with an income under $1,540. Shriver indicated that in 1965 over 35 million American families were "poverty-stricken" and untouched by existing programmes for aiding the poor. If, as Ferdinand Lundberg pointed out in his best-seller, *The Rich and the Super Rich,* one assigns a conservative figure of three persons to a family, then over 105 million Americans were living in poverty, or over half the existing population. Another study, Michael Harrington's *The Other America,* sets the figure much lower, at 50 million people, or roughly one-quarter of the population of the United States.

Canadian statistics reveal a similar situation. In 1961, as recorded by the Dominion Bureau of Statistics, approximately one family in four had an income of less than $3,000.[17] The main concentrations of poor families were in the Maritime Provinces, rural Quebec and Saskatchewan. Of 200,000 registered Indians of Canada, 75% of the families earned less than $2,000 a year.[18] The statistical picture that emerges concerning the extent of poverty in Canada varies considerably, depending on which yardstick is used. The Economic Council of Canada in 1968 stated that at least 4.2 million persons, or 29 per cent of the population, were poor if defined as "those using 70 per cent of their income for food, clothing and shelter. On this basis, low income families and individuals would include single persons with incomes below $1,500, families of two with less than $2,500 and families of three, four and five or more with incomes of less than $3,000, $3,500 and $4,000 respectively."[19] The Economic Council made a second estimate using as a criterion that a family is poor if sixty per cent of its income is spent on food, clothing and shelter. By this measurement it has been calculated that at least 6.6 million poor people live in Canada.[20]

Influenced by President Lyndon B. Johnson's example in the U.S.A., Canada declared her own war on poverty. A Manpower Mobility programme was set up to aid families to move to more affluent areas. An Area Development programme was inaugurated to encourage new industry in areas of low employment, mainly by inducements of tax concessions. Finally, Manpower programmes to train and re-habilitate adults in vocational training were established. In our technologically sophisticated society, a major aspect of the war on poverty involves training the unskilled or semi-skilled worker to aid him in securing employment. The Province of Quebec, however, has remained somewhat doubtful about the federal approach to poverty, reflecting the typical provincial suspicion of federal powers. As Quebec officially pointed out after a War on Poverty Conference:

> It may be nothing more than a sort of advertising technique, which dresses up under a new generic name a wide array of decisions and socio-economic measures which would have been implemented anyway. Or, because it naturally tends to be comprehensive, it may serve as a starting point for several new courses of action, integrated so as to form the instruments of a coherent policy.[21]

The major difference between Canadian and American approaches to poverty lies in the channels for dispersing funds. The American Office of Economic Opportunity operates under the control of the President of the United States, and can provide funds directly to local municipalities. In Canada the constitution requires that every effort of the federal government to supply funds for the war on poverty must be channelled through the provincial governments. There is no comparison between the American agency with its substantial funds and under the control of the President, and Ottawa's role as a co-ordinating body and statistical research centre.

Cost is obviously a key factor in any programme combatting poverty. If the government is to play Robin Hood, taking from the rich to give to the poor, it will redistribute income gained from taxation. In Britain, tight income and estate taxes initiated by the welfare state in 1945 have done much to equalize incomes. This is not true of the United States. Senator Joseph S. Clark explained the effect of an antiquated property tax structure:

The rich man pays local property taxes on what may be a tiny fraction of his accumulated wealth; the average-income man pays on what may be more than his accumulated wealth. As it affects individuals a more inequitable tax system could hardly be devised. And because the property tax is thus inversely related to the ability to pay, its limit is reached early—when it strikes too hard at the resources of the lower and middle income groups who bear the brunt of it.[22]

What about other forms of wealth? The story here seems to be somewhat similar. One estimate of stock and bond holdings in the United States is that 1.6% of the population owns more than 80% of all stocks, 100% of state and local government bonds, and 88.5% of corporate bonds.[23] It might be assumed that Uncle Sam gets a great chunk of the accumulated wealth through estate taxes, upon the death of one of the wealthy holders. But as Ferdinand Lundberg points out in *The Rich and The Super Rich,* the legislators of Washington deliberately leave loopholes which are used to funnel money away from government collection agencies: tax-free outright gifts, charity donations and trust funds. In vain has the United States Treasury in recent years implored Congress to close these gaps that have been estimated to cost around $15 billion a year in lost taxes.[24]

The tax structure in Canada has been examined in the Report of the Royal Commission on Taxation, the Carter Report, released in February 1967. This massive study combined four and a half years of study by over 150 tax experts, into six volumes and 2,576 pages. It contains a scathing indictment of the inequitable basis of the existing tax structure which, while heavily taxing the wage earner, does not bear down so hard upon dollars earned on the stock market or in real estate. The viewpoint of the Commission was that "a buck was a buck" regardless of how it was acquired, and therefore each earned dollar should be subject to taxation without any tax concessions for the manner in which it was gained. Like other unwelcome Royal Commission reports, the Carter proposals were smothered under a barrage of protest that arose from a minority of the population which felt threatened by its recommendations. It has been estimated, for example, that the "public ownership of corporate stock is for the most part in the hands of about 2.9 per cent of the people who file income tax returns."[25] A sequel to this important question of how best to share the national wealth developed when Finance Minister Edgar Benson proposed to create the financial substructure of Prime Minister Pierre Trudeau's Just Society through the introduction of tax reforms. Protest to his proposals came from a number of special interest groups who stood to lose particular privileges.

The "Robin Hood" concept works only within certain limits. Social insurance schemes designed to alleviate poverty collect money by regressive taxes on wages and salaries, which often exceed benefits available from the scheme. These taxes, too, bear more heavily on the poor than on the wealthy. That is, "any redistribution of wealth takes place among the social strata below the wealthy."[26] This broad generalization was borne out by the findings of the Carter Commission which reported that, "The net effect of the whole fiscal system in Canada is a redistribution of income from those earning between $4,500 and $7,000 to those with incomes below that level."[27]

But how about private welfare measures by employers? Richard M. Titmuss, a British scholar, has claimed that the proliferation of private welfare measures tends to increase inequality. Benefits of such schemes as sick leave, medical care, holiday expenses, training grants, expense accounts, are untaxed or only lightly taxed so that the real cost is thus borne by the government. For example, Titmuss estimates that private tax-exempt pension schemes alone cost the British government far more in uncollected taxes than the entire Exchequer cost of national insurance pensions.[28] Pension or Trust schemes that can take advantage of the government regulations by circumventing taxation are openly advertised in Canada, and tend to reduce the effectiveness of national schemes.

The increasing popularity of the idea of a guaranteed annual wage indicates that there are many concerned individuals who wish to eliminate poverty in Canada. The Senate

Committee investigating poverty, under the direction of Senator David Croll, reported in October, 1971 and supported the idea of a guaranteed annual wage. But to treat the problem of poverty simply in terms of money, as has been done here, is neither complete nor completely realistic. Additional factors will appear as we look at other aspects of the social spectrum.

1. Stan Fitzner, *The Development of Social Welfare in Nova Scotia,* Province of Nova Scotia Centennial Project for the Development of Public Welfare, 1967, p. 9.
2. The main change was in the administration of poor relief. Virginia had organized English-style ecclesiastical parishes in 1641. By the 1780's the unit of administration in the United States had become the county: this reflected the separation of church and state, with poor relief being a civil responsibility. In any event, the parish system was ill-suited for use in large, sparsely populated areas.
3. *Toronto Globe and Mail,* 25 October 1969.
4. *The Report from His Majesty's Commissioners for Inquiring into the Administration and Practical Operation of the Poor Laws* (London: Published by Authority, 1834), p. 46.
5. Charles Dickens, *A Christmas Carol* (Boston: Educational Publishing Company, 1898), pp. 16-17.
6. Robert H. Bremner, *From The Depths* (New York: New York University Press, 1964), p. 47.
7. Richard B. Splane, *Social Welfare in Ontario, 1791-1893* (Toronto: University of Toronto Press, 1965), p. 67.
8. Ralph E. Pumphrey and Muriel W. Pumphrey (eds.), *The Heritage of American Social Work* (New York: Columbia University Press, 1961), p. 133.
9. Province of Ontario, *Sessional Papers,* 1891, no. 18, p. 220.
10. Fitzner, *The Development of Social Welfare in Nova Scotia,* p. 47.
11. Kenneth McNaught, *A Prophet in Politics* (Toronto: University of Toronto Press, 1959), p. 38.
12. "Report of the Committee on Evangelism and Social Service," *Journal of Proceedings of the Tenth General Conference of the Methodist Church, October 2-17, 1918* (Toronto: William Briggs, 1918), p. 342.
13. John Bauman, "The Scope of the Poverty Problem," *Current History,* November, 1971, p. 284.
14. Samuel I. Rosenman, comp., *The Public Papers and Addresses of Franklin D. Roosevelt,* 13 vols., (New York: Random House, 1938), 4: 19-20.
15. See T.W. Tanner, "Microcosms of Misfortune: Canada's Unemployment Relief Camps Administered by the Department of National Defence, 1932-1936," M.A. Thesis, University of Western Ontario, 1965.
16. *Report of the Royal Commission on Price Spreads* (Ottawa: King's Printer, 1935), p. 110.
17. "Profile of Poverty in Canada," mimeographed, prepared by Special Planning Secretariat, Privy Council (Ottawa: December, 1965), p. 21. For details see J.R. Poluluk, "Characteristics of Low Income Families," mimeographed (Ottawa: Dominion Bureau of Statistics, 1965).

18. Martin O'Connell, "Breaking the Cycle of Poverty In Indian Reserve Communities," *Indian-Eskimo Association of Canada Bulletin* 6 (November 1964) pp. 3-4.
19. Economic Council of Canada, Fifth Annual Review: *The Challenge of Growth and Change* (Ottawa: Queen's Printer, 1968), ch. 6. Cited in W.E. Mann (ed.), *Poverty and Social Policy in Canada* (Toronto: Copp Clark Publishing Co. Ltd., 1970), p. 54.
20. Ian Adams, *The Poverty Wall* (Toronto: McClelland and Stewart Ltd., 1970), p. 16.
21. "Quebec's Statement to the War on Poverty Conference–December 7-10, 1965," pp. 21-22, cited in B. Schlesinger, *Poverty in Canada and the United States* (Toronto: University of Toronto Press, 1968), p. 39.
22. B.L. Berry and J. Meltzer, eds., *Goals for Urban America* (Englewood Cliffs, N.J.: Prentice Hall Inc., 1967), p. 41.
23. Ferdinand Lundberg, *The Rich and the Super Rich* (Toronto: Bantam Books, 1969), p. 13.
24. *Toronto Globe and Mail,* 24 March 1970, p. B2.
25. Ian Adams, *The Poverty Wall,* p. 134.
26. *See* Harold L. Wilensky and Charles N. Lebeaux, *Industrial Society and Social Welfare* (Toronto: Collier Macmillan Canada Ltd., 1965) p. xiii.
27. Ian Adams, *The Poverty Wall,* p. 135.
28. Richard M. Titmuss, *Essays on the Welfare State* (London: George Allen and Unwin Ltd., 1958), p. 69.

2

Trade Unions and Unemployment

I believe now, as I have all my life, in the right of workers to join unions.

F.D. Roosevelt

To bring into focus the growth of modern industrial trade unionism, it is necessary to consider the general economic environment in which it originated. At the end of the eighteenth century, there was great unrest among the workers of Great Britain. In the pre-industrial agricultural society, there had been a community of interest and a general sharing of aims and activity among landowner and farmer and peasant, so that even the lowest-paid farm labourer could feel a sense of personal interest and achievement in his daily work. In the new factory system, however, labour was impersonal and the labourer was beneath his employer or the factory-owner, in a new and rigid vertical organization of social classes. Workers moved in masses to the northern manufacturing towns, pulled by the dubious attraction of wages and pushed out of the agricultural villages by the enclosure acts which had forbidden them to keep livestock on village-owned land. And once in the mushrooming cities, they were frequently overworked, underpaid, and housed in hovels.

The new social science of political economy served to justify this new economic order. Political economists argued that prosperity would come if businessmen were left free to pursue their own interests; this philosophy of laissez faire did bring prosperity, at least to the owners of factories and machines. It took some time before the bewildered workers realized that they were not to share in this new wealth but instead they, as part of labour, were themselves a commodity to be bartered. For political economy was buttressed by English common law which held that a combination of workers to improve their conditions was a "conspiracy" to interrupt the natural laws of supply and demand. And conspiracy was punishable by the law.

UNREST AMONG THE WORKERS

It was a turbulent age. Britain was constantly at war with Napoleon. In 1798 French troops supported a nationalistic uprising in Ireland, and by 1799 the British government was in a mood to tighten up the laws against conspiracy. The real fear of the government of the day was that the idea of a revolution might spread from France to England. At this time Parliament was composed of members of the landed aristocracy, who understood that in union there is strength and, while preserving their own solidarity, sought to ensure that the working classes did not combine as a group. Even the revered Royal Navy was infected with the revolutionary virus, and mutinied at the Nore and Spithead when ordinary sailors sought to improve the terrible conditions on the lower deck. The mutineers sought to prevent vindictive retaliation by the authorities by pledging an oath of allegiance to stick together. This produced a government reaction in the passage of a parliamentary Act which prohibited such unlawful oaths, providing for a penalty of up to seven years imprisonment. This Act would later prove very useful in combatting industrial unionism.

Soon afterwards, reports began to filter in of workers in London and Lancashire combining in an attempt to increase wages. A further crackdown resulted when a Combination Law was enacted in 1799 and amended in the following year. Essentially the object was to prevent employees from combining to force an employer to grant their demands; to this end, the Combination Laws largely repeated what already existed in common and statute law, with the addition of a provision for summary trial, providing for a maximum of up to two months of hard labour as punishment. In the hands of determined employers these new laws could be used effectively to crush potential union activity.

As might be expected, a similar anti-union attitude existed in North America. In the Nova Scotia Act of 1816, there appeared a complaint about

> the great numbers of . . . journeymen and workmen, in the Town of Halifax, and other parts of the Province who have, by unlawful Meetings and Combinations, endeavoured to regulate their rate of wages and to effectuate illegal purposes.[1]

In Philadelphia, eight workers were tried in 1806 for "combination and conspiring to raise their wages," and upon conviction were fined the then princely sum of $8 each.

A nervous British government maintained a spy system in industrial districts, under the supervision of the Home Office. In 1819, tension increased sharply when an army unit of militia cavalry charged into an orderly group of families demonstrating in favour of labour unity. This inglorious military charge took place in St. Peter's fields in Manchester and, to mock the recent victory of Wellington over Napoleon, was termed Peterloo. Responsible reformers began to agitate to change the repressive policy of the government. Results of this agitation included the introduction of civilian policemen in place of the brutal military and the repeal of the Combination Laws in 1824. But what the law gave in 1824, it took back the following year. For while by 1825 unions were legal and could bargain with employers for wages, strikers were punishable in the Courts for "molesting and obstructing."

In the United States, Philadelphia remained the seedbed of unionism and, in 1828, a group of unions formed a federation called the Mechanics Union of Trade Assemblies. The American goal was to secure free education for children and to prevent the callous exploitation of child labour. Those early unionists could not have envisaged that the curse of child labour would blacken the name of American industries until, well over a century later, it was finally effectively outlawed in 1938 on a national scale. However, some immediate success was encountered in the 1820's in pressing for public education, and Workingmen's Associations were formed to press for "equal, universal education."

Legislation regulating working conditions in factories was pioneered in Britain. It was mainly inspired by the humanitarian Lord Shaftesbury, who had the necessary social prestige to persuade his fellow aristocrats in Parliament to abandon laissez-faire policies, in order to help children and women in the factories. Shaftesbury exemplified the motivating concept of noblesse oblige, which implied that the wealthy should have a sense of responsibility to the poor. A great leap forward in bettering industrial conditions in Britain was made with the Factory Act of 1833, which applied only to textile mills, but did introduce effective state regulation of working conditions. Children under thirteen in textile mills were restricted to a 48-hour week and a system of enforcement was set up by establishing the first inspectors paid by the State. By 1847, a ten-hour day for textile mills was prescribed by Parliament. In contrast, Massachusetts did not legislate the same factory conditions until 1874. Due to the federal political structure in the United States, industrial reform was difficult, and the American industrialist could and would pick up and move his industry to states that were more lax about passing legislation, whenever factory acts for employees met with his disapproval.

TRADE UNIONS

It was in the 1830's that the real basis for modern unions was laid, when two distinct traditions developed in Britain which would later emerge in North America. In the woollen industry of the West Riding of Yorkshire, the Nonconformist tradition planted by Methodism took strong root. A century later, in Canada, the Social Gospel preached by J.S. Woodsworth, the father of the Co-operative Commonwealth Federation, would be in this tradition. The other strand of union activity was the secular variety that originated with

Robert Owen, who is frequently termed the father of British socialism. Owen pioneered many ideas concerning the improvement of working conditions, but the particular organization which he inspired, and which was significant for unionism, was the Grand Consolidated Trades Union. This was not a union of the type with which we are now familiar, but an association of men from many different trades. Owen felt that it would be possible to develop what is now termed "workers' control" in industry and to establish a chain of co-operative ventures to replace normal business concerns; in general his proposals advocated a kind of communism, or communal living. The aim of his giant G.C.T.U. was hardly calculated to win the sympathy of employers, who were described by Owen, himself a mill owner, as "the ignorant, idle and useless parts of society."

Owen's call for working-class unity was heeded in 1834 by a group of farm labourers in the village of Tolpuddle, Dorset, who decided to form a lodge of the national union. Unfortunately, they made the mistake of insisting that each member swear a secret oath not to reveal union business, and they were sentenced to seven years transportation under the 1799 Act prohibiting Unlawful Oaths. In 1837, however, a wave of public indignation forced the government to bring back these "Tolpuddle Martyrs" from Australia, and three of the five later emigrated to Upper Canada. In the history of unionism, these villagers from Tolpuddle blazed a world-wide trail that alerted workers on two continents.

Legislation to improve working conditions continued in the 1840's, notably with the Mines Act of 1842 forbidding the employment in coal mines of all women, and of boys under ten. But the main thrust in this decade was in the direction of political action, for many working men felt that by obtaining the right to vote, they could influence Parliament to remake the entire industrial structure. From 1838 to 1848, the Chartist movement agitated for political reform which would include working-class representation. This large-scale political organization took precedence over grassroots union organizations working for small gains concerning wages and working hours, and when it collapsed in 1848, militant union activity was postponed for the next thirty years.

Two children in a Yorkshire coal mine, Ann Ambler and William Dyson, being drawn up to the surface

The first employment for a child in a mine was usually to open and close the air door as wagons passed through the tunnel

Reproduced from Children's Employment Commission, *Mines*, London, 1842

While there was less industrialization in North America during this time, progress was being made in the development of unionism. Printers were organized in Upper and Lower Canada, with Quebec City having a local branch as early as 1827, followed by Montreal and Hamilton in 1833. Toronto's Typographical Union has had a continuous history since 1844. George Brown, editor of the *Globe,* led the counter-attack of employers against unionism. Yet, by the 1850's every newspaper in Toronto seems to have been organized. A struggle ensued to maintain a minimum wage of $7 per week and a ten-hour day, with the unionists disciplining any member who worked below the agreed rate. By the mid-1860's, there were also printers' unions in London, Saint John and Halifax.

In the United States at this time, moderate progress was being made concerning legal recognition of unions. The Massachusetts Supreme Court ruled in 1842 that the charge of criminal conspiracy did not apply to unions which used legal means to achieve their ends. The Massachusetts ruling was an interpretation of legal responsibility for union activity similar to that of Britain. In practice, it meant that the use of a strike was virtually outlawed for it was claimed that strikes restrained the employer's right to trade.

The "new model" craft union of the mid-century was the Amalgamated Society of Engineers founded in Britain in 1851. This model was really a moderate friendly society emphasizing benefits connected with sickness and death. Such unions catered to the more affluent "aristocracy of labour" found in the skilled trades. As early as 1853 the Amalgamated Society of Engineers had established an overseas local in Montreal, as British immigrants brought trade union practices with them. While this started the trend to internationalism for Canadian unions, it was far from typical of the period. During the 1850's most of the Canadian unions that existed were purely local in character.

In 1860 the Iron Moulders became the first American union to found a local in Canada, and they were followed by the Cigar Makers in 1865. During the late 1860's there were a significant number of unions in Canada affiliated to American unions, including the typographical unions which joined the larger body in the U.S.A. There was an obvious advantage in securing a union card from an American organization, as it opened up employment opportunities within the United States for those seeking jobs. Furthermore, American unions gained status by using their small Canadian membership to warrant the term "international union," as in the case of the International Typographers Union. But the bulk of the unions in Canada continued to remain local in character, as for example the shipbuilding unions in Victoria and Halifax. Only slowly were associations of local trades unions formed into local trades councils in the larger cities.

In Britain, unionists were becoming increasingly aware that the Master and Servant Act reflected attitudes that regarded employer and employee as not equal either socially or legally. But before pressure could be brought to bear on Parliament to amend the discriminatory Master and Servant law, an unexpected disaster threatened the whole trade union movement, when some union members in Sheffield used force against non-union men. These "Sheffield Outrages" inflamed public opinion and a Royal Commission was established to investigate trade unionism in 1867. Five trade union leaders agreed to co-operate to ensure that the Royal Commission gave a fair hearing to their cause, and they appointed one of the eleven commissioners.

While the commission was sitting, another problem for the unions arose when the legal decision on a case then before the courts stipulated that trade union funds did not have legal protection. This meant that if a dishonest union official ran off with its sickness and unemployment funds, a union could not sue for damages. Not surprisingly, subscriptions to unions dropped. A minority report of the commission investigating unionism advocated that unions be given legal protection for their funds and, even more importantly, managed to influence public opinion in this direction. This was tremendously significant: English public opinion was in 1867 about where American opinion towards unions would stand in 1937, seventy years later, after the massacre of union pickets by Chicago police at the Republic Steel plant.

THE REFORMS OF THE 1870's

Against this somewhat depressing background of outrages, investigations and loss of membership, the British Trades Union Congress was formed in 1869. It came into being soon after the passage of the Second Reform Bill had placed a preponderance of voting power in the hands of the working class. The T.U.C. was formed to exert political pressure on Parliament to reform laws unfavourable to trade unions. William Gladstone's Trade Union Bill of 1871 was disappointing as it left union members liable to criminal prosecution for picketing. Gladstone's rival, Benjamin Disraeli, was helped to political victory in the election of 1874 by the resulting working-class backlash. By 1875, Disraeli's ministry had repealed the legislation on picketing, and substituted a significantly worded Employers and Workmen's Act for the detested Master and Servant Act. No longer were employees treated as potential criminals when they were held to have committed a breach of contract. Furthermore, for the first time employees were to be tried in civil courts, like employers, and not in criminal courts. This Act of 1875 has been termed the Magna Carta of British trade unionism. Picketing was legalized, the Act stipulating that it was legal for a group of workmen to do anything that was permitted to the ordinary citizen acting alone.

Parallel developments took place in Canada where both the 1871 and 1875 British Acts were eventually adopted. In 1872, Toronto printers struck for a nine-hour day or 54-hour week. Their employers, headed by George Brown of the *Globe,* offered a sixty-hour week. Legally, Ontario unions at this time were in the same position as British unions had been in the grim days of 1791, for the achievement of Confederation in 1867 had meant that British laws no longer automatically applied to Canada. Brown laid formal charges against thirteen of the union leaders, who were then arrested for criminal conspiracy. A mass protest meeting, involving 10,000 workers, was held outside the Ontario legislative building at Queen's Park. These protesters knew that Gladstone in Britain had, the year previously, made British unions legal. Turbulent demonstrations continued and an intense parliamentary battle concerning the rights of labour began in Ottawa. Sir John A. Macdonald saw his way clear to "dish the Liberals," by passing through the Canadian Parliament the Conservative legislation based on the Gladstonian Liberalism of 1871. George Brown, editor of the *Globe,* addressed a protest meeting of employers in Toronto and cried out, "Crush out the aspiration of employees! Stamp out the movement! Ostracize the union men and drive them from Canada!"[2] However, the Toronto trade unionists, supported by John A. Macdonald's legislative action, won their strike, and this became the first significant piece of successful political agitation by Canadian unions. The Liberal party in Canada gave tit for tat in response to John A. Macdonald's opportunism when, in 1876, they adopted the main features of Disraeli's trade union measure of 1875; neither Liberals nor Conservatives in Canada showed much reluctance to snap up ideas from either of their namesakes in Westminster.

THE AMERICAN APPROACH

In the U.S.A., political action was rejected by Samuel Gompers, the founder of the American Federation of Labour, in favour of immediate economic gains. Gompers sought to divorce unionism from politics, which was considered by many Americans to be a dirty game. When Gompers organized a federation of unions in 1886, he was undoubtedly guided in his philosophy by the experience of an earlier group known as the Knights of Labour.

The Noble Order of the Knights of Labour had been organized in 1869. It was an industrial union open to all working men, which generally organized on a plant basis, and had as its purposes, as stated in the platform,

> to secure to the toilers a proper share in the wealth that they create; more of the leisure that rightfully belongs to them; more societary advantages . . . all those rights and privileges necessary to make them capable of enjoying, appreciating, defending, and perpetuating . . . good government.[3]

Such idealism was complemented by the more practical objective of educating the employer into granting an eight-hour day. Yet the law of the land made it difficult to make such progress. The lawyers of large American corporations had discovered the usefulness of the famous Fourteenth Amendment, originally intended to give civil rights to freed Negro slaves, which stated:

> No State shall make or enforce any law which shall abridge the privileges or immunities of citizens of the United States; nor shall any State deprive any person of life, liberty or property, without due process of law.

Corporation lawyers sought to have their corporate clients defined as citizens of the United States in order to block union activity. Conservatively minded courts of law willingly accepted this definition and also interpreted "property" to include profits. The businessman's philosophy of laissez faire and anti-unionism was thus given federal constitutional sanction.

Gompers, in founding the American Federation of Labour, sought to avoid conflict with politicians and the law courts. Skilled workers were organized, under tight discipline, to press for gains under the slogan "more now." Restricting recruitment to craft or skill groups had a particular advantage: as these workers possessed a specific skill they could not be readily replaced if they went on strike, and this consideration could compel employers to bargain with them. Furthermore, the men in a particular craft had a community of interest which tended to produce a tightly knit group when the time came to bargain with an employer. Immediate objectives of the union included higher wages, shorter hours, and prohibition of convict labour. In Canada, the unions became affiliated with the American Federation of Labour and formed a national governing body in 1886, termed the Canadian Trades and Labour Congress.

The Knights of Labour, who had mushroomed from a membership of 100,000 to 700,000 in a single year, suffered a severe setback in 1886. A change in method by some of their leaders to anarchist tactics produced, in addition to a rise in membership, a disastrous incident in Chicago. A badly planned general strike for an eight-hour day resulted in an anarchist throwing a bomb in the Haymarket, which killed eight policemen. Public opinion connected the Knights with the incident, and the trade union organization was undermined and ultimately collapsed.

The widespread American belief in rugged individualism meant that public opinion in general favoured employers, and strikes for improved working conditions were seen as an attack on employers' sacred and inalienable rights. At the same time, the cause of the unionists was weakened by the tidal waves of immigrants arriving from South and East Europe who furnished cheap labour to industrialists. Between 1890 and 1914, over twelve million New Americans arrived from Italy, Austro-Hungary, Poland and Russia. To property-less peasants, who had first to learn the language of the new country, unionism seemed to prevent them from bartering their labour as they saw fit in the new land of opportunity. Native-born American workers resented the newcomers for the low wages at which they could be hired, and the story of American labour is checkered with violence. During the decade from 1895 to 1905 there were over 35,000 strikes, many of them resulting in bloodshed.

Canadian labour history was affected by events in the United States. The burst of union activity under the auspices of the Knights of Labour had collapsed by 1900. From the wreckage of these industrial unions, new central organizations were formed called "Trades and Labour Councils," the title indicating that craft unions and the unskilled were coming together. As one might expect from the economic nationalism inherent in John A. Macdonald's National Policy, it was Ontario who dominated the trade union situation. Generally speaking, Canadian labour after 1880 tended to be organized on an all-inclusive basis. The controlling Trades and Labour Congress accepted any union group, with the possible exception of a company union, which was a dummy organization run by an employer. Despite this flexible policy of attracting all types of labourers, the total number of Canadian union members in 1901 was only 8,381.

THE NEW UNIONISM

The difference in outlook between Canadian and American union organizations was attributable, in the main, to the influence in Canada of the "new unionism" in Britain. Britain in the late 1880's was the scene of a sustained drive to organize the semi-skilled or unskilled worker. A Marxist-inspired group named the Social Democratic Foundation supplied much of the agitation for an eight-hour day. "New" unions were formed, which were general unions in the sense that they recruited workers of all grades of skill. It was in the interest of all workers, reasoned the union leaders, that the unskilled should be organized. The inclusion of unskilled labourers in general unions could prevent the existence of blackleg or scab labour used by employers against the unions. Very prominent in this drive for "new unions" were the Dockers and Gas Works employees.

But the real spark that started the union drive in the 1880's came from a group of badly underpaid and over-worked girls in London's East End. What the Tolpuddle Martyrs were to the 1830's, the girls of Bryant and May's match factory were to the late 1880's. In 1888 the conditions in this factory were publicized by a fiery socialist, Mrs. Annie Besant, who wrote an article called "White Slavery in London." In London, a publicity campaign was soon mounted for improvement of conditions for the match girls. The girls went on strike and, in the face of mounting public indignation, the employer capitulated to their terms.

Such working girl solidarity so impressed the dockers in the east end of London that they struck for better wages and, over a period of a month, over 150,000 men came out on strike. A campaign was launched to obtain "a tanner (12¢) an hour." Support came from the Roman Catholic Archbishop Cardinal Manning, who formed a peace committee and aided the cause of the dockers. Help arrived from as far away as Australia, where dockers contributed thousands of pounds to a strike fund raised to aid their London counterparts. This strike which tied up the world's largest port ended in victory for the strikers. As a result of this situation, there ultimately emerged the Dock, Wharf, Riverside and General Labourers union with a powerful membership of 18,000 men.

UNIONS IN NORTH AMERICA

In contrast to the course of events in Britain, it was the skilled workers who organized in North America during the 1880's. Canada in these years was influenced by both her American and British heritages and was also particularly affected by the world-wide depression from 1873 to 1895, when the sale of primary products suffered badly in a world market.

While Canada had yet to experience widespread industrialization, the influence of the British experience with factories was seen in the campaign by trade unionists to secure Factory Acts that regulated conditions of employment. For a time it looked as if improvement of Canadian working conditions might founder on the contemporary political issue of Dominion-Provincial rights, as it was unclear which level of government had jurisdiction. In 1882 a federal commission of inquiry investigated working conditions in mills and factories in preparation for a Dominion Factory Act, but soon afterwards the issue was seen as a provincial matter. In Quebec and Ontario the legislatures enacted provincial measures that prohibited the employment of girls under 14 and boys under 12. Quebec's Factory Act of 1885 set a maximum of 72 hours of work per week while Ontario, in the following year, restricted the hours of labour for women and children to sixty per week. While in the absence of an efficient system of inspection these regulations could be evaded, nevertheless this factory legislation constituted an important precedent. Politicians in Canada showed that they were willing to adopt the British pattern of controlling those employers who abused the privilege of laissez faire through inhuman working conditions.

During the 1880's, the bulk of Canadian unionists belonged to well-established unions which were affiliated to an American parent organization. There was also, however, a form of nationalism at work in the efforts made to strengthen the power of such local branches. Unionists attempted to improve labour conditions by forming municipal organizations known as labour councils. Canadian unions barely survived this period of depression, but did, nevertheless, achieve a first for North America by organizing a national convention in 1886. Thus the founding of the Canadian Trades and Labour Congress preceded that of the American Federation of Labour by three months. The Canadian organization settled in 1892 on the name Trades and Labour Congress of Canada. The new organization was perhaps more Ontarian than Canadian, for it was not until after the depression ended in 1897 that New Brunswick and Manitoba participated. Meanwhile, Canadian industrialists copied the tactics of their American counterparts in encouraging the immigration of European peasants as a source of cheap labour.

AMERICA IN THE 1890's

In the United States, bloody battles became a familiar feature of strikes. What was, for example, supposed to be a model company town at Pullman, Illinois, saw the eruption of a clash that ultimately involved the President of the United States. Because of the financial impact of the depression, shareholders at the Pullman Car Company decided to slash wages in order to maintain dividends, while at the same time, raising the rents charged on company houses. This situation brought to the fore Eugene V. Debs, the organizer of the American Railway Union. Debs sought to stop all trains on which Pullman cars were being used. In retaliation, the railway employers' organization became determined to resist the strike organized by Debs, and even sought Presidential intervention on the grounds that the federal mails must be kept moving. By the use of court injunctions and federal troops sent by President Cleveland, the strike was broken. Later investigators of the Pullman strike have tended to blame the Pullman Corporation for the clash, but public sympathy was behind the employer. This general attitude was reflected in the way American courts virtually sided with employers against labour; in this respect American unionists were less fortunate than their cousins in Britain where the relative impartiality of the courts was respected. In short, industrial feudalism had taken root in the United States, principally in the form of company towns. A company which owned a town, built by itself to accommodate its own employees, was prone to regard "outside interference" as an affront to its property rights. As late as 1933, for example, the federal Secretary of Labour, Frances Perkins, was forcibly prevented from speaking in the streets of a Pennsylvania coal town.[4]

Steelworkers in Pittsburgh felt the power of their overlords. In 1892, Andrew Carnegie's plant at Homestead was under the control of a manager named Henry Frick. Frick sought to lower wages by 22 per cent and informed the Amalgamated Association of Iron and Steel Workers that henceforth workers would be working under a non-union system. A strike followed. Frick called in the Pinkerton Detective Agency to break this strike. Three hundred armed Pinkerton's men, or so-called detectives, approached the plant on barges on a nearby river: the strikers resisted and, after a grim gun battle, forced the detectives to retire. But the ostensible victory of the union produced a swift reaction in a society where property rights were sacrosanct. Troops were now ordered in to protect strike breakers and in this way the strike was defeated. It proved to be over forty years before another determined bid was made to promote union solidarity among steelworkers.

As central European immigrants who were suspicious of unions provided a source of easily exploitable labour, so did the children of the United States. In the total labour pool were approximately two million child workers who frequently worked ten hours a day for six days a week. Child labour was badly abused in the United States, due to the absence of adequate State control. A writer named John Spargo described the horrors of the situation in *The Cry of the Children* (1906). He told of the sixteen-hour day worked in the cotton mills by thousands of little girls between ten and twelve years old. The working conditions were so hazardous that one surgeon alone claimed to have amputated the fingers of over one hundred children. Spargo told of nine-year old boys, hunchbacked and deformed from crouching in the coal mines, receiving a wage of fifty or sixty cents a day.

The number of full-time child workers employed in

industry was estimated at approximately one and a half million, while part-timers far exceeded this number. Due to the federal Constitution, it was difficult for reformers to secure adequate laws to prohibit child labour. South Carolina, for example, finally worked up to a twelve year age minimum for factory labour, but permitted exceptions where this limit imposed a hardship on the family. Not until 1909 did an American State–Delaware–provide that "no child under the age of fourteen shall be employed or suffered to work in any gainful occupation." It was not until much later, in 1938, that legislators agreed to stop the abuse of children in an effective manner. A long-protracted battle about children lasted until the New Deal of Franklin Roosevelt.

At the turn of the twentieth century, the contrast in both North America and Britain between labourers' wages and employers' fortunes was glaring. It was, of course, an age in which there was no income tax or estate tax. In Edwardian England, the wealthy exhibited what some economists called, with some understatement, conspicuous consumption. But even this elite was considerably outshone by the so-called robber barons in the United States where, it was estimated in 1904, ninety per cent of the national wealth was in the hands of ten per cent of the people. Palatial homes were built by families such as the Vanderbilts, Morgans, Duponts and Rockefellers; in Toronto, Sir Henry Pellatt's lavish Casa Loma boasted bath fixtures made of fourteen carat gold.

THE ATTACK ON LABOUR AND THE RESPONSE

In Britain, trade unionism suffered a severe setback at this time with the Taff Vale decision of 1901. This case involved strikers belonging to the Amalgamated Society of Railway Servants who tried to close down a company railway. The Taff Vale Company's general manager promptly planned to import blackleg or scab labour from the anti-union National Free Labour Association. This manager then sued for damages against the strikers and, as even the Government's chief labour conciliator G.R. Askwith commented, seemed to like "litigation for its own sake." Ultimately the case reached the final court of appeal in the House of Lords. Their lordships handed down a decision which attempted to cripple the labour movement, by declaring that a union was liable for all damages suffered by an employer against whom a strike was called. Working men assumed, not unreasonably, that the legal decision was basically a class decision, with the intention of weakening the union movement. This legal decision, besides costing the Railway Union £25,000 in damages, threatened by implication to bankrupt the entire union movement. The extremity of the situation at last galvanized the conservatively minded Trades Union Congress into seeking political redress by supporting the struggling infant Labour party. In the election of 1906, the trade union movement helped to elect 26 Labour members who then applied pressure to the ruling Liberal government. Almost immediately, a Trades Disputes Act of 1906 restored the right to strike without fear of incurring unreasonable financial liability.

Events in Canada followed a similar course in the early years of the century. In 1900, Quebec City shoemakers were locked out by their employers. Employers insisted that their workers sign a "yellow dog" contract, which was an agreement that no attempt would be made to form a union after work was resumed. Archbishop Bégin was asked to arbitrate in the dispute. Citing the *De Rerum Novarum* of Pope Leo XIII, the Archbishop announced that workers had the right to organize. This entrance by the Roman Catholic church into the field of organizing unions culminated in 1922 in the formation of the Canadian and Catholic Confederation of Labour.

In 1902, the American Federation of Labour decided to purge the Canadian Labour Congress. All rival unions to those of the A.F. of L. were to be expelled from the Canadian organization. In terms of numbers, this expulsion affected only a minority, but the significant aspect is that these workers loudly proclaimed their Canadianism. This was the first time in industrial history that self-proclaimed patriots had been evicted from a trade union organization by their fellow countrymen, at the insistence of foreigners based in another country. Yet it must be noted that the American domination of unionism, under the guise of internationalism, had probably more reality for the Canadian unionist that the political nationalism espoused by politicians. The economic pull towards integration within a continental setting so much deplored in contemporary society has long been present. Yet, at the same time, Canadians did not take kindly to direction from the United States. As one historian of the union movement has commented:

> From 1897 on, it [the Canadian Labour Congress] kept trying to get the international unions, or the A.F. of L. on their behalf, to turn over to the Congress the dues these unions paid the A.F. of L. on their Canadian membership. It finally solved this problem by getting the international unions to affiliate their Canadian membership direct, which they began in 1906. The A.F. of L. persisted right down to 1955 in chartering local unions in Canada. It also made repeated unsuccessful attempts to deny the C.L.C. the sole right to charter local Trades and Labour Councils, and it took the Congress 35 years (1910-1945) to win complete victory.[5]

Yet it is only fair to point out that probably only large American unions had the necessary staff and experience to protect the general interests of employees in Canada.

At the same time, however, there was also an influence from British unionism which remained particularly strong in the political sphere. It has not generally been recognized in Canada that an infant Labour party was born at the same time as that of Britain. In 1900, two independent Labour members were sent to the Canadian House of Commons. Nanaimo miners elected Ralph Smith, and A.W. Puttee was returned for Winnipeg. A difficult problem in labour reforms was posed, however, by the Canadian constitution, which split power between the federal government and the provinces, with the latter having the responsibility for legislation on property and civil rights. Union leaders relied upon meetings with government ministers to press for legislation favourable to labour; this was similar to the strategy of the Lib-Labs in Britain who were working men elected under the auspices of the Liberal Party in the years when there was no union support for a Labour party. These union Leaders in

Britain and Canada came, however, to a similar conclusion about the need for direct political action.

In 1903, a new Canadian Congress president, John Flett, declared that meetings with the Dominion Government were useless and that Canadian Labour should follow the British example and elect Labour representatives to Parliament. By 1906, the first official "Labour" M.P. was elected to Ottawa when Alphonse Verville was returned for Maisonneuve, Montreal. Verville was President of the Trades Labour Congress and hoped for "at least a dozen" Labour members in the next Parliament.

Yet the counter-pull of the American tradition of non-political activity could be seen in the reaction of the Trades Labour Congress. Reared on the philosophy of Samuel Gompers, this organization was not likely to become politically militant. It is worth considering in this regard that one major reason for the great success of W.L. Mackenzie King in Canadian politics was that as a "labour expert," he realized that A.F.L. principles precluded direct political activity. So Alphonse Verville was doomed to disappointment, when the Trades Labour Congress adopted an equivocal line of action. The Congress endorsed sending Labour representatives to Parliament and the Provincial Legislatures, and its provincial executives were to summon provincial conventions of trade unionists and sympathizers to set up "the necessary associations." After this, however, the Congress retreated out of the picture, having "recommended" its own platform of principles for "this independent effort."[6] It is important to note that, unlike the Trades Labour Congress in Britain, after 1900 there was no effort made to finance large-scale political activity by union funds. Yet the practical result was to launch a Canadian Labour Party in Ontario, Quebec, Manitoba, British Columbia and Nova Scotia. The only real success of this party, however, was in Ontario in 1919 when eleven candidates were elected to the provincial Legislature.

GOVERNMENT INTERVENTION

In 1900 a Federal Department of Labour was established and in September of that year the first *Labour Gazette* was published. The first editor, W.L. Mackenzie King, claimed to be Labour's friend. King was active in promoting the Industrial Investigations Act of 1907, which proposed that federal conciliators were to be called into industrial disputes, before strikes or lockouts could be considered. Compulsory arbitration under governmental auspices thus became a unique feature of Canadian labour legislation. This approach was principally aimed at cases involving essential or municipal services, such as mines, transport, gas or water works. Sir Wilfrid Laurier commented on the legislation of his Minister of Labour, W.L. Mackenzie King, by saying that "We do not propose to make arbitration compulsory. We say that it will be sufficient for the time being to provide for a compulsory investigation."[7]

There was possibly some advantage for the tiny trade union movement in this government action, for employers who had often refused to meet with union representatives were now compelled to agree to conciliation, and this in itself opened up the possibility of employer recognition of unions and collective bargaining. This labour legislation had great political potential for the federal government; Ottawa could gain in public popularity, pulling chestnuts out of the industrial fire, while claiming to be merely a neutral referee protecting the people's interests. Not surprisingly, labour viewed compulsory arbitration with an air of suspicion that turned, with experience, into one of anathema.

The unique flavour of Canadian collective bargaining is a legacy from the liberal belief of W.L. Mackenzie King that the State should be included in industrial disputes. King expounded his philosophy in fuzzy Gladstonian prose in 1918 in a book entitled *Industry and Humanity*. King was considered to be a labour expert and had gained experience in the U.S.A. while being employed by the Rockefellers. Although some critics felt that his idea of co-operation implied employer-dominated company unions, he maintained an air of moral rectitude that convinced the Canadian electorate that he had their best interests at heart. In this context it is interesting to reflect that, when the Second World War began, the Canadian Parliament passed an Order-in-Council on November 7, 1939, extending industrial investigation to all essential industries. By contrast, in the United States and Britain the governments generally relied upon the co-operation of their trade union leaders to ensure a whole-hearted war effort.

Britain's Liberal Party was dying in the pre-1914 period. Trying to steer a middle course between a socialistically inclined mass of working-class voters and the employers who supplied Liberal party funds, proved too much in the long run. In 1909, a Sweated Labour Act regulated conditions for women employees in certain notorious industries, such as box-making and tailoring. Cases had come to light of old women working eighty hours a week slivering wood with razor blades, so as to make "seeds" for cheap "raspberry" jam. Tailors earned roughly ninety-eight cents a day for cutting and stitching a complete man's jacket. Annual paid holidays even for trade unionists did not come until 1911. And not until 1913 did the Liberal government stir itself to repeal the anti-union Osborne judgement of 1908, that pro-hibited trade unions from financing the Labour party, and so kept Labour weak.

Strikes were widespread and troops were frequently called out to repress them. Militancy came into the labour movement when syndicalist ideas were imported from France. George Sorel, the syndicalist leader, shaped the philosophy of the general strike as a means of paralyzing the economy of a country. He thought of the general strike as a political weapon for winning control of the State or, failing that, for uniting the working class. By 1914, a British general strike was being planned by what was termed the Triple Alliance, comprising Transport, Railway and Mining unions; only the outbreak of war on August 4, 1914, saved the paral-ysis of the economy.

Up to the beginning of the war, Canada continued to benefit from the Laurier boom which had started in 1897. Labour conditions were to a very significant extent tied to the tremendous spurt of economic activity generated by railway building. During the decade of 1904 to 1914, there was never less than 3,000 miles under construction at any one time. Year after year employment was available for up to eight thousand men, working on surveys or in pick-and-shovel gangs. Unionism, however, was not encouraged. In the booming logging industry employers did not object when the reliable French-Canadian logger was displaced, as often happened, by a cheaper Sifton Sheepskin.[8] The high turnover of labour can be judged from the revealing comment of one lumberman that, "We now have three crews, one coming in, one working, and one going out." A sharp increase had occurred in union membership by 1914, when 150,000 men were enrolled, but even so, over 90 per cent of all workers were not members of unions.

THE IMPACT OF THE GREAT WAR

With the coming of war, Canada blossomed out as a major supplier of munitions which, by 1918, were valued at a total of $10,500,000,000: this figure equalled all governmental expenses by Ottawa between 1867 and 1932.[9] Canada thus entered the ranks of industrialized nations as a result of the Great War and, having secured a more diversified economy, left behind the days of small factories serving a local market under tariff protection. As Britain declined economically, North America prospered: by 1918 the United States was the leading creditor nation of the world. Furthermore, the cloak of patriotism tended to give a respectable flavour to large wartime profits which, by 1919, were perturbing many union men.

During the latter stages of the war, tension was rising in many industrial states. In October 1917, the Bolsheviks seized power in Russia, and reaction in the West to this event tended to fall along class lines. Upper-class politicians like Winston Churchill wanted Allied military intervention in Russia in 1919: labour leaders like Ernest Bevin insisted on a hands-off policy. Beginning in the spring of 1919, the British cabinet received weekly reports from the Home Office Directorate of Intelligence about trade unionism and the Labour party. Obviously the suspicions of a century earlier, that the worker could not be trusted and had to be spied upon, had not died in ruling circles. Similarly, in Canada the Royal North West Mounted Police entered a new phase of activity as undercover agents for the federal government in

Ottawa by burrowing within the labour movement.

But if the fear of radicalism among the workers occupied the governments of Britain and Canada, it was also true that in the United States there was an even greater panic. From 1919 to 1921 there occurred what was later termed the Big Red Scare, with accompanying outbursts of intolerance. An American historian, R.K. Murray, has written, "This was an era of lawlessness and the disorderly defence of law and order, of suspicion amid civil conduct—in a very literal sense a reign of terror." In this social climate, unionism was forced on the defensive.

Shouts of "Down with Bolshevism, down with the Reds" led to mobs roughing up union members. This kind of public hysteria gave a golden opportunity to the super-patriotic one hundred per cent American to pin labels like "Red" "Commie" "Bolshie" on ambitious working men. The goal of a closed or union shop now became "Un-American." A sensationalistic press printed imaginative horror stories, as for example of the situation "in Petrograd [where] the Bolsheviks had an electrically operated guillotine that lopped off five hundred heads an hour."[10]   When the Boston Police went on strike they were openly called Bolsheviks. From now on, trade union organizers on both sides of the Atlantic had to guard against being smeared as unpatriotic and/or communists. Ernest Bevin in Britain was particularly vulnerable to this latter charge, as the active British Labour party aimed to change the fabric of society by socialist means.

The most significant labour event in Canada at this time was the Winnipeg General Strike of 1919. At issue, according to the judgement of the Royal Commissioner Judge H.A. Robson, K.C. who later conducted the investigation, was the question of collective bargaining. Working men who had just fought a war for democracy were resentful and hostile towards the businessmen who had stayed at home to make war profits, and sought decent working conditions for themselves and higher wages to match rising costs. In addition the concept of industrial unionism within One Big Union had taken root in the Canadian West and its first real trial of strength was in Winnipeg, where employers refused to recognize any union that represented the metal workers.

Thirty-five thousand workers went on strike and most of the city's essential services were stopped for at least part of the forty-two days of the strike's duration. Canadian Mounted Police were called in to break the strike, and ten strike leaders, mainly British-born socialists, were legally charged with conspiring to introduce Russian Communism into Canada. Seven were convicted and sentenced to imprisonment. The federal government rushed two pieces of legislation through Parliament: an amendment to the Immigration Act of June 6, 1919 which was principally designed to get radical British unionists out of Canada as fast as possible, and an amendment to the Criminal Code in Section 98 which was intended to make police surveillance of unionists much easier. This amendment defined "unlawful associations" so loosely that it made any effort to provide any "governmental, industrial or economic change" suspect. For example, if a person attended a meeting of an unlawful association, a prosecutor would "in the absence of proof to the contrary" assume that he was a member of such an unlawful association. In other words, this section 98 reversed the basic assumption of English law, that a person was innocent until proved guilty.

Like the Tolpuddle incident, the Winnipeg strike produced martyrs to the cause of organized labour. Generally speaking, the Winnipeg General Strike has been considered as leading to the rise of J.S. Woodsworth. Whether or not his role in the strike justified Woodsworth's reputation as a crusader, however, has been disputed. Woodsworth's biographer, Kenneth McNaught, sees his hero as a knight in shining armour who emerges from an active role at Winnipeg to lead the gallant charge on injustice. A contrary point of view has been taken by D.C. Masters in his monograph entitled *The Winnipeg General Strike* and also by Professor Roger Graham, the biographer of Arthur Meighen, Minister of Justice at the time. The stand of these two critics is essentially that Woodsworth used the strike as a springboard for his later political career. That is, union leaders influenced by the Social Democratic Federation doctrine went to prison, the militancy died down and the Methodist brand of middle-class Canadian socialism survived to provide an influence in the later formation of the Co-operative Commonwealth Federation. While some of the causes and effects of the Winnipeg General Strike are debatable, there is no doubt that Canadian trade unionism was dealt a severe blow. Trade union membership steadily declined from a high of 378,000 in 1919, and would not reach this figure again until 1937, nearly twenty years later.

By 1921 there was a considerable difference in the political attitudes of labour movements in Britain and in North America. American unions continued to express belief in capitalism and sought economic improvements by collective bargaining with employers, while at the same time seeking to exert pressure on the two main parties for general legislation favourable to labour. On the other hand, British unions were now out to change the fabric of society by socialist means. The sickening mass slaughter on the Western Front had made working men determined to justify this sacrifice by making a better Britain. Due to the ravages of war and economic decline, drastic changes were occurring in the economy. In the 1920's widespread unemployment became a permanent feature of the labour scene and was never to drop below a million until the wartime Dunkirk crisis of 1940. Politicians showed little imagination in dealing with declining staple industries such as shipbuilding, coal and textiles, or in stimulating public projects. King George V tried to encourage the Lloyd George government to open up opportunities for public employment of those without work, and displayed a grasp of reality well ahead of his ministers. The King suggested emergency public works with projects such as road-making, land reclamation and reforestation to meet the claim of those who sought work and not charity. These ideas were eventually embodied not in British legislation but in the American New Deal.

In the 1920's American union members did not share in what has been depicted as the prosperous Roaring Twenties. Organized campaigns by industrialists sought to establish "open shops" where anybody was hired and union organizers found it difficult to promote solidarity among the workers in a plant. Membership in American unions declined from 5.1 million in 1920 to 3.6 million in 1929. Steelworkers often worked an 84-hour week. In Elizabethtown, Tennessee in 1927, girls worked 56 hours a week for 18¢ an hour: when these girls organized in protest, their strike was smashed by a combination of local vigilantes, company militia and state troops. Meanwhile, the Supreme Court found two child-labour laws unconstitutional, rejected a minimum-wage law for women and sustained yellow dog contracts. (Yellow dog contracts hired workers on the understanding that they would not join a union.)

While union membership also dropped in Canada, there was one interesting trend. In 1927, a number of union organizations, including notably the Canadian Brotherhood of Railway Employees, combined to form the All-Canadian Federation of Labour. Dedicated to both industrial and national unionism, this group later became the political arm of the labour movement, in support of the Co-operative Commonwealth Federation. The "national" emphasis in an "All-Canadian" Congress of Labour fitted into the political mood of the 1920's, although later international unions reasserted their dominance in Canada.

In Britain, labour was very restless, particularly the miners who were seeking nationalization of the mines. A Royal Commission of 1921 under the chairmanship of Lord Sankey endorsed nationalization. Annoyed that Lloyd George, the Prime Minister, did not act on this recommendation, the miners renewed plans for a general strike. As on the eve of World War One, the mining, transport and railway workers combined in the Triple Alliance. Only the miners, though, showed real determination about striking, and after several months they were forced to return to work at lower wages. This failure helps in understanding the renewed attempt of the miners to use the power of a general strike five years later.

By 1926, a further reduction of wages was imminent for the miners. Coal owners announced the absolute necessity of the miners tightening their belts, and the desperate workers received a sympathetic hearing from their fellow unionists. Once more a strike by the Triple Alliance was proposed. The miners' executive was led by Arthur Cook, a fiery Welsh Communist who coined the slogan, "not a minute on the day, not a penny off the pay," and the blunt-speaking Herbert Smith.[11]

When the General Strike came, it was found that the Government had prepared emergency plans. An organization for the Maintenance of Supplies was headed by Winston Churchill, who also edited the government newspaper, *The British Gazette*. The middle class rallied with patriotic eagerness to grapple with a national crisis, and many students fulfilled childhood ambitions by driving trains and buses. As in 1921, the labour front cracked when the transport and railway workers deserted their mining colleagues. It was November before the miners were compelled to capitulate, but then the mine owners set terms for rehiring which mocked Arthur Cook's defiant slogan, by increasing the hours of labour and lowering the rate of pay.

The General Strike of 1926 was a major crisis, but it was not "general" in the sense that all union members were called out. Only about one-sixth of the labour force was on strike, and essential services such as electricity and retail food distribution continued. Its effects were powerful enough, however, for a badly shaken Conservative government to be persuaded by employers into an act of revenge. In 1927 the Trades Disputes and Trades Union Act was passed, making any "sympathetic" or "general" strike illegal. But more important was the clause about a union member "contracting in" to a financial levy for the Labour Party. This meant that now a trade union member had to be asked if he would contribute, a drastic change from the earlier "contracting out," where he had to explain why he would *not* back the Labour Party. Pressure from fellow workers or sheer lack of interest might prevent a man from contracting out; but the same lack of interest, plus the fact that withholding a political contribution would increase his wages, could prevent a worker from contracting in. This action by the Conservative government reduced the Labour Party's income from the trade union affiliation by a third.

In the rebuilding of union power, a key figure to emerge was Ernest Bevin. Bevin's outlook was sufficiently broad to see the need for co-operation with industrialists, in order to resolve the root problem of technological unemployment.

Such co-operation was essential for any hopes of restored prosperity, as politicians seemed to lack the necessary imagination to revive Britain's obsolete staple industries. Fear of revolution prompted the familiar Conservative reaction of purchasing security; it was fear of violence and not concern for human charity that really produced the idea of the "dole." The names under which subsistence was paid to the unemployed varied, but the system of a "government handout" remained constant. In 1927, an official committee under Lord Blaneburgh studied the problem and, in the mistaken view that the peak of unemployment had been reached, recommended unlimited relief for all the unemployed as a statutory right. The eventual result of this Blaneburgh recommendation was the bankruptcy of the unemployment fund in 1931, despite massive financial transfusions from the Treasury.

Britain in 1931 had a so-called National Government which cut the pay of civil servants and the Royal Navy. History repeated itself when, as at Spithead during the Napoleonic Wars, the Royal Navy mutinied at Invergordon. Methods used in dealing with the rebels of the Navy were similar to those employed to repress unionists after the 1926 General Strike. All sailors stationed at Invergordon at the time of the mutiny, whether strikers or not, were singled out for special treatment: identification numbers were issued that in the future identified these potential "trouble-makers" to their future commanding officers.

THE DEPRESSION

In the 1920's, Britain's economic problems had been basically due to technological obsolescence. Large staple industries such as shipbuilding, mining and textiles could not find enough customers. When the full impact of the depression was added to Britain's woes, over 3 million workers, or 20 per cent of the working force, were unemployed. The government's unemployment benefit amounted to 29s. 3d. ($7.20) per week for a married man with three dependents, a sum which was subsequently increased to 36 shillings in 1936. This dole was just enough to keep an unemployed man from a state of revolution.

Revolution seemed possible in the U.S.A. when, by 1932, the depression was becoming worse and no dole existed for the unemployed. Yet the mood of America in the winter of 1932-3, just before the inauguration of Franklin Delano Roosevelt, was surprisingly apathetic. An authority on this period, William Leuchtenburg, has written:

> Both American and European observers were astonished by the strangely phlegmatic response of Americans to the depression. In England, thousands of British workers marched on Buckingham Palace and Downing Street, and in Newfoundland, a mob broke into the cabinet chamber in St. John's, and roughed up the Prime Minister; but in the United States, a country thought of as the land of lawlessness, most of the unemployed meekly accepted their lot.[12]

Ordinary Americans seemed to have lost faith in their economic system, and it is a tribute to F.D.R.'s awareness that one of the first phrases he uttered as President was that "the only thing we have to fear is fear itself." Professor Leuchtenburg notes, in his definitive study of the New Deal, that Franklin D. Roosevelt was essentially a conservative repairing a damaged economy. Although critics of the New Deal were to condemn it as socialistic and un-American, it was fear of socialism that prompted legislative action. As another writer has observed:

> The Marxist intellectuals were more powerful than they knew. They scared businessmen, conditioned the voters to extensive Governmental intervention, channelled normal human compassion and inadvertently helped save capitalism by moving everyone from Mr. Roosevelt to the bankers just far enough to the left for them to see the social significance of decisions traditionally regarded as purely private.[13]

Roosevelt saw the need for action and a large number of legislative measures were passed into law in 1933. To union members the National Industrial Recovery Act offered a chance to improve their working conditions. Wages and hours of work were to be regulated under industrial codes; this showed an astonishing change of philosophy in a country which prided itself on laissez faire and rugged individualism. A.M. Schlesinger has summarized the impact of this legislation in this way:

> ... N.R.A. accomplished a fantastic series of reforms, any one of which would have staggered the nation a few years earlier. It established the principle of maximum hours and minimum wages on a national basis. It dealt a fatal blow to sweatshops. It made collective bargaining a national policy and thereby transformed the position of organized labour. It gave new status to the consumer. It stamped out noxious trade practices. It set new standards of decency in American life. It helped to break the chain of economic fatalism. It accustomed the country to the feasibility of government regulation and taught people to think in terms of national policy for business and labour.[14]

When the Supreme Court ruled N.R.A. unconstitutional, the momentum of opposition to this move was sufficient to generate another Magna Carta for labour, the Wagner Act of 1935. This Act guaranteed to workers the right to select unions of their own choice, and also set up a Labour Relations Board to arbitrate labour disputes. Senator Wagner, commenting on his own legislation, said that workers could now decide for themselves, free of the pressure of an employer, whether or not to join a union, and which union. Once a majority of the workers had selected a bargaining agent by majority decision, employers were required by law to bargain "in good faith" with that union. This Act proved to be influential for Canadian policy; in the same year, the provinces of British Columbia and Nova Scotia adopted its principles. Alberta followed in 1938, Saskatchewan and Manitoba in 1940. Ontario's Legislature passed a Labour Relations Act in 1944, although by then the federal government had already pioneered in national collective bargaining in essential wartime industries.

UNIONS VERSUS CORPORATIONS

Against this general background of legislative activity, American union organizers renewed their assault upon the chief corporation strongholds represented by individual companies such as General Motors, Ford and United States Steel. In 1936, the federal government was trying to play the role of an impartial referee administering a code of rules. That corporate tool known as a "company union," which was essentially anti-union in its objective, would no longer suffice. It was in this setting that the tactical method of a sit-down strike was to prove so effective.

The idea of the sit-down strike had been born in 1934 in the General Tire plant in Akron, Ohio. A local union president, Rex Murray, felt that it was safer for strikers to sit down beside their machines than go outside and picket; while local police would not be slow to attack workers, they might hesitate if the employers' machines could be damaged. Two years later Akron was the birthplace of the Committee for Industrial Organization which was planned as a grass-roots organization to unite all workers in major industries. When rubber workers went on strike in 1936, they were backed by sympathetic unions of Mine Workers, Garment Workers and Printers who made funds available for resistance. This situation caused a tussle inside the union movement: the parent organization, the A.F.L., espoused a philosophy of craft unionism which was opposed by the infant C.I.O.'s principle of "industrial unionism"—the organization of all workers in one place into one union. John L. Lewis, the Miners' Leader, argued that big corporations had to be faced by big industrial unions. With the support of the Wagner Act, the old Committee for Industrial Organization broke with the A.F.L. and a new organization was established known as the Congress for Industrial Organization, and a campaign launched against monopolistic big business interests. This attempt to organize workers into industrial unions produced a violent reaction among employers. Corporations mobilized private armies of thugs and local police to resist unionization of the steel, textile, electrical and automobile industries.

Lewis led the C.I.O. crusade and America watched with

interest as he arrived, in person, to tackle the automobile companies of Detroit. On December 28, 1936, General Motors employees in Cleveland "sat down" on the job: in February, 1937, General Motors surrendered. The membership of the United Automobile Workers leaped from 30,000 to 400,000 and a similar achievement was made the following year when United States Steel surrendered like General Motors, and the Steelworkers, organized from scratch, had an instant membership of 325,000. Unions rapidly developed to cover other American industries. United Rubber Workers organized Firestone Tire and Rubber and by the end of 1937, the United Electrical and Radio Workers had organized General Electric, R.C.A. Victor and Philco.This effort at organizing the mass of American workers in industry was aided by the Fair Labour Standards Act of 1938, designed to put "a ceiling over hours and a floor under wages." It fixed forty hours a week as the working week and forty cents an hour as the minimum wage. The pendulum of power in industrial plants, so long weighted in favour of the employer, was now rapidly changing to benefit the worker. Furthermore, at long last child labour was outlawed in American industrial plants.

In 1939 Walter Reuther, head of the United Automobile Workers G.M. division in Detroit, led tool and die makers out on strike at a crucial time when the company was retooling for new models. This strike launched the auto workers on a wave of new triumphs.

Conditions in Canada parallelled those of the United States; frequently the same companies and unions operated on both sides of the border. Oshawa was the scene of a struggle in 1937 over admission of the C.I.O. to a plant of General Motors. Ontario Premier Mitchell Hepburn ordered the Ontario Provincial Police to break the strike, and labelled the C.I.O. as a communist organization; the resignation of two members of Hepburn's provincial cabinet followed from this incident and the strike was successful in securing union recognition and a 44-hour week.

CANADA MOVES TO THE LEFT

One unique Canadian development in the 1930's was the formation of a new political party, the Co-operative Commonwealth Federation. The impetus for a new political group came from delegates of labour and farm organizations in the four western provinces and Ontario. In 1933 a convention was held at Regina where a small group of intellectuals from the universities drafted a Manifesto, or statement of policy. The opening paragraph described the new party in these words:

> The C.C.F. is a federation of organizations whose purpose is the establishment of a Co-operative Commonwealth in which the principle regulating production and exchange will be supplying of needs and not the making of profits.

A socialistic program was proposed in the fourteen-point Manifesto, with item seven calling for the establishment of

> A National Labour Code to secure for the worker maximum income and leisure covering illness, accident, old age and unemployment, freedom of association and effective participation in the management of his industry or profession.

This movement blended the agrarian radical tradition of Western Canada with the socialist philosophy of Great Britain. Yet in an age when trade unionism only included approximately fifteen per cent of the skilled and practically none of the unskilled workers, the political movement could not expect mass support from labour. Furthermore, the socialist dogma expounded proved to have little appeal in Catholic French Canada or in the Maritimes.

Labour conditions during the depression were similar in all large industrial centres. In Canada as a whole, from 500,000 to 600,000 unemployed men and women were on public relief in 1935. That year was an election year and Prime Minister R.B. Bennett, a millionaire corporation lawyer, was infected with a radical virus and launched a radio tirade against:

selfish men, and this country is not without them—men whose mounting bank rolls loom larger than your happiness, corporations without souls and without virtue— these fearful that this Government might infringe on what they have grown to regard as their immemorial right of exploitation will whisper against us. They will call us radicals. They will say that this is the first step on the road to socialism. We fear them not.[15]

R.B. Bennett lauched Canada's version of the American New Deal. He pushed through minimum wage legislation, the 48-hour week and a weekly day of rest. The electorate, however, took a somewhat sceptical look at R.B. Bennett's late conversion to the cause of the underdog and proceeded to vote him out of power. In contrast, Franklin Delano Roosevelt in 1936 was returned to power with massive union support. The C.I.O. unions gave $700,000 to finance his campaign, the Democratic party's largest benefactor being the United Mine Workers who provided $469,000.[16] By 1937 the main union bargaining position had been achieved in the United States.

The furious American debate within the trade union movement over the relative merits of industrial and craft unionism created problems in Canada. The Canadian Trades and Labour Congress was faced with a virtual ultimatum from the American Federation of Labour, which represented the majority of Canadian unionists, to expel the C.I.O. unions. Those unions which were expelled in 1939 formed a Canadian C.I.O. Committee which, later that year, agreed to unite with the All-Canadian Congress, an organization which had long been at loggerheads with A.F.L. unionism. This merger of union organizations produced the Canadian Congress of Labour, set up in 1940, which rapidly expanded to become the second largest labour body in Canada. Possibly the main reason why union membership increased so rapidly in Canada after 1939 was that the federal government, given new powers by the wartime emergency situation, now endorsed the idea of collective bargaining. World War Two did for Canadian unionists what Franklin Delano Roosevelt's New Deal legislation had achieved for American labour.

EXPANSION DURING WORLD WAR II

During the 1940's, trade union membership in both Britain and Canada increased by leaps and bounds, with Canadian membership doubling between 1940 and 1945. The production of vast quantities of military equipment necessitated by the war pulled Britain and North America out of the economic slump. Ernest Bevin, the trade union leader, was Britain's Minister of Labour and mobilized workers for the war effort so effectively that by 1943, two-thirds of Britain's labour force between the ages of 14 and 64 was either engaged in war production, or in the armed forces. Bevin devised what he called "manpower budgets" which distributed the labour force according to wartime needs; this ignored the traditional emphasis on financial budgets.

In Canada, labour responded splendidly to the fight against fascism. The Congress of Labour that had been formed in 1940 co-operated with the government in developing war production. Canada organized a Department of Munitions and Supply, which had unlimited authority to control raw materials and issue contracts to private industry. Canada's total material production trebled between 1939 and 1945. During this time, Mackenzie King's Liberal government passed Order-in-Council P.C. 1003 dated February 17, 1944, which set up machinery for collective bargaining and made it uniform throughout Canada. In the same year, the Ontario Legislature established a provincial Ontario Labour Relations Board. With the blessing of the federal government, the Congress of Labour organized the mass industries during the wartime period, and union membership doubled to reach a total of 711,000 by 1945. Unions gained national prestige as war workers, including many women, backed the fighting men.

As trade unionism increased during the Second World War, so did the strength of the C.C.F. Party. In 1943, the C.C.F. party formed the official opposition in the provincial Ontario and British Columbia legislatures. The following year saw the C.C.F. take office as the government of Saskatchewan, forming North America's first socialist government. By 1945 a high point was reached when twenty-eight federal members were returned for the C.C.F. in the federal general election. But as prosperity increased in Canada in the postwar era, enthusiasm for socialism declined.

A noteworthy achievement of Mackenzie King was the introduction in 1941 of a federal Unemployment Insurance Act. This measure was strongly influenced by British experience, particularly in the concept of contributions being paid jointly by employer, employee and the government. Like Britain's scheme, it was centrally controlled from the national capital, whereas in the United States each of the then forty-eight states had developed its own Unemployment Insurance scheme, subject to general supervision from Washington. Mackenzie King used his political adroitness to get the Canadian provinces to release, at a time of national crisis, their right under the B.N.A. Act to control social welfare.

During World War II the British union movement not only gained a large increase in recruits, particularly women, but it also gained in national acceptance. In 1945, an electorate that had grown weary of a dominant Conservative party gave the Labour party a large majority. When the **Labour Government repealed the Trade Disputes Act of 1927,** this meant that once more workers had to "contract out" of a union. This was revenge upon the Conservatives and provided an immediate increase in political funds for the Labour Party. Even when the Conservatives returned to office in 1951, they dared not carry out a threat to re-enact the Trade Disputes Act of 1927. Trade unionism had become an accepted power in the land.

A very different pattern emerged in the U.S.A. where unionism was on the defensive. After the unions, with one major exception, adhered to their promise not to impede the war effort by strikes, the postwar period saw a wave of strikes. As the economy shifted to a peacetime basis, former war workers were often paid less. At the same time, the Republicans in 1946 had gained control of the Congress and despite President Truman's effort to veto the legislation, passed a Labour Management Relations Act. Generally known by the names of its conservative sponsors, Taft and Hartley, this Act banned closed shop agreements and placed restrictions on the right to strike and on picketing. There was to be a 60-day cooling-off period for industrial disputes and union leaders were required to take a non-Communist oath. Obviously, this was the start of an effort to draw the teeth of labour. The Act contained also a provision to force union members to act as scab or blackleg labour, by requiring them to work on projects that were being struck by other union workers.

Canada experienced a similar disruption of employer-union harmony after World War II. In 1945 a closed shop was sought at the Ford plant in Windsor. Eventually 11,000 men went out on strike and, under pressure from Ford and the underwriters who insured their property, the federal government was drawn into the dispute. Royal Canadian Mounted Police converged on Windsor. As public opinion was on the side of the strikers, the company and Ottawa decided to retreat by accepting the idea of a return to work without reprisals, and an arbitrator was appointed. Out of this situation emerged what was termed the Rand formula, which made union membership voluntary but union dues compulsory for its members. It thus fell short of the closed shop but improved union security.

The Ford strike was the most prominent of a wave of strikes in 1946. In Quebec the giant of the cotton industry, Dominion Textile, was struck. The president Blair Gordon, supported by Premier Maurice Duplessis, labelled it a communist conspiracy, but ultimately union recognition was conceded. The strike in Quebec that had the most far-reaching effects started in the town of Asbestos in February, 1949. The giant American corporation of Johns-Manville rejected the demands of the Canadian and Catholic Confederation of Labour for higher wages and improved safety conditions in the mines. Underlying the issues involved in the strike were deeper currents that reflected the emergence of Quebec into the industrial twentieth century, with the accompanying desire to be mistress in her own house. American and English-Canadian capitalism had long dominated industry in Quebec and from the late 1930's, industrial corporations had been upheld by the political power of Maurice Duplessis and his Union Nationale Party. So when the strike came at Asbestos, Duplessis sent provincial police to help in breaking it. Violence erupted as physical force was used on strikers. There followed a dramatic moment when the Roman Catholic Church, led by Archbishop Joseph Charbonneau, condemned the crushing of the social aspirations of the working class. Duplessis's power in the Vatican succeeded in having Charbonneau exiled to British Columbia. After much hardship, the asbestos miners won their fight; this victory proved to be one for the trade union movement of Quebec in general, and generated the movement which led to the Quiet Revolution of Quebec.

THE CLIMATE DURING THE COLD WAR

During the 1950's, American unions received much bad publicity. The climate of public opinion was unfavourable; this was the time of Senator Joseph McCarthy's crusade to reveal the secret hordes of reds and pinks in the United States. Dave Beck and James Hoffa were charged with misappropriation of funds and few noticed that Robert Kennedy, counsel for the Senate Rackets Committee, stated that "less than one-half of one per cent of the 430,000 union leaders" in America were guilty of criminal activity. In the face of the hostility which unions faced in the 1950's, the A.F.L. and C.I.O. mended their differences, in order to present a united front. In 1954 George Meany, a conservative trade unionist, became President of the combined A.F.L.–C.I.O. federation.

In 1959, a Labour Reform Act was secured, through the efforts of Democratic senators. This was intended to be a new bill of rights for labour; it guaranteed the use of the secret ballot for election of union officials and protection for union funds, and made it illegal for Communists to take office.

In Canada during the 1950's there were many major strikes of lengthy duration, in industries ranging from Dominion Textile to mining, railways and logging. Possibly the most significant came in 1955 when the plants of General Motors in Ontario were closed. The United Automobile Workers stopped for 148 days the operations of General Motors, a name symbolizing the branch-plant dependence of much of Canada's industry. This strike demonstrated the increasing power of Canadian trade unions.

The principle of the A.F.L.–C.I.O. merger in the U.S.A. was extended to Canada in 1955 when a Canadian Labour Congress was formed. The new body incorporated most of Canada's unionists and had approximately a million members. At first the Canadian Catholic Federation did not join the new body, but events in Quebec forced a re-evaluation of this policy. Maurice Duplessis there sought to restrict union activity by interpreting very rigidly the laws governing the right to strike; this caused the Canadian Catholic Federation to join the Canadian Labour Congress in political opposition to the Quebec government. At its first convention in 1957, the C.L.C. adopted a compromise policy on political action. Provincial union branches were left free to pursue whatever line they wished. Meanwhile, the Executive of the C.L.C. explored co-ordination of action with legislators, and this resulted in the New Democratic Party being formed in 1961. This alliance of the C.C.F. and the trades unions in the formation of the N.D.P. represented a new kind of political involvement for Canadian unions. True to its A.F.L. traditions, the Congress did not specifically affiliate with the new political party, yet as Dr. Eugene Forsey has pointed out:

> The relationship is much the same as that between the British Trades Union Congress and the British Labour Party. Indeed it is hardly too much to say that the founding of the New Democratic Party represents the triumph of the British tradition of direct political action, brought to Canada by British working-class immigrants in their baggage, over the non-partisan A.F.L. tradition. It is one of the marks of the independence of the Canadian labour movement from the American, with which it is otherwise in so many ways, so closely associated.[17]

The type of socialism found in the New Democratic Party reflects the British Nonconformist brand, stemming back to the influence of the Wesleyan Chapels in Britain. Both J.S. Woodsworth and Tommy Douglas were ministers, and it is possible that the atmosphere of moral fervour which surrounds the party may do something to change the tone of Canadian politics.

The major example of labour support for the N.D.P. to date was seen in the election of a new leader, Stephen Lewis, to head the Ontario party. At the 1970 Convention it was the labour delegation, representing about 45 per cent of the total voting strength, that ensured the election of Mr. Lewis. The union strength derived principally from two international unions, the United Steelworkers of America and the United Auto Workers, who provided nearly two-thirds of the union delegates. The Canadian director of the U.A.W., Denis McDermott, ensured solid support for the new leader and stated that "Lewis knows as much about the rank-and-file union member as I do."[18] It is too early yet to tell whether Canada's emerging labour movement will follow along British lines in selecting leaders. For Canadian unionism is a hybrid, seeking British-style political power but based on the economic strength of traditionally non-political American-style unions.

A specific objective of the N.D.P. as the political arm of the trade union movement is to ensure the abolition, on a national scale, of all ex-parte injunctions. Such an injunction is a restraining order against a union, issued by a judge, on evidence of an employer without hearing the union's side of the case. This type of legal coercion exerted by an employer has long been abandoned in Britain, has been made very difficult in America, but survives in much of Canada.

Unions in Canada are still relatively weak, as only around 30 per cent of the total working force has been organized. Of this number, 72 per cent are enrolled in international, generally American-based unions. According to a report in the *Globe and Mail* of March 9, 1970, approximately 35 million dollars is being paid annually by Canadians to American unions. The formation of the New Democratic Party and its support by unions clearly indicate, however, that Canadian unionists have aspirations to achieve a political, social and economic order which can repudiate American domination.

Total membership of Canadian unions remained static in the early 1960's as recruitment became difficult for two major reasons. First, white-collar workers have not been effectively organized because of their aversion to the working-class low-prestige connotations of the very word "union." The number of such employees has been growing rapidly due to increasing white-collar urban immigration from Britain, Germany and Holland, and to technological change that is decreasing the proportion of workers engaged directly in production. George Orwell once commented rather tartly on the difficulty of organizing the white-collar employees: "You cannot have an effective trade union of middle-class workers because in times of strike almost every middle-class wife would be egging her husband on to blackleg and get the other fellow's job."[19] William H. Whyte emphasized in *The Organization Man* that it is corporations who create the social status of their white-collar workers, and require group conformity to the idea of "company loyalty." On the other hand, anti-union feeling may just be a basic middle-class characteristic.

Another main reason for static union membership is the desire of many communities and some provinces to attract industries by the presence of "cheap non-union" labour. The problems of organizing Canadian workers have been further intensified by the New Canadians from a rural background who have been reluctant to join Canadian unions. For example, attempts to organize workers in the building trades in Toronto led to violence, and eventually to the formation of a new type of union. The Italian workers engaged in the pouring of concrete for construction of apartment buildings formed their own Italian Union. This union of Italian workers was not affiliated with any North American union organization.

Unionism has been greatly affected by the advent of automation. An educational publication issued by the headquarters of an American union summarized the impact of recent technology in this way:

A new industrial revolution has shaken the world. Machines can talk to and direct other machines. Human labour is becoming an anachronism. All previous social beliefs are begging for exhaustive scrutinization. . . The typical union opinion leader is the shop steward, but his role is being diminished as contracts and programs become more technical. To restore vitality to the local union, extensive labour education undertakings have to be initiated. For this is where the future of labour lies. The brain has taken the place of the pounding fist.[20]

ECONOMIC SECURITY

A worker's desire for security and for a just payment for his labour is usually expressed in the demand for a minimum wage sufficient to guarantee an adequate standard of living. In Britain six hundred years ago, the regulating of wages and prices under the Statute of Labourers of 1351 was intended to ensure that benefits went in the opposite direction, that is, that the labourer could not take advantage of a shortage of labour. The emphasis of this Statute thus was on setting a maximum rather than a minimum wage. Elizabethan England also tried to regulate prices and wages in favour of the employer. This trend was temporarily suspended by the Speenhamland system, inaugurated in 1793 but eliminated by 1834, of subsidizing the lowly paid labourer from local rates. At no point was there serious consideration by legislators of a minimum wage law until the twentieth century. In 1908, Winston Churchill set up boards to regulate wages and conditions in notorious "sweated industries" such as box-making. Three years later, in 1911, the recently formed Miners Federation struck for a minimum wage. Alarmed at this development, the Liberal government established local boards under impartial chairmen to set minimum wages. In Detroit, Henry Ford offered to pay a minimum of $5 a day, a princely sum for a worker in those days. Ford raised to new heights the concept of mass production, where high productivity made possible the payment of high wages. In the aftermath of World War One, the British miners secured a government subsidy to maintain their wage structure. Ernest Bevin in 1920 created a new precedent in successfully arguing before a Board of Inquiry for an adequate wage for dockers, and won both prominence and a minimum wage.

It was World War Two that produced the conditions in which Canada established minimum wages. In 1940 minimum wages were established for war industries, with an executive order, P.C.7440 of June 19, making provision for cost-of-living adjustments. As had happened in the social upheavals in Britain in the wake of the First World War, Canada's pattern after the return of peace saw the minimum wage idea become entrenched. In 1949 the minimum wage level was raised to 75 cents an hour. Also, in the postwar decade, the idea of ensuring an adequate wage level for a family was encouraged by supplementary benefits. By the middle of the 1950's, over 5,225,000 Canadian children were receiving $400 million in baby bonuses, and 755,000 old age pensioners were receiving $360 million yearly. In addition, the seasonally unemployed claimed benefits of over $200 million.

The next great leap forward came in the 1960's. In 1963, the Minimum Wage Act established for the first time in Ontario minimum wage rates for both male and female wages. Then, in 1965, a minimum hourly rate was set of $1.25 for industries under federal jurisdiction, and this was higher than most provincial levels. In Ontario, the Employment Standards Act of 1968 was put into effect, with emendations, on October 1, 1970. By the terms of this Act, workers were divided into two categories: those engaged in construction, for whom the minimum rate was $1.75, and employees in general industry, for whom the rate was $1.50. This legislation provided for increases in April 1971 to $1.90 and $1.65 for the two categories.[21] The increasing minimum wages of the 1970's, when contrasted with the decreasing maximum levels of pre-industrial Britain, seem to indicate a slow but definite movement towards the welfare state in Canada.

1. Eugene Forsey, "History of the Labour Movement in Canada," *Canada Year Book* (Ottawa: Queen's Printer, 1967), p. 773.
2. Charles Lipton, *The Trade Union Movement in Canada, 1827-1959* (Montreal: Canadian Social Publications Ltd., 1968), p. 32.
3. Norman J. Ware, *The Labour Movement in the United States* (New York: D. Appleton and Company, 1929), p. 378.
4. Samuel E. Morison and Henry S. Commager, *The Growth of the American Republic*, 6th ed., 2 vols. (New York: Oxford University Press, 1969), 2:229.
5. Forsey, "History of the Labour Movement in Canada," p. 776.
6. Ibid., p. 780.

7. R.C. Brown and M.E. Prang, *Confederation to 1949,* Canadian Historical Documents Series, vol. 3 (Scarborough, Ontario: Prentice-Hall of Canada, 1966), pp. 131-132.

8. Ibid., pp. 80-81. The term "Sifton sheepskin" was derived from the activity associated with Clifford Sifton, who organized the recruitment of European immigrants. Canada helped to establish a North Atlantic Trading Company with headquarters in Hamburg to seek out "the stalwart peasant in a sheepskin coat." Undoubtedly Canada gained many fine citizens this way but critics pointed out that Sifton was primarily interested in ensuring a flow of cheap labour. Statements by Sifton in 1922, when he looked back, tend to support this interpretation for he said:

> If one should examine twenty people who turn up at Hamburg to immigrate he might find one escaped murderer, three or four wasters and ne'er-do-wells, some very poor shop keepers, artisans and labourers, and there might be one or two stout, hardy peasants in sheepskin coats.

According to Sifton, the booking agencies in Hamburg "winnowed out this flood of people, picked out the agriculturalists and peasants and sent them to Canada." Five dollars per head was paid for a farmer. Rising political opposition in Canada forced Sifton to abandon the scheme.

9. A.B. Hodgetts, *Decisive Decades* (Toronto: Thomas Nelson and Sons (Canada), 1958), p. 520.

10. Robert K. Murray, *Red Scare: A Study in National Hysteria, 1919-1920* (Minneapolis: University of Minnesota Press, 1955), p. 36.

11. Smith once rebuffed Prime Minister Lloyd George during a wage dispute with, "Ye silly old booger, are ye daft?" Margaret Cole, "Growing Up Into Revolution," cited in W.R. Hitchcock, *Twentieth Century: The Great Issues* (Belmont: Wadsworth Publishing Company, 1969), p. 118.

12. William E. Leuchtenburg, *Franklin Delano Roosevelt and the New Deal, 1932-1940* (New York: Harper and Row Publishers, Harper Torch Books, 1963), p. 26.

13. Caroline Bird, *Invisible Scar* (New York: Pocket Books, 1967), p. 139.

14. Arthur M. Schlesinger, Jr., *The Age of Roosevelt,* 3 vols. (Boston: Houghton Mifflin, 1959), 2:167.

15. Brown and Prang, *Confederation to 1949,* p. 246.

16. Leuchtenburg, *Franklin Delano Roosevelt and the New Deal,* p. 188.

17. Forsey, "History of the Labour Movement in Canada," p. 781.

18. *Toronto Globe and Mail,* 15 October 1970.

19. D.J. Williams, *Strike or Bargain* (Toronto: Copp Clark Publishing Co., 1969), p. 32.

20. W.L. Abbott, *Our Union Heritage* (Akron, Ohio: United Rubber Workers Education Department), p. 31.

21. There are student rates listed in this legislation to cover employees under 18 years of age. Student rates apply to employment during the school vacation or part-time employment of not more than 28 hours per week. For the two general categories outlined in the text the rate since April, 1971 has been $1.30. But students should check the various special classifications to find the minimum rate applicable to particular types of employment such as messenger boys. The rates discussed apply to Ontario only.

3

Medicine, Health
and Insurance

The best doctors in the world are Doctor Diet,
Doctor Quiet, and Doctor Merryman.

Jonathan Swift

Vast changes have taken place in the field of medicine and
the role of the medical practitioner during the long history of
man's efforts to take care of his health. The present image of
the medical practitioner as a revered and white-gowned
professional is a recent phenomenon, and both his status and
his training were very different nine hundred years ago.

THE ORIGINS

European universities of the twelfth century offered the
study of medicine to interested students. All instruction was
given in Latin and the ability to read this language was the
main difference between the university surgeon and the
humble barber, who frequently knew more about the practical side of anatomy and surgery. After a papal decree of
1163 forbade the clergy to shed blood, the barbers had added
surgical duties to their original job of cutting hair. (The
familiar barber's pole of red and white stripes symbolizes the
blood that was spilled and the bandages that were used.) This
combination of functions was given royal sanction when in

1461, Edward IV of England granted a charter to barber-surgeons. In 1506 the barber-surgeons of Edinburgh were incorporated into a controlled body and that city began to establish its reputation as a medical center. Henry VIII passed the first medical registration act in 1511 and the preamble of this document condemned medicine practised:

> by a great multitude of ignorant persons using sorcery and witchcraft to the grievous hurt, damage and destruction of the King's liege people, more especially of them that cannot discern the uncunning from the cunning.

Bishops at this time still supervised the registration of medical men. In many ways, though, it seemed that the Christian Church had impeded the development of medical knowledge; disease was regarded as a punishment for sin, requiring prayer and repentance. A crippled child as a "victim of sin" was viewed as the product of divine intervention. Even more important was the belief that the human body was sacred and should remain inviolate, so that dissection was forbidden by the Church. Henry VIII liberated medicine from the control of the church by founding the secular Royal College of Surgeons in London in 1540. By this charter, the religious guild of barbers in London was amalgamated with the university surgeons, and in effect practical surgery thus improved its status by association with the Latin language. Members of the London corporation were accorded the right to call themselves Masters (colloquially, Mister); and British surgeons today still use the prefix "Mr." as opposed to the "Dr." that is revered in North America. Edinburgh continued to innovate in the field of medicine by forming a Faculty of Physicians and Surgeons in 1599; this was the first time that the two branches of medicine had been united.

Hospitals originated in the resting places provided by monasteries for pilgrims, where monks gradually began to take care of the sick and the lame. Monastic endowments financed the establishment in London of the early hospitals of St. Thomas's and St. Bartholomew's; after the Reformation, Henry VIII provided a secular endowment to continue support for St. Bartholomew's.

Fear of sickness was common, and justified, in the medieval world. The prospect of childbirth terrified women right up to the nineteenth century, as hygienic methods of disinfecting hands and clothing were unknown to the midwives licenced by the Church. City-dwellers faced the devastating periodic visits of the plague. Bubonic plague, known as the Black Death, carried off about one-third of the population of England in the fourteenth century. (This estimate is only approximate, as statistics for the period are unreliable: Norwich, presently estimated as having a population of 6,000 at that time, was reported to have lost 57,000 people.) The consequences of the Black Death were very serious for the Church, which was shown as being unable to placate the God who sent this destruction, in spite of prayers by the Pope and the priests. Survivors began to turn to investigating self-help measures and anticlericalism increased. Local administrative units, based on the parish and the town, became responsible for health measures. The Justice of the Peace developed into an authority for determining leper and plague tolls and calling for the assistance of doctors. A Justice of the Peace was the unpaid administrator of most health measures—certification of disease, reduction of "nuisances" (any activity dangerous or harmful to property-owners), sale of food, river pollution, garbage disposal, burial of the dead. World-wide epidemics of cholera also occurred periodically, originating usually in Asia. "Cholera" was a broad term that covered many acute diarrhoeal diseases. Leprosy was also common in England and its victims were confined, with those having other contagious diseases, in hospitals known as Lazar Houses.

It was early recognized that prevention is easier and more effective than cure; at least, there was no shortage of health laws in medieval England. Cleaning of the streets was advocated in laws of 1297 and 1309; the condition of food was regulated under a law of 1298 and prevention of water pollution in laws of 1345, 1357 and 1383. In 1388 England passed its first sanitary act for "removal of nuisances," followed in 1443 by a plague order recommending quarantine and cleansing. But to be effective legislation must be enforced and, as we are now learning in North America, measures of this kind relating to pollution or contamination must be backed by compulsion.

The Reformation caused an upheaval in the control of welfare measures for the sick. After Henry VIII had suppressed the monasteries, the Tudors found that some alternative provision had to be made for the ill and the indigent, and during the reign of Elizabeth I, Poor Laws required individual parishes to provide medical relief for these people. In general, though, England was left without a system of nursing, and it is therefore understandable that nursing had no distinctive part in the development of England's North American colonies. Of the Pilgrim Fathers who landed at Plymouth, Massachusetts in December 1620, half were dead within three months, and similarly the settlers at Jamestown, Virginia reported suffering from "cruell diseases, swellings, fluxes and burning fevers."

EARLY PIONEERS IN MEDICAL AND HEALTH PRACTICES

New France led the way towards effective nursing in the New World. Jacques Cartier who sailed up the St. Lawrence in 1535-6 was helped by friendly Indians to overcome the problem of scurvy among his crew: a brew containing spruce or hemlock tips provided vitamin C, and enabled Cartier to nurse his crew back to health. Unfortunately, Cartier did not record the Indian medicine for later generations of seamen who continued to suffer from scurvy on long voyages. The first hospital in North America, the Hôtel-Dieu of Quebec, was established by French Augustinian nuns; the first white woman to arrive in Montreal, Jeanne Mance, founded the Montreal Hôtel-Dieu in 1644. The complementary provision for medical care was provided in New France by the warrant given to Jean Madry of Quebec City in 1658 to establish the Mastership of Barber-Surgeons. Once the religious zeal of the seventeenth century had died down, there appears to have been a lull in the growth of medical activities on both sides of the Atlantic until the nineteenth century, when new religious orders of nuns appeared who specialized in nursing. In Ireland in 1831, the Sisters of Mercy started to staff hospitals as did the Devonport Sisters, founded by the Church of England, in 1848. But there was no professional training or modern nursing until later in the century.

In the American colonies, doctors were ill-trained and expensive. In 1662 Rhode Island adopted British legislation that required the overseer of the poor, or Justice of the Peace, to care for the health of the poor; in practice, however, this meant summoning the cheapest and usually the most incompetent physician to minister to the sick pauper. Hardy pioneers survived in spite of, and not because of, the provision of medical facilities in the New World.

Epidemics of smallpox raged across both Britain and North America in the seventeenth and eighteenth centuries. Hospital buildings as we know them began to be built in the eighteenth century. Guy's Hospital, London, was built to take the overflow from St. Thomas's and was followed, in 1745, by the building of the Middlesex Hospital. In North America Quakers founded a Philadelphia almshouse in 1713 which developed into one of the earliest hospitals in the American colonies. Primitive conditions existed within these hospitals: Bellevue Hospital in New York originated as a "pesthouse" in 1794, and the lunatic asylum of Bedlam was one of the sights of London, where visitors went to be amused by the antics of madmen exhibited in cages.

Public health measures were virtually non-existent at the beginning of the nineteenth century. The Dark Ages lasted longer than most historians have recognized, if judged by standards of cleanliness and sanitation. From 1309 onwards, one reads of ordinances dealing with disposal of sewage, but the allied problem of water pollution was considered to come under the common-law concepts of public nuisance and malicious damage. By the middle of the eighteenth century, Improvement Commissions had been established by special Acts of Parliament to improve urban conditions, but they usually did not have authority to drain and sewer districts.

Military doctors were responsible for the main advances in health care that were made in the eighteenth century. A Scottish doctor, Sir John Pringle, helped to develop rules for army camp sanitation and ventilation. Similarly, a naval doctor, Dr. James Lind, discovered that fresh lemon juice could prevent scurvy and Captain Cook put this medicinal discovery into practice during his long voyages to Australasia. Also, British Army doctors were the first skilled medical men to come to the British North American colonies. The regimental doctors often gave free medical and surgical treatment to the poor and some of them stayed on as civilian practitioners when they retired from the Army. The garrison surgeon in Quebec, James Fisher, sought the introduction of a strict system of licencing, and the support of priests to urge people "to avoid the promiscuous use of large bleedings, violent and drastic purgative medicines and keeping their houses too close and hot."[1]

In 1788 a stiff ordinance was passed in Lower Canada to eliminate unlicenced practitioners but this did not much curtail incompetency. The story was much the same in Upper Canada. In 1795 the first Medical Act stated that no one should practise medicine unless he was examined by a board of surgeons, which was to be chosen from His Majesty's Hospital and the surgeons of the regiments. Yet little could be done to establish standards when few qualified non-military doctors came to the Canadas. The Medical Act of 1795 was repealed in 1806 and medicine was thereafter unregulated in Upper Canada. As late as 1815, there were not more than forty qualified men practising medicine in Upper Canada. In the Maritimes, an effort was made by the Nova Scotia Act of 1828 to exclude "ignorant and unscrupulous persons from the practise of physic and of surgery." Thus, until the 1830's the British Army garrison doctors continued to be the leading medical men. In 1829, however, the enthusiasm and experience of Scottish graduates of the McGill General Hospital helped to establish the McGill Medical Faculty, and this medical center began to train doctors in the Canadas.

THE EARLY NINETEENTH CENTURY

Surgery was still a crude skill in the early nineteenth century. A visitor to H.M.S. Victory, Admiral Nelson's flagship now berthed at Portsmouth, England, can see the medical arrangements used at the Battle of Trafalgar in 1805. On the gun decks there are bags of salt available as a first aid cleanser for "minor" wounds, like the loss of a couple of fingers. The "serious" cases went below decks to the cockpit, painted red to minimize the presence of blood and provide a psychological boost to casualties waiting for the surgeon. The only light came from lanterns of one candle-power, which provided the dimly lit setting for amputating limbs without the benefit of anaesthetics. One suspects that it might have been necessary to administer Navy rum to immobilize the patient while a couple of "Jolly Tars" held him in position. When in 1810 the Admiralty finally agreed to aid in the cause of hygiene by issuing soap, naval regulations specified that a seaman had to request it, and for each issue an appropriate sum was to be deducted from the seaman's wages.

It is revealing to study the small stature of soldiers and sailors of the early nineteenth century. The bunks in the sleeping quarters of British Army forts and the low ceilings in naval wooden ships reveal that their inhabitants' height could not have exceeded five feet. The poor physique of Britain's soldiers and sailors provided a strong argument for the introduction of regulations concerning factory conditions, for the wartime soldiers and sailors were recruited from factory workers and their children. The argument based on the patriotic need to defend Britain with healthy men was difficult for factory owners to resist, and industrial conditions were regulated by Acts of Parliament with resultant improvement in the height and weight of children in textile mills.

In spite of the Acts of Parliament, the Industrial Revolution continued to spawn slums, unsanitary conditions and disease to such an extent that the average age of death of a factory hand in Manchester was seventeen. Yet little was done to ameliorate these conditions in an age when laissez faire reflected the philosophy of businessmen and politicians. Unless a national catastrophe threatened, for example, it was unlikely that the men of affluence would vote taxes to control effluence lying in urban cess pools and open ditches. It is hardly surprising, therefore, that about half the children born in London died before the age of five.

By 1832 a national crisis had arrived when cholera visited

England, and the death rate in the major industrial cities increased by 50 per cent. In that year a Royal Commission was appointed to investigate the Poor Laws. The secretary of this Commission was the Benthamite Edwin Chadwick, who felt that poverty was often a result of sickness. Chadwick seized the opportunity to improve health services by using the New Poor Law of 1834 to provide basic medical care for orphans, the aged and the infirm. The Poor Law Commissioners argued that the taxpayer would save money if preventative medicine lessened the need for workhouse treatment, whereupon Parliament authorized the appointment of a medical officer to assist each elected Board of Poor Law Guardians.

Chadwick, who was to become known as the Father of Sanitation, fought an uphill battle in his struggle to secure "the greatest good for the greatest number." The real problem was that the elected municipal councils established under the Municipal Act of 1834 had become public bodies where vested interests vied for control. Political oneupmanship replaced concern about cleaning up the unsanitary urban conditions; the city corporations, private water companies, cleansing boards and Poor Law Guardians sought to protect their interests, while resisting any form of centralized supervision.

Chadwick used his authority as a Poor Law Commissioner to launch an official enquiry into contemporary conditions. In 1842 appeared his famous "Report on the Sanitary Conditions of the Labouring Classes of Great Britain" which described the appalling sanitary conditions in England and Wales, and emphasized the health hazards presented by polluted water and unsanitary sewage disposal. The doctors who conducted the investigations cited instances where houses were surrounded by human waste, and were approached by walking on raised bricks. Cesspools were found in the lowest parts of the towns which were cleaned only twice yearly, and then by men using buckets who deposited the mess into the nearest river. Chadwick advocated the introduction of water closets and of sewer pipes flushed by water flowing at high velocity.

Chadwick's efforts were aided by a pressure group called

DEATH RATES PER HUNDRED IN PRESTON
1838 - 1843

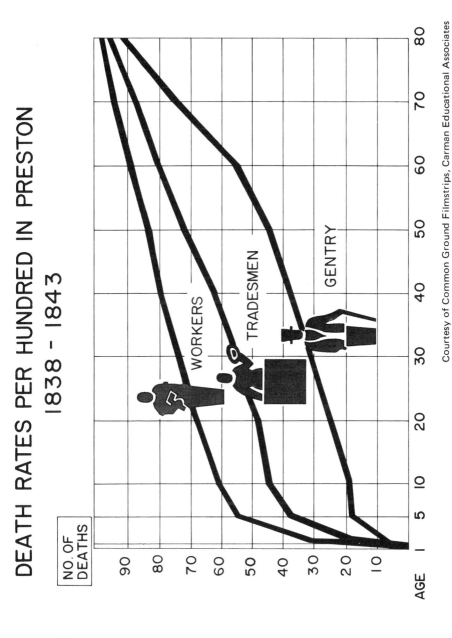

Courtesy of Common Ground Filmstrips, Carman Educational Associates

93

the Health of Towns Committee, which tried to popularize the view that "the heaviest municipal tax is the fever tax." A Health of Towns Commission of 1843 found that in a certain part of Manchester, "thirty-three privies served 7,095 persons," for a ratio of 215 persons per privy. Political efforts were made to secure a General Sewage Act and to create a supervising national Board of Health, but these ideas were strongly resisted by local vested interests who feared the introduction of compulsory directives that would limit their power. It was argued that health measures would interfere with private property rights: this argument still has its supporters in the 1970's.

The indefatigable Chadwick continued to tilt his lance. A Report on Intra Mural Interments of 1843 provided a new shock to the public. Evidence showed that the land in Russell Court, near Drury Lane in London, had been raised several feet by continuous burials. In London, a fixed quantity of 203 acres was allocated for cemeteries and an annual 52,000 bodies were added to these already crowded cemeteries. Unfortunately, the obvious need for more cemeteries was impeded by a bitter rivalry between the Church of England and the Nonconformists. The Church of England resisted the view of Nonconformists that they should be allowed to bury their dead in parish churchyards. Burial was seen as a sacramental rite, so that corpses were interred by members of that religious sect to which the dead had belonged. Parliament had learned that any attempt to control interments produced political uproar. Chadwick did not succeed in stopping the chaotic and unsanitary burial practices, and it was not until cremation of bodies was gradually adopted after 1876, that the problem of the disposal of England's dead was resolved in a way that was not a health hazard to the living.

Several of the revelations of Chadwick's report concerned burial clubs. These were established by groups of working men to pay the funeral expenses of members and their families from a common fund accumulated by regular payments by the members. Funeral arrangements were in the hands of private undertakers who used moral blackmail to induce mourners to pay for lavish and unnecessary funeral ceremonies. (The present practices of the American funeral parlour industry, revealed in Jessica Mitford's *The American Way of Death,* obviously have antecedents going back well before the huckstering of this century.) Chadwick's revelation that a few desperately poor working men sought to get their contributions out of the burial club by killing one of their own family, forced a shocked Parliament to authorize his proposal that, in order to protect children, there should be a registration of births and deaths, with a medical officer certifying the cause of death. Chadwick's persistence was probably the main reason why the Registration of Births and Deaths Act was passed in 1836, replacing the practice of a priest recording such information in a parish register.

Chadwick pressed on with his crusade. He arranged for the production of the first glazed earthenware drainpipes in England, and tried to prove that taxpayers would save money if there were sanitary engineering to lower the number of the sick receiving Poor Law relief. And in 1848, a new wave of cholera panicked the British Parliament into creating a national Board of Health. This action constituted a landmark in the history of world health, for by its creation Parliament acknowledged responsibility for ensuring the health of the nation. Noted social reformers, such as Chadwick and Lord Shaftesbury, were members of it. However, the Board of Health was weak, as it was set up on a five-year trial basis, and had only one inspector to cover England and one to cover Scotland. Bitter opposition to the introduction of the Board of Health prevented it from having any power in London, and its activities were confined to trying to persuade provincial authorities to provide sewers and uncontaminated water.

Private water companies and the administrators of cemeteries complained of the "socialism" preached by the Board of Health. Members of Parliament were under pressure from their local constituents who were interested in ensuring that Parliament did not prolong the Board's life; as an embittered Lord Shaftesbury wrote after the Board was destroyed in 1854, "Its sin is its unpardonable activity." Certainly the efficiency of the Board's investigations into local incompetence and indifference contributed to its demise. For example, it is easy to understand the squirming of local authorities when a report was issued about the fever epidemic of 1849, stating the causes to be "insufficient supply of water, overflowing privies . . . privies in the cellar the effluvium of which penetrated into every room of the house . . . cesspools soaking into cellars . . . matter oozing through walls of houses."[2] It is not surprising that 4,251 Londoners died of cholera in August, 1849 and 6,644 persons in the following September.

NORTH AMERICA AT MID-NINETEENTH CENTURY

Conditions in the large urban centres of North America were similar to those in Britain. New York streets were embellished by piles of manure and mud left for weeks at a time. Sewage was removed by bucket from cesspools or permitted to lie in the open ditches that ran down many streets. By 1857, New York had installed sufficient sewers to cover only a quarter of the city. Outbreaks of typhoid, dysentery and typhus were continual; the cholera plague visited the city in 1832, 1849 and 1866. After the last visitation, Boards of Health were set up on the 1848 model of Britain. A Cincinnati Board of Health report told of a two-storey tenement which housed 102 people, for whom one privy was available. But some progress was being made: after 1866, hogs were no longer allowed to roam the streets of New York.

The United States was still predominantly agricultural before the Civil War. This economic situation tended to place emphasis upon the traditional family services of the physicians rather than the large-scale health problems produced by industrialization. One significant American medical contribution occurred in 1844 when the first use of anaesthesia was recorded. Soon afterwards, James Simpson of Edinburgh discovered the use of chloroform as a general anaesthetic. American medical schools compared poorly to those of Scotland with the result that many Scots graduates, or graduates of Trinity College, Dublin, emigrated from their crowded homelands to make a career in America.

A History of the Medical Profession in Upper Canada,

1783-1850 by Dr. W. Caniff indicates that graduates of Scottish universities provided the largest group of qualified medical doctors in Upper Canada. A future Prime Minister of Canada, Dr. Charles Tupper, took his medical training at Edinburgh, before returning to Nova Scotia as a practising surgeon. Surgery at that time in Canada usually took place as an emergency operation in makeshift surroundings, and the payment for professional service was usually by kind rather than by cash. Charles Tupper would be called to a farm where a labourer's leg had been crushed by a fallen tree: while attending to the casualty, without the benefit of an anaesthetic, he was expected to provide a reassuring dialogue with the surrounding throng of agitated onlookers. These conditions did not encourage trained doctors to tramp the backwoods, and increasing numbers of quacks were in circulation.

Unfortunately for the qualified doctors of the Canadas, the politicians sided with pressure groups who sought to allow anyone to practise healing. The nineteenth-century belief in free trade was applied to the health field. Homeopaths, for example, argued that orthodox medical men favoured unnecessary purgings and bleedings, with the result that, in 1859, the House of Assembly of the Canadas gave legal recognition to homeopaths and eclectics. Outraged doctors did not receive any help from the legal profession, whose members welcomed the chance to secure new business from lawsuits. The camaraderie of the doctors and lawyers, stressed later in "the professions," is possibly of more recent vintage than usually assumed. In Quebec (Canada East), the state of medicine can be judged from the complaint of a doctor practising in St. Andrew who recorded, "I am annoyed by a noted bonesetter, who, mainly I believe from possessing the happy knack of dislocating his own thumb . . . gulls the public with the belief that no case . . . can withstand his manipulations."[3]

In the House of Assembly, the irate Dr. Nelson commented "the quack is an audacious and not over-conscientious personage, not seldom immoral in his habits, and generally a canting hypocrite." Unfortunately for the doctors, it was difficult to attract additional skilled men to the Canadas in the first half of the nineteenth century. Although the McGill medical faculty was sending out competent graduates, there were many irresponsible medical schools providing worthless diplomas which cast suspicion on all qualifications. The danger to patients is obvious to us but the protests of contemporary doctors went unheeded.

Some idea of the uphill struggle to introduce adequate health services can be gained from the example of the Toronto Asylum for the Insane. From the time the institution was planned, there was widespread political jobbery. In 1854, the building was erected—on marshy ground which soon became a cesspool, and contractors built a cheap drain that did not connect to the main sewer. The Superintendent, Dr. Workman, spent a lifetime trying to prevent political pressure from interfering in his efforts to modernize the building.

Medical training in the United States was poor by European standards. Yet unlike the Canadian doctors, the physicians managed to form a national association. The American Medical Association, founded in 1847, was composed of delegates from state medical associations. From its beginning the A.M.A. was dedicated to the idea of free enterprise and it still clings to a laissez-faire attitude.

THE LATE NINETEENTH CENTURY

During the second half of the nineteenth century, there was a great improvement in the quality of nursing care. It was certainly time for reform: apart from the religious orders discussed earlier, the only women employed in hospitals were disreputable. Hospital wards often were staffed by drunken prostitutes. In workhouse infirmaries the poor were cared for by old and incompetent members of the institutions. It was only when public opinion was outraged by nursing incompetence during the Crimean War, which started in 1853, that a great change occurred.

When *The Times* of London finally revealed the appalling conditions at the Crimean base hospital at Scutari, the British public insisted that the War Office do something. Cholera, typhoid fever and dysentery were killing three times as many soldiers as the battles. The real enemy was the filthy condition of the base hospital, and the incompetent nursing by untrained orderlies. Florence Nightingale, who had studied scientific nursing in Europe, offered to take charge and thirty-eight nurses accompanied her in the relief mission to the five thousand patients. Florence became a national heroine as she supervised the clean-up and began a new kind of care for the wounded. The fame of the "Lady With The Lamp," visiting all wards each evening, was carried back to Britain.

Inspired by the reforms in Army nursing, the Royal Navy organized the Royal Naval Medical Service and now assistant surgeons were rated as "gentlemen" with wardroom privileges. The role of an army or navy surgeon was changing to emphasize preventative medicine. Florence Nightingale continued her crusade in peacetime and established the first Royal Commission in British history to enquire into the food, housing and health of the peacetime soldier. In 1861, organized physical training began at the Army base at Aldershot. Britain wanted to give Florence Nightingale a national funeral in Westminster Abbey when she died in 1910, but she had emphatically stated a different request. Her coffin was carried to her family grave in a country churchyard by six sergeants of the British Army, for which she had done so much. The concept of scientific nursing had been spread throughout the world. In Ontario, the first training school for nurses, The Mack Training School, was founded in 1874 by a Dr. Mack with the advice of Florence Nightingale. And in the United States the birthday of Florence Nightingale, May 12, was established as National Memorial day.

The quality of training for doctors also improved dramatically during this period. A Medical Act was passed in Britain in 1858 that set up a General Council to supervise the training and registration of doctors. Before this time only about one "doctor" in three took the trouble to obtain any qualifications at all. After 1858, unlicenced practitioners could be prosecuted, and the process had begun of turning a rough group of surgeons into socially acceptable gentlemen. A key figure at this time was Dr. John Simon, Medical Officer to the Privy Council, who sought to improve sanitary conditions. As a doctor himself, and unlike Edwin Chadwick, Simon was able to continue the crusade for improved sanitary conditions without arousing hostile opposition. He appointed the first sanitary inspectors, then known as "Inspectors of Nuisances." Simon's Report of 1865 emphasized the continuing disgusting conditions in British cities. Populations, forced to drink polluted water, were ravaged by cholera. Acts of Parliament followed, but in the absence of a coercive power they were ineffectual. As with so much Victorian legislation, general laws which merely advised local authorities to take action did not work.

During the 1860's, a select committee of the House of Commons investigated rivers. Following its report, parts of the River Thames were cleaned up, but the reason probably had little to do with the main activity of the committee. The truth was that the smell from the Thames made it necessary to keep the windows of the Houses of Parliament closed. With M.P.'s literally holding their noses, it was not long before sewers were installed that carried sewage to ebbtide thirteen miles below London bridge, and parts of the Thames were cleaned up by 1865. One can speculate that the lesson to modern ecologists and anti-pollution groups should be fairly obvious. If in North America all pollutants could be diverted into the nearest river flowing past State or Provincial capitals, supplemented by the widespread pollution of the Potomac at Washington and the Ottawa River, then remedial action should quickly follow.

Smoke pollution was legislated upon in British Parliamentary Acts of 1819, 1847 and 1863 which concerned the amount of acid content permissible in smoke issuing from manufacturing plants. These Alkali Acts sought particularly to control chemical manufacturers in Cheshire and Lancashire. One of the significant aspects of these political efforts to control chemical manufacturers was that attempts were made to scientifically define at what point the smoke became a dangerous health hazard. The lesson was being learned that specific rules, enforced by inspectors, were the only way to control manufacturers. While the preventative facet of medicine was making headway in the control of the environment, there was similar development in the curative aspect.

Progress was being made in the 1860's in the field of surgery. A young London surgeon advanced the surgeon's craft by solving the problem of infection in incisions made during operations. Lister used carbolic acid as an antiseptic and the appalling post-operational loss of life diminished. It is true that surgery was still a crude business compared to modern twentieth-century standards. Surgeons were prone to regard fatalities as a kind of inevitable result of the intervention of God, not of a lack of skill and techniques. Nineteenth-century operating rooms relied upon natural daylight for illuminating the operating table, with the daylight admitted through windows above the surgeon.

In Canada, one result of Confederation in 1867 was to encourage medical co-operation through a Canadian Medical Association which sought to consolidate provincial bodies. Dr. Charles Tupper, a prominent Father of Confederation, was elected as the first President of the C.M.A. However, according to its official historian, the Canadian Medical Association had a lean time until the boom years of the Laurier era after 1896.

Canadian doctors sought to have an Act passed by the federal government that would copy Great Britain's Medical Act of 1858. Ontario doctors did succeed in securing a provincial Parker Medical Act of 1865 that was almost a literal copy of that of Great Britain, and provided for a Medical Council to prescribe standards. Lawyers soon saw to it that the Parker Act was extended, in 1869, to include the excluded homeopaths and eclectics. But with the formation of the Canadian Medical Association, a strong medical lobby was mounted at Ottawa that produced the Act of 1872 giving to the medical profession the right to regulate its own discipline and registration. The real significance of the federal legislation is indicated by the fact that the Ontario Medical Register of 1871 showed 1,177 men registered, but it was known that at least 500 more "doctors" practised in defiance of the law. Doctors distrusted politicians and their point of view was voiced in 1874 by the President of the Canadian Medical Association:

no greater blunder can be committed in this democratic age than seeking medical legislation, as the sympathies of legislators generally . . . are in favour of quackery and free trade in medicine.[4]

Ridding the profession of quackery was the main concern of the C.M.A. but it would be some years before this was accomplished.

BRITISH REFORMS OF THE 1870's

In the Britain of the 1870's, there was considerable progress in the field of public health. A Royal Sanitary Commission of 1871 proposed administrative changes which led to the establishment of Local Government Boards, the successors of the ill-fated Board of Health, to co-ordinate sanitary, public health and poor law services. The Local Government Boards were dominated by the Poor Law Guardian element, a pressure group composed of the medical staff of the Poor Law hospitals. Based on the recommendations of the Sanitary Commission of 1871, the Public Health Act of 1875 was passed. This very significant Act consolidated all the previous piecemeal legislation on sanitary matters. It provided for compulsory officers of health in towns, a measure long overdue. Also in 1875, the first postgraduate course in public health in England was introduced at Cambridge University, where the idea had been borrowed from Trinity College, Dublin. Finally, in 1888, a Medical Officer of Health was required to have a diploma in public health.

Public health was related to the purity of food and drugs. Unlike earlier parliamentary legislation since the time of Henry VIII, the successive Pure Food and Drug Acts of 1872 and 1875 were intended to be enforced by Parliament. There were legal loopholes in this legislation, but in general it served Britain fairly well in reducing the worst commercial abuses until 1955, when a new comprehensive Food and Drug Act was passed. In North America there was no real attempt in the nineteenth century to control the adulteration of food or drugs, or to reduce misleading advertising concerning them.

Water pollution was again tackled by Britain's Parliament

in 1877 with the passage of the Pollution of Rivers Bill. Opposition to the bill came from manufacturing interests who managed to weaken the restrictions on liquid refuse. But the discharge of untreated sewage into any stream was forbidden, and the disposal of sewage and solid matter was placed under restrictions that lasted until a new Act was passed in 1928. The national newspaper, *The Times,* strongly supported the anti-pollution drive, stating in its edition of August 27, 1877, that "England is a land of streams. . . . Corruption is spreading . . . by ignorance and neglect. . . . We must convince towns [that] sewage is a valuable manure." In the crusading fervour of the 1870's, the British Parliament investigated existing schemes for health coverage and life insurance. (The business of selling life insurance is, of course, directly related to the expected longevity of the insured.) Some of the testimony before a select committee was most revealing as to why commercial life insurance companies bothered to sell penny policies to the poor. A spokesman for the Royal Liver Company, one of the largest, bluntly stated that "intelligence and education are of no account in the [insurance] trade, in fact a man's success . . . is much in proportion to his coarseness, ignorance and unscrupulousness."[5] Insurance salesmen tapped the gambling instinct of Englishmen by proposing that a man have a flutter by putting "sixpence on grandmother." The parliamentary investigating committee attacked the unscrupulousness of the Prudential Insurance Company, the largest life insurance firm in England. The committee noted that "the company issues of necessity stamped policies [but] allows its agents to represent them as a sort of Government guarantee."[6]

The concept of a Friendly Society can be traced back to the mutual aid arrangements of the medieval guilds. The Friendly Societies of the nineteenth century had a function similar to that of insurance companies, in helping the poor to weather sickness or pay for burials. These non-profit, voluntary, self-help organizations by groups of workers were viewed with approval by Parliament. Unfortunately, the Registration Act of 1875 which was intended to help the Friendly Societies was loosely worded, and failed to distinguish adequately between reputable voluntary societies and commercial insurance companies. Although the burial policies (known as assurance policies) were not covered by the Registration of Friendly Societies Act, this did not worry the commercial organizations. Assurance companies ignored the Act and posed as "registered friendly societies." The Royal Liver Company became the Royal Liver Friendly Society. This type of misrepresentation bears out the later statement of Sir William Beveridge that "disregard of legal niceties in pushing business among the poorest classes has been the mark of industrial life [insurance] offices throughout their history."[7]

LATE VICTORIAN IMPROVEMENTS IN HEALTH CARE

The status of medical practitioners was rising on both sides of the Atlantic in the latter part of the nineteenth century. In Britain, the Royal Army Medical Corps was formed in time to serve in the Boer War. (And to serve in a category appreciably different from that of their medical forefathers at the Battle of Agincourt four centuries earlier, when doctors were ranked with drummers.) The status of medicine in the United States also took a sudden leap forward with the establishment of the Johns Hopkins Medical School at Baltimore, Maryland in 1893. The quality of training in this school equalled European standards, and the example of Johns Hopkins inspired other medical schools to do likewise. The Carnegie and Rockefeller foundations provided the money for more research and for improvement of American training. Reports on the health situation financed by foundation grants shocked the public and enabled the medical profession to outlaw "irregulars" like homeopaths, eclectics and osteopaths. The standards of medical training improved dramatically although in 1906, the American Medical Association still rated only half of the existing 160 medical schools as satisfactory. In Canada, the long struggle to secure a national Act to regulate medicine had been hampered by the British North America Act, which allowed the provinces to control medical education. Finally, in 1894 the provinces agreed to allow the passage of a Dominion Act to permit the medical profession to enforce standards in training establishments.

The shining example of the Johns Hopkins medical centre in the U.S.A. undoubtedly aided the cause of the doctors. Further efforts of the Canadian Medical Association to get Ottawa to exercise some authority over sick Indians and seamen, and over the adulteration of food, were ignored by federal politicians before World War One.

NURSING AND PREVENTATIVE MEDICINE

Nurses had a struggle greater than the doctors had to secure professional status. Several European countries established the pattern of using an advanced course to train midwives, which Britain copied in the Midwives Act of 1902. British infant mortality which had stayed fairly constant for thirty years at around 150 deaths per 1,000 births, was cut to 128 per 1,000 and then halved again by the 1930's. This improvement was partially due to the care possible in the average family, reduced from the six children of a Victorian household to two children by the 1930's. Similarly, in North America infant mortality declined by two-thirds, while life expectancy increased from forty-nine to fifty-nine years. In Britain, midwives were trained to work under the general supervision of doctors and a "district nurse" handled a delivery in the mother's home. A trend in the opposite direction was evident in the United States, where doctors insisted on handling obstetrics and the licencing of midwives was discontinued in many states in the 1920's. It is interesting to note that in 1960, the average British infant mortality rate was below that for the United States (which, in turn, was slightly below that for Canada).

General nursing today is still inspired by the Nightingale model, with a matron or superintendent responsible for all nursing within a hospital. Yet several of Florence Nightingale's principles were contrary to practice today: she resisted centralization and fought the idea of registering nurses, which would, in her view, "standardize mediocrity." Only after Miss Nightingale's death could the advocates of registration make much progress. The first Nurses Act to regulate training in England and Wales was not secured until 1919.

Canadian nursing was influenced by the models of both Britain and the United States. The American influence has been most noticeable in the organizational features of the profession. In 1896 a Nurses Associated Alumnae of the United States and Canada was formed, which became the American Nurses Association in 1911. The American fondness for degrees resulted in universities offering a bachelor's degree in nursing by 1916. A familiar professional pattern now began as master's degrees and doctorates were offered to professional nursing administrators. Particularly in the United States, this has led to a pattern of full-time chiefs and part-time Indians, as many trained nurses leave to raise a family and then return as part-time help.

Preventative medicine became increasingly important in the twentieth century. After numerous attempts to control the American interstate traffic in food and drugs, President Theodore Roosevelt secured a federal Pure Food and Drug Act in 1906. This was a notable achievement in the land of free enterprise, even if a legal loophole about a "distinctive name exception" allowed manufacturers to continue to ship more or less what they pleased. Also in 1906, a School Feeding Act was passed in Britain which provided for meals and milk to be distributed in the elementary schools, despite the cry that this was "socialism." The parents seemed, however, to welcome this "socialistic" trend of permitting local authorities to provide poor children with meals. Concern for undernourished children in Britain's schools was long overdue, as 124,000 children died during the year of 1906, and it was estimated that over 50,000 children died needlessly every year. In 1907 medical inspection of children was authorized in an attempt to control diphtheria epidemics. An attempt was also made to eliminate vermin on slum children. It should not be thought that Parliament was suddenly horrified at the state of health of poor children, as the concept of laissez faire was still strongly ingrained in the Liberal Government. Rather, it was the skilful politicking of a civil servant, Sir Robert Morant, that enabled a school medical service to be established, by the ruse of burying it in a much larger Act dealing with educational housekeeping measures. Sir George Newman became the Chief Medical Officer of the

Board of Education and spent a lifetime seeking continued improvement in health care in the schools, until his retirement in 1935. Newman preached that healthy children would make more receptive pupils and a healthier and happier adult work force.

THE STRUGGLE OVER INSURANCE

In 1910 began a political struggle over the attempt of David Lloyd George to pass a National Insurance Act, intended to help adult workers when they were sick. This Act was basically copied from Bismarck's health scheme in Germany, where medicine and basic maintenance were provided for workers, but many modifications to the original model appeared in the National Insurance Act of 1911. Initially Lloyd George hoped to introduce a state-run scheme using the organization already built up by the reputable Friendly Societies. However, insurance companies, led by the Prudential company, lobbied intensively to ensure that commercial firms known as Industrial Assurance companies, which specialized in burial insurance, would participate and be ranked with Friendly Societies as Government agents. The pressure of the insurance lobby forced Lloyd George to modify his proposals, and in the final form of the Act the commercial assurance companies ranked with Friendly Societies as government agents. In theory there were 20,000 approved agencies divided approximately equally between the old fraternal societies (friendly societies) and assurance companies controlled by insurance companies. In practice, the large organizations such as the Prudential rapidly obtained a lion's share of the business.

From 1911 until 1945 the Assurance companies successfully prevented any comprehensive national coverage developing under a Ministry of Health. The 1911 Act proved a bonanza for insurance companies such as the Prudential who skilfully exploited their position as government agents. The legislation specified "non profit" agents and to conform to this requirement, insurance companies organized "non profit" assurance sections of their organizations. It was a brilliant manoeuvre, in a business sense, as it provided leverage for getting into the homes of the poor to sell profitable life insurance policies. Salesmen operated as government agents, dispensing the benefits of the National Health scheme, while paying regular visits to their clients to collect the three-pence contributions. In effect, insurance companies had 70,000 collector-salesmen whose salary was paid mainly by the State. A collector of premiums would deliver a thirty-shilling benefit, as a government grant; then he would immediately press for a new life insurance policy. The spectre that was raised of a loved one being buried in a potter's field made it easy to sell burial policies of £10 to £15. British assurance-insurance companies resisted the idea of any government payments being made to widows or orphans, as this would curtail the sale of the £10 to £15 policy to ensure a "respectable" funeral. Insurance companies formed a tremendously strong political lobby because they had direct contact with most of the working class. Furthermore, their business efficiency compared favourably to the government's bungling of unemployment insurance, a point the insurance spokesmen were not slow to reiterate. It took the social upheaval of the Second World War to finally break the grip of the insurance companies.

Doctors' incomes rose after 1911, when they gained an assured income from patients. The medical profession had to fight hard, however, to prevent itself being controlled by the Approved Societies. A doctors' strike was attempted in 1912 and the British Medical Association won concessions. Patients could select their physician from a panel of doctors and the doctors had representation on the local insurance committees that administered the scheme. A decade later, the secretary of the British Medical Association outlined the improvement in the position of doctors:

> When I compare it [the National Insurance Act of 1911] with the old club system at 2s 6d or 3s 6d per year; with doctors tumbling over each other in a horrible Dutch auction to get clubs even at that price so as to keep competitors out; with the bribery and corruption that went on in connexion with the election of doctors to these clubs. . . I can confidently say that not one doctor

in a thousand who is doing national insurance work would go back to the old system.[8]

How was the British health scheme of 1911 viewed on the other side of the Atlantic? One observer in Canada commented in the *Canadian Medical Association Journal* of 1912, "a spirit of charity will be replaced by a cold official atmosphere. When physicians become civil servants . . . the rich will be the gainers and the last state of the poor will be worse than the first." The fear of doctors becoming civil servants is understandable, but hardly in accord with the position of British doctors at that time. In the United States, the insurance lobby was easily as strong as its British counterpart although unlikely to become a government agent. American insurance companies paid salaries of up to $100,000 to executives whose names were used for prestige purposes and whose salaries were paid for by increasing the premiums to policy holders. J.P. Morgan controlled the New York Life, the Mutual Life and the Equitable—three of the largest companies. Apostles of free enterprise who followed J.P. Morgan's leadership were unlikely to welcome positive action by the State, unless of course it increased profits. The climate of North America was not ripe for any national health schemes, or for appreciating the efforts of Lloyd George in putting the State into health care.

DEVELOPMENTS AFTER 1914

It was the Great War of 1914-1918 that gave the medical profession a chance to make rapid progress in terms of techniques. Young medical officers in the Army and Navy were able to bypass the peacetime apprenticeship system whereby a surgeon reached middle age before he was fully certified for practice. The bloody results of battle made necessity the mother of invention: blood transfusions and new anaesthetic procedures were put into practice for the first time. In the base hospitals, orthopedic surgeons developed special centres for the treatment of physical handicaps. In the war factories, the introduction of first-aid facilities and canteens helped to keep the work force healthy and well-fed. Free diagnosis and treatment of venereal diseases were established when a British Royal Commission recommended the Venereal Diseases Act of 1917 and criticized the advertising of quack remedies.

The blood bath of the Great War ended on November 11, 1918, and in the following year the British government decided to establish the long-awaited Ministry of Health. This Ministry was intended to extend preventative medicine to the whole population, particularly in view of tuberculosis among discharged soldiers and postwar flu epidemics. Once more political opposition developed to prevent a national approach to the health of the nation. The medical branch of the Poor Law administration joined with the insurance lobby to resist a health insurance scheme that might undermine their power. The attitude of the insurance companies was clearly expressed by their news organ, the *National Insurance Gazette,* in an article dated June 15, 1918: "politicians and governments can be pressed and the more urgent we are the more likely to get what we want. To put it bluntly we must be importunate." Instead of becoming the top national authority on health, the Ministry of Health was forced into the secondary role of an advisor. In the straitened economic conditions of postwar Britain, successive governments were inclined to think of economy rather than health benefits. Lloyd George's promise about making a land fit for heroes was becoming a hollow mockery.

British doctors were forced once more to fight to prevent the insurance lobby from controlling their activity. Physicians at this time were not particularly well-paid: in 1920, seventy-five per cent of them earned less than £500 a year. The capitation fee, or annual amount allowed per patient, went up from 8s 6d to 11s in 1920, in the face of a threatened mutiny from doctors, then down to 9s 6d per patient in 1922. The low level of doctors' salaries was largely due to the insurance companies who, in their role as government agents, sought to keep costs to a minimum. These companies deliberately kept insurance benefits low, as this encouraged workers to apply for the higher state unemployment benefits, and thereby saved the funds of the insurance company. A sick worker would therefore often maintain the fiction of being available for work, so that he could draw unemployment pay. Furthermore, the problem was compounded by the fact that, as the Fabians had long argued, unemployment and inactivity made people prone to sickness. This vicious circle led to deceptive practices. The colloquial term "on the fiddle" became popular in the 1920's, implying the efforts of a worker to manipulate payments from the National Insurance Act (the club) or unemployment benefits (the dole). Workers who wished to get some time off sought medical certificates, and married women between the ages of 20 and 25 made particularly excessive claims. Doctors who certified a worker as sick gave him or her approval to get fifteen shillings a week from an approved society; the societies resisted what they considered excessive claims and sought "medical referees" to investigate these claims. The local doctor was caught in a political vice, for if he was too conscientious, he lost patients to other doctors who built a reputation for putting people on the club. In areas suffering from a high rate of unemployment, there was tremendous social pressure on doctors. In effect a doctor could be forced, by social pressure or his own humanitarian instinct, into helping patients to use the "club" as a form of dole.

After World War One, school clinics began to appear where nurses and doctors tended sick children. No insurance company ever braved the wrath of mothers by condemning this "socialistic" practice. Similarly, by 1924 milk was being widely distributed in the school system, but this was due less to a concern over health, than to the political lobbying of the depressed dairy industry. Britain was slow, however, to implement the immunization which had enormously reduced mortality due to diphtheria in both the United States and Canada.

CANADA IN THE POSTWAR PERIOD

Canada came out of World War One with a new sense of national pride, which was reflected in the desire to found a Royal College of Physicians and Surgeons. Another reason for seeking to strengthen the professional organization of the Canadian Medical Association was that many Canadians felt that the rich province of Ontario was overstocked with doctors. In this climate of opinion, the Canadian Medical Association meeting of 1920 passed this resolution:

Whereas Canada has now assumed the status of nationhood within the British Empire . . . it is now the opportune time to promote a closer alliance between the medical men of the Old Country and those of Canada . . . it is resolved . . . to consider the problem of a Canadian College of Physicians and Surgeons.

A questionnaire to all Canadian Medical Association members produced a wide spectrum of opinion:

"A good idea but a little premature." "The University of Manitoba strongly endorses the proposal and offers its unqualified support." "The Maritimes feel that the time is not ripe for the formation of such an institution." "The medical schools in Ontario, while expressing sympathy with the idea, have considerable doubt as to its timeliness. With this opinion McGill concurs." "A few medical societies doubt the wisdom of multiplying organizations." "The medical associations in Western Canada favour action."[9]

This diversity of opinion also reflected the shifting balance of power within the Canadian Medical Association. During the 1920's the McGill medical faculty ceased to dominate the Association and the influence of the West began to be felt. Most French-Canadian doctors did not join the C.M.A., belonging instead to the Association des Médecins de Langue Française du Canada. The difficulty of organizing a College of Physicians and Surgeons was compounded by the Canadian constitution which made medical matters a provincial responsibility and it was 1929 before Quebec agreed to help to overcome the constitutional hurdle.

Canadian medicine achieved world prominence during the 1920's. Sir Frederick Banting and Charles Best were the first men to extract insulin for the treatment of diabetes, and Banting received the Nobel prize for medicine in 1923. Until 1918 Canadian doctors had normally gone to Britain or continental Europe for post-graduate training but now this trend was diminishing with the development of such centres as the Banting and Best Institute of Toronto and the Montreal Neurological Institute. Furthermore, there was considerable growth in the number of good research centres in the United States available to Canadians. At the same time it should be pointed out that ties to Britain remained strong as immigrant doctors reinforced the professional interests of Canadians trained in the United Kingdom, and friendly relations existed between the medical associations of the two countries.

A most important recommendation was made in 1928 by a Canadian parliamentary select committee that investigated possible insurance against unemployment and sickness. The committee saw these two conditions as interrelated, just as Lloyd George had in 1911. While accepting the constitutional right of the provinces to pass their own social legislation, this committee said that there was nothing to stop the federal government from contributing grants to the provinces for such purposes. The real significance of this recommendation did not become apparent until twenty years later, when the federal government insisted that it had a role to play in the creation of a welfare state. As will be discussed later, the potential federal-provincial deals that this proposal opened up have transformed the social character of Canada.

THE EXPANSION OF SERVICES

Dentistry in Britain, which had developed in the nineteenth century under the control of the Royal College of Surgeons, lagged behind its American counterpart. An indication of the difference in status of the dentist in North America is that he is called "Doctor," while his counterpart in England is not. At the time that Britain passed the Dentists Act of 1921, there were only 5,800 registered dentists and over 70 per cent of children had dental decay. North American dental standards were higher than those of Britain, where concern over dental care spread slowly. The number of British dentists tripled in the inter-war period of 1919 to 1939 and 1,582 school dental clinics existed at the beginning of World

War II. Yet when dental care became the province of the state with the passage of the National Health Act of 1946, it seemed that every citizen of Britain needed "free" dentures or extractions.

Hospital administrative practices began to change amid the economic and social pressures of the Great Depression of the 1930's. Hospitals in the United States had been frequently run on a charitable basis under religious auspices. With the introduction of pre-payment arrangements termed Blue Cross plans, the methods of financing hospital care changed drastically. Blue Cross plans arranged contracts with hospitals that provided hospital service instead of merely a cash indemnity. With the financial problem largely solved for many subscribers by these plans, modern hospitals began to become the logical centres for recovery from sickness. During the 1930's there was a shift from home nursing to care in a hospital, where expert medical knowledge and skill was readily available.

Canada began to lead the United States in extensive planning for medical insurance during the late 1930's. During the Depression, physicians were overwhelmed by requests for their services, illustrating the theory that unemployment and sickness are twin facets of the same social problem. In 1935, the Ontario Medical Association negotiated an arrangement with the Ontario Department of Welfare. Medical services were provided for 350,000 persons on relief, at a contract price of 25¢ per month for each individual. This was the first time in Canada that public money had been paid for the medical relief of the poor and unemployed. In 1936, doctors in British Columbia put political pressure on the provincial government to plan for a pre-paid, non-profit medical scheme. Similarly, the Canadian Medical Association welcomed health insurance plans, although understandably retaining its fear that state patronage might strengthen the case for state medicine. What delayed the further development of nationwide plans was the continual federal-provincial wrangling over responsibility and finance. But in spite of these difficulties, in 1939 Canada introduced a Blue Cross plan for hospital care which was sponsored by the Provincial Hospital Association.

On the eve of World War II, preventative medicine suddenly became headline news in the United States. During 1937 there were 73 deaths from uncontrolled poisons, which resulted in the passing of the Federal Food, Drug and Cosmetic Act of 1938. A Food and Drug Administration set up inspection centres in several large cities to prevent further catastrophes.

WORLD WAR II AND ITS EFFECTS

Britain took stock of her hospital accommodation in 1939, in view of the casualties expected from air raids. There were still one million paupers in the country, with over half of this number receiving medical treatment in the 388 workhouse infirmaries. There were also 137 general hospitals, generally larger in size than the workhouse infirmaries, with total bed accommodation existing for 207,000 patients. Fortunately the casualty rate from air raids never attained the predictions of prewar experts, or Britain would have been unable to cope with the need for both normal and war-induced hospital services. During World War II new techniques of treating patients were developed. Plastic, orthopedic and neuro-surgery were developed and miracle drugs such as penicillin and sulpha compounds were widely used. In earlier wars approximately 75 per cent of the wounded died: in World War II, over 80 per cent of the wounded recovered. Also, during the war the social class structure of Britain tended to become less rigid and, in turn, this meant that a continuing national approach to health problems became possible.

The example of Britain's Beveridge Report, which sold over 65,000 copies in North America alone, helped to inspire Ottawa to establish in 1942 an Advisory Committee on Health composed of high-ranking civil servants. This advisory committee proposed that the federal government should aid provincial governments to set up comprehensive health schemes. In the light of the later opposition of the medical profession in Saskatchewan to implementing this plan, it is interesting to note the positive attitude of the Canadian Medical Association in 1943. Dr. Routley, General Secretary, appeared before a special parliamentary committee and stated:

We visualize for Canada a system of health insurance which will be more all-inclusive, efficient and sound than any which has ever been devised and operated anywhere. It should place much emphasis on the prevention of disease and the development of a high degree of physical fitness and should include complete modern diagnostic and curative services.[10]

As had happened so often before, the main obstacle to introducing comprehensive medical coverage was the constitutional issue. The provinces had the power, Ottawa had the money. Unfortunately, in 1945 there was no general agreement on financing comprehensive provincial health schemes and the issue lay dormant until 1960, except for some piecemeal grants for special purposes.

Britain's new Labour government elected in 1946 soon enacted a comprehensive National Health Act to go into effect in 1948. This health scheme was a compulsory one that covered all aspects of medical, surgical, optical and dental services. All health facilities were to be included in the scheme. Labour's blueprint was the famous Beveridge Report of 1942, although in framing the Health Insurance Act, Parliament ignored the plea that reputable Friendly Societies be allowed to participate. Insurance-Assurance companies were to be swept aside anyway, due to the bitterness engendered by their activities. But the Labour Government also swept away all other agencies. The National Health Plan was to be administered in a State scheme and once again, as in 1912, the British Medical Association rose in revolt. Doctors claimed that they were bitterly opposed to the idea of becoming civil servants, but their resistance collapsed when Aneurin Bevan, the fiery Minister of Health, agreed to pay for the good will of the medical practice. Despite the furor, Britain's national health scheme started on schedule. At the same time, many disgruntled British doctors emigrated and were to play an important role in fighting against state medicine in Saskatchewan fifteen years later.

In the United States in 1945, President Truman failed to pass a health insurance plan proposing compulsory and prepaid medical, dental and insurance coverage. The Beveridge Report had been read by American insurance executives and they had noted the planned demise of their British counterparts; Truman thus encountered intense opposition from the insurance lobby and the American Medical Association, both wedded to free enterprise. Congress did, however, start to allocate grants to states and cities for the construction of hospitals in 1946, and hospital care became the backbone of American medical services.

In Canada, the Medical Association took a different attitude from that of the A.M.A., stating that Canadians did not feel that voluntary medical plans were sufficient. Ottawa continued to study the possibility of a complete health insurance plan, watched closely by doctors' organizations who sought a non-political Health Commission. Dominion-Provincial conferences continued to discuss how health insurance was to be financed. In April 1957, there was an "Act to Authorize Contributions by Canada in respect of Programmes administered by Provinces, providing Hospital Insurance and Laboratory and other Services in Aid of Diagnosis." This long-winded name was intended to spell out to the electorate what federal politicians were doing. It is interesting to see a British point of view on the snail-like progress in Canada since 1943. An article in the *British Medical Journal* in 1958 said that trying to compare Canadian to British schemes was impossible, for Canada was not a national entity in terms of dealing with health insurance, and even some Canadians overlooked the fact that the health of the population is a provincial responsibility. Furthermore, noted the British observer, there was no real philosophy concerning the welfare state in Canada, as politicians and physicians were still watching the British health scheme to see where flaws existed. It might be added that Ottawa also had an eye on the American scene for, in 1958, Canada finally copied the American practice of giving grants for hospital construction. The Canadian federal-provincial financing was based on the usual pattern of splitting the costs on a 50:50 basis. Unlike in Britain, hospital ownership and management were left untouched.

Generally speaking, Canadian politicians copied American ideas in health insurance. Canadian doctors themselves, however, have always enjoyed a close association with their British colleagues. In 1955 there was a joint meeting, the fourth of its kind, of the Canadian Medical Association and the British Medical Association. And in 1954 the general practitioners of Canada had copied a British precedent in forming a College of General Practitioners.

DEVELOPMENTS IN THE 1960'S

American ideas on health insurance seem to be a modified version of the type of German legislation of the Bismarckian era of the 1880's, or the 1911 British health scheme that was copied from Germany. Health insurance in the United States has meant the advance financing of medical expenses by individual or employer-employee contributions. Private agencies administer contracts where the benefits are spelled out. There are about 900 commercial insurance companies involved and an additional 800 plans known as the independents. One independent plan has achieved nationwide fame, the Kaiser Foundation Health Plan which covers 200,000 people. The Kaiser plan provides top-quality medical care for fees that are 20 to 30 per cent below comparable schemes. These so-called "voluntary" plans have supporters that deride "compulsory insurance," paid for by general taxation, as State dictatorship or socialized medicine. Blue Cross and Blue Shield schemes are non-profit organizations that arrange hospital and physician services respectively.

Until recently, persons over 65 in the U.S.A. were paying nearly twice as much for medical premiums as younger people, yet their income was estimated at a third of the average. President Eisenhower had managed to pass the Kerr-Mills Bill providing federal aid to a state that would initiate "Medicare" programmes for the aged. Despite bitter opposition from the medical lobby, President Lyndon Johnson extended the Medicare coverage to a health insurance plan for men and women over 65. The Johnson legislation of 1965 provides compulsory hospital insurance but other medical coverage is voluntary.

By the mid-1960's, the fastest growing aspect of health insurance in the U.S.A. was for major medical expense

Courtesy of Ed Arno and LOOK magazine

LOOK 9 8-70

ED ARNO

"I'm sorry, but under the terms of your group policy, you don't collect unless the entire group is sick."

protection. An individual insures himself for a large sum of up to $20,000 to cover health costs, but this financial coverage is misleading. Usually the insurance agency requires the beneficiary to pay a "deductible" amount of up to $500 annually, with an additional "co-insurance" feature that limits the agency's responsibility to 75 to 80 per cent of the costs above the deductible minimum. Critics claim that the system discourages early diagnosis and treatment and inflates health insurance costs; defenders of the system reply that it gives protection against large catastrophic claims and saves paperwork in processing small claims. It can be reasonably argued that health plans that offer "services," such as the

119

Blue Cross schemes, are preferable to those which offer cash indemnities, as costs are apt to be lower to a member of a group that has an arrangement with a hospital.

Canada in the early 1960's was still having constitutional squabbles over the financing of provincial health plans. It was clear by 1960 that federal-provincial tax-rental agreements were breaking down. Quebec insisted that Ottawa withdraw from the provincial area of responsibility, but federal politicians refused. Successive conferences worked out compromises that replaced the tax-rental arrangement by a proportional sharing of yields from succession duties, income and corporation taxes. Equalization grants were to be given to the less prosperous provinces, a type of financial bribery to stay within Confederation that had been started by John A. Macdonald. The justification that all Canadians should have reasonably equal living standards was resisted, however, by the wealthier provinces—Ontario, Alberta and British Columbia—who would finance this process. Ontario claimed that by the federal proposal of 1963, it would provide 49.5 cents of each dollar collected by Ottawa, and that the proposed federal plan to work out Medicare on the basis of national "average costs," would mean that the liberal regime of Joey Smallwood in Newfoundland, for example, would receive a sum in grants greater than the total cost of Medicare in that province.

To solve this problem, Prime Minister Lester B. Pearson launched a new wave of activity and Ottawa offered to withdraw from hospital insurance and turn over the revenues to the provinces. Furthermore, in 1966 the federal government decided to copy the successful launching of Canada's first comprehensive health coverage by the Provincial C.C.F. government of Saskatchewan. Canada's "Medicare" was to start on July 1, 1968 with federal aid being supplied to provincial plans that were to be non-profit and universal in coverage. Taxation would have to be increased to finance Medicare and the Progressive-Conservative opposition, the provinces, and some public opinion opposed such a move. Mr. Pearson then utilized his diplomatic talents at the Constitutional Conference of February, 1968, to smooth over the storm. In 1970, the scheme was still not in effect in Quebec which has been the most vehement opponent of Ottawa. After the provincial government's insistence on Quebec's constitutional right to be "maître chez nous" was modified to accept a federal-provincial medical plan for the province, the doctors themselves resisted. The province's four thousand specialists demanded an opting-out clause in the legislation, and went on strike. The response of the Quebec National Assembly was to pass Bill 41, a coercive measure intended to force the specialists back to work; however, political turmoil in the autumn of 1970 obscured the medical struggle. It will be interesting to see, though, if this latest struggle over health care results in doctors being driven from Quebec, as predicted by Dr. D.L. Kippen, president of the Canadian Medical Association.

THE BATTLE OF SASKATCHEWAN

The battle in Saskatchewan over health services, which began in 1942, provides a significant background to the present state of medical insurance in Canada. In 1943 the College of Physicians and Surgeons of Saskatchewan endorsed health insurance, saying in the words of Sir William Beveridge that they wanted to ensure "the care of every citizen from indigent to millionaire," from the cradle to the grave. In 1944 the Co-operative Commonwealth Federation party won the provincial election in Saskatchewan on a platform which included "state medical services." Premier Tommy Douglas assumed the portfolio of Minister of Public Health to implement this promise and established a Commission to survey health services. This Commission was headed by an internationally known authority on the social history of medicine, Professor Henry E. Sigerest of Johns Hopkins University. The gist of the commission's findings was a recommendation that a "socialized medical service" be implemented when financial aid was available from the federal government. The findings of the Sigerest Commission received a favourable reception from the Canadian Medical Association.

From 1945 to 1960, Saskatchewan's government delayed further action on state medicine until the federal-provincial struggle over power and finance would be resolved. Pending the introduction of a province-wide health scheme, Saskatchewan introduced in 1946 an experimental Swift Current Regional Health Plan involving 53,000 persons. In 1947 hospitalization became free for all Saskatchewan citizens, a move which met cries of "regimentation" and "socialism"; it is noticeable, though, how other provinces followed suit, with the federal government seizing the opportunity to encroach upon the provincial responsibility for hospitalization by stressing its role as a financial fairy godmother. In 1959 Premier Douglas assured the provincial medical association that no steps would be taken without consultation, but also stressed basic principles upon which the future provincial plan would be founded, such as universal coverage and centralized administration. It was an election year in 1960 and the affluent doctors of Saskatchewan, buoyed up by a prosperous economy, decided to fight the proposed health coverage. Not only did this decision reverse the stand of the College of Physicians and Surgeons of Saskatchewan of 1943, but also it reflected the determination of some doctors who had emigrated from Britain, to refight the battle over state medicine lost earlier at home. During the prosperous 1950's, the doctors had organized profitable voluntary organizations known as Medical Services Incorporated and Group Medical Services, and they did not want to lose these sources of revenue.

Doctors rolled up their sleeves to fight on the Saskatchewan hustings in 1960. A campaign chest was raised by assessing doctors $100 each and the C.M.A. added $35,000 more. This doctors' fund for political purposes exceeded the amounts available to either the C.C.F. or Liberal parties. But the doctors proved inept politicians, in effect aiding their political opponents by extravagant charges which either antagonized or amused the electorate. For example, it was rumoured that the Pope had rejected a similar health plan in the U.S.A. as contrary to the beliefs of the Roman Catholic Church. The President of the College of Physicians and Surgeons of Saskatchewan, Dr. H.D. Dalgleish, saw the proposed Act as a "civil conscription of the medical profession." The College of Physicians and Surgeons depicted the virtues of "free enterprise" versus "state control" and, like their political mentor Winston Churchill in 1945, lost the support of the electorate.

Despite the resistance of the doctors' official organization, the Provincial C.C.F. party in Saskatchewan won the election of 1960. Dr. W.P. Thompson, a distinguished biologist, was then appointed to become chairman of an Advisory Planning Committee on Medical Care. The Thompson Commission included representatives from the College of Physicians and Surgeons, who took the stand that state medicine would drive good men out of the study of medicine. Unfortunately for the advocates of such a view, this prediction was not supported by British experience. Professor Richard Titmuss of the London School of Economics reported in his *Essays on the Welfare State* that in the University of London, 73 per cent of the medical students were the sons or daughters of doctors. Moreover, as it happened, the number of doctors in Saskatchewan actually increased after the introduction of state medicine.

When the Saskatchewan Medical Care Insurance Act received Royal assent on November 17, 1961, the starting date was set for April, 1962. Premiums were set at the low rate of $12 per year for a single person and $24 for a family, with general revenues defraying the rest of the cost. The Battle of Saskatchewan rose in intensity as in May 1962 Dr. E.W. Barootes, the representative of the College of Physicians and Surgeons on the Thompson Commission, thundered: "Never since the days of Charles II has there been [such] legislation reversing the civil rights and liberties of citizens."[11]

A doctors' strike started on July 1, 1962 when 700 physicians took their holidays. It must be pointed out that the College of Physicians and Surgeons had set up an emergency service of 225 doctors, indicating that the doctors were concerned about the continuance of medical services during their political struggle. But a violent reaction of the news media outside the province condemned the self-centered attitude of the physicians and further inflamed public opinion within Saskatchewan.

The Saskatchewan government airlifted 90 British doctors into the province on a temporary basis to help maintain essential services. Lord Taylor, a British physician and an architect of Britain's National Health Scheme of 1945, acted as mediator between the government and the striking doctors. Concessions were made to enable doctors to deal indirectly with the Medical Commission, by using insurance agencies as non-profit intermediaries; the doctors felt they could use these agencies as launching pads for a resumption of free enterprise, should there be a change of government. Lord Taylor who negotiated a settlement to the 23-day strike was much wiser, as he knew from experience in Britain that once the state scheme was adopted, no politician dare try to put back the clock. The American Medical Association took a keen interest in the Saskatchewan struggle, as their executives realized that this state scheme was the thin edge of the "socialist" wedge in North America. Finally, nearly twenty years after comprehensive health coverage had first been recommended for Canadians, the dream became a reality in the Saskatchewan of 1962.

CANADA ACCEPTS MEDICARE

Other provinces began to move in the direction of a comprehensive scheme for medical care, although more on a voluntary than a compulsory basis. Medical insurance lobbies were more successful in Ontario and Alberta than in Saskatchewan. The Hall Royal Commission in Ontario recommended a comprehensive Health Charter that would deal with "all" medical needs, but this proposal was considerably diluted. To make the provincial schemes profitable, the insurance agencies participating in them decided to weed out bad risks by limitations, deductibles and co-insurance. For example, while Saskatchewan provides coverage for all people in the province, Alberta's plan covers only 10 per cent under a subsidy plan, paying one-third of medical costs. Ontario instituted two schemes to provide total health coverage, the Ontario Health Services Insurance Plan (O.H.S.I.P.) for physicians' services, and the Ontario Hospital Insurance Plan (O.H.S.C.). For a family the total premium in 1971 was $309 per year, considerably above the more comprehensive Saskatchewan plan. Ontario's coverage did not cover prescription drugs or dental care in the dentist's office, and OHSIP paid only 90 per cent of the 1969 Ontario Medical Association schedule of fees. This fee schedule was only recommended, and therefore not subscribed to by all medical practitioners. The New Democratic Party of Ontario promised to reduce the yearly fees for a family to $120, and to cover all medical fees by eliminating the 10 per cent paid by the patient—they felt that doctors could afford to drop this "double billing" in view of an average net income of just under $31,000 per year. The Conservative government of Ontario began the process of reviewing the structure of the program, realizing, it seems, that "socialized" medicine does not mean supplying public funds to insurance companies or overly entrepreneurial doctors. The Ontario election of October, 1971 extended the mandate of the Conservative party which, in the following session, announced that there was to be free medical coverage for persons over 65 years of age. Under the new Ontario Health Insurance Plan (O.H.I.P.) to be introduced on April 1, 1972 the total premiums are to be reduced to $264 a year.

The doctors of Newfoundland and British Columbia accept 90 per cent of the local medical tariff as complete payment. In Manitoba, the New Democratic Party campaigned in 1969 with a promise to reduce premiums for the provincial medicare scheme, and the newly elected NDP government under Premier Edward Schreyer reduced the family premium from $9.80 to $1.10 per month.

The use of the word "premium" in health schemes is rather deceptive, as personal payments are really a regressive personal tax used to support the program. This eases the burden on the general revenues of the provincial treasury but is unrelated to the ability to pay, as it bears heaviest on the poorest-paid labourer. One other general feature of provincial plans like those of Ontario and Alberta, is the participation of insurance agencies, reminiscent of the 1911 British National Health Scheme. Under the federal Medicare Scheme, the use of private insurance firms as agents is to cease in July, 1972. It will be interesting to see if Canadian insurance companies can outlast their British counterparts who survived for 34 years as government agents dispensing public funds.

HEALTH HAZARDS

It might be thought from what has been said about the advances in medicine and health care that our generation is indeed fortunate compared to earlier generations. Undoubtedly progress has been made in scientific research and its application to medical techniques. Yet increased longevity of human life is being threatened by an increasingly unhealthy environment. During the past twenty years a new threat has emerged in the form of unprecedentedly widespread air and water pollution. When Thor Heyerdahl navigated the Atlantic in a reed boat in 1970, he reported seeing plastic bottles, oil blobs and garbage floating hundreds of miles from the nearest shore. Professor D.A. Chant, Chairman of the Department of Zoology at the University of Toronto, has declared that the threat to our environment is serious enough to raise the possibility of man failing to survive unless the pollution question is given the attention it deserves. Children may well have no future if they are literally engulfed in industrial waste and human sewage. At least effective filtration and chlorination can cope with sewage, but plastic and glass containers and many industrial pollutants are virtually indestructible. Once again the solution appears to lie in political action to restrain polluters and, as a recent precedent, it would be hard to improve on the example of London's experience.

The word "smog" was coined to describe a combination of smoke and fog, and the substance it denotes has long been familiar to many industrial cities where blast furnaces pour out exhaust fumes. In December of 1952, a disastrous smog killed 4,000 people in London, England and started a national outcry. Most British homes burned coal as a source of heat and the sulphur contained in this soft coal was emitted from chimneys as choking sulphur dioxide. In the Clean Air Act of 1956, rules were laid down concerning the type of fuel that could be burnt, and these restrictions were impartially enforced. London bird watchers have since reported that the number of species that inhabit the city has doubled.

In contrast, it has been rumoured that around Los

Angeles even the birds cough. California pioneered in American air pollution legislation in 1960 when the seriousness of the air pollution, principally from car exhausts, finally stirred public opinion. The problem had been recognized earlier, but automobile manufacturers tended to dismiss the idea that their metal monsters were in any way responsible for the acrid fumes that affected the nose and eyes of urban residents of the Sunshine State. In 1953 the Ford Motor Company wrote to a Los Angeles supervisor that:

the Ford engineering staff, although mindful that automatic engines produce exhaust gases, feels these waste gases are dissipated in the atmosphere quickly and do not present an air-pollution problem. Therefore, our research department has not conducted any experimental work aimed at totally eliminating these gases.[12]

On June 4, 1961 New York State finally warned the major automobile manufacturers to install anti-fume devices on their cars or be compelled to do so. Public relations representatives of the automobile manufacturers hastily explained that this thinking certainly conformed to their own public-spirited plans. At the same time, the claim of some experts that the internal combustion engine has been the most important single cause of air pollution has not been answered by these public relations men with that firm degree of certainty exhibited by the Ford engineering staff a few years earlier.

The Clean Air Act of 1965 introduced a federal plan for the United States to regulate motor vehicle emissions. Exhaust standards were issued in 1968 and it has been proposed that a penalty of up to $10,000 per day for violators be imposed. Canada is watching the American experiment with interest and copying the main features. It is to be hoped that we will draw also on British precedents in the field of air pollution if we are going to secure clean northern air. There is little doubt that a legal precedent of 1306 could be used most effectively: to encourage compliance with legislation, a violator of a British law that prohibited burning coal in a furnace was prosecuted, condemned and executed. But

Canada is not merely watching developments elsewhere, for Ontario has led North America by its Air Pollution Control Act with a fine of $5,000 maximum for the first offence, and $10,000 for the second.

Politicians did not take water pollution seriously in the United States until 1965. Prior to this time, there had been a Rivers and Harbours Act in 1899 forbidding discharge of solid refuse from ships, and an Oil Pollution Act of 1924 regulating oil discharges in coastal waters. But the first real federal legislation to control more than merely waste products from marine engines, or relatively small amounts of garbage dumped overboard, stemmed from legislation passed in 1948. At this time individual states were given power to set pollution standards and in 1956 a Water Pollution Act provided federal grants for research. The apex of this legislative effort was reached by the Water Quality Act of 1965, which helped to establish control of water in all states. In Canada, Ontario's Water Resources Commission has been active in promoting research and public interest into this most serious problem.

The United States and Ontario share the Great Lakes and the related pollution. Lake Erie has been declared "dead" and polluted almost beyond redemption. It has been the victim of detergent phosphates, raw sewage and industrial waste products. Further west, Canadian physicist C.E. Hollborn recently reported that detergents were turning Lake Winnipeg into a "giant bucket of suds."[13] There is no secret about which industries have achieved a remarkable record in polluting sources of water. Chemical companies, detergent manufacturers, primary metal industries, paper and textiles, petroleum refining and untreated municipal sewage—all have made their contribution.

New challenges to our total environment have emerged in the past twenty years that will have to be faced not in the future, but now. And these challenges must be faced with all available resources and expertise, if man's environment is to be clean enough to allow him to enjoy any fruits of the long struggle for health care.

1. Hilda Neatby, *Quebec: The Revolutionary Age, 1760-1791* (Toronto: McClelland and Stewart, 1966), p. 236.
2. Great Britain, *Report on the Epidemic of Cholera, 1850* (Parliamentary Papers, 1850, Appendix E.) p. 127.
3. *British American Journal,* 1847, 3:81.
4. Hugh E. MacDermot, *History of the Canadian Medical Association* (Toronto: Murray Printing Co., 1958), 1:62.
5. *The Spectator,* 23 May 1874, p. 656.
6. Ibid.
7. W. Beveridge, *Voluntary Action: A Report on Methods of Social Advance* (London: George Allen and Unwin Ltd., 1948), p. 58.
8. *Journal of the American Medical Association,* 1921, vol. 76. Cited in G. Newman, *Building A Nation's Health* (London: Macmillan and Company, 1939), p. 419.
9. MacDermot, *History of the Canadian Medical Association,* 2:92.
10. *House of Commons Special Committee on Social Security, Minutes of Proceedings and Evidence, 1944 Session* (Ottawa: King's Printer), p. 138.
11. *Regina Leader Post,* 3 May 1962. Cited in E.A. Tollefson, *Bitter Medicine* (Saskatoon: Modern Press, 1963), p. 104.
12. David R. Newman, "Air Pollution," *Current History,* August 1970, p. 19.
13. Gordon Mitchell, *Sick Cities* (Baltimore: Penguin Books, 1969), p. 114.

4

Housing and the Development of Cities

Great mischiefs daily grow and increase by reason of pestering the houses with divers families, harbouring of inmates and converting great houses into several tenements and the erection of new buildings in London and Westminster.

Elizabeth I, 1593

This statement could easily be applied to urban problems of our age. These problems have a long history and in this chapter it is proposed to sketch their historical background; the discussion will emphasize the physical arrangements regarding shelter that have been essential to man's health and well-being.

EARLY PATTERNS

The Romans were excellent city planners and evolved the idea of a grid pattern of streets that has been used so extensively in the United States. Military engineers laid out straight Roman roads, preferably on high ground, so that troops on the march could watch for enemies. In their houses the Romans introduced the idea of central heating by means of furnaces, as well as that of a thick wall of thermal capacity to radiate heat long after the fire had burned low. With the decline of the Roman Empire, urban culture languished until revived in the development of medieval towns.

130

The need for protection was a prime factor in the location of many medieval towns in Britain. A town huddled close to the protection of a castle. The townspeople surrounded their settlement with a town wall, and at dusk strangers were prevented from entering the gateways by massive wooden doors. Inside the town wall, the town developed in a random fashion, as the use of the land mainly depended upon the economic activities of the inhabitants. The town of

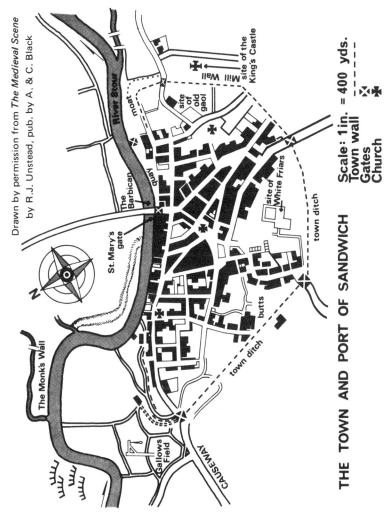

Drawn by permission from *The Medieval Scene* by R.J. Unstead, pub. by A. & C. Black

THE TOWN AND PORT OF SANDWICH

Scale: 1 in. = 400 yds.
Town wall
Gates
Church

Sandwich in Kent is preserved largely as it developed four centuries ago, because as its river silted up this great medieval port ceased to grow. The plan reproduced in this chapter indicates the unplanned arrangement of the streets of the town. This plan also indicates the important role played by the church in the life of medieval cities. If a settlement grew sufficiently to warrant the building of a cathedral and thus became the seat of a bishop, it was then called a city. Leading cities were relatively small by modern standards; for example, two leading cities of the Middle Ages, Bristol and Norwich, each had only approximately 30,000 people.

Cities did not grow up as isolated blobs on a map but reflected the economic activity of the surrounding countryside. Medieval cities had a surrounding hinterland for, in a predominantly agricultural economy, the land was an accepted setting for community life. Metropolitan influence exerted by these cities began to spread with the expansion of trade and commerce in the sixteenth century, and eventually reached the New World of North America.

William Penn planned the city of Philadelphia in Pennsylvania during the seventeenth century in a rigid grid pattern, with straight North-South and East-West streets intersecting each other at right angles. This pattern made it easy to sell rectangular building lots or plots to incoming settlers. The founder intended his city to be a "holy experiment" in establishing a community of brotherly love, and he hoped to develop five public squares that would provide green areas for the enjoyment of the residents of his city. Further north, in New England, the towns reproduced the traditional English village green in the form of a central common, surrounded by distinctively styled white frame churches and houses.

New France soon developed an architectural style of stone houses with steeply angled roofs that was suited to the harsh winters of a northern climate and to the available building materials. The population was at this time surprisingly urban: the census taken in 1666 revealed that almost half the total population of 3,418 persons lived in the three growing towns of Quebec, Three Rivers and Montreal.

All the early towns in the New World, with the exception of Philadelphia, developed piecemeal from farm villages or port villages, with the topography of the land determining their irregular layouts. The first and only settlement that was constructed as a project of the British government was the naval base of Halifax, founded in 1749. The construction of Halifax was planned for reasons of imperial defense as a counterweight to the French fortress of Louisburg, in a century that believed in planning: a city of 10,000 was organized on paper, and carpenters were brought to the harbour of Chebucto to begin construction.

When the United States of America was formed, its founders intended to have a capital city worthy of the new nation. A French engineer, Major Pierre Charles L'Enfant, was entrusted with producing a basic plan for the city of Washington and dreamed of providing many open areas in his spider-web pattern. But by the late eighteenth century, commercial interests were very influential in the government, and this was reflected in the preference for profits before beauty. L'Enfant refused to produce a properly engraved plan for Washington as he feared that hasty real estate promotion would prevent the execution of his plan. This fear was well-founded, as even the federal government was more interested in the opportunity for land speculation than in co-operating with the planner to ensure that his plans were faithfully carried out. Benjamin Latrobe, who supervised the construction of public buildings in Washington, commented bitterly on the private buildings that were erected in what were intended to be open areas. Similarly, in Philadelphia the five public squares planned by William Penn were never used exclusively for the intended purpose of recreation. Civic planning ran counter to the prevailing American attitude about the commercial value of land.

ECONOMIC CONSIDERATIONS AND PLANNING

Land was the readiest source of new wealth in America. The public domain was sold by the treasury of the new nation to land companies who, in turn, offered it for resale at a profit. It can be contended that American cities planted in a newly discovered wilderness were "history-less" and, therefore, that cultural considerations were never important relative to economic considerations. Many jerry-built buildings were constructed and merely intended to serve their purpose for a limited amount of time. What brought some order to these American cities was the standard layout of rectangular blocks of land in a grid pattern, which facilitated land speculation and transfer of property. By permitting lots to be marked out long before anyone knew the natural features of the land, the grid plan encouraged the idea of future growth and thus increased land values. Thomas Jefferson's travels abroad provided him with learned justification for the chequer-board pattern in antiquity, but it is unlikely that cultural considerations weighed very heavily with the City Fathers of New York. When, in 1811, New York City's Planning Commissioners blocked out the future development of the city, they merely extended the gridiron pattern, while providing revealing reasons. New York decided that deep, narrow lots did not "waste" land, while the idea of diagonals or oval shapes, such as had developed in Bath, England, was set aside as "frivolous."

In York, the new capital of Upper Canada after 1791, a less commercial attitude towards land use was noticeable. In the first place, the Loyalists had migrated to an area which was under the protection of Britain, and this permitted military surveys to be made of the land. The first official plan for York envisaged four squares, with each square having two rows of four houses facing it. Those government buildings that were erected may not have been particularly elegant but they showed the influence of official planners. Governor John G. Simcoe contributed the straight military roads, known now as Yonge and Dundas streets, that were intended to aid the colony to repel a Yankee invasion. London was envisaged as the administrative site of Upper Canada and soon displayed the planning that has since earned for it the title of the "Forest City."

Old London had benefitted from the Georgian era in which residential planning was a dignified function of a civilized community. In the eighteenth century, numbers of graceful Georgian houses were built around public squares, and London and Bath still arouse the admiration of those who seek beauty within the city. Elsewhere in Britain, Birmingham originated the idea of a building society in 1781,

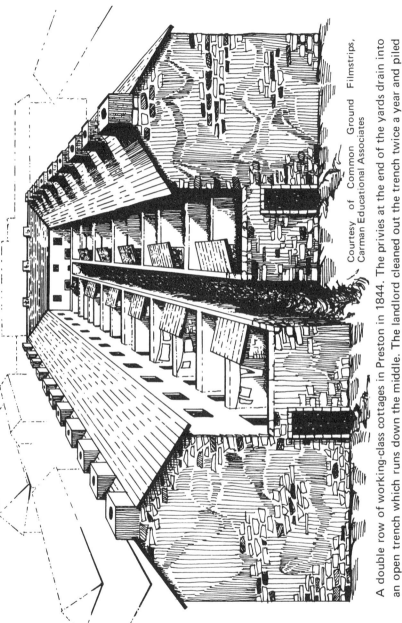

A double row of working-class cottages in Preston in 1844. The privies at the end of the yards drain into an open trench which runs down the middle. The landlord cleaned out the trench twice a year and piled the contents near by

Courtesy of Common Ground Filmstrips, Carman Educational Associates an organization intended to finance private house building by regular contribution to a voluntary organization. Building societies rapidly multiplied in number. But this era was really the calm before the storm, as the industrial revolution drastically changed attitudes towards the provision of housing.

HOUSING THE INDUSTRIAL WORKER

During the industrial revolution there was a population boom in areas that had earlier been almost exclusively rural in character. Towns such as Manchester and Sheffield mushroomed rapidly. In one sense new industrial cities were being created but no cathedrals were built to justify the term "city," as fulfilling the spiritual needs of the working masses was not considered very important by exponents of laissez faire. Factory entrepreneurs required a large number of cheap houses which could be rented to their labourers. Builders saw the chance for quick profits by cramming rows of two-storey houses, often back to back, around a factory or mineshaft. Back-to-back housing meant that the houses were only one room deep, measuring about 11 feet by 11 feet 6 inches. There was no back garden as the backs of these dwellings converged upon a courtyard provided with one communal tap. Because cheap material was used in construction, a slum problem soon appeared. The walls of the houses were not impervious to damp, and toilets, where they existed, were often shared.

Yet it was not only the expanding urban areas that turned parts of Britain into a nineteenth-century wasteland. The physical landscape was changed as ugly man-made hills were formed from the waste material deposited from mining coal or china clay deposits. These tips, as they are called, are found from Cornwall to South Wales, from Northern England to Scotland. One of these ugly and dangerous tips was brought to the world's attention in 1967 when the slag heap at the village of Aberfan collapsed, engulfing a crowded school. Construction of railway embankments in the nineteenth century made deep gashes in the land, as engineers sought to provide even gradients for the locomotives. Whereas the medieval city had existed within a green hinterland,

136

the industrial revolution produced black ugliness near many of the rising metropolises. To compound urban problems, there was no local political administration in most of the new urban regions until the passage of the Municipal Corporations Act of 1835. Housing reformers therefore had an uphill struggle to persuade the dominant factory owner that places like Manchester or Birmingham were not merely industrial hives of men and machines.

A few enlightened individuals had formed, in 1830, the Society for Improving the Condition of the Labouring Classes. This organization sought to ameliorate the physical condition of workers by stressing the need for adequate housing and, from 1844 onwards, had as its president the eminent social reformer Lord Shaftesbury. Benthamites led by Edwin Chadwick added their voices to the agitation for reform, and inspired the Health of Towns Commission of 1842. From this Commission Parliament learned, for example, that in the densely populated county of Lancashire, which was the hub of the cotton textile industry, only one town had a public park. A young novelist, Benjamin Disraeli, also drew attention to the need for education and leisure in factory districts in his novel *Coningsby* (1844). Another writer who was to achieve a different type of political fame, Friedrich Engels, produced a detailed indictment of Manchester in his *Condition of the Working Classes in England in 1844.* Manchester, the largest city in Lancashire, eventually showed some evidence of civic concern when three parks were established in 1846, mainly due to donations received from wealthy men.

By 1851 even royalty was joining in the struggle to secure better houses for the workers. Queen Victoria's husband, Prince Albert, inspired the building of a model block of workers' houses at the Great Exhibition in London. That year of 1851 saw the passage of two relevant pieces of legislation: The Labouring Classes Lodging Houses Act, which gave local authorities power to expropriate land in order to build lodging houses, and the Common Lodging Houses Act which encouraged local authorities to inspect and regulate this type of building, and which was sponsored by that indefatigable reformer, Lord Shaftesbury. Unfortunately the term "lodging houses" was not clearly defined to mean either collective or individual houses and these Building Acts made little progress in the face of vested interests. But 1851 was a notable year in several aspects of housing, as one enlightened textile manufacturer, Titus Salt, built a model village at Saltaire in Yorkshire, which was well-planned and showed an attempt at architectural style.

THE NEW REPUBLIC

North America did not have major industrial blight during the first half of the nineteenth century, although there were slums. As immigrants entered the ports of Boston and New York during the 1830's, they were often herded into these developing slum areas. An indication of the filthy conditions can be gleaned from the fact that pigs and geese were encouraged to roam the muddy streets as scavengers; in Charleston, South Carolina, even vultures were protected by law because of the role they fulfilled in removing the remains of dead animals.

During the 1830's, certain cities began to acquire distinguishing characteristics. New York had already acquired its reputation as the city of hustle and bustle. Asa Greene, a noted resident, recorded in 1837 that to cross Broadway:

> you must button your coat tight about you, see that your shoes are secure at the heels, settle your hat firmly on your head, look up street and down street . . . to see what carts and carriages are upon you, and then run for your life.[1]

New York City was the point of entry for most immigrants, and long and narrow Manhattan Island was not suited to accommodating a rapid growth of population. Wealthier inhabitants moved northwards out of the island's lower end, where their former homes were converted into tenements, but even then:

> The intense housing shortage caused basements, attics, and lofts to be rented. As a measure of the resulting congestion, the density of the seven lower wards of Manhattan increased from 94.5 to 163.5 persons per acre

138

in the period from 1820 to 1850. In 1843, a survey found 7,196 persons living underground in New York. Within seven years . . . the cellar dwelling population of the city had increased to 29,000.[2]

Before 1850, over ninety per cent of the population of the United States was concentrated east of the Mississippi River. The completion of the Erie canal in 1823 encouraged the growth of cities like Cleveland, Detroit and particularly Chicago, incorporated in 1833. One of Chicago's early mayors, William Ogden, represented New York investment interests and vigorously pushed the roads and railways out into Chicago's agricultural hinterland. Chicago had become the centre of the meat-packing industry by the 1840's and urban growth was rapid, with real estate interests predicting that the cities on the Great Lakes were the future hub of the nation. Congress facilitated this rapid growth by its land policies. By an Act of 1796, a policy had been established that public land should be sold at public auction. To avoid considerable paperwork, land was disposed of in units of 640 acres to large-scale buyers. In reaction to this policy, poor people began the practice of squatting on public land, and regarded physical possession as more important than a legal title. Following the War of 1812, a wave of human migration took possession of the land in the lower lake states, and Congress was impotent to enforce its regulations. The legal position was eventually tidied up in 1841 when Congress gave squatters in the Ohio Valley a chance to purchase "their" land.

TORONTO THE GOOD

To the north of Lake Ontario, the capital city of Upper Canada was growing steadily. A reporter of the *Illustrated London News* recorded in 1847 that, "Toronto, the capital of Canada West, during the past 30 years, has advanced from a small village of wooden houses, with a few hundred inhabitants . . . to a city of elegant and commodious brick and stone buildings, with 20,000 inhabitants." At this time, was Toronto Good? As the largest national influx was of Irishmen, it is perhaps understandable that there was a ratio of approximately seven inns for every church that graced the city in 1848. On the other hand, the established conservative tradition of respect for the law provided relatively honest government in comparison to the American scene. Yet civic action to implement planning had certainly languished since the town was first established, despite the admirable plan for the lakefront. A permanent broad promenade had been planned along the whole shore, to be called the Mall, and a Royal patent had been issued in 1818 to permit the development of thirty acres of land. Failure to implement this plan had serious consequences for Toronto, when a railway boom occurred between 1852 and 1857. The lakefront area was shown on the map as "Reserved for the Public as a Promenade" and, in 1854, construction of this public esplanade actually began. Then the Toronto Council yielded to the pressure of the railway interests and the area was taken over as a marshalling yard. In the 1850's, towns in central Canada competed vigorously to secure railway connections, and railways could secure sweeping concessions that included free land, tax exemption and the best sites in the city. Ironically, the railway age was also a period when culture flowered. Toronto acquired its fine St. Lawrence Hall and University College, while Chicago even built an opera house.

AMERICAN EXPANSION

Leisure was provided for in the public parks that became increasingly important to community health. In 1853, New York City started to construct what would become known as Central Park. Real estate interests pressured politicians to fight against this "misuse" of valuable land. On the other hand a well-organized movement of interested citizens stressed that the park would serve as "lungs" or "ventilators" in the city. Frederick Olmstead, a landscape planner who had travelled extensively, sought to bring natural beauty to the city for, as he remarked, "what we want is tranquillity and rest to the mind." By 1861, Olmstead had completed the first real park built in the U.S.A., and this inspired other American cities to copy his model. This interest in parks developed at a crucial time, for the United States was about to embark on a great boom period of expansion.

With the Civil War over, Western expansion continued until the crash of the stock market in 1873. As Lewis Mumford, the dean of urban studies, has explained, the factory and the railroad were the generating agents—and the pace of urbanization increased as the rhythm of industrialization increased. Millions of European immigrants arrived, drawn mainly by the lure of what was supposed to be free land, but settling instead in the eastern cities, crowded into tenements that rose near the factories. Slum landlords derived an annual income of between twenty and thirty per cent on their invested capital. It was Manchester all over again, as railroads cut through the middle of cities, with the clouds of smoke being supplemented in Pittsburgh by blast furnace fumes, or in Chicago by the stench of stockyards. Squatters' clubs sought to obtain the lion's share of the public lands of the west, with the aid of financial support from eastern banking interests. The Homestead Act of 1862 reflected the fact that politicians were trading public property for votes, and appealed to the American dream about speculative profits. Indeed, a leading authority has claimed that the frontier thesis of Frederick J. Turner is basically inaccurate because by 1870, "the supply of free, arable, humid land was exhausted . . . twenty years earlier than the date he [Turner] assigned."[3] The land may have been idle but it was not "free," as defined by Frederick J. Turner and his disciples, just because the census figures and population density did not determine who held title to the land. Turner's basic assumption that the frontier existed until 1890 was understandable, for it was not until 1890 that the United States Census Bureau declared that the frontier had officially disappeared, meaning that a minimum density of two persons per square mile existed over the west.

American experience in homesteading was watched keenly by the Dominion of Canada that emerged in 1867. Canada decided that her western development should serve "the purposes of the Dominion," and that the cost of expansion could be defrayed from the sale of land. Canada copied the mechanics of the American system of laying out townships of six miles square, subdivided into 36 sections of 640 acres. Under the Dominion Lands Act of 1872, a settler could obtain a quarter-section of 160 acres after fulfilling certain residential requirements and paying a $10 fee. Those sections which were odd-numbered upon the plans of the official surveyors were reserved for railway grants. But before homesteading could gain in momentum, the Great Depression started in 1873 and discouraged immigrants from crossing the Atlantic.

VICTORIAN REFORMS IN BRITAIN

On the other side of the Atlantic, the social conscience of a few individuals caused attention to be focused on the appalling conditions within the British slums. Prominent among these reformers was Octavia Hill, the grand-daughter of the Benthamite, Dr. Southwood Smith. Continuing the family interest in improving slum areas, Miss Hill borrowed money to buy three slum houses in Marylebone, London in 1864 and made them habitable. She stated her philosophy as "you cannot deal with people and their houses separately," and sought the co-operation of her tenants to maintain the property. Her venture was run on a business basis and was both a financial and moral success; soon other landlords began to seek her advice. A new profession was developed as she founded the Society for Women Housing Managers in England. For over twenty years, Octavia Hill managed a district of more than five thousand slum dwellings, while continuously emphasizing the need for public service rather than maximum profits. Her pupils spread out all over Britain and the United States, publicizing the methods of sound property management which emphasized the need to keep buildings in a state of sound repair.

Slowly, Parliament was drawn into the campaign to clean up the slums. In 1868 the Torrens Bill proposing that local authorities be given power to demolish individual unsanitary houses, was enacted into law. In 1875, Octavia Hill published her book *Homes of the London Poor* and showed that the largest private agency had, in the thirty-year period from 1843 to 1873, built accommodation for only 26,000 people.

Miss Hill pointed out that this was only "half the number which is yearly added to the population of London."[4] She welcomed the housing legislation proposed by the Home Secretary Richard Cross, and stated, "This is an enabling Bill. . . It will put in our power collectively [a means] . . . to clear away foul places. Let it be distinctly understood that we had not got this power [before] Mr. Cross' Bill."[5] The Bill became the famous Artizans' and Labourers' Dwellings Improvements Act of 1875, known familiarly as the first Cross Act, and was the first real parliamentary recognition that slums were a national problem. Cross attacked the problem of the blighted downtown area, where the reduced value of the land made it possible to have large-scale demolition and reconstruction. The national treasury was to loan money to municipalities who could throw the cost of improvement schemes on local taxes.

Cross cited figures which showed that in London, "for every twelve children who grow up healthy in the rich district, only one child grows up [healthy] among the poor,"[6] and pointed to one district in London where not one house had escaped an annual death by fever. Newspaper editors immediately encouraged public opinion to support Cross. A reporter for *The Spectator* who described the overcrowded areas known as the "rookeries" recorded, "drainage is impossible . . . . the soil being too putrid, the death rate of adults is double the average . . . . children die like flies in the summer, four out of five perishing before they are five years old."[7] Cross's legislation was quickly passed through Parliament. As the legislation was only intended to cover England and Wales, it is significant that all the Scottish M.P.'s banded together, regardless of party, to ask that its provisions be extended to cover Scotland.

The Mayor of Birmingham, Joseph Chamberlain, rose to national prominence by his energetic use of the power provided by the Cross Act. Usually Joseph Chamberlain appears in Canadian history books as a wicked villain whom the noble Sir Wilfrid Laurier opposed; but this interpretation is apt to do a grave injustice to a man who started a family tradition of promoting slum clearance. Chamberlain borrowed £1,650,000 for clearing ninety-three acres of slums, occupied by eighteen thousand people. Chamberlain himself guaranteed another £10,000. When the improvement scheme was finally completed, Birmingham had dignified new streets named Corporation Street and New Street which enhanced civic pride. Critics claimed that Chamberlain did not build houses to replace the slums he had removed, but there was no disputing that he focused national attention on what would one day be called "urban redevelopment." The land that was cleared was leased to tenants for seventy years' duration and, since 1954, Birmingham has become rich as the leases have reverted to the municipality.

The Cross Act of 1875 was a milestone in British social history with significant political overtones, as it established the reputation of the Conservative party for being concerned about the housing of the poor. Various Royal Commissions and further Acts of Parliament followed during the rest of the century, but did not dull the lustre of the most effective housing legislation of the nineteenth century. It is true that the Cross Acts were typical Victorian measures in seeking to encourage local authorities by permissive legislation rather than by mandatory enforcement. But the fact that public money was used to help in securing homes for the poor represented a breakthrough in social enlightenment. Significantly, the word "housing" began to appear in statutes during the 1880's: this word, derived from Tudor times when "housing" meant dwellings provided for the workers by the rich, was coming to mean the State organizing housing for workers.

Parliamentary Acts on housing were supplemented by the activities of philanthropic bodies, or what have been called "five percenters." Housing trusts were established by such men as George Peabody who, in 1862, constructed model tenements, while two model villages were constructed at Bournville, in 1879, by the Cadbury chocolate company, and at Port Sunlight in 1888 by W.L. Lever, the soap king. These ventures were merely token gestures in solving the national housing problem, but did reveal an attitude more enlightened than mere building for speculative profit.

Furthermore, the model accommodation set an example that inspired emulation, in particular with reference to bathrooms. The upper classes of Victorian England were rather prudish about certain facilities, and many Victorians felt that the idea of a communal bath was rather disgusting. Bathrooms did not become common features in large homes until the end of the century.

HOUSING NEW AMERICANS

Much more disgusting than shared baths, however, were the conditions in New York's "dumb-bell" apartments constructed from the 1870's on. These structures were the answer of New York builders and landowners to the tidal wave of European immigrants that poured into the city. The dumb-bell was a unique American solution to the problem of how to crowd approximately two hundred people into a space 25 feet by 90 feet. This stacking of human beings was permitted by the Tenement House Law of 1879, which ironically had been intended to tighten up the provisions of an earlier tenement law of 1867. Under this law, an example of New York's setting the trend in trying to initiate housing reforms, a window was required in the bedrooms of new tenements. The "dumb-bell" buildings, which managed to comply with these requirements, were named after their shape. An indentation in the middle of the building combined with a similar indentation of the next tenement to provide an airshaft about ten feet wide. This gap was supposed to provide the light and ventilation required by law. The dumb-bell structure was specifically designed to take advantage of the standard sized 25 feet by 100 feet New York lot, and ingeniously met the stipulation that 10 feet must be left behind the building. Into these dreary, six-storey buildings, human beings were concentrated, and with ten tenements to a block, an ordinary block of dumb-bells contained as many as 4,000 people.

An American journalist, Jacob Riis, focused attention on New York City's teeming immigrant neighbourhoods in his best-seller *How the Other Half Lives* (1890). Riis used the metaphor of the multi-coloured quilt to describe the complexity of population patterns in New York:

A map of the city, coloured to designate nationalities, would show more stripes than on the skin of the zebra, and more colours than any rainbow. The city on such a map would fall into great halves, green for the Irish prevailing in the West Side tenement districts, and blue for the Germans on the East Side. But intermingled with these ground colours would be an odd variety of tints that would give the whole the appearance of an extraordinary crazy quilt. From down in the Sixth Ward, upon the site of the old Collect Pond . . . the red of the Italian would be seen forcing its way northward along the line of Mulberry Street to the quarter of the French purple on Bleecker Street and South Fifth Avenue, to lose itself and reappear, after a lapse of miles, in the "Little Italy" of Harlem, east of Second Avenue. Dashes of red, sharply defined, would be seen strung through the Annexed District, northward to the city line. On the West Side the red would be seen overrunning the old Africa of Thompson Street, pushing the black of the negro rapidly uptown, against querulous but unavailing protests, occupying his home, his church, his trade and all, with merciless impartiality.[8]

The tensions within New York City amid appalling living conditions caused an inspector of building plans named Lawrence Veiller to urge the creation of an investigating State Tenement Commission. In 1900 Theodore Roosevelt, the Governor of New York, created this Commission to investigate the tenement accommodation of approximately two and one quarter million people, more than two-thirds of the city's population. With their first Report, the Commission condemned the dumb-bell as providing accommodation "unknown in London or any other city in Great Britain." Dumb-bells were prohibited by the subsequent New York Tenement House Law of 1901, which established a permanent Tenement House Commission that recruited 166 building inspectors within two years. Benthamism had finally arrived in New York. During the next twelve years, over half a million complaints of building violations were investigated. Yet the enforcement of minimum standards of safety and health did not solve the basic problem of overcrowding. A few philanthropic efforts were made to build model tenements, such as Brooklyn's Riverside Apartments, but the apparent need to maintain a "five per cent" annual profit forced the rents to be higher than ill-paid workers could afford. Population density in the notorious Tenth Ward tenements was estimated at 750 persons per acre, which is about fifteen times what present-day planners consider suitable for comfortable living.

Conditions were not much better in the rapidly developing Midwest cities. Slums proliferated between 1880 and 1900 in the age of the industrial "robber barons," who were inspired by the belief that the maximum public good is naturally realized through individual aggrandizement. With the railroad network complete, investors began to seek quick profits in the urban areas. Promotion of a town was deemed a civic virtue; this practice casts suspicion on the accuracy of many of the local histories that were produced, particularly as some of these "histories" were commissioned by local Chambers of Commerce. This age that believed in Social Darwinism was not likely to be concerned with death in the slums. Fast-growing Indianapolis, with a population of 75,000 in 1880, had toilet plumbing for just ten per cent of that number. Chicago's stench led its million inhabitants of 1890 to refer to the "infinite stink." As land values had rocketed in the business district of the Loop up to three and one half million dollars an acre by 1890, tenement building was restricted to the areas unwanted by business interests. The "wonder of the West," Chicago, had only 629 miles paved of its total of 2,048 miles of road. Yet, as with the earlier nightmare city of Manchester in England, reformers began to appear who set to work to clean up the excesses of the Chicago urban jungle.

At the World's Fair in Chicago in 1893, a group of architects presented an example of beauty, order and symmetry by blending the exhibition buildings into a miniature city. The City of White Palaces gave rise to what was termed the City Beautiful movement, as a wave of dissatisfaction swept America, and inspired numerous city plans for beautification efforts and the creation of parks. But the infant profession of city planning was ignored by investors, who generally believed in laissez faire and felt that the less government the better. Possibly the business community was still annoyed at the action of Congress in financing its first venture into the housing field in 1892 by an appropriation of $20,000 for launching a survey of slums.

Another feature of this period was the type of semi-feudalism introduced in the company town. Company housing had developed in Western Pennsylvania around the coal mines and steel production centres. Large corporations built and rented primitive accommodation to their employees, and the term "company town" acquired a stigma in the United States. For a short time, it looked as if reform might take place when a planned model community at Pullman, Illinois, set a new trend. George Pullman, who had a monopoly of production of railway sleeping cars, made a paternalistic experiment in town planning with the object of illustrating the virtues of the private enterprise system. Pullman claimed that it was strictly a business proposition to act as both employer and landlord, but a result of this ethic was that when he cut the wages of his employees in 1893 to maintain profits, he did not cut rents. Pullman workers suddenly realized the very narrow limits in which benevolent feudalism operated. The outcome was the famous strike of 1894 which had the effect of retarding any idea of further ventures in town planning by private industry, particularly during the existing depression.

URBANIZATION INCREASES IN CANADA

Canada had company towns in the form of logging camps, and settlements near pulp and paper plants or mines. Yet as Canada was still primarily agricultural before the boom that started in 1897, the country did not have widespread manufacturing in such areas as textiles or heavy industry which spawned industrial feudalism. There were some exceptions such as Hamilton, Ontario which was to be Canada's Pittsburgh and soon acquired the mass-produced monotonous housing so familiar in American and British industrial towns.

Urbanization was increasing, as the census of 1891 showed a large increase in towns during the previous decade, with the official explanation that this was "caused to a considerable extent by the growth of places which had not attained a population of 1,500 in 1881."[9] Toronto more than doubled its population from 86,415 in 1881 to 181,215 persons by 1891.[10] The railway network that had done so much to open up Canada was frequently poorly located in the urban areas. Railroad yards and tracks despoiled the city cores of Montreal, Toronto, Calgary and Vancouver. Before the First World War, a visiting Englishman recorded his impressions of Canada's two largest cities:

> the British part of Montreal is dominated by the Scottish race; there is a Scottish spirit sensible in the whole place—in the rather narrow, rather gloomy streets, the solid, square, grey, aggressively prosperous buildings, the general greyness of the city. . . . Even the Canadian habit of loading the streets with heavy telephone wires, supported by frequent black poles, seemed to increase the atmospheric resemblance to Glasgow.[11]

When he passed on to Toronto, the following impressions were recorded:

> Toronto "pronounce T'ranto please" is difficult to describe . . . . the largest British city in Canada (in spite of the cheery Italian faces that pop up at you out of excavations in the street). . . . It is situated on the shores of a lovely lake: but you never see that because the railways have occupied the entire lakefront. So if, at evening, you try to find your way to the edge of the water, you are checked by a region of smoke, sheds, trucks, wharves . . . railway lines, signals and locomotives.[12]

In the boom years of the Laurier regime, immigrants arrived in large numbers and housing became scarce in such cities as Toronto and Winnipeg. Governor-General Earl Grey encouraged Canadians to take an interest in housing for the worker and, being familiar with the British trend towards town planning, arranged for competent lecturers to visit Canada. The result was the first Canadian Housing and Town Planning Congress which was held in Winnipeg in 1912. A private company, the Toronto Housing Company, was formed to provide working-class accommodation and it pressed the Ontario Legislature to encourage the provision of housing in cities. The subsequent Ontario Housing Act of 1913 was the first legislation of its kind in the Dominion. Under this Act, as amended in 1914, a municipal council could, if it was satisfied that additional housing accommodation was needed, guarantee up to eighty-five per cent of the bonds of a building company. This legislation enabled the Toronto Housing Company to issue one million dollars worth of bonds and build Riverdale Courts in East Toronto, providing 204 apartments for rental. The venture, though limited, was an immediate success: in 1972 a few of the original residents are still in occupancy.

AMERICA WRESTLES WITH URBAN PROBLEMS

Before World War One, Canada had a predominantly British flavour and this contrasted to the melting pot further south, where more complex urban problems existed. By 1900, New York, Chicago and Philadelphia each had over a million people. America claimed to believe in the concept of the melting pot in forming a nation, and the public school system supported this vision, but the residential patterns were definitely at odds with it. Italian and Polish districts frequently provided a culture within a culture. More significant were the developing black belts of Chicago and Harlem, where slum property accommodated a high-density ghetto of coloured people. Still further south, politicians did not mince words when they proclaimed white superiority. A City Ordinance in Birmingham, Alabama of 1919 reads:

It is a misdemeanor for a member of the coloured race to move into . . . or having moved into to continue to reside in, an area of the city . . . generally and historically recognized at the time as an area for occupancy of the white race.

Racial prejudice made a mockery of the assimilation or melting pot theory. Even more important than any political concepts of Americanization was the way in which the "trickle down" theory of housing worked in practice. Deteriorating older residential areas were sold to newcomers and, in turn, waves of Irish, Jewish and European peasants passed these areas on to black people. For as coloured people sought to settle in the cities, white residents moved outwards into the suburbs and this produced lower property values in a ghetto area. Zoning statutes could be manipulated for purposes of racial or class segregation.

This pattern was reinforced by the changed attitude to city planning once the City Beautiful movement had receded by about 1910. Paradoxically, in view of the ugliness created by the railways in North American cities, some of the solid and lasting achievements of the City Beautiful movement were the massive ornate railroad terminals like Penn Station in New York, Union Station in Washington, and Union Station in Toronto. The change for the worse was foretold when city planners began to become professionals concerned with efficiency. Permanent planning commissions developed within a structure of municipal government that was mainly concerned with building codes and transportation problems. American zoning laws had little to do with community planning, as they sought to protect existing property values and naturally received the support of property owners. The question of whether a zoning ordinance would be put into effect depended mainly on whether property owners would gain financially. As pecuniary gains rarely result from changing the use of land from industrial or business purposes, it was the residential areas that were the main target for zoning. Zoning requirements were subdivided into character, density and height zoning. Character zoning entails a distinction between residential, business and industrial use; density, the amount of land that buildings may occupy; height is usually related to the width of the street. Height regulations were particularly relevant on Manhattan Island as skyscrapers could block out light and air from adjoining areas. Before World War One, the leading apostle of restrictive legislation concerning housing was Lawrence Veiller. Veiller authored "model" housing laws and was founder and secretary of the National Housing Association, which advised housing groups throughout the nation. On the other hand, Veiller energetically condemned as "socialistic" any idea of a positive approach being taken by the government in the form of a building program. Private enterprise therefore continued to supply accommodation for individuals who could afford to pay for it, rather than seeking ways of relieving the crowded tenements by constructing units that could be rented by workers.

Yet in the years before World War One, there was one man whose radical ideas have since inspired a number of housing reformers. Henry George was an American who had been shocked at the contrast between wealthy homes and the bleakness of the slums. To finance his proposed reform, George evolved the idea of the "single tax" on the increased value of land. He argued in his best-seller *Progress and Poverty* (1879) that since economic progress entailed a growing scarcity of land, the idle landowner was receiving "unearned increments" at the expense of labour. Therefore, the landowner gaining from rentals should be taxed to finance public works.

THE GARDEN CITY

George's thoughts on keeping down the cost of land had influenced the thinking of an Englishman, Ebenezer Howard. Howard wondered whether it was possible, by holding down land costs, to shift the emphasis in housing from concern over property values to concern over tenants, and then from the individual to the community. The concept of building a model Garden City developed, with the city to be its own landlord. The land on which the city was to be built would be low-priced agricultural land and would be owned by the community as a whole. A private corporation would administer the city under a charter limiting dividends to five per cent on capital actually invested, and use the unearned increment on land to finance municipal improvements. All building leases would specify building requirements and green areas were to be preserved throughout the city. Howard publicized his ideas in a book entitled *Tomorrow: A Peaceful Path to Social Reform* (1898) which proposed blending the best features of town and country in a balanced community, instead

Courtesy of Radio Times Hulton Picture Library

Heart of an Imperial Empire: London's East End in the 1880's

Courtesy of the Greenwich Libraries, Spurgeon Collection

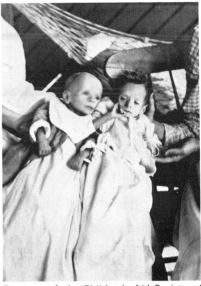

Courtesy of the Children's Aid Society of Metropolitan Toronto

The cry of the children: match-seller in London, England (above, left) and babies taken into the care of the Children's Aid Society in Toronto

Courtesy of the Children's Aid Society of Metropolitan Toronto

Courtesy of the Children's Aid Society of Metropolitan Toronto

"It is hard to remove the impression that the Children's Aid Society exists solely for the purpose of taking children from their parents . . . . [Rather,] the object in forming a society is not to take children away but to encourage and persuade negligent parents to love, protect and provide for their children, so that removal would not be necessary."

J.J. Kelso, 1905

Courtesy of the Public Archives of Canada

The Single Men's Association parading to Bathurst Street United Church, Toronto, 1930's

Courtesy of the Library of Congress

New England factory life: "Bell-Time"

Lumbering camp, Ontario, October 1895

From a photograph loaned to the Public Archives of Canada

Miners'
strike,
South
Porcupine,
c. 1910

Courtesy of the Rev. W.L.L. Lawrence Collection, Ontario Archives

Courtesy of the Public Archives of Canada

W.L. Mackenzie King
(centre) with Archie
Dennison (left) and
John D. Rockefeller
(right) while studying
industrial relations
under the auspices
of the Rockefeller
Foundation, 1915

Courtesy of the Foote Collection, Manitoba Archives

"Bloody Saturday": streetcar being overturned during the Winnipeg General Strike, 1919

Memorial Day Massacre, Sunday May 30, 1937. Outside the Republic Steel plant in Chicago, police killed ten strikers and wounded ninety others

Courtesy of the United Steelworkers of America—AFL-CIO/CLC

Courtesy of the *London Free Press*

Tolpuddle Martyrs' Shrine, London, Ontario

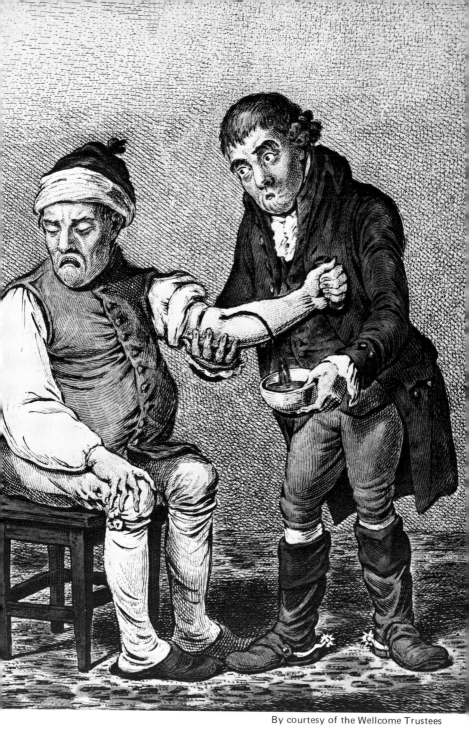

By courtesy of the Wellcome Trustees

"Blood Letting: Breathing a Vein": 1804 engraving by H. Humphrey

Courtesy of the Centre Jeanne-Mance, Hôtel-Dieu, Montreal

Jeanne Mance (1606-1673), who founded the first hospital in Montreal in 1644. She was the first white woman to arrive in Montreal, and has been credited with saving the colony three times

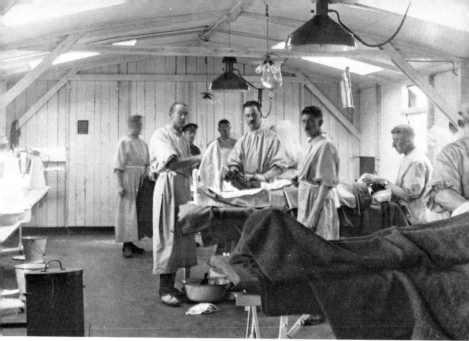

Courtesy of the Public Archives of Canada

Operating room: no. 3 Casualty Clearing Station, July 1916

Wounded Canadians en route for Blighty, July 1917

Courtesy of the Public Archives of Canada

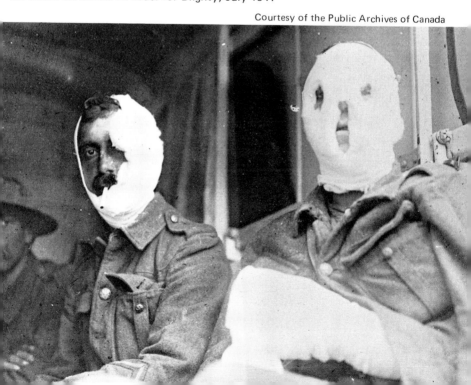

Courtesy of the Toronto Star Syndicate

Modern methods of disposal: roadside scene near Toronto (above) and industrial wastes on Lake Superior

Courtesy of Central Mortgage and Housing Corporation

Courtesy of the Metropolitan Toronto Central Library

reet scene in Barkerville, British Columbia, before the great fire of 1868

typical North American subdivision

oto by Roberts; reproduced by permission from Bonner, *Our Recent Past,* ©1963 Prentice-Hall Inc.

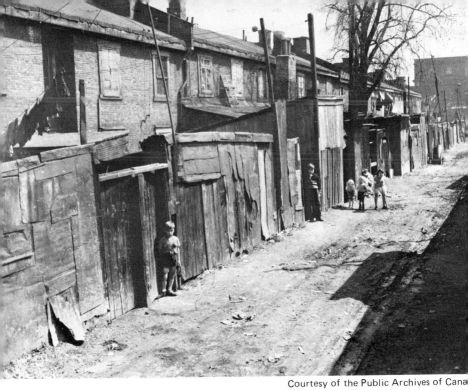

Courtesy of the Public Archives of Cana

Point St. Charles district, Montreal, 1946

O'Keefe Brewery Staff in the 1890's

Courtesy of the Metropolitan Toronto Central Libra

Courtesy of the Library of Congress

"A Sermon on Temperance"

Interior of a saloon, March 1912

Courtesy of the Western Development Museum, Saskatoon

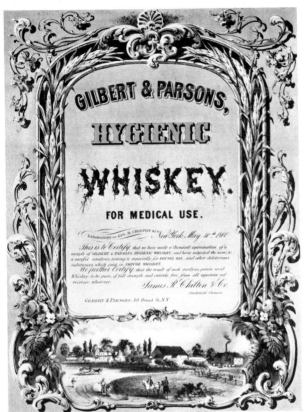

Courtesy of the Library of Congress

(left)

Advertisement for whiskey, 1868, hereby certified to be "pure, of full strength and entirely free from all injurious admixture whatever"

(below)

Bar of the Fairy Glen Hotel, Dwygyfylchi (nr. Pehmaenmawr) Wales

Courtesy of the British Tourist Authority

of an ill-organized urban sprawl. The size of the Garden City was to be limited to 30,000 people, enclosed in a permanent green belt upwards of three miles long to separate urban from rural functions. Local farmers in the surrounding hinterland were to provide the basic food needs of the city, a service function which would also aid in checking rural depopulation. Howard foresaw Garden Cities being set up throughout England, providing a way to check the continued growth of the huge, congested industrial cities. However, prophets rarely have honour in their own country, and Howard was no exception. The socialist intellectuals of the Fabian Society dismissed Howard's ideas as futile and impractical, with George Bernard Shaw describing this amazing man as an "elderly nobody."

But intellectuals are sometimes wrong in their assessments and time was to demonstrate the Fabians' misjudgement. A Garden Cities Association was formed and the first city was started at Letchworth, thirty-five miles from London, in 1903. The architects, Raymond Unwin and Barry Parker, strove to avoid the mechanical stereotypes which were indicated in Howard's sketches of a diagrammatic city. A density of only 48 persons, or 12 houses, per acre was planned. Industrial planning set the factories on the northeast side of the town, so that the prevailing south-west winds would blow smoke away from the houses and prevent air pollution.

The Garden City idea represented the culmination to that point of England's contribution to solving the housing problem. While nearly all continental town housing was tenemental, England produced the first low-density garden city with single-family houses. An English line of development led from the garden city paternalism in the Lever development of Port Sunlight and Cadbury's Bournville, to Letchworth with its municipal ownership of land. A trend was evident that led away from the earlier, unrestrained operations of land speculators. Letchworth also showed the inadequacy of planning for "health" only. The regulations passed by local governments had ensured that each house built was sanitary, but there was no concern with harmonious blending for the sake of beauty.

The city of Letchworth, however, became the mecca for housing and planning reformers. On a wave of enthusiasm an International Garden Association with world-wide membership was launched, with Ebenezer Howard as president. Letchworth had shown that an entirely detached planned community could be constructed on a virgin site and survive, but this was not the lesson that some admirers drew. For example, the impact upon the United States has been well summarized:

> "garden villages," "garden suburbs" and "garden homes" became the fashion after 1910 . . . .Most of the conceptions that were part of [the] Garden City . . . were initially applied by businessmen who were not unduly concerned with creating a good community but who foresaw large real estate profits. The term "garden city" was often used to describe any planned new community that preserved a natural setting.[13]

A more significant legacy in Britain was left by the first parliamentary legislation concerning planning. By the terms of the 1909 Housing and Town Planning Act, local authorities were empowered to prepare a plan to control the urbanization of new land. In the same year of 1909 the first formal programme in town planning was established at the University of Liverpool, indicating that planning was acquiring a professional status. While the idealism of the age envisaged Letchworth's twelve houses to an acre, private builders ignored Ebenezer Howard's ideas before World War One. Municipal authorities built houses for rent but they were responsible for only five per cent of the total number of dwellings constructed and, as the taxpayer was paying for their construction, they owed little to the garden city idea. But sound ideas have a way of embedding themselves in the conscience of social reformers, so that in later years men would be inspired to adopt and adapt the revolutionary thinking that inspired Letchworth.

154

BRITISH WORKING-CLASS HOMES

There was need for change, as can be gauged by the fact that in Scotland in 1911 over forty per cent of the population lived in two-roomed houses, with the proportion rising to approximately half the populations of Glasgow and Dundee.[14] The rapid urban growth and rising land prices produced by industrialization had created in Scotland four- and five-storey tenements, similar to those that were a feature of New York City. What were termed flats in Scotland often consisted of the notorious "single end," comprising one room, or of one room and a kitchen, with no bath and only one toilet shared by several families. Yet even with these low standards, private enterprise could not provide sufficient accommodation at a rent the working classes could afford to pay.

British residential building actually slackened after 1911. In 1913, David Lloyd George started a "Land Campaign" to get the British government into house-building by lending money to local authorities for building homes for agricultural labourers. But the outbreak of war in 1914 caused building virtually to cease for its duration. During 1917, the Ministry of Reconstruction, studying postwar needs, estimated that 796,000 new homes were needed in England and Wales plus another 115,000 for Scotland. The appalling conditions that prevailed in a Scotland that was sending her sons to die on the Western Front were outlined by the Royal Commission on Housing that reported in 1917.

These are the broad results of our survey: unsatisfactory sites of houses and villages, insufficient supplies of water, unsatisfactory provision for drainage, grossly inadequate provision for the removal of refuse, widespread absence of decent sanitary conveniences, the persistence of the unspeakable filthy privy-midden in many of the mining areas, badly constructed, incurably damp labourers' cottages on farms, whole townships unfit for human occupation in the crofting counties and islands, primitive and casual provision for many of the seasonal workers, gross over-crowding and huddling of the sexes together in the

155

congested industrial villages and towns, occupation of one-room houses by large families, groups of lightless and unventilated houses in the older burghs, clotted masses of slums in the great cities.[15]

Much of the postwar unrest would stem from the realization of returning soldiers that the ideals for which they had fought were not reflected by their habitations.

POSTWAR PLANNING

In 1918, Canada's federal government made its initial venture into the housing field. By an Order-in-Council passed under the War Measures Act, the sum of twenty-five million dollars was loaned to the provinces for the purpose of re-lending to municipalities. This sum financed the construction of approximately six thousand homes of moderate cost. The United States had entered the Great War and also found, by 1918, that the federal government had to arrange to provide housing for armaments and shipyard workers. Government loans financed the building of ten thousand houses. This wartime action in the field of housing established a precedent for federal aid, as well as providing an opportunity for American architects to experiment for the first time with community planning identified with the Garden City movement.

Welwyn Garden City in England was founded in 1919, the second Garden City. Located closer to London than Letchworth, it was to become known as the first satellite town because a large percentage of its residents commuted to work in London. The British government at this time was trying to establish a postwar housing policy. Raymond Unwin, the architect of Letchworth, wrote a pamphlet called *Nothing Gained by Overcrowding* which planned for two-storey houses ranging in size from 755 to 1,150 square feet. Britain sought to construct badly needed houses under the terms of a Housing and Town Planning Act of 1919, usually termed the Addison Act after Dr. Christopher Addison who, as Minister of Health, controlled the housing programme. Before the Addison Act, planning had been permissive in character but now every council that controlled an area with a population over 30,000 was required to prepare a town planning scheme. Local authorities were encouraged to build working-class houses with the aid of subsidies from the Treasury and, between 1919 and 1921, 176,000 new houses were built. But the promise of Prime Minister David Lloyd George to make "a land fit for heroes" began to encounter stiff opposition. For one thing, despite the desperate need for housing, the building unions would not relent on refusing to allow returning heroes to become bricklayers' apprentices. A government scheme to train 50,000 unemployed ex-servicemen failed because, after two years of negotiation, the building unions refused to accept the promise of a guaranteed work week. Heroes might fight the enemy but were not allowed to lay a brick to build their homes. Also, in 1921 there was a public outcry at the excessive cost of the houses produced by the Ministry of Health and in June of that year the Government was forced to halt the Addison housing plan.

Housing now became a political football as the Conservative and Labour parties each claimed to be able to produce more, better, and cheaper houses. In 1923, the Conservative Minister of Health, Neville Chamberlain, pursued a policy of limiting subsidies to a maximum of £6 annually per house for twenty years, and urged private builders to build houses for sale or rent. For his Act of 1923, Chamberlain claimed immense savings for the British taxpayer, claiming that "the average cost of the new houses was between £400 and £450 depending on size, compared with an average for Addison of about £1,000."[16] Chamberlain was hoping also that the "trickle down" theory would allow the discarded homes of the prosperous to filter down to the poorer workers.

The Labour party was returned to power for the first time in 1924. A radical Clydesider, John Wheatley, took charge of housing and passed the housing act that bears his name. The Wheatley Act increased Chamberlain's subsidy by fifty per cent, from £6 to £9, while doubling the time period from twenty to forty years. Now the Wheatley and the Chamberlain schemes were running side by side until 1929, and it is interesting to compare the results.

From 1924 to 1932, the Wheatley Act produced 520,928 houses, of which approximately one-third were built as municipally owned homes for rental to workers. One important requirement in Wheatley's legislation was that each home was to contain a bath in a bathroom, a facility which used to be a luxury for working-class tenants. In 1929, the Conservatives reduced Wheatley's subsidy to £7.50. Then, on regaining power in the same year, Labour bumped the figure back to £9 again. The Chamberlain houses were somewhat smaller than those built under the more generous terms of the Wheatley scheme. Yet the reputation of the Conservatives for being willing and able to house workers, which dated back to the Cross Acts of 1875, was enhanced by Chamberlain's scheme. In 1932, as the Great Depression reached Britain, Chamberlain closed down the Wheatley Act while claiming that interest rates were now so low that private builders could afford to build without subsidies.

In overall terms, considering the quality and number of houses built, the Wheatley Act was the best housing legislation of the inter-war period. Labour also introduced, during a short period in power in 1930, the idea that housing subsidies should be dependent upon eliminating slums. A political race between the Labour and Conservative parties in building new houses was only one of the two sides of the housing problem. Eliminating slums was the aspiration of housing reformers who felt that tenants were not responsible for the deficiencies of their physical environment, like lack of air, no toilet or bath facilities or a surplus of dirt and disease. From this premise the social reformer argued that improvement of the physical environment would lead to improved social characteristics on the part of the former slumdweller. Yet to those investors known as slum landlords, the existing property was a valuable source of rent and, unfortunately, it was unrealistic to expect these landlords to be enthusiastic about abolishing slums. Overcrowding was widespread: the Census of 1931 showed that 1,110,000 families in Britain were not living in their own homes.

Yet it should be noted that Scotland did launch a drive to eliminate slums, under the auspices of local authorities, and in two years, 1933-1934, 15,797 houses were constructed that were specifically designated as replacing condemned houses. This achievement compared very favourably with the whole period from 1919 to 1932 when a total of only 19,699 houses were built for the whole of Scotland.[17]

Generally speaking, Canada did not have the widespread areas of slums that were so noticeable in Britain. In the west, for example, the towns had wide streets and large lots that tended to prevent overcrowding. At the same time, there were pockets of slums in the major cities and conditions were frequently very bad in the older cities of the Maritimes. In 1920, a Royal Commission investigated the mining industry in the Maritimes and recorded:

> That in view of the fact that the housing, domestic surroundings and sanitary conditions of the miners are, with few exceptions, absolutely wretched . . . it is therefore recommended that the Companies that own the houses put and keep them in proper repair and that a sewerage system be devised and installed whereby surface closets will be eliminated.[18]

Six years later, in 1926, another commission reported that little had been done, and outlined that, "water is either delivered by the operators in carts or has to be carried a distance. Where water is piped into the houses there is an almost total absence of bathrooms or closets, due, we are informed, to a lack of sewers."[19] Similar conditions were found in mining areas of the United States, where token gestures were made towards solving the housing problem of the 1920's.

In the postwar period a housing crisis for low-income groups had developed in New York City. The New York State Commission of Housing and Regional Planning pressed for legislation to improve this situation, with the result that the Limited-Dividend Housing Act of 1926 was passed. This Act provided tax exemptions for construction of apartments. It produced little in the way of construction, but was important because New York's State Board of Planning was encouraging multi-family dwellings. New York set the pace in American housing affairs and began to use zoning as the chief practical link between planning and housing.

American city planners assumed the existence of a transitory city whose growth would be motivated by the hope of

159

commercial gain. The market price for downtown areas was based on a projected profitable use of the land as a region capable of holding a high density of people. Zoning became the chief tool of the municipal planner for maintaining land and property values. In the 1920's, it was not yet clearly recognized that zoning was limited in its ability to correct urban problems and might even magnify them, if vested interests manipulated zoning laws for racial or class segregation. Ordinances were adopted that specified the minimum size of a lot and of the house that might be erected; these restrictions were intended to exclude less affluent people from prestige residential neighbourhoods. Manufacturers sought to create false land values, as districts that possessed only a few factories were designated for industrial use. Special interest groups exerted political pressure. Property owners challenged the constitutionality of zoning regulations that rigidly prescribed the use to which land might be put and cited examples of more flexible British ordinances. Finally a Supreme Court decision of 1926 held that zoning was a legitimate exercise by local authorities of the police power to ensure the orderly development of their community.

Professional planning of the 1920's began to shift away from the concept that the role of the planner was that of a social and aesthetic reformer, seeking a City Beautiful, to the idea that he was a technician seeking the City Efficient. American pragmatism guided efforts to develop techniques to promote community planning. Developers of subdivisions taught local authorities the need to establish standards for streets because, as a temporary owner of the land, the developer was inclined to skimp on facilities and leave the community to clean up his mess.

THE GREAT DEPRESSION

By 1929 easy credit practices for house purchasers emphasized a low down payment and an obligation to meet the full purchase price by large first and second mortgages at seven per cent and higher. Over-extension of credit for prospective home buyers contributed to the Wall Street crash of November, 1929 and after the crash residential building virtually ceased. As the depression lengthened, there were demands that the government do something in the way of public works to ease the problem of unemployment and stimulate the economy. President Herbert Hoover recorded that "the literally thousands of heart-breaking instances of inability of working people to attain renewal of expiring mortgages on favourable terms, and the subsequent loss of their homes, has been one of the tragedies of this depression." In 1932, over 273,000 people lost their homes and, during the next year, a thousand homes a day were being foreclosed. Land values collapsed, as it became apparent that the zoning of down-town areas for future profitable use had exceeded the needs of the community. In a mood of fear and frustration, many men began to look to Washington and urge that the federal government enter the housing field.

The New Deal era of Franklin D. Roosevelt produced a new agency to promote "public housing"—that is, to provide low-rental housing. In 1933, the Public Works Administration (P.W.A.) was established and was authorized to start slum clearance and low-rental housing. In the next four years, P.W.A. constructed 22,000 housing units before its activities were declared unconstitutional. This public housing endeavour was on much too small a scale to alleviate conditions. In the operation of the programme, federal funds were passed to the states who backed local efforts at slum clearance through the programme, and the term "urban renewal" entered into the planners' vocabulary. Temporarily, the opponents of "socialism" were too stunned by the magnitude of the depression to offer much resistance, as real estate and loan associations were in a desperate plight, while the building materials lobby actively encouraged the idea of future sales, in effect although not in ideology supporting public housing. In 1934 a Federal Housing Administration (F.H.A.) was established to improve housing standards, provide employment and stimulate the economy. The F.H.A. guaranteed mortgage loans to financial institutions, such as banks or insurance companies, and it is hardly surprising that it is today the major surviving agency of the New Deal. One critic has described the operations of the Federal Housing Administration as a system "which allows the government to assume the risks that in a free society are supposed to be assumed by the entrepreneur."[20]

There was a variation to this approach in Canada whose Prime Minister R.B. Bennett was a public radical who, in private life, was a millionaire capitalist. Canada passed a Dominion Housing Act in 1935 to stimulate loans to private builders, with the Federal Government providing one-quarter of the total loan of 80% of the value of the building, and this scheme financed 5000 units. No attempt was made in Canada at this time to produce public housing. By the terms of the National Housing Act of 1938, which replaced the 1935 measure, there was a provision for direct federal loans to aid in the construction of low-rental housing, but the municipality had to accept any operating losses. As the depression bore heavily on municipal finances, it is not surprising that this federal legislation did not serve to initiate any public housing.

After the American presidential election of 1936, Franklin D. Roosevelt spoke in his inaugural address of the "third of a nation" that lived in poor housing. Congress responded by passing the Wagner-Steagall Low Rent Housing Bill which provided the first permanent subsidy programme for housing in the United States. There was no doctrinaire reason for launching this new activity; rather, the construction industry was paralyzed by the depression and, therefore, Congress decided that low-rental housing might help to revive it. In this Housing Act of 1937, the opening section stated:

> It is the policy of the United States to promote the general welfare of the nation . . . to remedy the unsafe and unsanitary housing conditions and the acute shortage of decent, safe and sanitary dwellings for families of low income.

The poor were called "low income" families; while this label may have salved the conscience of social and political reformers, it did little to solve the problems of the poverty-stricken. But the commendable objective of the housing act was quickly recognized by the states, as all but five of them enacted legislation to permit public housing.

162

To supervise the program at a federal level, the United States Housing Authority (U.S.H.A.) was created. Emphasis was put on slum clearance by providing up to ninety per cent of the cost of clearing slums, but there was no equally necessary large-scale building program, although the major projects of the former P.W.A. program were completed. Yet the 1937 Housing Act stipulated that for every substandard dwelling that was eliminated, there should be a low-rental unit built. This "equivalent elimination" requirement tended to slow down the interest of municipalities in launching slum clearance schemes and served to firmly link federal public housing with slum clearance in the minds of the public. Yet the efforts to build low-cost rental housing had enthusiastic supporters among black Americans. As Gunnar Myrdal observed in his monumental study of Negro life, *An American Dilemma*, the U.S.H.A. gave Negroes a better deal than did any other major federal, public welfare agency. Negroes represented one-third of the total number of approximately 200,000 people who had benefited from public housing by 1941. When compared to the ten million homes that the U.S.A. built between 1921 and 1939, it is obvious that the significance of the federal program was in creating a social precedent rather than in the scale of construction.

In addition to efforts towards public housing, there was a less publicized effort to create a new environment for urban dwellers. Once again, Ebenezer Howard's Garden City inspired planners in the Resettlement Administration who, in 1936, tried to adapt the garden city principles to America. An imaginative plan was proposed which envisaged twenty-five garden towns. Franklin D. Roosevelt approved eight: Congress reduced it to five and three were actually built— Greenbelt in Maryland; Greenhills in Ohio; and Greendale, Wisconsin. Fierce opposition was encountered in the greenbelt developments from local real estate agencies who began to agitate that the houses, built at federal expense, should be sold on the open market. The result of this violent opposition has been summarized by an historian: "They [the houses] were fought by real estate interests . . . denounced as company towns . . . after the Second World War, they were sold at great loss by the government. Only 2,267 families were actually aided."[21]

The combination of public housing and greenbelt town construction aroused fierce opposition from pressure groups. The National Association of Real Estate Boards and building and loan companies began organized attempts to block further federal appropriations for public housing. In addition, in the late 1930's municipal planning boards began to include among their members laymen who were supposed to balance the opinion of professional planners, before proposals went to the municipal council. Realtors and businessmen were not slow to see this development as a way to slow down local planning policies. Yet at a national level, the idea of improving conditions in the slums persisted. A federal report of 1937 entitled *Our Cities—Their Role in the National Economy* introduced the term "urban redevelopment."

While the United States was moving into public housing in the 1930's, Britain was moving away from low-cost rental houses. With the Conservative party in power in the midst of a depression, the provision of public housing virtually ceased in Britain. The traditional bias of the Conservatives towards free enterprise was exhibited in their encouragement of private builders. Class bias was reflected in the language of the Town and Country Planning Act of 1932 where the word "town" meant suburbia, where the "better classes" lived. This Act merely consolidated earlier planning legislation. Guidelines for private builders were ignored at a time when the economic depression made governmental suggestions superfluous. There was very little coherent urban planning. It is true that after 1934, the building industry did begin to produce a substantial amount of housing, but it was located in southern England and not intended for lowly paid workers. Only the more affluent citizens could afford a four-roomed house at a price of £350 with a weekly payment of between 12s. 6d. and 14 shillings.

Between November 1918 and September 1939 approximately four million houses were built in England and Wales, of which about one-third were constructed with State assistance. Housing subsidies ceased in 1932 when the Wheatley Act passed by a Labour government was terminated, although the Census of 1931 had shown 1,110,000 families not occupying their own homes. Between the two World Wars, the Government spent in England and Wales £208,424,183 on housing, of which approximately two-thirds was spent under the two Addison Acts immediately after 1918.[22]

An interesting comparison exists between the methods employed for building houses in different parts of Great Britain between 1919 and 1939. Whereas private enterprise built approximately seventy per cent of all new houses in England and Wales, the reverse was true in Scotland, where more reliance was placed on municipalities constructing houses which could be rented to workers. Scotland was conscious of the inferior quality of its housing relative to its southern neighbour and placed little faith in the ability of private builders to rectify the situation, at prices which the bulk of the population could afford. Yet in the total British picture there was very little slum clearance in the 1930's, as municipal governments demolished or closed 272,836 slum dwellings, a figure which just balanced the 273,000 new houses built in that decade. In short, the Britain that went to war in 1939 had over two million citizens living in over-crowded slums. Adolf Hitler's Luftwaffe would prove to be a more effective slum clearance agent than any British endeavour.

THE RESULTS OF WARTIME PLANNING

During the Second World War, 200,000 homes in Britain were destroyed by enemy action and over three million damaged. Yet even as bombs devastated London in 1940, a new wave of planners was working to build a better Britain. The Barlow Report released in 1940 concerned the Geographical Distribution of Industrial Population, and sought to rebuild the blitzed areas along the lines recommended by Ebenezer Howard. Wartime conditions produced a willingness to think in national terms. The Town and Country Planning Association pressed for control of urban and rural development. By 1943 a separate government department was established under the name of Town and Country Planning. An

Interim Development Act exerted the authority of the planning department over the whole country. Winston Churchill's wartime government accepted the principle of dispersing people away from the congested cities into "overspill" communities surrounded by green belts. A leading planner named Patrick Abercrombie was commissioned to prepare the Greater London regional plan, which was subsequently designated as the Abercrombie Plan. This plan envisioned planning for ten million people, in a radius of thirty miles from the centre of London, with close co-operation with local authorities to ensure efficiency. By 1944, local authorities were empowered to acquire land in war-devastated areas with grants supplied by Westminster. Planning had become a key word. The geographical siting of new industries had become government policy by 1945, with the intention of aiding those areas that had suffered in the prewar depression. It was estimated in 1945 that approximately 750,000 new houses were needed, plus another 500,000 to replace slums.

The wartime United States was a prosperous country. By 1940 public housing authorities were concerned with providing houses for war workers. The private building industry had revived, but capitalists were taking no chances that the "socialist" Franklin D. Roosevelt might re-direct the public housing program into postwar competition with private industry. So in 1943, Congress insisted that temporary wartime housing should be disposed of within two years after the President had declared the "emergency" at an end. The shortage of accommodation produced rent control in all defense areas and, by the end of the war, over sixteen million units were controlled.

During World War II, Canada built more than 30,000 rental homes for servicemen which were administered by Wartime Housing Ltd. In 1944, Canada moved towards providing better housing conditions for civilians under the National Housing Act. This Act supplied federal loans to banks and builders to produce low-cost houses, or a fifty per cent federal grant to municipalities for the purpose of slum clearance. The Act furthermore made it a specific responsibility of the Minister of Finance to carry out investigations into housing conditions and possible remedies. Housing is an important item in stimulating Canada's economy, and the federal government aspired to keep residential construction going in the winter, as this activity employs a considerable labour force. The Central Mortgage and Housing Corporation (C.M.H.C.) was formed in 1945 as the federal agency responsible for administering housing activities. In 1947, Toronto became the first Canadian municipality to embark upon clearing a slum area and built the low-rental housing development of Regent Park.

Britain in the postwar period was smitten with a planning fever. The "housing problem" which had under normal peacetime conditions been the concern of the poor, had become a problem for all classes by 1945. A New Towns Committee was established that planned to produce twenty new towns, following the general Garden City concept, of a population between 30,000 and 50,000. Another influence was the American idea of a self-contained neighbourhood unit that included industrial parks. This activity produced the New Towns Act of 1946, followed in 1947 by a wider measure entitled The Town and Country Planning Act of 1946. By the latter measure, national control was to be exerted over land use and local authorities were to submit a plan that showed the redevelopment intended for the next twenty years. Each plan had to have the approval of the new Ministry of Town and Country Planning. Town planning became a national obsession as municipalities scrambled to hire planners. Unfortunately, the official stipulation that the outline had to plan for only twenty years meant that comprehensive planning was ignored, as municipalities sought to implement plans in the cheapest possible way. Once again the Garden City idea fell by the wayside. At the same time, it is true that experience had shown that planning must be flexible and planning must be conceived as a continuous process, for the future is not predictable, and specific long-range plans incur the hostility of property owners. The 1947 Act also adopted Henry George's idea of taxing the increase in land value in order to finance outlays on housing. This method of taxing land surrounding redeveloped areas incurred the hostility of the property owners being taxed. Furthermore, restrictions were placed on private land use that almost nationalized the right to develop previously undeveloped land.

From this planning activity came the commendable provision for green areas under the National Parks and Access to the Country Act of 1949. A national commission established ten national parks covering 5,246 square miles in England and Wales. Park planning authorities were encouraged to pay attention to tree planting and "removal of eyesores such as advertisements." While this conservation activity was most significant, the same praise cannot be bestowed upon cleaning up the urban areas.

Postwar shortages of materials led to a rationing system for concrete and steel, with prefabricated components being designed to produce mass housing. Yet the actual production of housing was far short of the Labour government's promise of 300,000 units annually. Labour continued its policy of the 1920's of encouraging municipalities to act as their own builders and 85% of the housing constructed between 1945 and 1950 was in this category. The results were disappointing as the annual rate was only half the production of the prewar years, which had averaged over 300,000 houses per year.

Allied to the deficiency in providing new homes was the difficulty created by continuing wartime rent controls, which magnified the problem of improving the slums, as the owners had little incentive to provide adequate maintenance. To compound the problem still further, housing took a back seat as the government tried to revive Britain's export trade by building power stations and factories. Factory owners insisted that their plants should be built within the cities on land cleared for redevelopment. Therefore the planned decentralization of industry was not really effective. Even the plans began to look obsolete as urban land values rose sharply, the population increased rapidly, and wider use was made of the automobile.

By the 1950's, there had been so much planning on paper and such limited results with residential housing that a general disillusionment set in with town planning. The electorate turned in 1951 to the Conservative party, who encouraged private builders and caused house construction to soar by competing with building by municipalities. Scotland continued to lag in terms of the inability of private enterprise to build houses for sale at reasonable prices and, therefore, Scots had to rely on rented accommodation, rather than following the trend discernible in England of purchasing new houses.

CANADIAN AND AMERICAN HOUSING AFTER 1945

Canada believed in relying on private builders. In 1945, an amendment to the Housing Act permitted several life insurance companies to form Housing Enterprises of Canada Limited which was supposed to develop rental housing. Not until 1949 was an amendment passed introducing the principle of subsidy for housing for sale or rental, which made Canada the last major industrial country to adopt public housing on a national scale. After 1949 the federal government supplied up to 75 per cent of the capital cost of a project, while the provinces supplied the balance. The chartered banks entered the housing field in 1954, when the Housing Act established the Central Mortgage and Housing Corporation as an insurance body to guarantee approved lenders against loss in the event of default. This financial stimulus to lending institutions caused a reduction in the down payment for a new house by about one-quarter, and encouraged wide-scale building.

South of the border, the nature of the building industry in the United States had changed from prewar days, when home building was on a small scale. After 1945, building became "big business," with 10 per cent of the builders constructing 60 per cent of the houses. Yet this private building did not affect the slum dweller. President Harry Truman had made slum clearance a major item of the Fair Deal of 1949 which presumably would give Americans what they had missed under the earlier "square" and "new" deals. The word "fair," as related to housing, only became possible after a Supreme Court decision of 1948 prohibited racial discrimination in covenants concerning housing. In his State of the Union address to Congress in 1949 Truman told the nation that "five million families are still living in slums and firetraps" and "three million families share their homes with others." It should be kept in mind, when reading of the subsequent course of events, that the tripartite system of government in North America makes it necessary to balance municipal projects against the financial power of the federal and state (or provincial) governments.

Congress responded to the challenge by passing the 1949 Housing Act which had the objective of "a decent home and suitable environment for every American family." It was this Act that introduced the concept entitled "urban redevelopment" whereby the federal government supplied funds to local authorities for the purpose of clearing away slums. To placate real estate interests, mortgage companies and private builders, who were bitterly opposed to public housing, Title I of the new Act allowed private interests to handle the building program. A procedure evolved whereby the legal concept of eminent domain permitted the local authority to implement plans by appropriating private property for public use, without the consent of the owner, although compensation had to be given. Then the federal government absorbed the financial loss involved in "writing down" the difference between the cost of the slums and the lower price at which the cleared land was sold to a private developer.

As in Britain, the business community cared little for the social planning of the government. Cleared areas in the centre of the city frequently were desirable locations for erecting blocks of offices. Ironically, in view of the anti-discrimination or open housing decision of the Supreme Court, some cities used slum clearance to remove non-white residents. For this reason, the rather cynical expression "Urban renewal means Negro removal" developed. Moreover, while the Housing Act of 1949 pleased private enterprise, it frequently made the plight of the displaced slumdweller even worse than before as he was forced to move into an already overcrowded adjoining area. Developers who erected luxury apartments as a sound investment frequently increased racial tension as they did not provide for the displaced Negro.

Also, as discussed earlier with regard to Britain, the maintenance of rent control made it difficult to clean up the slums. Rent control by the federal government was not terminated until July 30, 1951. The slow progress being made towards slum clearance was highlighted by the *Report of the*

Presidential Advisory Committee on Government Housing and Programs of 1953 which commented, "If we continue only at the present rate of clearance and rely on demolition alone to eliminate slums, it will take us something over two hundred years to do the job." Furthermore, as the housing shortage continued, the ownership of slum dwellings became very profitable. As the Advisory Committee reported to President Eisenhower, "the ugly business of slum racketeering" caused landlords to exert local pressure to prevent clearance programs. And as Negroes migrated into the northern cities, the middle-class whites fled to the suburbs.

In Chicago the drop in real estate values in areas formerly occupied by white residents caused political agitation by concerned property owners and real estate interests. In 1953, the Illinois Legislature was pressured into trying to legislate to prevent a fall in the value of property and, in the following year, political pressure was being exerted at Washington. From this situation was born the 1954 Federal Urban Renewal Program which emphasized the "renewing" of areas that were still liveable.

URBAN RENEWAL AND PUBLIC HOUSING

Urban renewal switched the emphasis from the use of the bulldozer to maintenance of what already existed by rehabilitation of homes. In one sense, it showed a realization that maintaining a constant market by planned obsolescence for such items as appliances and cars, had failed in the field of housing. The federal government paid up to two-thirds of the costs involved in bringing the facilities of an area up to decent standards, with better schools or off-street parking.

Canada copied American principles in the Canadian Housing Act of 1954, which stressed urban renewal and guaranteed loans. An amendment to the National Housing Act of 1956 permitted Central Mortgage and Housing to assist in financing urban renewal studies by a municipality, with the federal government paying 50 per cent of the cost of preparing a plan. It is important, however, to recognize that the initiative on planning has to come from the city government and, during the 1950's, a large number of civic plans were developed. Possibly it was easier to plan in Canada as the situation was not as potentially explosive as it was in the United States with its underlying racial tensions.

A number of American cities and states had to threaten real estate companies with revoking their licences if the practice of block busting did not cease. Block busting entailed the deliberate introduction of a coloured family into an all-white residential block, so that the whites would be encouraged to accept low prices for their homes, which were then sold to Negroes as prestige houses at high prices. Cities such as New York, Detroit, San Francisco and Baltimore suffered from this practice. Well-meaning whites also contributed to the racial problems involved in housing: white liberals who thought in terms of eliminating the ghetto sometimes incurred the hostility of Negro politicians. Slum clearance could be viewed by Negroes as a tactic intended to dilute the political power of non-whites. Where individuals of the same race are segregated, they tend to fuse together as a base of political power, in the same way that class interests bind white suburbanites. The American myth of the self-made man also emphasized the gap between the slum-dweller and the suburbanite, who usually felt that any individual worth his salt could and should raise his family out of the slums.

Some huge public housing projects were built, such as Fort Greene, Brooklyn which housed 3,400 families. But observers pointed out that while physically decent, the barrack-like blocks were socially similar to the slums they had replaced. American liberals who had been preaching since the 1930's that social regeneration follows improvement of the physical environment were muting their voices by the 1950's. Local renewal agencies were supposed to relocate the dispossessed tenants in "standard" housing within their means, but such housing was scarce in the cities. Municipal authorities were keen to get projects going and were impatient about handling the dispossessed tenant, who frequently moved to other slums. According to a study done in Philadelphia in 1958, over seventy per cent of displaced slum dwellers were relocated in remaining slums. Philadelphia is frequently cited as the leading example of a city that revitalized its downtown areas, with a planned commercial area known as Penn Center, and the preservation of historic town houses. But a town house that has been restored is not for the average Negro family, when priced around $50,000, and the displaced Negroes had the alternative of moving into sterile high-rise apartments, or relocating in other slums. Negroes facing racial and economic problems were frequently forced to double up in other ghettos and this led to bitter complaints about "urban renewal"; this phrase now covered all rebuilding efforts in the city.

The rise of luxury housing on former slumland, paid for by federal subsidies, was an anomalous trend in the country that prides itself upon being the land of opportunity for all its citizens. In effect, the federal subsidies meant that the poor were financing their own removal for the benefit of the wealthy. Public housing had been expected in 1949 to supply ten per cent of the nation's accommodation, but by 1959, it provided a mere one per cent, with 585,212 federal low-rental units. The real estate theory about housing eventually "trickling down" to lower income groups was being reversed by 1960.

Private builders built twelve million new houses between 1950 and 1960 without government aid. The F.H.A. financed over thirty per cent of these new housing starts, which displayed its other main role besides public housing. Life insurance companies and savings and commercial banks have been the principal holders of loans insured by the F.H.A. Sound commercial practices meant that most of the money was loaned to middle-class whites, for the American concept of class or social status is dependent to a large extent on one's address. Middle-class home owners seek to use zoning restrictions to keep out cheaper or less prestigious housing and particularly public housing because, as one writer has stated:

Life in the usual public housing just is not the way most families want to live . . . .Public housing projects tend to be very large and highly standardized in their design . . . .Each project proclaims visually that it serves the "lowest income group."[23]

Another reason for the American attitude towards these areas was provided by the U.S. Commissioner of Public Housing, testifying before Congress in 1960, who expressed the opinion that the stipulation that projects be racially integrated had made them unpopular. This view was a tragic commentary on the hope for integrating the 1,800,000 non-whites who, during the 1950's, had moved into the twelve largest cities of the United States. Those white Americans who could afford houses in the private market shunned public housing. The residential building industry and the real estate lobby stubbornly resisted federal subsidies to public housing projects. While construction unions did not oppose the idea of public housing, they did seek to keep Negroes from acquiring skills in the building trades.

MAKING CITIES FIT PLACES TO LIVE

In 1965 President Lyndon B. Johnson launched an appeal to make American cities liveable and successfully pressed for the establishment of a Cabinet-level Department of Housing and Urban Development. President Johnson noted then that over seventy per cent of America's population lived in urban areas, and that "each year in the coming generation, we will add the equivalent of 15 cities of 200,000 each." The following statement of President Johnson must have pleased the modern disciples of Ebenezer Howard:

> Let us be clear about the core of this problem. The problem is people and the quality of the lives they lead. We want to build not just housing units, but neighbourhoods; not just to construct schools, but to educate children; not just to raise income, but to create beauty and end the poisoning of our environment.[24]

The United States had a precedent for large-scale governmental assistance in the housing field in their successful program of aiding veterans which had provided over five million homes. Similarly, Canada had assisted veterans to acquire their own homes.

The Canadian federal government sought to improve the

housing situation by guaranteeing N.H.A. mortgages at a maximum of 6% interest from 1957 to 1959. Soon afterwards, in 1960, N.H.A. mortgages rose to 6¾% as the Conservative Government felt that this higher rate would encourage private lenders to loan money, and thus lighten the load upon the Central Mortgage and Housing Corporation. During 1964 the National Housing Act of 1954 was considerably amended to permit wider participation of the C.M.H.C. The Federal Corporation agreed to pay half the cost of implementing an urban renewal scheme prepared by a municipality. Provision was also made for a program of land acquisition in advance of a public housing project, with the C.M.H.C. loaning 90% of the cost.

The red tape involved in building public housing may have impeded interest in initiating projects; Canada has very complex arrangements for translating the idea for a project into bricks and mortar. Initially, a municipality has a project approved by the Provincial and Federal governments. Much time is taken up with accomplishing this progression through city committees and sub-committees to Provincial departments to the regional office of the C.M.H.C., which passes it to the C.M.H.C. national office. Authorization having been granted for a detailed study, the paperwork now moves back down the chain of command. With the plan accepted, a draft agreement is worked out between the various levels of government, and the municipality takes the first step of securing an option on the land, if it has not already purchased the necessary property. The municipal government is left to face any criticism by ratepayers, while the senior levels of government remain aloof, despite the fact that a provincial organization such as the Ontario Housing Corporation and the federal C.M.H.C. determine the criteria for the geographic location of developments.

Usually revisions to the plan become necessary at this point. The project plan now is circulated among about twenty government departments. Such authorities include the Conservation Authorities, Regional Development Associations, a provincial Water Resources Commission, Air Pollution Authority, Assessment Authority and the School authority. It has been suggested that this procedure is intended to justify the existence of some officials: work may be created for officials as well as for bricklayers. Needless to say, as the plan passes from "in" to "out" trays and then on to the next desk, costs are apt to rise from the original projections. It has been estimated that it takes from three to five years from the time that a housing project is approved by a municipal council until the first family moves in. On the other hand, as public funds are being used, there is probably little choice in the mechanics of handling the paperwork: large-scale housing projects are too open to criticism that they are not co-ordinated with local services. Yet even after allowance has been made for governmental bodies to be cautious in the use of public funds, there is still a vast improvement needed in imaginative planning. The *Report of the Federal Task Force on Housing and Urban Redevelopment* strongly criticized the lack of foresight in these terms:

> Lest there be a misunderstanding, the Task Force did find planning at work in urban Canada. But it frankly was disappointed and discouraged by it. So much of it was concerned with minutiae while the need for a grand urban design goes begging . . . .The urban scene seemed to abound with bureaucrats–but to be sadly lacking in dreamers.[25]

This Task Force that toured Canada's urban areas displayed a rather delightful awareness of the dangers of bureaucracy, for example when it proposed changing the name of C.M.H.C. to Canada Housing Corporation. The reason provided was that:

> In the view of the Task Force, Central Mortgage and Housing Corporation is a somewhat cumbersome mouthful which . . . leaves the Federal Government open to the play-on-word allegation that "it always puts mortgages before houses."[26]

Toronto is now the fastest-growing city in Canada and has played the Canadian equivalent of New York's role in pioneering in national solutions for housing problems. Consideration of Toronto's problems will highlight several aspects of the housing problem in built-up areas. Metropolitan Toronto increased in population from 900,000 persons to 1,650,000 in the twenty-year period that ended in 1962. During that time, the magnificent heritage of ravines and green areas steadily disappeared as builders sought to provide for this influx of people. At the same time, the outward flight of the middle class into suburbia meant that the downtown areas were frequently allowed to deteriorate. Eventually the process of building houses in green areas had to be reversed: city planners have been forced to encourage the demolition of houses in the congested areas, to permit small half-acre parks. In 1960 a policy was adopted of building parks within a quarter of a mile of each resident but, of sixty-two parkettes projected, only twenty-one have been completed in the past ten years.

Toronto was the first city in Canada to build a low-cost rental development, the Regent Park Apartments which were constructed in 1946 on former slum land. Further concern over housing was shown by the formation of the Metropolitan Toronto Housing Company Ltd., which supplies rental accommodation to senior citizens over sixty years of age. Since this company was established to take advantage of the provisions of the 1954 National Housing Act, over 1,600 units have been constructed. Yet the number of units constructed, for the aged and for the poor, is far from adequate. In effect, Canada has not undertaken major urban renewal or public housing projects, mainly because such schemes have depended on municipal initiative, in the absence of widespread participation by the federal government.

At the present time, some twenty Canadian cities are engaged in urban renewal studies with funds granted by the federal government. The term "urban renewal" was not officially copied from the United States until it was introduced into the National Housing Act in 1964, and municipalities were encouraged to tackle blighted or substandard areas. In 1960 the Metropolitan Toronto Planning Board had unveiled a comprehensive plan covering the years from 1960 to 1980 which called for the construction of 25,000 to 30,000 new subsidized rental units in that time. As subsequent events revealed, it is not the amount of public housing in Canada that is important as this is barely 1% of the total residential construction, but rather the passions that are aroused by the idea. Public housing in Canada meets some of the objections already described for the pilot projects built in the U.S.A., for example, the argument that socialism gives something for nothing to those who don't deserve it, and that high welfare costs can be attributed to the subsidies needed to support low-rental housing. But as the presence of the New Democratic Party testifies, Canadians may be less worried about the effects of socialism than many Americans. Also, Canadian cities generally lack the racial strife so closely related to American urban problems.

HELPING RACIAL MINORITIES

It appears that out of the 673,000 American families who have been helped by public housing, approximately half have been non-white. Real estate lobbies have fought this competitive form of providing shelter to the point where the total amount of public housing construction permitted by Congress, in any one year, is only 35,000 units for the entire U.S.A. The cry of "creeping socialism" has been advanced by real estate interests, although the public housing construction is handled by private enterprise and there is no lingering government control. Certainly the "creeping" aspect of housing being supplied by government action is well illustrated by the fact that it has taken half a century for such housing to advance from zero per cent to one per cent of total residential construction. President John Kennedy sought to forbid racial discrimination in 1962 by an executive order concerning Equal Opportunity in Housing under the control of the federal government. Unfortunately this Presidential order did not cover the bulk of the nation's housing and real estate organizations rallied to resist fair housing laws enacted by State legislatures. In California, the real estate lobby was responsible for the approach to housing seen in Proposition 14, which not only prevents enforcement of the state housing law, but also requires a statewide referendum before any additional fair housing legislation can be enacted. The Texas Real Estate Association conducted a similar campaign on

178

constitutional grounds in 1965 to prevent a fair housing law being passed.

Why? One reason could be that racial minorities have generally lived in the slums and provided a substantial income for owners of these substandard properties. After the 1967 urban riots, the Presidential Advisory Commission on Civil Disorders—referred to as the Kerner Report after its chairman, Illinois Governor Otto Kerner—stated, "White racism is essentially responsible for the explosive mixture that has been gathering in our cities since World War II." The Commission furthermore stated that "This is our basic conclusion: Our nation is moving towards two societies, one black, one white—separate and unequal." This trend was discernible during the period from 1960 to 1966 as the Negro population in American central cities rose by 2.4 million, a total which included about one million migrants. The Kerner Commission pointed out the significance of this development:

> By 1985, the Negro population in central cities is expected to increase by 72 per cent to approximately 20.8 million. Coupled with the continued exodus of white families to the suburbs, this growth will produce majority Negro populations in many of the nation's largest cities.[27]

It would seem that only action by the Federal Government can ward off confrontation. Yet there are real problems involved in directing mandatory integration, even if some of the liberal elements of both colours are willing to strive for national harmony. For example, President John F. Kennedy's executive order of 1962 covered only twenty per cent of new housing starts.[28] The method of financing giant developments usually includes conventional financing by private companies, which is not covered by the federal executive order. A suggestion has been made that new construction facilitated by the Federal Housing Administration and Veterans Administration should be identified by a sign proclaiming its availability to all ethnic groups. Yet, on the other hand, such signs "might discourage white purchasers or

renters who would go on to competing developments." [29]
One possible answer lies along the lines indicated by
Ebenezer Howard, that congested cities must be changed by
planned development of satellite cities, although many the-
orists like Jane Jacobs oppose this on the grounds that re-
locating people destroys their social milieu.

PLANNING FOR THE FUTURE

While Americans may seem understandably obsessed with the
problems of the present, there have been voices advocating
urban planning for the future. The crux of planning is land
usage and as early as 1912 Charles Beard, the economic historian, advocated a strengthening of municipal authority over
land ownership as the only way to ensure a habitable city for
men. An indication of what could be achieved is provided by
a comparison to Britain's policy between 1945 and 1965,
when well over two million apartments or houses were provided by local authorities, after completion of slum clearance
schemes. It is noteworthy that rather than preventing population congestion in cities, the tendency on both sides of the
Atlantic has been to build blocks of apartments on the
premise that this form of construction is the only economically feasible way of using expensive urban sites. Sociologists
have warned of the effects on children raised in the sterile
atmosphere of such surroundings; Ebenezer Howard must
occasionally stir in his grave at man's unwillingness to implement his concepts of the Garden City.

Planning has undoubtedly obtained professional status as
in the 1950's, Durham University in England initiated the
first degree program in Town and Country Planning; this was
followed soon afterwards by the Massachusetts Institute of
Technology giving formal recognition to Town and Country
Planning in the U.S.A. The terminology of planning, however, does not have the same meaning on both sides of the
Atlantic. For example, the term "decentralization" as
presently used in Britain means removal of people and work
places to less congested areas, while in North America this
term often means the outward rush of individuals to the
suburbs, a very different thing.

The Garden City approach must imply total planning, but this conflicts with the North American preference for private ownership rather than public-owned goods. People would rather have a second car to drive on the streets than better law enforcement to keep those streets safe; they would rather have a tiny lawn of their own than a large park. So the city council can ignore planning recommendations and deal with various services required by the taxpayer on an individual basis, such as those concerning transportation, education and utilities. While the planners may think in terms of making a rational use of land, this is not the motivation of other interested parties. Downtown merchants support urban renewal plans as a way to draw purchasing power back into the city, while investors and property owners view it as a means to bolster property values. A few isolated local situations have, however, occurred in cities like New York and Toronto where streets have been closed to permit open air cafes or street vendors, with an accent on people rather than on expanding a concrete jungle. But such development relieves rather than solves urban housing problems. Only decisive governmental action that directs the orderly development of satellite towns can overcome the political pressure from interests that do not want dispersal of people by relieving congested conditions.

The deterioration of the core of American cities combined with the flight of the wealthier citizens to the suburbs has created a serious problem. As most of the suburbanites are white, while the expanding population in the core of the city is black, a racial powder keg has been created. Furthermore, the long-established American pattern of autonomy in local affairs makes it difficult to plan effectively for all citizens in an urban region. Schemes for urban renewal are more likely to be settled along racial lines than on the basis of planning merit. This is quite consistent with the historical background for, as Lord Bryce stated after an exhaustive study of government in his classic *The American Commonwealth* (1888), city government has been "the one most conspicuous failure of the United States."

PLANNING IN CONTEMPORARY CANADA

A large Canadian city, such as Toronto, has a different background from most American cities. Some wealthy or middle-class Canadians prefer to live downtown and the creation of luxury apartments and townhouses has provided premium priced accommodation that supplements prestige residential areas, such as Rosedale in Toronto or the Mountain in Montreal. The legacy of the British mould of local government has created a tradition in which most citizens are aware of their rights. For example, the first mayor of the newly incorporated city of Toronto, William Lyon Mackenzie, quickly discovered that local citizens threaten political rebellion if they feel their tax dollars are not being spent wisely. Today, there are articulate citizens in the slums who can make their views known to the local politicians or the newspapers. The main inflow of new residents to the city, such as Toronto's Italian immigrants, has principally been of white people and has therefore not produced racial overtones that are common in northern American cities. Moreover, the immigrant migration to Toronto has reinvigorated the centre of the city by encouraging the establishment of good restaurants with a variety of different kinds of food that encourage trips downtown from the suburbs. The Italian community of Toronto now numbers in excess of 300,000, a size comparable to the city of Venice. Residential streets that were predominantly Anglo-Saxon now contain New Canadians who are apt to be more gregarious and have fewer inhibitions about painting their houses in purple or fire-engine red. In short, there is life and activity in the centre of Toronto's residential area. A recent wave of West Indian immigrants have added another colourful dimension by their well-attended annual Caribana festival, which indicates that even Torontonians now enjoy a calypso. These variegated population characteristics are mainly due to the increased mobility of people, who can migrate in comfort to their destination because of improved transportation facilities.

So-called dormitory towns have developed in Canada, the U.S. and Britain due principally to improvements in the speed of transportation. Men who work in New York City live in New Jersey; Londoners by day are residents of the seaside town of Brighton by night; many Torontonians now either ride the rapid transit system or drive to their homes in Toronto's hinterland. But these dormitory towns are not integrated garden cities, for industry or commercial activity has not dispersed into the new areas. There has been one attempt at introducing the satellite city concept into Canada but it has received a rather mixed reception.

Bramalea, to the northwest of Toronto, was planned to provide a satellite city which would be a self-sustaining community, complete with industrial core. Construction began in the 1950's on farmland. The development has grown to accommodate 20,000 persons and it is anticipated that within five years, there will be 50,000 residents. The private company that developed this area, Bramalea Consolidated Developments, was principally financed by the Eagle Star Insurance company and Close Brothers, a merchant-banking firm, both of England. Any idea of keeping land speculation down rapidly disappeared as local political manoeuvring took place. In 1957, a lot for a semi-detached house was worth $137.50: this figure climbed to $2,637.50 by the time essential services were provided. The government of Ontario cast a friendly eye on the development of Bramalea and, in 1967, decided to pay an average of over $6,750 for each of 1,666 lots. Ontario's plan called Home Ownership Made Easy (H.O.M.E.) envisaged the province keeping down land costs by purchasing a large quantity of land, which would be leased to builders or home owners. Ontario's second venture into Bramalea saw the Ontario Housing Corporation buying 4,602 Bramalea lots for townhouses at a cost of $4,000 per lot. A reporter for *Maclean's* summarized the situation as follows:

> The Ontario taxpayer is shelling out a huge speculative profit for housing lots in a development run by a private entrepreneur . . . .In the first H.O.M.E. deal, the O.H.C. bought single lots for $8,000 and sold them for $9,200 or leased them for $43.50 a month (which means that over a standard 35 year mortgage, the home owner will pay $18,270 to rent a piece of land he still won't own.) There should be a cheaper way to make housing cheap and

there is. In Saskatoon, the municipality has for years been buying large tracts of land, which it sells at cost. A serviced single-dwelling lot in Saskatoon costs about $3,500 compared to $9,200 in Bramalea . . . .The lesson of Bramalea, surely, is that if the developer is left to his own devices, driven only by the hunger for gain, he will produce an expensive, profitable mess.[30]

Toronto has not provided for satellite towns in its Metropolitan plan of 1966 that included the immediate hinterland of the city. There has been, however, a growing emphasis on the need to plan on a regional basis in Ontario. After five years of study, a *Metro Toronto and Region Transportation Study* was unveiled in 1968 and the conclusions published in a booklet called *Choices for a Growing Region*. Several plans were suggested to guide the orderly development of a 3,200 square mile region, from Oshawa to Hamilton and north to Barrie. Within this region the anticipated six million residents will be oriented towards Toronto by high-speed rail and road connections. A parkway belt will be provided five miles back from the lakefront to provide a major recreation area, stretching along the Niagara escarpment, with twenty-three "country residences" to accommodate 15,000 to 25,000 residents each. All of this planning is admirable but fails on a key issue that has continually frustrated town planners. These studies or plans are recommendations only, and implementation is not mandatory.

Despite such problems, in the eyes of observant Americans, particularly those living in border areas, urban Canada looks inviting. A revealing commentary is provided in a book entitled *Modern American Cities*:

> A traveller who merely crosses the border into Canada will soon see that these generalizations about the United States do not hold universally. In September, 1968 I visited friends in Toronto. Their apartment is a five-minute drive from downtown, but when you look out the windows the view is of green, grassy ravines, hills, and trees; you can watch black squirrels a few feet away. Looking out the window of my century-old house a

comparable distance from downtown Detroit, I could see nothing green except weeds overgrowing the sidewalk; parking lots surrounded me on three sides, and on the fourth was a street where lunatics drove 40 or 50 miles an hour with their horns raving.[31]

This American was delighted to find that, when he was thirsty, while listening to a "respectable" band near a "large and lovely park" in front of Toronto's City Hall, he could find a drinking fountain where "no one had tossed used chewing gum into the fountain." Canadians frequently disparage their own efforts in comparison to their neighbours to the south, but in terms of civic pride they often lead the Americans.

SOCIAL ATTITUDES AND POLITICS

North America has always held private land ownership in high esteem, while tenancy and public ownership are suspect. Private land ownership is so sacrosanct in public opinion and law, that respect for it is allowed to question the propriety of planning proposals and defeat community objectives. Conflicting pressure groups have ensured a lack of housing policy. The effects of this system of priorities on government supervision have been described by Donald G. Alexander, the legal counsel for the National League of Cities in the United States:

> Today we find the federal government in Washington controlling particular hour-to-hour details in carrying out individual local programs; we find responsibility for dealing with certain urban problems thrust upon states which have neither experience nor interest in urban affairs but seek only to increase their political powers through control of funds; and we find individual cities struggling valiantly to make their own complicated financing structure squeeze a few more dollars for urgently needed improvement programs because assistance is not available from any other level of government.[32]

Federal departments work at cross-purposes instead of co-ordinating their activities. The Department of Housing and

185

Urban Development seeks to stabilize conditions and improve home ownership in underprivileged areas. Yet federal tax laws stimulate a rapid turnover of property with a resulting neighbourhood instability, while the home mortgage insurance protection of the Federal Housing Administration encourages a flight to the suburbs. Emphasis on local property taxation, as a financial base for municipal government, means that a city council will welcome wealthy people living in apartments or the construction of office buildings, rather than being concerned with re-housing lower-income groups displaced by urban renewal schemes. In short, in our democratic societies we have tried to provide something for everybody, which means that there are no real national objectives in North America regarding solution to the housing crisis. The piecemeal approach to provision of public housing in Canada is indicated by the fact that for the twenty-year period, 1949-1969, only 42,600 units were completed, less than two per cent of the total housing starts in Canada. [33] The planned number of low-income units was expected to rise from 27,500 in 1969 to 35,000 in 1970. The latter figure is as high as that permitted by Congress in the entire United States, and Canada's "commitments for these two years will amount to 75% of all production undertaken in the last twenty years." [34]

But if there is no apparent housing problem of a national scope in Canada, there is a recognition that local housing problems exist. A federal Task Force on Housing and Urban Development was established in 1968 to survey the Canadian scene. A brief submitted to this Task force by the Ontario Division of the Community Planning Association commented that "problems are not a new phenomenon but can be traced to a long history of entanglement of 'red tape', lack of co-ordination between the various levels of government and lack of interest by the non-involved sections of the population." [35] The community planners went on record as favouring the creation of a Federal Department of Housing and Urban Development, similar to the American precedent, which was to have "the undivided direction and attention of a Cabinet Minister." Also, it proposed that Provincial Governments establish equivalent bodies because by the terms of the

B.N.A. Act this basically is a provincial matter. Certainly there appears to be a need for a federal cabinet minister to speak for national planning objectives. In the past, individual cabinet ministers of the federal government were apt to use the opportunity for politicking; the control of a comprehensive program needs to be under the direction of a full-time cabinet minister. The appointment of Robert Andras as Federal Minister Responsible for Housing in May, 1969, was a step in the right direction and he has displayed awareness of the larger social issues involved. In the House of Commons on April 21, 1970, the Minister stated that his Public Housing Program included provision for social and recreational facilities in both new and old public housing projects such as, for example, the introduction of day care nurseries.

A medley of voices is heard on the subject of the need to maintain and improve our cities. Such groups include financial institutions, newspapers, downtown merchants, owners of real estate, academics, city planners and city politicians. Recently, a new voice has been heard—the newly-formed residential associations of individual citizens who resist urban renewal. In Toronto the plans formulated by Mayor Philip Givens in 1966 for public housing have ground to a halt because of citizens' objections.

The example of one group, the Trefann Court Residents Association, has shown the power of such groups of citizens to resist City Hall. In 1966 Mayor Givens stated that "I warn you that all the king's horses and all the king's men couldn't put this thing [urban renewal] together again if it is dropped now." The Mayor continued, "Abandoning Trefann now would sound the death knell for all future renewal projects in Toronto. The senior Government would lose confidence in the city and refuse to co-operate."[36] This warning was ignored by the residents of Trefann Court who continued to resist plans for renewal in their area. And five years later, nothing remains of a grand plan of the Metropolitan Planning Board to set up 24 urban renewal areas, demolish 7,400 homes and 1,100 industrial buildings, and rehabilitate another 1,900 homes. Toronto's poor have not welcomed the spanking new high-rise barrack blocks which were to replace their homes. The area known as Don Vale was designated as

187

an urban renewal area in 1956, but, after fourteen years of public protest, was finally removed from this classification. The present Mayor, William Dennison, has indicated he would like to disband what remains of the Toronto Housing Authority.

The failure of urban renewal to make an impact on Toronto has been duplicated in Vancouver. Initially, in the mid-1950's, city planners viewed urban blight as purely a matter of economics. Bulldozers were used to level eleven blocks of a downtown section known as Strathcona which had been the home of two thousand people. In October of 1968 a decision was made to bulldoze the remaining 438 homes and at that point a public reaction set in. Chinatown residents living in this area began to resist the concept of concrete freeways and barrack blocks. A Strathcona Property Owners and Tenants Association (Spota) was formed and began to put political pressure on such prominent federal politicians as Paul Hellyer, who headed the Task Force on Housing. The education that these home owners provided to politicians was well explained by Robert Andras, Minister for Housing, when he stated that:

> These people have had a hell of a lot of influence on my view of urban renewal. They have faced the breaking up and the stamping out of a lifestyle. You can put up much prettier buildings, but where do the people go? The Strathcona situation proves that people do count and can be heard.[37]

In view of the determination of the Spota organization, it is not surprising that an economist helping to plot the future of Greater Vancouver said "the city hasn't done much—urban renewal is a joke."[38]

The increasing resistance to the plans of developers has been well illustrated by the latest political fight by concerned residents in the St. James Town section of Toronto. This high-rise complex was built by developers known as the Meridian group and comprises 5,099 units including 1,674 public housing units. On March 15, 1971, Toronto's Planning and Development Committee approved, despite vociferous

188

opposition from concerned residents, the construction of three 30-storey apartments just west of the development. The present 15,000 inhabitants lack parkland but the lawyer for Meridian argued that the "1.4 acres of local parkland for every 1,000 people . . . recommended by the Official Plan was only a guide and not a regulation."[39] Residents had sought to draw attention to their plight by a "paint in" whereby a street to be widened for the convenience of the developer was painted green to simulate parkland. It would seem that political pressure by irate tenants of high-rise developments can cause concrete to turn into grass, an interesting reversal of the usual process.

Many young Canadians who live in urban areas are beginning to seriously doubt whether they will ever be able to buy a house as real estate values continue to rise. One of the underlying causes for this sharply increased purchase price of houses is related to land speculation in Canada. The Federal Task Force on Housing noted that a speculator either purchases land on the fringe of urban areas and "waits for those socially created increments to catch up with his investment," or buys slum property and waits for the time "when governments expropriate it or private developers pay a large price."[40] The recommendation of the Task Force would have gladdened the heart of Henry George:

All profits from the sale of land should be treated as taxable income. In addition consideration should be given to a special tax in cases where ownership of land is transferred without improvements.[41]

It would seem that despite our pride in providing houses with modern facilities, we have a rather familiar historical situation on our hands.

1. Charles N. Glaab and A. Theodore Brown, *A History of Urban America* (Toronto: Collier-MacMillan (Canada) Limited, 1967), p. 84.
2. Ibid., p. 94.
3. Thomas Le Duc, "History and Appraisal of U.S. Land Policy to 1862," cited in Thomas Cochrane and Thomas Brewer, eds, *Views of American Economic Growth* (New York: McGraw-Hill, 1966), vol. 1, p. 307. The Turner thesis has been highly influential in the writing of history. In 1893, Professor Frederick J. Turner read an essay to a group of fellow historians entitled "The

Significance of the Frontier in American History." According to this essay, the lure of free land had drawn men out to a Western frontier where they developed certain traits, such as self-reliance—a love of freedom—restless energy. Historians eagerly embraced this environmental explanation of the American national character. The phrase that was to unlock America's past was "the significance of the frontier," and this blended well with the current mood of isolationism. During the 1920's the motion picture studios of Hollywood discovered the potential of the Wild West, which covered the Turnerian period from 1870 to 1890. Academia and popular culture often walked hand in hand until Adolf Hitler drew young Americans back to visit their European heritage.

4. Octavia Hill, *Homes of the London Poor* (London: MacMillan and Co., 1875), p. 72

5. Ibid., p. 4.

6. *The Annual Register: A Review of Public Events at Home and Abroad, 1875* (London: Rivingtons, 1876), p. 44.

7. *The Spectator*, 13 February 1875, 48:202.

8. Jacob Riis, *How the Other Half Lives* (New York: Charles Scribner's Sons, 1914), p. 25.

9. *Statistical Yearbook of Canada*, 1895, p. 167.

10. Dominion Bureau of Statistics, *Fourth Census of Canada*, 1901, 3:87.

11. Rupert Brooke, *Letters from America* (London: Sidgwick and Jackson, 1916), p. 51.

12. Ibid., p. 80.

13. Glaab and Brown, *A History of Urban America*, p. 290.

14. George S. Pryde, *Scotland From 1603 to the Present Day* (London: Thomas Nelson, 1962), p. 302.

15. *Report of the Royal Commission on the Housing of the Industrial Population of Scotland Rural and Urban* (Cd. 8731), H.M.S.O., 1917, para. 2232.

16. Bentley G. Gilbert, *British Social Policy, 1914-1939* (London: B.T. Batsford, 1970), p. 198.

17. *Annual Report of the Department of Health for Scotland, 1934* (Cmd. 4837), H.M.S.O., 1935, p. 25.

18. A.C. Dalzell, *The Housing of the Working Classes* (Toronto: the Social Service Council of Canada, 1928), p. 10.

19. Ibid., p. 10.

20. Jewel Bullush and Murray Hausknecht, *Urban Renewal: People, Politics, Planning* (New York: Doubleday and Co., 1967), p. 6.

21. C.N. Glaab and A.T. Brown, *A History of Urban America* (Toronto: Collier-MacMillan Canada Ltd., 1968), pp. 303-304.

22. Bentley G. Gilbert, *British Social Policy, 1914-1939* (London: B.T. Batsford, 1970), p. 148.

23. Catherine Bauer, "The Dreary Deadlock of Public Housing," *Architectural Forum* 106, no. 5 (May, 1957): 141-142.

24. Lyndon B. Johnson, "Message on Housing and Urban Development to the Congress of the United States," March 2, 1965, *Congressional Quarterly Almanac, 1965*, p. 1400.

25. *Report of the Federal Task Force on Housing and Urban Development* (Ottawa: Queen's Printer, 1969), p. 13.

26. Ibid., p. 73.

27. *Report of the National Advisory Commission on Civic Disorders*, cited in John E. Kersell and M.W. Cowley, eds., *Comparative Political Problems* (Scarborough: Prentice-Hall of Canada, 1968), p. 57.

28. J. Tager and P.D. Goist, eds., *The Urban Vision* (Georgetown, Ontario: Dorsey Press, 1970), p. 301.
29. Ibid., p. 301.
30. Walter Stewart, "The Wrong Way to Solve the Housing Crisis", *Maclean's*, February, 1970.
31. Ray Ginger, ed., *Modern American Cities* (Chicago: Quadrangle Books, 1969), p. 20.
32. Donald G. Alexander, "Liveable Cities," *Current History*, August 1970, p. 87.
33. *Urban Renewal and Low Income Housing*, Central Mortgage and Housing Corporation, vol. 6, no. 4 (1970), p. 8. Statement by Robert B. Bradley.
34. Ibid., vol. 6, no. 2 (1970), p. 12.
35. Ontario Community Planning Association of Canada, *Brief to the Task Force on Housing and Urban Development*, September 1968, p. 4.
36. *Globe and Mail*, 27 October 1970, p. 31.
37. *Maclean's*, January 1971, p. 25.
38. Ibid., p. 23.
39. *Toronto Telegram*, 16 March 1971.
40. *Report of the Federal Task Force on Housing and Urban Development*, p. 38.
41. Ibid., p. 39.

5

Wets and Drys
and the Demon Rum

Four and Twenty Yankees
Feeling mighty dry,
Took a trip to Canada
And bought a case of rye.
When the case was opened
The Yanks began to sing—
"To hell with the President!
God Save the King!"

American rhyme of the 1920's

As the above rhyme indicates, the liquor question is apt to play havoc with political concepts of sovereignty and nationality. Even within one nation the drinkers of alcoholic beverages (the "wets") have usually fought pitched battles with their fellow countrymen who, as "drys," have sought to restrict the flow of alcohol. The problem of whether or not to drink liquor has greatly influenced the development of social attitudes on both sides of the Atlantic, and only by tracing its history can the issue be brought into focus.

ENGLAND'S HERITAGE

Free beer and bread are still served today to visitors at England's oldest house of charity, at St. Cross Hospital near

Winchester. Known as the "Wayfarer's Dole," this refreshment dates back to the founding of a religious order for thirteen poor men by Bishop Henry of Blois in 1136; drinking Old English Ale, prepared by fermentation of barley mash, was an accepted feature of the medieval scene.

The social structure was changing by the sixteenth century as manorialism declined and a new "working class" emerged with somewhat different habits. Labourers were hired for wages and their desire to spend part of these on recreation and companionship led to the construction of a large number of ale houses. England's Parliament of 1552 passed the first law that attempted to control the number of what were termed common ale or tippling houses. The responsibility for issuing licences for drinking places was delegated to that unpaid Tudor civil servant, the Justice of the Peace. Liquor licencing was, then, from the beginning a local affair with the J.P. being exhorted to maintain a vigilant watch over local conditions. There was certainly need for such supervision, as Old English Ale was a potent brew. Furthermore, because of the impure drinking water available, even little children drank "small beer," a diluted version of the Ale.

Old English Ale was the "sack" consumed by the jovial Sir John Falstaff of William Shakespeare's *Henry IV*. Taverns were often places of entertainment as well where the customers, seated on the ale bench outside the tavern, listened to minstrels. But it would be misleading to depict the Tudor period as one of a totally Merrie England; there were problems with excessive drinking, as the Act of 1552 testifies. Furthermore, as this century of exploration sent sailors on voyages into the New World, a new habit was formed of drinking grog, or rum distilled from molasses.

A reaction to the era of heavy imbibing was inevitable, and after the Reformation the Puritans formed the first really strict dry lobby. In the early seventeenth century, Puritan self-discipline demanded that men abandon drunkenness and immorality and devote their hours of leisure to religious study. God-fearing Puritans saw rum and Romanism as equally evil and during Oliver Cromwell's Interregnum, sought to eliminate both. Puritans pressed for strict moral guidance, enacted as blue laws, that regulated the conduct of all citizens. During the latter part of the Cromwellian Republic, England was divided into twelve districts, each ruled by a Major General, who sought to discourage "profaneness and ungodliness" by prohibiting drunkenness and closing many ale houses. Total abstinence from taking alcohol was linked to a Protestant ideal that saw drunkenness as unethical conduct, since it inhibited the exercise of such virtues as self control, industry and thrift. Wine was much better used, from the Puritan's point of view, in celebrating the festival of the Lord's Supper for the greater glory of God. Yet the Puritans of England, strict as they were, could not be as rigid in enforcing their code of conduct on society as their brethren in Massachusetts, who had set up a theocracy in New England.

NEW ENGLAND AND NEW FRANCE

The New Commonwealth of Massachusetts was established under the direct rule of the godly. A student of the Puritan influence has recorded that:

> Of English-speaking communities that in which the discipline of the Calvinist Church-State was carried to the furthest extreme was the Puritan theocracy of New England....[The] vain custom of drinking to each other was forbidden to true professors of the faith.[1]

An early appreciation of the health benefits to be derived from abstaining from alcohol was recorded by an immigrant minister. The Reverend Francis Higgins said at Boston in 1630 that "a sup of New England's air is better than a whole draught of Old English Ale."[2] Initially the power of licencing sellers of wine or alcoholic beverages was in the hands of the Governor, but with the development of local government, this power passed to the county courts by 1647. After 1680 the permission of the selectmen of a town had to be secured before a licence could be granted. This trend towards tight local control of liquor represented a climate of opinion receptive to the idea of a temperance movement intended to

194

ultimately abolish the use of alcoholic beverages, either by persuasive encouragement to voluntary abstinence, or, if necessary, by legislative enactment.

In New France, the first temperance movement was launched by Bishop Laval and the Jesuit missionaries. Because of the demoralizing influence of liquor on the Indians, the use of French brandy as a trading commodity was prohibited in 1657. This law was enforced as, in 1661, two men were shot and one whipped for selling brandy to the Indians. Louis XIV tried to check the imports of brandy to New France by a royal ordinance of 1664 that charged "cent pour cent" on all imported liquor. This did not restrict the flow of imports, nor did the efforts of the Intendant Jean Talon to provide a local substitute of beer supplied from the brewery he built. The economic dependence of the colony on fur trading, allied to the competition of the cheap rum supplied to the Indians by Dutch fur traders from the English colonies, forced New France to have an equivocal attitude to liquor. Bishop Laval continued to disapprove of the sale of brandy on moral grounds, but the colony moved from total prohibition of this liquor trade to a licencing system. By the early eighteenth century, the liquor trade was well established in the colonies of the New World. New England's ships traded in West Indian molasses and rum while, in the Appalachian mountains, the American invention of moonshine, or corn liquor, was being distilled.

THE ERA OF EXCESS

Englishmen were also acquiring a taste for a new liquor. Soldiers who had served in European wars brought back to England a taste for gin, which was a Dutch invention. Queen Anne stimulated the distilling of gin when in 1702 she raised the tax on imports and lowered excise duties on the home product. An orgy of gin drinking began in 1721 that was to last for thirty years. During the 1730's, Parliament further encouraged the consumption of gin by allowing anybody to become a distiller and by keeping taxation low: the reason was a purely selfish one, as the dominant landed interest wanted to ensure that corn was consumed. Gin threatened to replace the Englishman's time-honoured beer and ale, although port, tea and coffee were available for the wealthy people who could afford these imported items.

Ever since Britain had been released from the Puritan grip after the Restoration of Charles II, the consumption of distilled spirits had been soaring. In 1684, the consumption of spirits was 527,000 gallons; by 1714, it was up to 2,000,000 gallons; by 1735, the amount had increased to 5,394,000 gallons and by 1750 it had doubled again to 11,000,000 gallons.[3] With the retail price of gin at a penny a quart, it is not surprising that gin shops offered to make a man drunk for a penny, or dead drunk for tuppence. London was the main centre for the gin trade and in 1743 over eight million gallons were being consumed in the metropolis yearly, with "every sixth shop. . .believed to be a dram shop."[4] As London had approximately seven hundred thousand people, the annual consumption of gin per person must have been about 11.5 gallons; and as children and women were not heavy imbibers, the average male consumption was probably around a gallon a week. All social classes drank heavily and this was the time of the "two-bottle parson" who could still preach after downing his port. Dissenting ministers were apt to claim that the Church of England parsons were going to hell: possibly the real question should have concerned their degree of sobriety on arrival.

By the early 1740's, excessive gin-drinking had helped cause the appalling death rate in London which was double the rate of births. The government moved reluctantly, and against the powerful landowners, to stop the worst excesses of gin. In the interests of maintaining public order, it finally decided to act. The Act of 1751 placed a high tax on spirits and the retailing of liquor by distillers and shopkeepers was stopped. With a subsequent reduction in the number of gin shops, the "trade" began to lose its constricting grip and the milder beverages of ale and beer began to be substituted. At the same time, the rise of the Methodist movement under John Wesley provided for many workers an alternative psychological outlet to liquor-induced intoxication.

196

THE NORTH AMERICAN SCENE

The crusading zeal of the Methodists crossed the Atlantic, where it reinforced the earlier Protestant ethic of abstinence so firmly rooted in New England. At the time of the American Revolution, the key area of New England was still remarkably homogeneous, as its 700,000 inhabitants were almost entirely of English origin. The Yankee had a deep religious conviction that he was answerable only to God, and his stern moral code prohibited travel or the serving of liquor in a tavern on the Sabbath. From such stern stuff had Oliver Cromwell formed his famous Ironsides and, when the battle for America's independence was joined, the King of England had his hands full. Support for New England's resistance came from rural areas where evangelical sects such as the Baptists and Methodists predominated, who were also inclined to view the Demon Rum with suspicion. It would be an oversimplification to view the overall struggle for independence as a conflict between the drys and the wets, but it is true that British troops could hold the larger ports or towns outside New England, where Episcopalian or Roman Catholics were generally tolerant of drinking. On the other hand, this does not mean that Washington's army did not imbibe as, at Valley Forge, each soldier was entitled to an official ration of a daily gill, or half a pint, of whisky.

Was the American War of Independence fought over the issue of "no taxation without representation?" If it was, then it is particularly ironic that the triumphant Republic soon faced an uprising from citizens who resisted the collection of liquor taxes by President George Washington. The trouble began when the federal government sought in 1791 to impose an excise tax on distilled liquor. Scots-Irish pioneers in Pennsylvania erupted in the Whisky Insurrection of 1794 which, though it has not received the same publicity as the Boston Tea Party, did necessitate Washington's ordering in 13,000 troops to support the tax collectors.

Taxes on liquor comprised part of the customs and excise that defrayed the main costs of government. So in the newer British colonies that were developing to the north of the American Republic, the liquor revenue loomed as an important item. By the Quebec Revenue Act of 1774 a system of licencing was introduced along with import duties that displayed a form of Imperial Preference: British brandy and rum were taxed at the rate of 3d per gallon, West Indian rum at 6d per gallon and American liquor at 9d per gallon. Following the division of the colony into Lower and Upper Canada, the system of licencing was extended to the upper province by its first Legislature in 1792, "except to retail liquor in jails or prisons." British authorities at home were also concerned about controlling liquor around this time, as William Pitt was seeking to finance the struggle against Napoleon. A duty on port wine imposed in 1798 forced the price up to nearly double the previous amount, with a quart bottle of port costing the then exorbitant price of 2s 9d. This tax was not only sound financing and patriotic, but probably also helped to get any lingering "two-bottle parsons" under control.

TEMPERANCE IN THE EARLY NINETEENTH CENTURY

Slowly the alcoholic condition of England was being improved. The increased availability of tea, coffee and cocoa contributed to sobriety by providing alternative beverages, and a milder type of beer became available when pale ale was developed at the town of Burton-on-Trent. Although this could not be foreseen at the end of the eighteenth century, pale ale would prove to be a most popular national drink. In fact, its fame had so developed by the twentieth century that, during the Second World War, the Royal Air Force bomber crews used the slang phrase "gone for a Burton" to indicate a comrade's death. A leading military hero of the early nineteenth century also had a taste for beer: the Duke of Wellington argued in 1828 that there should be a free trade in beer, so that the working classes would use it in preference to spirits. Encouraged by the Beer Bill of 1830, passed when Wellington was Prime Minister, over 30,000 beer shops opened in Britain.

Moderation is the quality suggested by the word "temperance" and this was the meaning of the word in relation to the use of alcohol until Temperance Societies began to form in the United States. A Temperance Society was organized at

Saratoga, New York in 1808, followed soon afterwards by the formation of the Massachusetts Society for Suppression of Intemperance. As used by these societies, the word "temperance" came to be a label for any movement that opposed alcoholic beverages. Prohibition was an extreme form of this movement which sought to secure complete abstinence by legal compulsion. In 1826, an American Society for the Promotion of Temperance was founded in Boston and seven years later this movement had over one million members, including many Congregational and Presbyterian ministers in Massachusetts. At this time the term "teetotalism" was added to the expanding vocabulary of the drys: temperance supporters indicated their total belief in abstinence by writing the letter "t" opposite their names on the temperance rosters. There was now a wide gulf between believers in the earlier voluntary abstinence from alcohol, and these teetotalers who regarded any backsliding with horror.

Religion was associated with the use of alcohol in the developing frontier of the 1830's where Methodist and Baptist circuit riders preached fear of hell and hope of heaven. When Protestant churches expressed their dislike of the Irish Catholic immigrants arriving in the New World, their way of condemning these Roman Catholics was to identify them with the Demon Rum. To many rural Methodists and Baptists, the evils of booze, Popery and city life were all part of the same wickedness. Ironically, the Protestant Irish immigrant helped to reinforce this prejudice, for the Ulster Temperance Society had been formed in 1829 and soon had twenty-five societies in Ireland and three in Scotland. Within one year the Ulster Temperance Society had also spread to Yorkshire and Lancashire in England, and the flow of Ulstermen to British North America carried the faith to the Maritimes and the Canadas.

Nova Scotia felt the impact of Temperance when Methodists at Beaver River formed the first society in 1828. Reinforced by its strong ties to New England, Nova Scotia was to become a strong temperance centre. New Brunswick, the neighbouring Maritime province, had its own liquor problems due to the development of trade with the West Indies, and the social effects of the return cargoes of rum and molasses. Whereas it had been said that gin was the fastest way out of Manchester, the fastest way out of the slums of Saint John, New Brunswick was through the medium of rum. Faced with a barren soil and a harsh climate, the Loyalist Province did not offer a very wide choice of occupations for the labourer. The irregularity, the unpleasantness and the dangers of seafaring, lumbering and shipbuilding encouraged hard drinking. New Brunswick was therefore ripe for a rapid growth of the temperance organization known as the Sons of Temperance, which spread northwards from the United States.

Lower Canada with its predominantly Roman Catholic population was not swept along by the Protestant passion for organizing temperance lodges, although individual curés sponsored similar activity in their parishes. Methodists resident in Lower Canada did, however, sponsor Temperance Societies. A monthly publication entitled the *Canada Temperance Advocate* was published in Montreal after 1835, and a convention of thirty societies was held in that city. Meanwhile, Upper Canada had formed its first temperance society in 1828, followed, three years later, by formation of a Temperance society in its capital of York. Colonial newspapers were an important influence in the formation of public attitudes and Egerton Ryerson, the editor of the Methodist *Christian Guardian*, actively promoted the temperance cause. There was also a political undercurrent, for reformers such as Ryerson, M.S. Bidwell, Jesse Ketchum and Dr. J. Rolph were also united in the temperance brotherhood. Possibly that irascible and unrepentant Tory, Colonel Thomas Talbot, had this potential political power in mind when he condemned the Methodists as those "Damned Cold Water Drinking Societies." Anglicans, who perhaps had less tradition of attempting to regulate the moral conduct of their neighbours than did the sects with American affiliations, generally stayed clear of the campaign to reform the wets.

Upper Canada at this time had a strong contingent of wets: by 1842 there had developed 147 distilleries and 96 breweries to serve a population of less than 500,000 people. In a society not far removed from the frontier, inns and bars provided a source of social relaxation: the temperance advocate, however, saw these institutions as a source of unmitigated evil. The lumbering industry produced near Bytown, the present site of Ottawa, a breed of men who provided a sharp contrast to the respectable temperance advocates. One area of Bytown was known as "Cork Town" and centred around a picturesque establishment called "Mother McGinty's Tavern." Working conditions for the lumbermen in this area were described by a witness appearing before a British Parliamentary Committee that investigated the timber trade:

> *Question*: Will you explain further in what way that depravity was exhibited?
> *Answer*: By drunkenness and brutality. The timber trade, by causing bodies of men to live in the woods in shantees, [small temporary buildings] places them beyond the good social effects consequent upon being surrounded by women, and the responsibility of being subjected to the laws of the country.[5]

The politicians in the legislature of the United Province of Canada were doubtlessly aware of the potential power of temperance advocates; the decision of 1845 to allow municipalities to have the money derived from the sale of liquor licences, was an early attempt to deflect the mounting dry lobby from carrying a province-wide prohibition measure.

SIGNING THE PLEDGE

The American campaign against the Demon Rum received a further impetus from the activities of the Washingtonian Society, which comprised reformed alcoholics. Starting from Washington D.C., the movement soon had lodges throughout the United States, with former wets making impassioned appeals for adults and children to "sign the pledge" of abstinence. As the Washingtonians began to diminish in strength by mid-century, the dry cause was taken up by a much more powerful movement. From Utica, New York, was launched the Order of Good Templars which spread out all over the United States and the Canadian colonies and even reached

Britain. Their emphasis was now on teetotalism and Good Templar lodges multiplied which, in turn, reinforced local temperance movements. In Britain, a new type of movement arose that concentrated on juveniles to sign a pledge of abstinence, and grew from a Band of Hope formed at Leeds in Yorkshire, a county renowned for its Methodist adherents. Bands of Hope soon sprang up throughout Britain. This movement built upon the climate provided by the earlier Anglican British and Foreign Temperance Society, of which Queen Victoria became the patron, that had pioneered the cause since 1831. Ireland supplied the greatest of the Temperance missionaries in Father Theobold Matthews of Cork, who left his triumphs in his native land of the early 1840's to carry the faith to England, and eventually to America by 1850. Father Matthews seemed to encounter some difficulty with the stubborn English but reflected the zeal of the international temperance wave. By the 1850's, Britain's temperance movement was sufficiently influenced by American examples to campaign for complete teetotalism. Yet in political terms, it was not possible to secure mass support for complete prohibition of drink, so the leading temperance organization, the United Kingdom Alliance, campaigned for limiting the hours in which the public houses might remain open, and for local prohibition by local option.

The United Kingdom Alliance, founded in 1853, was to profoundly affect the character of politics in Britain, because the working classes were directly affected by the pressure to close public houses. Although religion was not of much interest to them they saw quite clearly that Nonconformist fervour sparked the temperance drive. A historian who has studied this period noted that "After 1850 they [Nonconformists] with ever-increasing ardour...against...the pleasure or solace of drunkenness then became the most active crusaders."[6] At this time the United Kingdom Alliance supported any politician who would take the pledge to press for restriction of the liquor trade; but it was already becoming evident that if the Alliance ever supported a particular political party, they might drive any enfranchised wet workers into the arms of the alternative party. Yet while the Temperance cause in the United Kingdom was not too popular among the masses, progress was being made on the other side of the Atlantic.

American democracy had produced a considerable number of local by-laws to restrict drinking, under the policy of permitting local option. But this was not deemed sufficient to reform society, since teetotalers envisaged complete prohibition. As State Legislatures had the constitutional power to control all aspects of the liquor trade, a political campaign of evangelical fervour was mounted at the state level. New England led the way when the state of Maine passed a prohibitory law in 1851. In the neighbouring colony of New Brunswick, the ladies of Saint John were actively campaigning through their organization called the Ladies Total Abstinence Society. A political ally was available in Leonard Tilley, soon to be Premier of the colony, who as a dedicated abstainer secured the passage of a prohibition law in New Brunswick in 1855. The Act provoked riots among the wets in the city of Saint John that threatened public order and prohibition was quickly repealed. (This victory of the wets has rarely been mentioned in our history books in comparison, for example, with constitutional issues, like the rebellions in the Canadas of 1837. One wonders if Canadian history is truly as dry as some critics have claimed.) And in 1855 the adjoining colony to New Brunswick decided to forego prohibition in view of the uproar; Nova Scotia thought that it would be wiser to adopt strict licencing and local option laws.

CONTROLLING THE WETS

At the same time, the United Province of Canada was feeling the pressure of members of the Grand Lodge of Good Templars in Upper Canada. A committee of the United Province Legislature proposed a form of local option as a way to resolve the tussle between the wets and drys, and this was adopted in Upper Canada in 1853, with Lower Canada following suit two years later. In the following decade, the politicians were being pressed to pass tighter legislation by a new group formed at Montreal, the United Canadian Alliance for the Suppression of the Liquor Trade. Christopher Dunkin sponsored the resulting Temperance Act of 1864, which gave any municipal council the right to pass a by-law to prohibit the retail sale of liquor, if a majority in favour was recorded by popular vote. After Confederation, the Dunkin Act remained in force in both Ontario and Quebec, but during the early Victorian period Ontario showed much more zeal than Quebec in voting for dry counties and municipalities.

Strong drink was a significant factor in the life of Victorian England. Intolerable living conditions and employment, as depicted in the chapters on housing and unions, tended to encourage the use of alcohol as a sedative by the industrial working classes. Drunkenness was a common sight, particularly on Saturday night. The popular drinking song, *I Belong to Glasgow*, could have easily been applied to any large city in Britain during the nineteenth century. (I'm only a common old working chap,/ as anyone here can see,/ But when I get a couple of drinks on a Saturday,/ Glasgow belongs to me.) In the 1860's the liquor question threatened to divide Britain in two: not the rich and the poor as Disraeli had suggested, but rather the wets and the drys. The Temperance Societies tended to see their members as the respectable pillars of society; as Samuel Morley, a leading spokesman, stated, "the Temperance cause lay at the root of all social and political progress in this country."[7] On the other hand, the implication that the wets were a disreputable group aroused antagonism, particularly as public houses provided the major outlet for the relaxation of workers, while the aristocracy had long been accustomed to the use of alcohol.

Like their brethren in North America, the Temperance movement spear-headed by the United Kingdom Alliance sought to act as a political pressure group. A parliamentary candidate would be asked by agents of the Alliance to pledge himself to support the policy of controlling the liquor trade, and if he refused he would find the Alliance urging his supporters to vote against him. During the 1860's the small but powerful dry lobby pressed both Conservative and Liberal members to declare their position. Although the members of the United Kingdom Alliance tended to be Nonconformist middle-class merchants or skilled tradesmen, the liquor issue cut much deeper than a mere class or religious division. As will be discussed in the chapter on religion, most of the British masses were basically secularistic in outlook and on a matter such as alcohol, often took the wet position of wealthier individuals. Efforts to regulate the conduct of the nation aroused memories of Puritan blue laws and the wets conducted a stubborn resistance to the Temperance campaign. There were indications that history was going to repeat itself for the main body of the wet group appeared to owe a general, if sometimes confused, allegiance to the Church of England. It was true that the Church of England had its own Temperance movement, but this relied on persuasion and extensive literature rather than emphasis on complete abstinence. By the end of the 1860's, the Temperance movement was becoming politically identified with the Liberal party, while the Conservative party accommodated the brewers and their customers. After the passage of the Second Reform Act of 1867, which enfranchised many workers, the leader of the Conservative party, Lord Derby, openly declared that the Act would lead to more "beer barrel" influence, not a bad thing for a party that contained many brewers.

AMERICA GRAPPLES WITH THE PROBLEM

Beer drinkers were also beginning to rally in the United States, due principally to the immigration patterns. German immigrants introduced lager beers into the United States and formed an element that generally resisted the dramatic appeals of dry lobbyists. Irishmen were also prone to stiff resistance against the drys. At the same time, as the United States became more industrialized, its European immigrants, who were accustomed to drinking wine or beer as a matter of course, became concentrated in such large cities as New York, Chicago and St. Louis. In addition, the nineteenth-century faith in laissez faire provided a climate that enabled the liquor industry to expand in the 1860's. A vested interest developed as brewing and liquor concerns kept a sharp eye on the taxation policies of the federal government. President Abraham Lincoln passed the Internal Revenue Act of 1862 that placed a tax of one dollar a barrel on beer and twenty cents a gallon on spirits; this tax that procured increased revenue to finance the Civil War from the pockets of drinkers was bound to be popular with the drys. Furthermore, the way was now open to use liquor tax as the principal method of financing government revenues. After 1870, the liquor tax provided up to two-thirds of the entire internal revenue of the United States.[8]

Excessive drinking produced a second wave of Temperance reformers. In one sense, this movement was principally a reaction of rural America to the growing industrialism of the nation. Furthermore, the corruption involved in national political circles aroused the hostility of farmers. There was, for example, the Whisky Ring of 1875 that operated in St. Louis and defrauded the government of millions of dollars in taxes. President Grant's private secretary, Babcock, was found to be involved. It seemed that the liquor interests had entered into a corrupt alliance with politicians. To meet this combined evil, a Prohibition party entered the political arena to campaign for total abstinence.

An alliance was quickly forged between the Prohibition party and the most effective Temperance organization that was ever created, the Women's Christian Temperance Union (W.C.T.U.) formed in 1874. The union of these two bodies was cemented when Frances Willard, the founder of the W.C.T.U., welcomed the Prohibition party's support on securing female suffrage. The basic underlying theme of the W.C.T.U.'s philosophy was that women are the moral guardians of the nation, and the able Frances Willard began to organize the ladies for an attack on national immorality.

Supporting the W.C.T.U. was the International Order of Good Templars, the largest Temperance body in the world. By 1875, the world membership was up to 735,000; 200,000 of this number were in Britain. The British section caused a temporary rift in the movement when it seceded over its determination to see that coloured people were treated equally, a point of view that was not welcomed by Templars in the southern United States. Generally speaking, the British temperance movement of this time was more politically oriented than that of North America, and exerted a more powerful influence in the politics of the time.

PARLIAMENT TACKLES THE ISSUE

William Gladstone's Liberal government which was elected in 1868 was aided by an influential group of temperance advocates among his Nonconformist supporters. It was a time when some of these Nonconformists revelled in such ominous labels as the "New Model Army" and the "Puritans."[9] It should also be pointed out that, just as in the U.S.A., the politicians sought to placate the dry interest by their methods of financing government expenses. Gladstone, as the great maker of Victorian traditions of public finance, raised most of the State's income from customs and excise, principally by taxes on such articles as beer, spirits, tea, sugar and tobacco. Temperance societies were in general agreement with such a financial policy, while probably deploring the need for tea and sugar to be included. In 1872, Gladstone passed a Licencing Act designed to prevent adulteration of beer and to permit local magistrates to use their discretion in setting the closing hours of public houses. Such a policy was welcome to the United Kingdom Alliance as it enabled them to exert local pressure in what their President declared was a "holy war." Inside the Liberal party, a temperance advocate, Sir Wilfred Lawson, continued to urge that there should be a form of local option where a two-thirds majority of rate-payers could close public houses. But Gladstone was too wise to accept the invitation of the drys for an all-out war on the wets. A beneficial measure for the worker was passed when the payment of wages in public houses to coal miners was prohibited, for experience had shown that a publican, the proprietor of a public house, often secured a considerable portion of the weekly pittance that went for the support of a miner's family. The puritanical strand of thought within the Liberal party was pressing for control of "the trade." The police were given the right to search premises in pursuit of evidence that would show the practice of adulteration and, if a conviction was secured against a publican for an infraction of any laws, the magistrate was obliged to record this conviction upon the publican's licence. As the *Times* of May 12, 1875 commented, the Liberals' Act "treated the publicans rather as criminals to be placed under police supervision than as ordinary traders." This political manifestation of what was generally felt to be the influence of the Temperance movement reflecting the Nonconformist conscience, provoked Anglican Bishop Magee to exclaim that he would rather have England free than England sober. This sentiment in the Church of England was shared by over two hundred thousand licenced victuallers, who were in a strategic position to influence the thinking of the working classes, many of whom would vote for the first time in the election of 1874.

Many Englishmen resented the Liberals' pro-temperance legislation and publicans aided local wet candidates to defeat their dry opponents. William Gladstone exclaimed on hearing of his electoral defeat, "I have been borne down in a torrent of gin and beer." From this election of 1874 was to stem the identification of the brewers with the Conservative party, while the Temperance wing was now committed to the Liberal party. Benjamin Disraeli, the new Conservative Prime Minister, was a different type of man from his predecessor. Disraeli had once commented, when viewing some of his parliamentary colleagues, "These respectable elderly gentlemen can't stand the hours. They die off like flies. No man is fit for the House of Commons who has not in his youth led the life of a rake."[10] The Conservative government soon eliminated the right of the police to search public houses, and revoked the power of magistrates to use discretionary power in controlling the closing hour of public houses and recording offenses on the licencee's certificate.

Statistics reveal the seriousness of the "liquor problem" of England in the 1870's. The *Times* of May 13, 1875 stated that in the past year the amount of money spent in public houses was £146,000,000, approximately twice the amount of total government spending; of this total, £97,000,000 came from working men. Attempts were made to reform working-class habits by encouraging them to improve their minds at Trades Halls, but as the *Times* explained:

The working class. . .do not care for the books, the quiet games, the instructive lectures, the improving talk, the large national views, the tea and coffee. . . .They prefer stronger drink. . .more vigorous styles of talk and action.[11]

Such lamentations are still heard in our age, in the quiet of College faculty rooms or from ministers viewing their urban flocks.

A select committee of the House of Lords investigated the national scene and their report indicated that in 1875 there were 203,989 apprehensions for drunkenness. This situation was linked to the poor housing conditions, and this House of Lords Committee and the *Times* both endorsed the proposal of Joseph Chamberlain that the municipalities take over all the licenced premises, and use the profits for social reconstruction. The whole question was, however, fraught with political overtones, and wet and dry lobbies watched intently. The *Times* sent a reporter to the U.S.A. to investigate American methods of curbing the liquor trade, but they found no helpful guidance among the legislators at Washington, as indicated by this report in the *Times* of December 22, 1877.

From reading the rules. . .one would assume that Congress was a temperance society. . .however whisky has been sold under the name of "cold tea" and rum as "Roman Punch."

Considering the vigilance of such Temperance movements as the Women's Christian Temperance Union, it is understandable why the national legislators resorted to such subterfuges.

CANADA'S LEGISLATORS TRY THEIR HANDS

Canada was also beginning a cat-and-mouse game between legislators and Temperance interests, for the Dominion branch of the W.C.T.U. had been born in Owen Sound, Ontario immediately after the founding of the parent body.

When Alexander Mackenzie defeated John A. Macdonald at the polls in 1873, the dry lobby took heart for Mackenzie was a pronounced prohibitionist. A Royal Commission was appointed in 1874 to investigate the weaknesses of the existing Dunkin Act for municipal local option; the formation of the Dominion Alliance to co-ordinate temperance activity provided a national dry lobby led by a group of M.P.s who were also prohibitionists. Stubborn Prime Minister Mackenzie, though sympathetic, refused to take the political risk of pushing for national prohibition and so the first breakthrough came at the provincial level. In 1876, Ontario enacted the Crooks Act which provided that each riding in the province was to have a board of men appointed to issue a limited number of licences. The Crooks Act soon reduced tavern licences at the rate of approximately 433 a year and laid the foundation of the present Ontario licencing system.

On the federal level, the pressure of the Dominion Alliance finally secured national liquor legislation through the passage of the Canada Temperance Act of 1878. This measure, commonly called the Scott Act after the Secretary of State who sponsored it, applied the principle of the Dunkin Act concerning local option to the whole Dominion. Local plebiscites could be held in any city or county on petition of one-fourth of the electors at three-year intervals. A simple majority of the electorate decided whether the provisions of the Act would continue for another three-year period. Fredericton, New Brunswick became the first city to adopt the Scott Act, thus emphasizing its different character from the free-wheeling port of Saint John, but a much larger struggle was about to ensue. Underlying the problem of applying such legislation was the question of the respective constitutional powers of the provinces and the Dominion, under the British North America Act. Pandora's box was opened as a Dominion-Provincial struggle commenced for control of liquor legislation.

MORALITY AND CRUSADES

The contemporary climate of opinion in the United States was equally disturbed although somewhat different forces

210

were at work. The Temperance forces in the U.S. stepped up their efforts in the period between 1860 and 1880, when investment in the liquor business increased almost sevenfold. Country-bred Protestants viewed with horror the free-drinking "foreign" immigrants and the vices of the city. Liquor interests were criticized for maintaining a political lobby at Washington, and the Temperance forces claimed that the welfare of the nation's women and children was at stake. Prominent rural church leaders expounded the need to close the saloons to ensure the survival of American ideals. The W.C.T.U. exhorted school boards to endorse textbooks that promoted hygiene, a word which was synonymous with temperance, and, in turn, publishers began to fall in line. Medical statistics were supposed to prove that children conceived in drunkenness were mentally defective. Thus a popular book on hygiene *How to Live: Rules for Healthful Living* stated:

> Dr. Stockard has also shown in mice, on which he has experimented, the effect of alcohol on the germplasm is distinctly injurious. It is a fair inference that the use of alcohol by parents tends to damage the offspring.

The evils of alcohol were expounded in the school readers written by Dr. McGuffy, which sold nearly 122 million copies between 1836 and 1920, and conditioned children by temperance lessons such as "Don't Take Strong Drink." Publishers were a special target of the dry groups, as was indicated by the adoption by many British schools of a primer by Sir Benjamin Richardson entitled *Temperance Lesson Book*. On the American frontier, farmers' daughters became "schoolmarms" who formed a strong bridgehead for converting the next generation to the cause of temperance. The cleavage between the schoolmarms and the men they might have married, like lumberjacks, cowboys or miners, was accentuated by the fact that men engaged in these hazardous occupations frequently died early. Naturally the hard-drinking habits of these men were seen as retribution by the spinsters they had neglected. Village saloons were frequently crude places: a shack with a bar, a few tables and chairs and an array of spittoons. Frequently the cheap liquor was not protected by a brand name and the expression "pick your poison" had real significance. Churchgoing farmers and their families opposed these dens of vice so that, given the emotions that the Wild West saloon provoked, the less conspicuous practice of bootlegging becomes understandable. The expression "bootlegging" which now has wider connotations, derived from the practice in the mid-western United States during the 1880's, of carrying flasks concealed in boot tops. Spurred on by these devious devices of the wets, the forces of Prohibition continued to crusade against the Demon Rum.

Apart from moral or political considerations, the medical problem of habitual drunkards was becoming a concern to doctors on both sides of the Atlantic. In 1880, a medical doctor reported his findings after a tour of inebriate institutions in North America. The United States at this time possessed twenty-six such institutions, while Canada had only one curative institution at Belmont House Lunatic Asylum, where one wing was used for treatment of inebriates. In visiting the Fort Hamilton Inebriate Home at Brooklyn, New York, the visitor noted, "There are more American, Scotch and Irish than English and German patients, as the former are, as a rule, spirit drinkers, and the latter generally beer drinkers."[12] Britain had passed an Habitual Drunkards Act in 1879 on the urging of a Scottish doctor, that provided for curative centres to be established by local authorities; but there seems to have been little done until the government again stepped into the picture in 1898 to establish inebriate reformatories. The problem of alcoholism, viewed as a disease to be treated medically, was gaining increasing recognition, but the prohibition campaigns based on political and social factors still held the spotlight.

Canada was influenced both by the cultural influences concerning temperance emanating from south of her border, and by the British parliamentary battles of the 1870's between the wets and the drys. As in Britain, the leading brewers, such as the Molsons of Montreal and the Labatts and Carlings of London, were usually to be found in the Conservative and Anglican ranks. It had still not been finally determined whether control of liquor was a provincial or a federal matter: the Canada Temperance Act appeared to indicate that liquor legislation was within the power of the federal government, and the power of the Dominion to legislate on temperance was upheld in the decision of the Judicial Committee of the Privy Council of *Russell* v. *The Queen* (1882). But in the following year the whole question was reopened by another decision of the Privy Council, *Hodge* v. *The Queen*, which found Ontario liquor legislation valid, as it dealt with purely a local matter. Ontario promptly passed the Ontario Liquor Licence Act of 1884 which Prime Minister Macdonald disallowed. In this comic-opera sequence once more the question of just who had power to enact temperance legislation in Ontario was placed before the Privy Council, while the matter was held in abeyance in Canada. The struggle as to which level of government had power to enact liquor legislation really involved the question of who had patronage to dispense in Ontario, through the chance to appoint enforcement officers. Was this patronage to be controlled by Macdonald's federal Conservatives or Mowat's provincial Liberals?

The tussle continued between the two. All the Temperance bodies—the W.C.T.U., the Sons of Templars, the Presbyterian General Assembly, the Congregational and Methodist churches—placed pressure on both the Ontario and Dominion governments. That beloved delaying device of Canadian politicians, a Royal Commission, was established in 1892 to investigate the liquor traffic by conducting enquiries throughout Canada and the United States. Under the barrage of propaganda issued by the Temperance forces, the public was now being conditioned to accept "temperance" as synonymous with "prohibition."

THE DRYS INTENSIFY THEIR CAMPAIGN

Political parties based on the issue of prohibition existed in both the United States and Canada. They did not, however, secure much support at the national level. The high point of the American Prohibition Party came at the election of 1892, but then it polled only 271,000 votes out of a total of 12 million cast. The Canadian party, inspired by the Reverend Dr. Sutherland, did not make any national progress as a third party movement. One of its underlying political problems was that while the Roman Catholic, Episcopal and Jewish churches might endorse temperance, they opposed prohibition. Therefore the traditional apostles of abstinence, the Methodist, Baptist, Presbyterian and Congregational churches, were left to provide the main sectarian support for the Prohibition party which gradually faded from the scene. But the evangelical sects in the United States founded a more militant political machine when the Anti-Saloon League commenced activity in 1893.

Anti-Saloon League speakers were required to be fundraisers for the cause. They made "educational" appeals in churches which produced a collection for the cause as well as temperance pledges. This activity was supplemented by the activity of Carry (Hatchet) Nation who made a career in Kansas out of leading hymn-singing women into saloons, where they would shout abuse at "rummies" while their leader attacked the fixtures with an axe. Meanwhile, the more sophisticated ladies of the W.C.T.U. supported the campaign by some very efficient lobbying throughout North America. One of their most formidable lobbyists summarized the means she advocated:

> agitating through pulpit, platform, press and prayer meeting for the choice of temperance men as legislators. . . .appeal to their constituents in like manner to instruct these law makers to vote for temperance education in public schools. This should be universally and systematically done so that each legislator will feel this pressure before he leaves his constituents.[13]

The female drys discovered, as had the authors of school readers, that another powerful weapon lay in training children. Legions of children were trained to march and sing about the polling booths, whenever local or county plebiscites on liquor were held. Adult drys waited for known wets and sent their little children, clutching tiny American flags, into action.

214

"There he is children. Go get him." Swirling around the marked man in a wild elves dance, they sang with piping empty violence,

"Think of sisters, wives and mothers,
Of helpless babes in some poor slum,
Think not of yourself, but others,
Vote against the Demon Rum."[14]

In rural communities such a campaign by a disciplined army of prohibitionists was bound to make life uncomfortable for individual wets. Furthermore, American democratic practices tended to aid the Temperance advocates in, for example, the popular election of county courts. Prohibitionists focused their attention on gaining control of these offices so that liquor licences could be denied. It is not surprising, in view of these tactics, that by the turn of the century five rural states had been dried up by prohibition.

Simultaneous with the American movement of the nineties was an attack by the Canadian prohibitionists. Whereas under the American federal structure the control of liquor was a state's right, the constitutional issue had not yet been settled for the key province of Ontario. Pending the decision from the Judicial Committee of the Privy Council, the Temperance lobby exerted strong pressure on their potential ally Premier Oliver Mowat, a known abstainer. In 1894 Ontario had a provincial plebiscite on prohibition, accompanied by a strong campaign by the Temperance forces. A majority was secured in favour of prohibition and, swept along by this success, Mowat promised that he would introduce a prohibition bill as soon as the constitutional issue was clarified. The Temperance delegation was overjoyed at the news and gave three rousing cheers for the Premier of Ontario. Finally, in 1896, the Privy Council decision was rendered on the case of *Attorney General for Ontario* v. *Attorney General for Canada*, and Mowat was the victor. Ontario could pass temperance legislation within her borders, relating to local option, providing that it was applied to areas that had not already adopted the provisions of the Canada Temperance Act.

From the point of view of the wets, the Canada Temperance Act (Scott Act) created widespread dissatisfaction. It was claimed that the suppression of normal liquor outlets forced the business into the hands of bootleggers and that, as spirits contained a higher percentage of alcohol and could more easily be smuggled, there was a trend away from the milder beer or wine. Professor Goldwin Smith, the historian, made a close study of the workings of the Scott Act and concluded that the chief result had been:

> ...the substitution of an unlicensed and unregulated for a licensed and regulated trade. The demand for drink remained the same, but it was supplied in illicit ways. It was found by those who were engaged in the campaign against the Scott Act that the lowest class of liquor dealers were far from zealous in their opposition to prohibitive legislation. They foresaw that the result to them would be simply a sale for liquor without the license fee. Drunkenness instead of having diminished appears to have increased.[15]

The alliance of bootleggers and clerics, who both opposed legal drinking, infuriated many wets who felt that controlling their social habits was an infringement of their freedom. So when the Privy Council decision supported Sir Oliver Mowat, who had promised to pass a prohibition measure for Ontario, the battle lines were once more drawn. The drys sensed victory from their successful lobbying in Ontario and now began to intensify their activity.

The jubilant Temperance forces pressed for and obtained a number of provincial plebiscites that showed a majority in favour of prohibition; this campaign culminated in a nationwide plebiscite in 1898. To carry the prohibition campaign to a successful conclusion, an enormous amount of Temperance literature was distributed. For example, the Dominion Alliance alone distributed 8,757,000 leaflets and 10,000 posters, while the Dominion W.C.T.U. had separate literature mailings; this thorough program produced two copies of the prohibition message for every man, woman and child in Canada. The cry, now that Ontario seemed to be won, was "On to

Ottawa," where Oliver Mowat was now Sir Wilfrid Laurier's Minister of Justice. But the public proved to be apathetic, as only 500,000 voted in the much-publicized national plebiscite. There was a razor-thin majority of 13,687 for prohibition, but Quebec emphatically rejected the proposal by a ratio of over four to one. Sir Wilfrid Laurier pointed out to the Dominion Alliance delegates that only one-fifth of the electorate of Canada had bothered to vote and, therefore, a national prohibition measure was not practical politics. Temperance groups now returned to the fray at the provincial and local levels. It seemed that Manitoba would be the first province to enforce prohibition when the Methodist Church secured a provincial prohibition law. But the wets fought back, aided by the Ontario Licenced Victuallers, to defeat the liquor law at the polls. When, in turn, Ontario had an election in 1902, the prohibitionists were aided by their Manitoba allies, such as Dr. Carman of the Methodist Church, and campaigned vigorously to secure the election of drys. Yet despite frequent references to Mowat's pledge to secure prohibition, the drys of Ontario could not induce the returned Liberal administration to enact a province-wide prohibitory measure.

THE BREWERS IN THE TWENTIETH CENTURY

Prohibition did not succeed in Britain either. A prominent Liberal, John Morley, had called the prohibition cause "the greatest movement since the movement for the abolition of slavery." But in the Imperialistic mood of the 1890's, the argument of the Conservative Lord Bruce had more appeal: he argued that "every year the [liquor] trade contributes £40,000,000 to the revenue of the country, so that practically it maintains the Army and Navy, besides which it affords employment to thousands of persons."[16] Temperance advocates were, however, encouraged by a decision of the House of Lords in 1891 that declared that the licences of public houses were limited to one year at a time, and had to be renewed annually. This legal decision seemed to offer hope that the number of establishments selling alcohol could soon be reduced, and that total prohibition might follow.

217

The Conservative party took steps to ensure, however, that licencing was taken out of the hands of the local authorities by the Licence Act of 1904, which authorized the Justices of the Peace to meet in quarterly sessions to issue licences. The chagrin of Temperance advocates can easily be appreciated, and they were also up in arms at a further provision of the Act that authorized the creation of a fine to be levied upon the brewing trade to compensate pub owners whose licences were taken away. Sir Wilfrid Lawson of the United Kingdom Alliance said it was a "vicious principle" which endowed the devilish trade. Yet to the credit of the brewing industry, an effort was made to improve the quality of the public houses they owned and it was this factor that tended to draw the teeth from the attack of the dry lobby.

In the United States, the breweries who owned seventy per cent of the taverns were indifferent to the advantages to be gained from improved public relations. A barkeeper was evicted if sales dropped and the main objective of the approximately three thousand breweries was to carve out the largest possible profit while they could. Well-meaning friends of the brewers advised them to evade the criticism of the moral crusade of the Temperance lobby by closing saloons in red-light districts, but the warnings went unheeded. Improving conditions was opposed to the widely held conviction that drink was the most important cause of poverty, and that the drinker should be capable of self-improvement. Another theory was that of merchants who argued that if the worker spent less on alcohol, he could buy more dry goods. Hence businessmen backed temperance as a sound business practice that encouraged the virtues of work and efficiency. Saving their workers from the evils of drink was regarded as more important by businessmen than providing a decent environment in which they could relax. For, if the taverns were improved, the chances of getting a worker to buy dry goods might diminish even further. Furthermore, the Puritan virtues held by many of the employers were not shared by their overworked Roman Catholic labourers from Europe. Thus the tavern owners for a variety of reasons were in a poor position for resisting the final assault of the prohibitionists.

THE STRUGGLE IN AMERICA

In 1900 approximately twenty-three per cent of Americans lived in dry areas, mainly in rural states. Politicians at Washington sought to avoid the pressure of the Temperance lobby. Congress did, however, yield in 1901 to the patriotic appeal of the Anti-Saloon League that all alcohol should be prohibited in Army canteens. The League made a practice of lobbying inside the Democratic and Republican parties, supported by church members who endorsed this activity to secure national prohibition laws. In the six-year period after 1906, the same pressure on state legislators caused seven more states to enact prohibition. In that year of 1912, the Anti-Saloon League turned out on their printing presses 250,000,000 book pages of literature a month. In spearheading this attack, the Anti-Saloon League had some powerful allies. The American Medical Association backed prohibition as it feared the rivalry of patent medicines, laced with alcohol, might lose its members both patients and fee. Protestant churches in the midwest equated Rum with Romanism, and both with the evils of the alien city culture. For the census of 1910 had shown that those wicked city dwellers and the foreign-born together comprised over half the population: this imparted a new sense of urgency to the mission of the drys. William Jennings Bryan, the voice of rural America, explained his attitude towards closing saloons at a Democratic state convention in Nebraska. Bryan declared, "This is a moral question. There is but one side to a moral question. Which do you take?" This type of closed reasoning indicates the evangelical zeal of the Temperance advocate although, in company with the President and Bryan's fellow aspirants to the White House, Bryan avoided the temperance issue on public platforms whenever possible. In 1913, on the eve of the First World War, the drys secured the Webb-Kenyon Act which prohibited the transportation of liquor to dry states and gave them their first national victory. The large Eastern cities, however, were still wet.

THE ERA OF THE GREAT WAR

In Britain, the last major event in the liquor problem before the war occurred in 1908 when the Liberals made a last assault on the liquor industry, which they regarded as a Conservative pressure group: David Lloyd George increased liquor taxes, which was a popular measure among the drys in his Liberal party. Ontario had also had a last fling at the liquor question when, in 1911, the provincial Liberal party adopted an "Abolition of the Bar" programme. A Conservative supporter wrote to his leader about the activities of the Liberal leader.

> Mr. Rowell. . .is in our section just now. He with his family are touring in an auto, our township, taking with them from our town a couple of the leading "Abolition of the Bar" admirers and they are calling on all the Methodist clergymen. . . . I fear this claptrap cry will catch many a Conservative vote.[17]

Underlying the Temperance agitation in 1911 had been the desire to return to a simple majority in order to decide local option plebiscites, rather than the sixty per cent majority required by law since 1905. In this sense, the "Abolition of the Bar" campaign, aimed at limiting opportunities for drinking in wet areas, was a Liberal move to secure dry votes preparatory to repealing the Conservatives' three-fifths majority. In the subsequent election of December 1911, the Conservative party under Sir James Whitney was, however, returned again to power. Temperance supporters in Ontario were frustrated once more at the polls, but it was not to be long before wartime conditions began to create a climate where abstention from liquor would be seen as a patriotic act.

On August 4, 1914, Britain went to war and the wets-versus-drys struggle abated there. On the other hand, when in October of 1914 the first Canadian contingent of troops was stationed at Salisbury Plain in England, a new era in Canada's liquor struggle began. General Hughes, Canada's Minister of Defence, insisted that the canteen used by these troops should be dry; the absence of alcohol would make this training camp the only dry one in the British Isles. Soon afterwards, the Dominion government at home was forced to admit that Canadian troops had not only secured liquor, but had created disorders in neighbouring English towns. Because of this unrest among the supposedly dry Canadian troops under his command, British General Alderson authorized wet canteens which, considering that most of the soldiers were British-born, seemed to be a reasonable solution. When the news reached Canada, a howl of protest resulted. General Hughes resented being overruled; the President of the W.C.T.U. personally chastised Prime Minister Robert Borden; the Moderator of the Methodist Church led those who sent indignant telegrams to Ottawa, questioning General Alderson's "moral right to treat Canadian motherhood in such a shameful way." Part of this hysterical reaction was due to the wartime fervour of sacrifice, self-denial and righteous indignation aroused by the battle against the Prussian monsters; Canadian troops must be mentally and physically fit to grapple with the Hun. Furthermore, the ladies in Canada were well aware that the American Armed Forces, although they had not yet joined the War, were prohibited the use of alcohol. For in April 1914, Josephus Daniels, Secretary of the Navy and a dry, had prohibited the use of liquor by sailors. The Navy thus joined the American Army which had long had dry canteens and, to ensure the world's soberest fighting forces, Congress now added dry zones of a five-mile radius around military camps. The mood of America too was one of promoting self-sacrifice, and the General Federation of Women's Clubs put a ban on such dances as the tango and the hesitation waltz. This sombre mood still prevailed in 1919, when the Methodist Church would not approve a decorous dance step enticingly called the Wesleyan Waltz.

Sacrifice was also called for by David Lloyd George, Britain's Chancellor of the Exchequer in 1915, who provided patriotic ammunition for the Temperance advocates. Britain had traditionally been a country of wets but, as Lloyd George explained, "Drink is doing us more damage in the war than all the German submarines put together." Lloyd George proposed a dual solution of high taxation on alcoholic beverages and complete control by the State of the liquor trade in certain key industrial areas. Increased taxes were voted down but state control of liquor was authorized under the Defence of the Realm emergency regulations, passed in May 1915. A central control board was established to restrict the number and opening hours of public houses, and purchase on credit at public houses was forbidden. In the city of Carlisle, the local authority moved in to establish direct control of public houses, which still exists in 1972, despite Lloyd George's claim that it was to be a wartime emergency measure. Yet even after the passage of the legislation to control drink, Lloyd George stated on October 29, 1915 that "We are fighting Germany, Austria and Drink; and, as far as I can see, the greatest of these three deadly foes is Drink." The statements of this leading British politician, which included speculations about a plan to nationalize the liquor industry, were given considerable publicity by the temperance groups in Canada.

The Temperance movement in Canada was closely related to the campaign to extend the franchise to women. This combination of goals has already been noted for the W.C.T.U. in the United States and, during the Grear War, the related Dominion sisterhood began to agitate for the vote. The advocates of female suffrage may have counted on the ladies adding to the dry vote on any future referendum concerning national prohibition, for the considerable success obtained in drying up many municipalities by the local option provisions of the Canada Temperance Act was seen as merely the first step towards total prohibition. Meanwhile pressure on provincial governments resulted in Saskatchewan becoming, in 1915, the first province to enact prohibition as a wartime measure.

The Demon Rum was now under fierce attack, for the Canadian Temperance lobbies had additional arguments to present during wartime. The vast sums of money spent on alcoholic beverages should, it was argued, be diverted to pay for the war. The factory worker and farmer behind the fighting man should not be so unpatriotic as to consume strong drink that would cause absenteeism and inefficiency.

Naturally, brewers, distillers and some trade-union leaders resisted the cries of their enemies whom they termed the "sin-hounds": but they were fighting a losing battle. Even British Columbia which had formerly been unresponsive to Temperance activity had, by 1915, accepted the idea of local option for the duration of the war. And in 1916 there was an "over the top" campaign by the prohibitionists which was considerably influenced by favourable news from the United States.

Woodrow Wilson was re-elected in 1916 mainly because of his promise that he would keep America out of the war. Following Wilson's victory, William Jennings Bryan threw political caution to the wind as he realized that he would never be President. Bryan now used his influence in rural America to aid the drive for prohibition. Further evidence of the rising dry campaign was provided by the druggists of America who dropped the words whisky and brandy from the list of drugs included in the Pharmacopoeia of the United States. Furthermore, Allied propaganda in America furnished drys with ammunition for patriotic attacks on those breweries that had German names, despite the support that German-Americans had given Wilson in his election campaign. Although America was not yet involved in the war in 1916, the mounting influence of their drys intensified the impact upon a Canada whose increasing exertions in the Allied cause had led to further restrictions on liquor.

Once more the Methodist, Baptist and Presbyterian churches launched a crusade for prohibition in individual provinces. On July 1, 1916, under the pressure of the Temperance and Moral Reform League of Alberta, that province closed beer parlours and liquor houses. Only Temperance beer could be sold in Alberta—this beverage contained less than 2½% alcohol. Manitoba followed the same path, while the Dominion Government aided the temperance cause by passing a law making it an offence to send liquor into any dry province. The campaign continued with a rally held by the Dominion Alliance on November 20, 1916 at Massey Hall in Toronto. The resolution adopted at this rally neatly combined patriotism and prohibition, for it concerned:

...preventing any impairment of the efficiency of our country's manhood, in the Dominion's present great effort to aid the Empire in her self sacrificing struggle for the principles of honour and justice and liberty, the Dominion [therefore should]...be earnestly urged to enact as a war measure, a law prohibiting the manufacture of intoxicating liquor....The question of maintaining or repealing the same to be submitted in a referendum to the electors after the war, but not before the expiry of three years from the time of the act going into force.[18]

But while the climate was becoming more favourable for securing the desired action by Ottawa, there was not yet complete conviction that such a drastic step would aid the war effort.

In 1917 the United States entered the war and American war hysteria provided further ammunition for the dry lobby. German troops were reported to have committed atrocities while under the influence of alcohol and this cast an unfavourable light on Hun brewers in the U.S. By this reasoning, it became unpatriotic to drink beer produced by German-American brewers like Pabst and Busch. The real reason for this campaign can be seen in the politics of the key state of Ohio, where the German-American vote of Cincinatti and Cleveland had defeated the state referendums on prohibition of 1914, 1915 and 1917. What added fury to the assault of the drys was the revelation that German-American brewers had financed newspaper coverage to fight the drys' "over the top" campaign. Patriotism may be the last refuge of scoundrels but, in this particular instance, it served the drys' purpose of equating winning the war with undermining the power of the German-American brewing interests. Alcohol was also condemned by the President of the American Medical Association who stated that his organization disapproved of it, either as a beverage or as a therapeutic agent. This action by the A.M.A., like the similar condemnation of alcohol in the previous year by the druggists' organization, was probably based more on eliminating unwelcome competition from the manufacturers of "strong" patent medicines, than on any moral point of view. Yet, to the dry lobby, this official medical endorsement of their campaign for prohibition was a godsend. This wave of wartime abstinence promoted a desire to reserve grain for badly needed food rather than spirituous liquor and was bound to reinforce the successful dry lobby of Western Canada.

THE SPIRIT OF SACRIFICE

The war was lasting much longer than Canadians had anticipated, and by 1917 a higher percentage of native-born Canadians were enlisting in the army. Yet the number of volunteers was deemed inadequate and Sir Robert Borden decided to introduce conscription. To carry this conscription measure through Parliament, women were enfranchised, giving them an important voice in the affairs of the nation. Canadian mothers and wives were naturally concerned about protecting their loved ones from the vices of Europe. And the terrible bloodletting in the disastrous Passchendaele campaign in the fall of 1917 heightened the spirit of sacrifice. With this background, it is possible to understand the final successful drive of the prohibitionists in North America.

More than two-thirds of the American states had adopted prohibition laws. When Congress was debating the wisdom of introducing national prohibition, Congressman Cooper of Ohio cited Lloyd George, who was now Prime Minister of England, as seeing the liquor trade as a greater enemy than Germany or Austria. The war fever enabled the Prohibitionists to carry the Eighteenth Amendment prohibiting intoxicating liquor in the United States, with both Republicans and Democrats endorsing the view of the Anti-Saloon League that this was not a party issue. The historic day for approving prohibition came on December 18th, 1917. Canadian politicians could no longer resist the intense Temperance pressure for a similar measure and six days later, an order-in-council prohibited the manufacture in Canada of alcoholic beverages of more than 2½% alcoholic content. Canada's prohibitory measure was to last for the duration of the war and for one year after peace had been declared. The prohibition applied to all provinces, except Quebec who refused to accept it, and Ontario's native wine was exempted in the interests of the Niagara fruit belt.

Patriotic zeal had finally carried prohibition in North America. To the pre-war emphasis on protecting children and females had been added the wartime demand for protecting young men who were serving their country far from home. Yet even as the drys rejoiced in 1918 there were early rumblings of a counter-offensive, for the situation overseas was rather different from the newly dry North America. An American intelligence officer serving in France wrote in September 1918, "Place full of newcomers, trying to dry up France in one evening. Also full of tarts, with Yanks falling in en masse."[19] The problem of the "returned man" would become increasingly evident in future years as the heroes returned to America; the family's conception of what Daddy did in the Great War often differed from the way Daddy remembered it.

On January 29, 1919, the Eighteenth Amendment was ratified by the states and the U.S.A. became dry. Yet even while bowing to the dry lobby, Congress had ensured that the law could not completely be enforced. For in the Eighteenth Amendment, the weasel word "intoxicating" was used rather than "alcoholic" and, while it was easy to prove alcoholic content, it was far more difficult to prove drunkenness. To close this loophole, the Volstead Act, named after Congressman Andrew Volstead of Minnesota, was passed. This Act, to come into effect on January 16, 1920, defined the word "intoxicating" as ½% of alcohol by volume. However, the dry lobby still could not secure a ban upon drinking in homes, particularly as many Senators drank. Furthermore, all people in all classes of society did not partake of the spirit of self-sacrifice in which prohibition was passed. The Volstead Act was not to take effect for one year, and this enabled people who could afford it to stock up their cellars: for example, the Yale Club with prophetic insight laid in a fourteen-year supply of liquor. It might seem reasonable to assume that, with the war over, the political and emotional climate would have been more favourable to the wets. But as the German menace receded, a new villain was found in the Communist menace released by the Russian Revolution. Alben Barkley of

Kentucky said that he knew of nothing else in the world which contributed so much to Bolshevism as the pernicious doctrine of the wets.[20] At the National Convention of 1919, the leader of the Anti-Saloon League expressed similar sentiments when he said that, while the President wanted to make the world safe for democracy, the business of the Church of God was to make it sober everywhere.

Similar sentiments were being expressed in Canada as was shown by the response of Ottawa to the idea that Bolsheviks had plotted the Winnipeg General Strike. Yet even the idea of linking Bolshevism to the need for continued prohibition was not an appeal that would attract returning soldiers, who were harder to convert to prohibition than were the wartime legislators. This changed postwar situation was recognized by one of the leading Temperance advocates when he stated that "With the signing of the Armistice, it was at once seen that it would again become necessary for the temperance forces to become active in the Dominion sphere."[21]

Quebec, however, showed signs of weakening at the end of 1918 and only drew back from the brink of prohibition by permitting the exemption of wine and beer. The other provinces permitted the manufacture, but not the sale, of spirits, beer and wine.

During the driest days in Canada's history, there were many Canadians who remained confirmed wets, and among these was Stephen Leacock. Leacock was a humorist but definitely not of the dry variety, and his publicized address, "Brewery Bay, Orillia" did little to placate the local drys. As his biographer David Legate says, "After the majority of Canadian provinces in 1918 misguidedly decided to follow in the wake of the U.S. Volstead Act and bring prohibition to Canada, Leacock became a 'wet' crusader with a vengeance. Pernickety he may have been about payment for most of his public appearances, but he made it a principle not to accept money for anti-prohibition speeches."[22]

For the first time since the War of 1812, large numbers of Americans began to take an interest in crossing the Canadian border. Ironically, the automobiles built by Henry Ford enabled tourists to move northwards to obtain liquor at the same time that Ford was backing the Anti-Saloon League.

Canada's trade increased by leaps and bounds as "export companies" supported the effort to serve the thirsty Americans. Within the United States there was a growing sense of frustration, heightened by a split within Protestantism between the fundamentalist groups supporting rural Progressivism and the urban Social Gospellers. For example, in 1920 William Jennings Bryan spoke for rural America when he asked his famous question, "If you cannot get alcohol enough to make you drunk, why do you want alcohol at all?" Rural drys seemed to be forcing their ideas upon the recalcitrant urban section of the nation. Even individual families were split by the liquor issue, as when Ex-President William Taft became Chief Justice of the Supreme Court in 1921 and sternly enforced the law, while his own wife and family ignored it. The American Medical Association suddenly rediscovered the therapeutic value of whisky and beer: this tacit admission that they had been wrong in 1917 was resented by some prohibitionist politicians. By the terms of a compromise measure, the Willis Campbell Act of 1921, a doctor was limited to writing no more than a hundred prescriptions for therapeutic liquor in a ninety-day period. Even at the level of the White House there was a problem because President Warren Harding had brought his "Ohio gang," a group of poker-playing hard-drinking cronies, to Washington. Now the Department of Justice dealt in graft from bootleggers, while dispensing pardons like a medieval Pope. Rum and Romanism were appearing in strange places.

ILLEGAL SHIPPING AND DRINKING

Rum-running became a Canadian occupation that rivalled the more traditional vocation of fishing on the Great Lakes and on both sea coasts. Between 1918 and 1922 imports of British liquor into Canada increased six times, as Canada became a pipeline to the United States. The term Rum Row was used to describe the Canadian "fishing" vessels that lined up outside the three-mile limit of New York City, where the American federal government lacked jurisdiction. International complications developed when Lord Curzon, Britain's Foreign Secretary, objected to American efforts to expand territorial limits beyond this three-mile limit and also to applying the Volstead Act to British vessels. A compromise was worked out in 1924 whereby visiting British ships could carry liquor under seal, while the U.S. Coast Guard had the opportunity to chase and search the fast Canadian rum-runners within one hour's steaming distance from the shore. As Canadian "export houses" began to reap huge profits from the liquor trade, and as respect for public order diminished, provincial governments began to see the need to discard their prohibition laws. Quebec and British Columbia adopted in 1921 a system of placing liquor sales under direct government control. Manitoba followed in 1923, Alberta in 1924, Saskatchewan in 1925 and Ontario and New Brunswick in 1927. American tourists grew to love the Canadian outdoors. The provincial governments, who controlled the liquor revenues, had publicity campaigns that stressed the warm welcome and traditional hospitality of Canadians.

But there were problems. Prime Minister W.L. Mackenzie King, who presided over this Canadian assistance programme to thirsty Americans, ran into the problem of a customs scandal in 1926. The liquor traffic across the border was reaching new heights despite King's assurance to Alberta's W.C.T.U. in the previous year, that he would give it serious consideration. The "official" exports in 1926 comprised more than one million gallons of spirits, which provided revenue welcomed by provincial treasurers. Unfortunately for Prime Minister King, a Parliamentary Committee uncovered evidence that certain customs officials were permitting additional liquor to be smuggled into the United States. It looked as if the government would be unable to continue in office in view of the Opposition's impending vote of no confidence, expected to be supported by the Western Progressives, who were' aghast at this moral crime. Prime Minister King was equal to the occasion, however, for he diverted Canadians' attention to the wicked impropriety of the Governor General, Lord Byng. For Lord Byng, being an Englishman, had some strange notion of treating each political party with impartiality and felt that Arthur Meighen, Mackenzie King's Conservative opponent, should have the chance of forming a

A L C O H O L

The **DRUNKARD** is subject to
**Tuberculosis, Venereal Diseases,
Delirium Tremens, General Debility.**

The DRUNKARD has children threatened with
Tuberculosis, Rickets, Insanity, Epilepsy.

ALCOHOLISM

MEANS DEATH TO THE NATION

Reproduced by permission from "Principles of Hygiene," published by the Government of the Province of Quebec c. 1925

government as he possessed a larger party following. King quickly diverted the attention of Canadians to the idea that Lord Byng was treating him as a colonial. The seriousness of this constitutional crime in Canada was soon demonstrated to be much more important than mere smuggling of booze, for King returned triumphantly from the election of 1926, while Byng retreated to England.

While the temperance lobby had died down after 1918, England was enjoying a considerable improvement in the standard of behaviour of her drinkers. Due to the impact of the Great War, the hours and number of public houses were reduced. Taxes on liquor were raised during the war to very steep levels, raising the price of a bottle of Scotch whisky from its prewar level of 3s 6d to 25s, an increase of over 700 per cent. Yet the drink trade was not ruined, for as public houses became more respectable, they attracted a wider clientele. In Southern England numbers of roadhouses were built to cater to motorists, while village taverns began to cater to a brisk week-end trade. The English pub was increasing in status in the 1920's at the very time when Americans were having considerable problems with wets who refused to be drys, and would even break the law to resist their conversion. The term "speakeasy" came into vogue, denoting a bootlegging establishment whose door was opened to those who whispered the right word. In New York City the number of speakeasies was double that of the legal saloons that had existed before Prohibition. Citizens bought "do-it-yourself kits for the home moonshiner" and turned out bathtub gin. Governor Alfred E. Smith of New York State saw the futility of trying to enforce prohibition in a large metropolitan area and, in 1923, repealed the state law. Smith would pay the penalty five years later, when as the Democratic Presidential candidate, he was violently resisted by the dry Protestants of America, on the grounds of his unsuitability both as a wet and as a Roman Catholic.

Protestant drys had not, however, anticipated several developments within the United States that made Governor Smith's action seem justified. Brewers were producing regular beer, then removing most of the alcohol in it to make the beverage conform to the "near beer" of the Volstead Act.

231

This removed alcohol was shipped with the legal product to enable the purchaser to "spike" the beer back to its original condition. Similarly, under Section 29 of the Volstead Act the manufacture of fermented fruit juices was permitted. The California wine industry flourished as it produced "wine tonics" of high alcoholic content but little medicinal value. Emigrants from Europe in New York City, Chicago, Boston, Philadelphia and Pittsburgh suddenly felt the need for an increased supply of these Californian tonics. This desire does not seem unreasonable when one keeps in mind that a Pittsburgh steelworker slaved 12 hours a day, 7 days a week, for a total of 84 hours. As Samuel Gompers, the leader of the American Federation of Labour, stated, the prohibition of beer seemed like class legislation that hurt the worker, not the rich.

But more serious was the deterioration of respect for law and order. Only 4,500 agents were recruited to enforce prohibition and these, because they were not covered by civil servant competitive examination conditions, were usually appointed through patronage and presented ample opportunities for graft. The federal government soon found itself in the uncomfortable position of having to prosecute some of its own enforcement officers on charges of taking bribes. Among the visitors to speakeasies were many emancipated women, and this development tended to undermine the drys' argument that women, as moral guardians of the nation, were opposed to drink. A further problem emerged because of the variation in the quality of liquor served in speakeasies. Just as Appalachian moonshiners had discovered a way to give a real "kick" to their product by adding dead rats or bad meat to the corn mash, of nearly half a million gallons of so-called whisky and gin seized and analyzed in New York in 1927, ninety-eight per cent contained poisons. Over sixty people died of wood poisoning in that one city alone. It might be thought that there would be general agreement on the need to eliminate the production of such poison, but this was not the view of one newspaper reader. The influential Hearst press gave prizes for readers' solutions to the liquor problems, and one letter endorsed the practice of trying to kill drinkers. A dedicated female dry suggested selling poisoned liquor through the bootleggers so that hundreds of thousands would die; these casualties would be worthwhile, she thought, for they would ensure proper enforcement of the law. This suggestion, although somewhat extreme, did point up the fact that law enforcement was impossible when millions of Americans wanted to disobey the law of the land. With billions of dollars involved in the liquor trade, underpaid American policemen were paid off in protection money. Large cities could not enforce the law in an atmosphere where the need for corruption and graft by bootleggers was accepted as inevitable by citizens.

THE WETS COUNTERATTACK

In 1926, concerned Americans launched an Association Against the Prohibition Amendment (A.A.P.A.). This organization copied the tactics of the Anti-Saloon League and flooded magazines with lurid accounts of bootleggers. Drinking was seen as "striking a blow for liberty." The middle classes of America were becoming receptive to the idea that no central government could legislate upon their moral behaviour.

There was one group of Americans who could use prohibition as moral justification of their social attitude. White Southerners, while ostensibly in favour of prohibition, at the same time used the odd drunk Negro as an example of the need for white superiority. For the 1920's were a time when bigotry flourished. The rapid growth of the Ku Klux Klan opposed to "niggers, Jews, Catholics and foreigners" displayed an ugly side of life that flourished in a decade when respect for the law did not. In the Presidential election of 1928 such prejudices were displayed to the nation. The Roman Catholic Alfred Smith campaigned on a wet ticket against Herbert Hoover, the Republican candidate, who supported prohibition.

During that election year the printing presses of the Women's Christian Temperance Union at Evanston, Illinois, produced ten million copies of a pamphlet detailing the wet record of Al Smith. Once Smith had been nominated at the Democratic Convention, an attack came from Bishop James

Cannon Jr., a Methodist clergyman, who reflected the rural values of America. In the liberal weekly *The Nation* of July 4, 1928, the Bishop urged his·fellow Democrats to vote for the Republican candidate, as "Governor Smith is personally, ecclesiastically, aggressively, irreconcilably Wet." A whispering campaign developed that stressed Smith was a Roman Catholic and incited Americans of the "one hundred per cent type" not to vote for him. Smith's anti-Prohibition views were anathema to the dedicated drys within the Protestant churches. So although Al Smith succeeded in carrying the Northern cities, he was resoundingly rejected in the rural sections and Herbert Hoover became President.

The drys rejoiced at this victory of 1928 but it was to be their last triumph. America was going wet; for example, in that year it was estimated that doctors made forty million dollars out of writing medicinal prescriptions for liquor. Furthermore, the Association Against the Prohibition Amendment now formed a women's section, led by such fashionable society matrons as Mrs. Pierre du Pont and Mrs. Coffin Van Rennselaer. Repeal now became a social movement endorsed by the smart set who popularized the idea of serving cocktails before dinner. A new hero was discovered in the rum-runner; one of these, Captain William McCoy, became famous for the high quality of his cargo and has been commemorated in the phrase "the real McCoy." In spite of the changing mood of the country, President Herbert Hoover approved the Jones Act which finally put teeth into the Volstead Act by stipulating maximum penalties for a bootlegger's first offence of five years in jail and a $10,000 fine. The Department of Justice took over the duty of enforcing the provisions of the Eighteenth Amendment, a duty fairly easy in sympathetic rural areas but very difficult in many cities. When the biggest bootlegger in the business, super-gangster Al Capone of Chicago, was jailed, he claimed—not without some justice— that he was performing a public service in supplying liquor. Across the border Canadians were performing a similar function for frustrated American wets, but did not often go to jail.

Even Nova Scotia, a province long known as a Temperance area, deserted the dry cause in 1930 by repealing its prohibition law. Only Prince Edward Island was now left to uphold the cause of Temperance. It is true that the Canadian government did make a real effort to check the flow of liquor into the United States after 1930, in line with President Hoover's efforts to enforce the law south of the border. Yet the American Wickersham Commission which investigated the Prohibition experiment reported in 1931 that "Liquor revenues of the Canadian government increased four times during prohibition, while consumption of the Canadian population almost halved."[23]

It is hard to imagine the staid Prime Minister Mackenzie King being identified closely with the American Roaring Twenties but, statistically speaking, the country he led seems to have made a major contribution to the frolics of that era. It is true that the provinces controlled liquor within their borders but it is also true that the federal government acted to ensure that it was the governments that secured all available liquor: by the federal Importation of Intoxicating Liquors Act of 1928, the importing of liquor into any province was forbidden unless it was consigned to His Majesty, the Executive Government, or a government agency vested with the right to sell liquor. As Prime Minister Mackenzie King ensured that provincial premiers had a monopoly on the control of liquor, with the attendant revenue, it is not surprising he was a respected politician. The significance of liquor as a political issue in Canada can only be understood when one keeps in mind that our "export companies" supported the supremacy of the drys in the United States.

With the onset of the Great Depression the wets in the United States gained many new allies. The revival of the beer and liquor industries was seen as one way to revive employment. Businessmen now saw taxes on liquor as a way to ease the heavy taxation on their own enterprises and such prominent industrialists as John D. Rockefeller Junior deserted prohibition. Furthermore, the distress in the large cities gave a new sense of determination to urban workers and by 1931 there was an ugly mood in industrial areas. Alarmed employers soon decided that legalizing beer was one way to relieve class hatred. Against the newly militant wets, the loyal prohibitionist was helpless. In 1932 Franklin Delano

Roosevelt campaigned on a promise to eliminate prohibition and his presidential victory was seen as a victory for the wets. On February 20, 1933 the Twenty-first Amendment repealed prohibition and, when the Amendment had been ratified by the requisite number of states, the problem of liquor control was in that year passed back to local authorities.

North America was now back to where it had been before World War One. The liquor issue was not dead, however, as some western states and the province of Prince Edward Island continued to be dry. The issue was still very much alive in Ontario, where there was a split in the provincial Liberal party about the provincial laws governing the sale of beer, wine and spirits. The leader of the Ontario Liberals, Mitchell F. Hepburn, adroitly used the liquor issue to win the election of 1933. In his campaign to the electorate, he stressed to temperance advocates that the Conservative party was wet, while inside his party he encouraged acceptance of the Liquor Law passed by the same Conservatives. There were other issues involved in his election, but his victory did indicate that the rural vote in Ontario was influenced by the implication that farmer Hepburn was ostensibly dry. In the few years that remained before World War II captured the attention of Canadians, the major problems for most workers were unemployment and an adequate diet, rather than the liquor question.

WARTIME DEVELOPMENTS

The wartime emergency between 1939 and 1945 caused the federal government of Canada to introduce controls over liquor and beer. Under War Order No. 14 of November 1, 1942 the production of distilleries was commandeered to ensure an adequate wartime supply of industrial alcohol. Prime Minister Mackenzie King explained in a broadcast of December 16, 1942 that the consumption of spirits had increased by 37½% since the start of the war, and beer consumption was up by 60%. Consumption of alcohol was climbing, despite sharply increased taxation. Ottawa felt it was necessary to restrict production and this was accomplished under the Wartime Alcoholic Beverages Order which limited the supply of wine and beer, while ensuring that spirits were no stronger than 70 per cent proof. Prime Minister King outlined the need for wartime controls in a way which sounds far less militant than the statements made during World War One. King appealed for support for his policy of a moderate temperance approach to the liquor problem in these terms:

> As we all know, many persons, young and old, merely accept stimulants because they think it is expected of them... To most sensitive natures it requires more courage not to yield to some social habit, or fashion or custom, than it does to face physical danger.[24]

King abstained from all intoxicating liquor during the balance of the war as an example to his countrymen.

Members of the Canadian Armed Forces overseas were also engaged in learning to drink in moderation. As a result of the Allied defeats suffered in 1940 which pushed the Allied forces back to Britain, most Canadians overseas spent much of the war in a Britain where visiting the "pub" was an accepted social custom. The impact of this wartime experience can be readily seen today in the numerous Canadian versions of the pub, which range from the inside of a Canadian Legion Hall to a hotel beverage room to a converted basement. Any postwar immigrant from Britain has likely had the experience of being told by a Canadian ex-serviceman about the virtues of the pubs that both left behind. After 1942, American troops also became wartime guests in Britain. It became relatively easy, two years later, to distinguish between the G.I. who had become acclimatized, and the new arrival who drank as if the pub were going to close or go dry at any moment. The new arrival was not to be criticized in view of his country's history in enforcing liquor legislation, particularly as this had involved successful attempts to provide the world's soberest fighting men. Events seemed to be coming full circle. Descendants of stern Puritan emigrants were returning for a twentieth-century refresher course.

LEGAL AND MEDICAL ISSUES

In any discussion of past and present attitudes towards alcohol, it must be emphasized that excessive drinking can be a serious problem. For example, the law on both sides of the Atlantic subscribes to the idea that drunkenness can produce temporary insanity, as seen in the attitude to unpremeditated murder committed under the influence of intoxication: in England the charge is changed to manslaughter, and in the United States to one of murder in the second degree. Even more significant is the recognition that alcoholism is a medical problem that requires treatment. The change in emphasis from moral guidance to medical treatment for alcoholics is a recognition of the gravity of the liquor problem. Britain, Canada and the United States all have a problem of alcoholism among segments of their population. The tragedy of alcoholics, estimated as numbering up to five million in the United States, attests to the magnitude of this disease; in Canada the Addiction Research Foundation of Ontario, founded in 1949, has estimated that the figure is about 30 out of every 1,000 drinkers. The efforts of Alcoholics Anonymous, an organization composed of drinkers with a medical problem, display the need for restoring health to these adults. Any organization that seeks to solve the problem of alcoholism deserves our commendation. The traffic policeman who seeks to prevent fatal accidents attributable to drunkenness needs support from the public at large. For the claim of the dry over the centuries that the drinking of alcohol can produce family tragedies is not without foundation, and the continued activity of Temperance groups serves to remind us that drinking can lead to tragedy as well as enjoyment.

According to surveys made by the Canadian Institute of Public Affairs,[25] the percentage of the population who are drinkers of alcoholic beverages has increased steadily since 1943. The Maritimes contain the largest percentage of drys, while the West has the greatest percentage of wets; among religious denominations, the Anglican and Roman Catholic Churches have had a higher percentage of wets than the

United Church. This information is consistent with the historical development of Canada.

MODERN CANADA

Canada has maintained a more powerful dry lobby than appears to be the case in the United States, judging from the beer advertisements which appeared on television until a change of legislation in 1971. A Briton or American was doubtless fascinated by his first sight of a Canadian beer commercial. Young actors and actresses sang and cavorted in a manner that displayed a real zest for life. By implication, we were led to understand that a certain brew had produced this remarkable burst of energy: but, unlike other commercials, the product was never seen. Recently, however, attitudes towards the consumption of alcohol seem to have been growing more relaxed in the major cities of Canada. This is not to imply, though, that the old political attitudes of Ontario have died. Since Premier George Drew introduced cocktail lounges into the province after World War II, the Conservative party has sought to reassure the dry voter. The Chairman of the Ontario Liquor Control Board has never been an average social drinker. As *The Toronto Telegram* of Wednesday, September 2, 1970 pointed out, the only two jobs barred to a drinker are the Presidency of the Ontario Temperance Federation, and the Chairmanship of the Ontario Liquor Licence Board. Such political caution seems to fly in the face of all the modern talk about the need for expert knowledge and experience. Yet there are signs that a drinker may yet climb to the leadership of the provincial body that controls him.

The liquor question continues to make the headlines. When President Nixon disturbed Canadians by his new economic policies in August of 1971, he particularly annoyed distillers. Mr. Nixon applied his ten per cent surcharge to imports of rye whisky from Canada, while desiring to discuss with Prime Minister Pierre Trudeau the issue of Canadians' failure to imbibe bourbon. According to the *Globe and Mail* of October 2, 1971:

The Nixon administration wants to change drinking habits on both sides of the border. . . .The United States gained a piddling $1.2 million from selling [879,645] gallons of bourbon to Canadians. . .while Canada earned $165.2 million from whisky sales [of 23 million gallons] south of the border.

Judging from the record, Mr. Nixon may have difficulty legislating changes in drinking habits. It is enough to make the red-blooded American voters of 1972 unite under the slogan, "Drinkers of the world unite! You have nothing to lose but your rye."

This chapter has merely sketched some of the highlights of the controversial subject of drinking alcoholic beverages and it is hoped that more detailed studies will emerge from other historians. For has there been any other subject in Anglo-American-Canadian history which has produced the spectacle of Yankees rushing up to Canada to drink the health of the King of England?

1. Richard H. Tawney, *Religion and the Rise of Capitalism* (New York: Mentor Press, 1954), p. 111.
2. John C. Miller, ed., *The Colonial Image* (New York: George Braziller, 1962), p. 16.
3. Goldwin Smith, *A History of England*, 3rd ed. (New York: Scribner's, 1966), p. 448.
4. Christopher Hibbert, *The Roots of Evil: A Social History of Crime and Punishment* (New York: Funk and Wagnalls, 1968), p. 43.
5. Great Britain, *Report of the Select Committee on the Timber Duties* (House of Commons Sessional Papers, XIX, 1835), p. 178.
6. Kenneth S. Inglis, *Churches and the Working Classes in Victorian England* (Toronto: University of Toronto Press, 1963), p. 47.
7. G. Kitson Clark, *The Making of Victorian England* (London: Methuen and Company, 1965), p. 128.
8. Andrew Sinclair, *Era of Excess: A Social History of the Prohibition Movement* (New York: Harper and Row, 1962), p. 101.
9. J.F. Glaser, "English Nonconformity and the Decline of Liberalism," *American Historical Review* 63: 356.
10. Harold E. Gorst, *The Earl of Beaconsfield* (London: Blackie and Son, 1900), p. 53.
11. *Times* (London), 18 January 1887, p. 9.
12. Stephen S. Alford, "Habitual Drunkards Act of 1879" (Paper read before the Social Science Association, London, England, February 2, 1880), p. 17.

13. Sinclair, *Era of Excess,* p. 107.
14. Ibid., p. 108.
15. J.A. Stevenson, *Before the Bar* (Toronto: J.M. Dent and Sons, 1919), p. 82.
16. Ebenezer Howard, *Garden Cities of Tomorrow* (New York: Transatlantic Arts, 1951), p. 41.
17. Charles A. Muna to Whitney, 16 August 1912, Whitney Papers, Ontario Department of Public Records and Archives, Toronto, Ontario.
18. Ruth E. Spence, *Prohibition in Canada* (Toronto: Ontario Branch of the Dominion Alliance, 1919), 191; 485.
19. Sinclair, *Era of Excess,* p. 118.
20. Ibid., p. 127.
21. Spence, *Prohibition in Canada,* p. 490.
22. David Legate, *Stephen Leacock* (Toronto: Doubleday Canada Limited, 1970), p. 96.
23. Sinclair, *Era of Excess*, p. 198.
24. H. Reginald Hardy, *Mackenzie King of Canada* (Toronto: Oxford University Press, 1949), p. 253.
25. Alcoholism Research Foundation, *Statistics of Alcohol Use and Alcoholism in Canada: 1871-1956* (Toronto: University of Toronto Press, 1958), p. 7.

6

Religion, Secularism
and Social Policy

*Said Waldershare, "sensible men are all the same
religion." "And pray what is that?" inquired the
prince. "Sensible men never tell."*

Benjamin Disraeli, *Endymion*

In the summer of 1970 crowds of American tourists converged on Plymouth, England. Official celebrations were
being held to commemorate the 350th anniversary of the
departure of the Mayflower. A Canadian reporter recorded an
interview with a local Anglican vicar who was opposed to the
celebration.

> I don't think they [the Pilgrim Fathers] deserve it. They
> were a miserable lot, thoroughly bigoted, most un-
> pleasant. In Massachusetts they were active in witch hunt-
> ing and massacring Indians.[1]

Obviously the achievements of any particular religious group
can be controversial.

THE SETTING

The survey in this chapter of the influence of Christianity
upon social reform is not intended to approve the role of any

one sect, or alternatively of those who do not have a religious affiliation. It is primarily concerned with the impact upon social policy of both Christian and secular reformers. The relation of the institutional church to poverty was discussed in Chapter One: here we are principally concerned with individual Christians who sparked movements that made contributions to social reform. As education has usually been considered the key to resolving social issues, this chapter will also examine some of the religious influences upon the development of education.

Many modern social problems emerged from the industrial revolution, with England being the first country to feel their impact. In the pre-industrial eighteenth century, Anglicans held a monopoly on places at England's two universities of Oxford and Cambridge, as well as at such "public schools" as Eton and Harrow and at most of the local grammar schools. The leaders of the nation came from an aristocracy that viewed education as a privilege to which they were entitled as preparation for their role of the ruling class. This Tory outlook was mitigated somewhat by the spirit of paternalism which implied that privilege carried responsibilities for helping the lower orders of society. However, noblesse oblige, port, and prejudice all tended to enforce the status quo, and the shattering impact upon society caused by the industrial revolution took the slumbering Church of England by surprise.

Political revolution was in the air in the second half of the eighteenth century, and John Wesley has been credited with preventing a revolution in England after 1760 by channelling discontent into religious forms. Wesley was conservative by nature and so was the Methodist movement he originated. In England, he rode into churchless industrial areas, preaching salvation by faith to the working classes. This was a hazardous undertaking; Wesley was stoned and abused for bringing the good news of the love of Jesus into industrial districts. Yet his sincerity won him many converts, as in the textile towns of the West Riding of Yorkshire. Workers, overworked and underpaid, felt that somebody cared about them. Within the Methodist circles, "brothers" and "sisters" learned to organize benefit clubs that loaned money to members in need. Furthermore, these groups taught men to read in order to have the Bible accessible to them. Men who were educated in the Chapel formed a working-class intelligentsia from which many trade union officials were drawn.

CAMP MEETINGS, CHURCH AND CHAPEL

As early as 1772 a group of Methodists from Yorkshire carried the faith to Cumberland County in Nova Scotia. Miners from Cornwall, another Wesleyan stronghold, emigrated to the United States. The American Revolution, however, loosened the tie between these Methodists in the United States and those in Great Britain. In the rural environment of America, an indigenous movement developed unique aspects such as the camp meeting, a form of revivalist gathering which often lasted for several days and provided pioneers with an emotional outlet.

When the province of Upper Canada was formed, American circuit riders carried the Methodist faith into pioneer communities there. Impassioned revivalist oratory against the sins of frivolity, dancing and drinking was welcomed by poor farmers, partially because such emotional outpourings served as a protest against officials in the capital of York and the established church they seemed to represent. The ruling caste, later labelled the Family Compact, was usually resented by the pioneer farmer. Religious affiliations thus came to imply different social classes. After the War of 1812, the heavy British immigration tended to blur distinctions based on religion, yet the early pattern persisted. The Anglican and the Presbyterian churches concentrated on serving the larger established centres like York or Kingston, where their well-trained ministers preached to wealthy and respectable congregations; itinerant Methodist preachers established contact with frontier communities. But as the total community grew in sophistication and wealth, the Methodists in turn became more conservative, constructing church buildings and adapting themselves to the needs of the business and professional classes.

Paradoxically, in North America the democratic spirit was often accompanied by a tendency to be intolerant

244

towards different religious practices; Britain did not claim to be democratic, but had learned to tolerate religious diversity. England had bitter memories of the laws of Cromwell's Republic and thought herself well rid of serious Puritans, who deplored the wickedness of mere pleasure. During the eighteenth and nineteenth centuries the established Church of England was generally tolerant of human frailty, particularly by comparison with the rigorous Methodists or the watchful Presbyterians in the Kirk of Scotland. This casual attitude towards religious observance made visitors wonder if England could even be considered a Christian country.

And if church or chapel attendance was taken as a measure of Christianity, then active believers were in a minority in Britain. Leaders of all denominations bemoaned the estrangement of the bulk of the working population. A Congregationalist leader wrote, "the bulk of our manufacturing population stand aloof from our Christian institutions."[2] Another observer, Friedrich Engels, recorded that in Manchester there prevailed an almost universal indifference to religion. Part of the trouble was that the Church of England had been slow to evangelize in the new industrial cities of the North. While it was supposed to be the national church, the Anglican church was too conservative to rise to the challenge posed by the new urban areas produced by the industrial revolution. Life was a brutal struggle for the factory hand and miner, who were understandably not interested in spending what little leisure time they had in listening to sermons. In the cotton-spinning districts of Lancashire, the immigrants from Ireland were apt to forget their Roman Catholic faith. Priests talked of a Catholic "leakage," while Irish workers talked of taking the "fastest way out of Manchester," oblivion through alcohol.

The religious sects formed by those who did not accept the teachings of the Church of England were called Nonconformist. An intense rivalry existed in Britain between these two main branches of Christianity, with both factions claiming to have greater national support. Because of the conflicting claims of religious leaders, Parliament decided to make an official investigation. On a particular Sunday in 1851, a religious census was taken. One of the revealing conclusions was that, "the masses of our working population . . . are never or but seldom seen in our religious congregations."[3] The reason was given as both a feeling that "religion [was] a purely middle-class luxury" and also "a genuine repugnance to religion itself."[4] This attitude reflected a widespread feeling that middle-class church- or chapel-goers were snobs and their ministers hypocrites. A plumber who wrote to the *Methodist Times* satirized the call of Christians to the non-worshipping masses:

> We want you, the working "classes" to attend our church; but you must not forget that you are the working "classes", and you must not on any account presume to be on an equal footing with ourselves, as you don't belong to our "set", and you should be grateful to us for our condescension in asking you to come at all.[5]

It is hardly surprising that the government report of 1851 concluded that members of the working class could best be described as "unconscious secularists."[6] This census was taken only in England and Wales; it is significant for understanding Canadian attitudes that observers of the working classes in Scotland noted that some workers there displayed an intense interest in religious dogma.[7]

EVANGELICALISM

In 1878, Parliament passed a Factory Act that decreed all textile mills must close "the whole of Christmas and Good Friday." Factory inspectors and parish priests had recommended this legislation, as they found it impossible to persuade some factory owners to observe Christian holidays. Humanizing or Christianizing the factory system was one of the "good works" engaged in by the Evangelicals, a group comprised of both Methodists and Low Church Anglicans.

The nineteenth-century equivalents to the modern crusades of Billy Graham were usually held in Exeter Hall, London. For most of the nineteeth century, this building was the centre of evangelical activity in Britain. In 1840 the first Anti-Slavery World Convention was held there. Soon

246

afterwards Lord Shaftesbury, a great evangelical philanthropist, presided over the first meeting of the Ragged School Union, which will be discussed in the chapter on education. Each year there were "May Meetings" which brought Anglican, Nonconformist and undenominational missionaries together. Sometimes as many as twenty-two meetings were held in a single day in the numerous rooms, which resounded with applause and hymn singing. But Evangelical fervour did not lead to church union and many doubted its authenticity: Exeter Hall was sometimes called the Hall of Humbug.

Christian virtues were in evidence in the reform of the so-called "public schools" that served the upper classes of Britain and are associated with the name of Dr. Thomas Arnold, headmaster of Rugby. Public schools were changed from "nurseries of vice" to nurseries of Christian gentlemen under a system of using older students as prefects to maintain discipline. Thomas Arnold stressed first, religious and moral principles; secondly, gentlemanly conduct; thirdly, intellectual ability. These ideas reflected the influence of John Locke, the philosopher, who had stressed that in educational matters the formation of character was more important than learning. Disciples of Thomas Arnold carried his ideas throughout an expanding net of private schools termed "public schools." Students at these boarding schools learned to "play the game" by exerting self-discipline on the sports field, while spiritual development was inculcated by daily attendance at chapel. Critics emphasized the limitations of this muscular Christianity yet, in a very real sense, these Victorian institutions trained the elite administrators of an expanding British Empire. The idea of training an elite in the Anglican and English tradition took root in the Canadas when at York, in 1831, Upper Canada College first opened its doors to train Christian gentlemen.

DIVERSITY OF FAITH

There were other types of religious influence carried across the Atlantic. Large numbers of Irishmen entered North America in the first half of the nineteenth century. Roman Catholics settled on the northeast coast of the United States, giving rise to the group known as the Boston Irish, while Protestants from Ulster usually made their way to Upper Canada. There were also Scots of Presbyterian, Roman Catholic and Baptist affiliations arriving in Upper Canada. Methodists and Baptists came from all parts of Britain, and many Englishmen claimed a vague connection to the Church of England. In the New World these immigrants tended to substitute religious sect for social class. Anglicans classified as "High" could look down on "Low" church Anglicans. Methodists who belonged to the Episcopal branch condescended to the mere Wesleyans, and despised the Primitive branch of the family. After the shattering impact upon Presbyterians of the Great Disruption in Scotland in 1843, supporters of the Free Kirk could detest other Scots who belonged to the Church of Scotland. In the eyes of the purists, the fact that the national church in Scotland had been willing to accept patronage from the state made it almost as bad as the Church of England.

The Anglicans claimed to be the established church in British North America. Staffing such an establishment proved to be difficult, as clerics in England were hesitant about leaving the comfort of their homes to pioneer in the colonies of the Maritimes or the Canadas. Men from the Celtic fringe showed less reluctance to emigrate and were often found in charge of the Church of England in Canada; the Scots-Irish contingent, as a result, exerted an influence on the Anglican Church far beyond its numbers. Canadian history books see nothing strange about Bishop John Strachan, a Scot, leading the Anglicans in Upper Canada while many Irishmen served as parish priests. Yet, "when Americans discover in Canada outstanding positions in the hands of Scots and Irishmen enthusiastic Protestants . . . they rub their eyes."[8]

The major difference, however, in the religious foundations of Canada and of New England lay in the type of Roman Catholic faith that took root in Quebec. The religious faith of New France has been described as "a kind of nineteenth-century Methodism in a seventeenth-century Catholic setting."[9] In the seventeenth century Jesuit Fathers established a mission to the Huron Indians around the southern edge of Georgian Bay, in what is now Ontario. Their missionary zeal reflected a different approach towards the native people of North America from that of New England. As Will Rogers once pointed out, paintings of the Pilgrims show them kneeling in prayer with muskets at their side. The prayer, Rogers explained, was for Divine help in getting something the Indians owned; the musket was to ensure that help was forthcoming.

Religious sects reflected social and national characteristics. The survival of the French-Canadian culture was linked to the Roman Catholic faith; seven classical colleges were founded between 1803 and 1832 to provide a flow of educated French Canadians who would enter the priesthood, law or politics.

THE CANADAS

In Upper Canada the main struggle over who should control education took place between Bishop John Strachan and Egerton Ryerson, the Methodist leader. Strachan was the dominant influence in the province until the 1830's and introduced the concept of quality education in grammar schools staffed by Anglican or Presbyterian teachers. Ryerson as an editor and educator attacked the exclusiveness of Strachan's educational structure and sought elementary education for all citizens. In 1841, the newly united Province of Canada tried to group Roman Catholics and Protestants under a Common School Act.

But in an age that believed in some form of religious instruction in school, it was obviously going to be difficult to decide whether to use the Douai Bible or the King James version. The great difference in the cultural outlook of the two former provinces necessitated a "dissentient clause" which allowed parents of either faith to make their own arrangements under trustees of their choice. In effect, this allowed separation of Catholics and Protestants and this is the point of origin of the two parallel school systems established in Lower Canada (Quebec). In 1843 an amendment was made to the law by the passage of an Act for the Establishment of Common Schools in Upper Canada which introduced a new concept of "separate schools." By the terms of this Act, only applicable in Upper Canada, it became unlawful to compel a child in a common school to read from any religious book, or join any religious exercise, to which his parents objected. Furthermore, if the teacher were Protestant "the Roman Catholic inhabitants shall have a separate school, with a teacher of their own persuasion." It seemed to Roman Catholics that Upper Canada intended to have all pupils in common schools under one management, only reluctantly "separated" on a religious basis when a parent insisted upon it. A great deal of distrust and misunderstanding was to flow from these early decisions about education in the United Province of Canada.

Denominational and ethnic distinctions helped to give meaning to the elusive quantity of a nineteenth-century Canadian identity. Transplanted Churches of England and Scotland had an official air and tended to represent the affluent in the cities; Toronto was possibly an exception with its prominent Methodists, exemplified by Timothy Eaton. As in Britain and the United States, Methodism in Canada had splintered into different organizations. In 1867 there were seven distinct Methodist groups in Canada, and Methodists felt that their voice would be strengthened if they amalgamated. By 1884 a new united Methodist Church of Canada had gathered together virtually all the individuals calling themselves Methodists. Church unification provided a stronger base in Eastern Canada from which to send preachers to the West, as well as strengthening the possibilities of social reform in the growing cities.

THE CHALLENGE OF SECULARISM

In Britain several attempts were made in the nineteenth century to provide the masses with a substitute for Christianity. Robert Owen, often called the father of British socialism, said in the 1820's that "all the religions of the world are in error." Owen financed Halls of Science to cultivate social science for the social improvement of mankind. Churchmen counter-attacked with the aid of local magistrates, who were often clerics, and sought to imprison "social missionaries" and prevent their public meetings. By the 1840's it looked as if the social missionary movement had been crushed. One social missionary, however, refused to accept this type of repression. George Holyoake continued to lecture and was accused of blasphemy and sentenced to jail, but his integrity slowly won great respect.

In the 1850's Holyoake encouraged a group of weavers to help themselves through co-operation; this group at Rochdale started the co-operative movement, which has since developed into the largest retail organization in modern Britain. The encouragement of workers' organizations was only one facet of Holyoake's activities, his beliefs developing from the statement of Tom Paine in *The Rights of Man* that "religion teaches men to be good."[10] Holyoake argued that the only way to do good was through material acts in this world. Such a view accorded well with those workers who felt that charity towards one's neighbour was the most important aspect of a religious life. Holyoake called the movement he launched "Secularism," and by 1856, there were thirty-six different Secularist societies organized from London to Glasgow.

Many of Holyoake's ideas were ahead of his time. He explained to workers in industrial districts the need for Saturday to be a Secular Sunday. His first reason was the need for recreation, because as he commented, "Had Moses foreseen the manufacturing system, instead of saying 'six days' he would have said 'five days shalt thou labour'." The other reason concerned air pollution, for he argued that a two-day break would enable the industrial smog of blast furnace fumes to disperse. Holyoake would have heartily approved of the air pollution index idea developed recently in North American cities.

Like the Christians, the groups known as Secularists had schisms. One radical exponent of Secularism was an Englishman named Charles Bradlaugh who attacked organized religion. Bradlaugh was a gifted orator who attracted large crowds and whose aggressive style can be judged from this attack on Christian beliefs:

it is one of the most ridiculous declarations of faith imaginable . . . a belief in Father, Son and Holy Ghost . . . The Father is somewhere in heaven, the Son sits at his right hand, and the Holy Ghost flies about in the bodily shape of a dove. What a curious picture to present to any reasonable man . . . a father begets a son from nothing, and a dove proceeds from the two of them . . . .[11]

By contrast, the other national leader of Secularism, Holyoake, refused to attack Christianity, and many clergymen appreciated his integrity, non-theistic though it was. For example, in 1861 the Reverend Samuel Earnshaw of Sheffield preached a sermon that indicated his sympathy for Holyoake's condemnation of what he called "predatory" Christianity. The sermon stated:

Great efforts are now being made to win back the masses . . . We read of monster congregations assembling in St. Paul's and in Westminster Abbey . . . working men will not go to these monster meetings . . . glaring inconsistencies in the lives of Christians must be done away with, in such things as tricks of the trade, short weights, deceptive advertisements.[12]

A number of clergymen in the nineteenth century were taking a critical look at the capitalistic structure. One group known as Christian Socialists sought to broaden the appeal of the Church of England by establishing the "Kingdom of Christ" as the true authority within the business and industrial community. The time was 1848, the year in which Karl Marx and Friedrich Engels issued their *Communist Manifesto* calling for workers of the world to unite. Charles Kingsley and J.F.D. Maurice sought to substitute Christian conviction for the revolutionary appeal of Marxism, using some methods not far from those advocated by Marx: they organized co-operative workshops which stressed profit-sharing, and Kingsley even sounded like Marx in his statement that the Bible had been used as "an opium dose for keeping beasts of burden patient."[13] Not all members of the clergy, however, held such views. In the United States, Henry Ward Beech intoned in a sermon of 1877:

252

It is said that a dollar a day is not enough for a wife and five or six children. No, not if the man smokes or drinks beer . . . But is not a dollar a day enough to buy bread with? Water costs nothing.[14]

An Anglican minister named Reverend Stewart Headlam was curate of a church in Bethnal Green, a very poor section of London. He attended Secularist meetings during the 1870's as an observer and his admiration for this "splendid humanitarianism" carried him to the point where he preached that the Secularists had in fact absorbed some of the best Christian truths, which the churches had been ignoring. Headlam sought to draw the Secularist movement within the fold of the church. In 1882, he preached at Westminster Abbey that "Christ [was] the greatest of all secular workers . . . who could utter scathing . . . words against the rich, the respectable, the religious."[15] Like many another social crusader, Headlam found it difficult to move the inertia of a large, conservatively minded church.

THE SALVATION ARMY

The 1880's saw a religious revival that was to have a profound and world-wide impact. The Salvation Army was born, and took over the main Hall of Science in London, where Bradlaugh had earlier branded the group "a mixture of enthusiasts, lunatics, and hypocrites." The military organization of the Salvation Army was appropriate for that age when victorious British Imperialism was painting the map of the world red; William Booth, founder of the Salvation Army, made striking use of brass bands, uniforms, flags, army ranks and methods.

General Booth had been a pawnbroker and had seen misery in the slums at first hand. In 1878 he started his career as an evangelist on the streets of Whitechapel, one of the poorest districts in London's East End. Despite physical opposition from some onlookers, he quickly gained converts who spread his ideas. From these humble beginnings a respected world organization was launched, and William

253

Booth eventually received the honour of the freedom of the City of London, and an honorary doctorate from Oxford University.

Physical opposition from drunks or gangs was only one of the early hazards. In 1884 alone, 600 Salvationists were jailed by the authorities for disturbing the peace by preaching in the streets, yet street corner services persisted. Wherever distress or unhappiness was to be found, so was the Salvation Army. Their slogan was "drowning men need ropes not tracts." Help was given to alcoholics, prostitutes, and ex-convicts; homes were created for children and the aged. In 1890, William Booth wrote a best-seller about social problems entitled *In Darkest England and the Way Out,* which included imaginative proposals for fighting poverty. One of his ideas was the promotion of emigration, and such schemes sponsored by the Salvation Army provided Canada with many new citizens.

The Salvation Army in Canada was launched by two Englishmen in London, Ontario in 1882. When the two men held their first street meeting they encountered the usual opposition of hooliganism and official condemnation. One year later, in 1883, a detachment of three Salvationists arrived to open an outpost near Dundas, Ontario and the communique of the Captain reported, "a howling mob received us and threatened to tar and feather us."[16] Hostility was not limited to the civic authorities in Ontario, who feared disturbances of the peace, but also came from church leaders. The spectacular evangelistic methods of the Salvation Army aroused the ire of established denominations, who feared the competition. Street meetings were an uncomfortable reminder to middle-class Methodists that they had once been famous for camp meetings. Claims of the Salvationists that they could reach the churchless only served to point up the failure of the Protestant denominations in urban slums. An alarmed Methodist admitted in the *Christian Guardian* in 1884 that his denomination was accused of being, "the institution of the wealthy and respectable class, neglecting the poor and vicious class."[17]

One of the reasons that the Salvation Army was a powerful evangelical force was its recognition of the equality of women, for women have normally been the backbone of any Christian congregation. The Ontario campaign of the Salvation Army was very successful, but more opposition was encountered in Quebec, where its teachings irritated Roman Catholics, although gradually an appreciation of the good works of the Army began to grow. By 1900, the campaign in the East was changing into one of consolidating gains. It was now time to carry the crusade into the West, with the cry of Hallelujah! Today the movement is known throughout Canada. In the slums of the big cities, the Harbour Refuges provide what Booth called "shelter from life's storms."

THE SOCIAL GOSPEL

The Salvation Army had arrived in North America at a time when rapid industrialization had produced social problems there which had been experienced earlier in Britain. Salvationists reinforced the concern about society that was expressed in the "social gospel" of some Protestant churches. The principles of the social gospel movement were drawn from both British and American sources to inspire, within the United States, a conviction that Christianity should be concerned with the quality of human relations on earth. American Protestantism showed signs of moving from concern about the individual to concern over society at large. The "new" or "liberal" theology endeavoured to bridge the gap between traditional Christianity and modern thought, and envisaged co-operation between labour and management within the capitalist framework. Liberalism rejected socialist ideas of state action and in the Protestant America of the 1870's, reform became the objective as it had in the reform wave in Britain during the 1830's and 1840's.

Washington Gladden, a Congregational minister, is considered the father of the social gospel. Gladden sought to make Christ important in the new industrial America, and declared his own intention to deal with real human beings rather than with ideas or words. Added to his belief in man's ability to progress, was the concept that the universal presence of God would promote industrial harmony. Individual selfishness was sin: men were to be educated to prefer social good to private advantage and Christ's love would remove all obstacles. Such thinking was a hopeful sign in an America where Social Darwinism was encouraging the notion that the economically strong should crush the weak and thus improve the human species. Social gospellers came from the Congregational, Unitarian, and Episcopal churches, as well as from the northern branches of the Baptists, Methodists and Presbyterians. The movement of social gospel teachings did not reach its height until the turn of the century.

A basic weakness existed in the position of those ministers who preached the social gospel. They saw themselves as educators who taught Christian principles in sermons, but their churches were financially dependent upon wealthy men who were not keen to see their ministers follow up their Sunday preaching with weekday political activity. Furthermore, clerics who thought they saw the reforms needed were usually not interested in administering programmes of relief. The long-ingrained Protestant tradition of the separation of church and state emphasized that secular voluntary agencies were to be the instruments of social action. Settlement houses in the slums inspired by clergymen usually became increasingly secular as their activity developed. In short, the social gospel might launch the ship but it needed businessmen to keep it afloat.

The illusion that America of the 1890's was still rural and Protestant persisted, and a Protestant social gospel was rising in an America no longer very Protestant. As a torrent of immigrants poured into the expanding cities of New York, Boston and Chicago, far-reaching structural changes took place in American society. The influence of Catholicism and Judaism grew as the immigrants came, and these long-established faiths soon adapted to life in America. Some Protestant ministers became alarmed at the influx of "foreigners" who seemed to threaten their America. However, many ministers raised in a rural America responded to the challenge of new populations by going into urban districts. Their effort was similar to John Wesley's mission to the British masses in the eighteenth century.

256

THE LATE NINETEENTH CENTURY

In order to appreciate the changing attitude towards religion in the late nineteenth century it is necessary to briefly review the political background in Britain and Canada. Religious leaders saw elementary schools as the place where Christian morality should be inculcated. But the question raised about the role of religion in schools supported by public taxation was basically the familiar controversy over church-state relations. In Britain, the tussle between the Church of England, Nonconformist churches, and secularists was essentially resolved by the Education Act of 1870. The urgently needed additional schools were to be placed under the control of locally elected Boards of Education, hence the term Board School. In these Board Schools, there was to be non-denominational religion offered at the end of the day, so that any parent who objected might withdraw his child without impeding the regular school programme. This solution was called the Cowper-Temple clause after the Member of Parliament who had proposed it.

The Cowper-Temple principle was then copied in Canada to resolve a heated conflict in Manitoba, where Roman Catholics had opposed the efforts of the Provincial Legislature to eliminate their schools. To suit their purpose the Protestants of Manitoba had borrowed an American principle that no state aid should be given to any school in which a church doctrine was taught. A constitutional crisis developed as to whether a province had the right to eliminate the guarantee given to Roman Catholics in 1870 that their religious beliefs would be respected. After protracted legal arguments, the question was referred to the Privy Council at Westminster, then the highest court of appeal. Ultimately the Privy Council ruled that the Catholic schools had to be restored. Sir Wilfrid Laurier resolved the constitutional crisis by co-operating with the Manitoba premier in restricting religious instruction to the end of the day between 3:30 p.m. and 4:00 p.m. Canada was in the fortunate position of being able to watch developments in Britain and America and adapt the solutions evolved in the older countries to her own needs.

The process of industrialization in the United States produced a familiar response towards religion among urban workers. The apathy displayed by the majority of British workers towards formal religion was paralleled by their Protestant counterparts in the New World. A college professor who embraced the social gospel summarized the position of wage workers in Chicago.

> There is no place in the average . . . church for the poor man unless it is in the position of janitor . . . few of the average Chicago preachers go out of their way to preach the gospel to the poor—of course "good" people who are "rich" establish mission schools for "bad" people who are "poor".[18]

The situation in New York was the same as in Chicago. Bakers sent petitions to clergymen in New York asking them to preach on the need for bakers to have the Sabbath free of work. The secretary of the bakers' organization concluded from the lack of response that:

> Relying on what the sabbath may do to assist in enforcing sabbath laws is equal to relying on a rain of manna that may make work superfluous . . . . Those gentlemen [the clergymen] are more interested in the movement of boodle than in the movement of labour.[19]

Walter Rauschenbusch, a Baptist minister, was an outstanding leader in the 1890's in the campaign to promote social concern among Protestants, and wrote a book called *Christianity and the Social Crisis.* Half a century later, this book influenced a young minister seeking social change as he strived for civil rights long overdue to his people. Dr. Martin Luther King, the Negro leader, said that Rauschenbusch's book "left an indelible imprint on my thinking."[20]

Rauschenbusch was known as an exponent of Christian socialism, which went further than the social gospel in its advocacy of state action to redress social injustice. A Christian brotherhood emphasizing equal rights was to support a democratic distribution of economic power. A spiritual revolution had to precede this new society to prevent the rise of atheistic Marxism. Like many other intellectuals since the nineteenth century, Rauschenbusch envisaged putting Christ into a Marxist framework. This "new" evangelism pointed out that:

> The moral teaching of the church in the past has dealt with private and family life . . . . It has nothing to say about the justice of holding land idle in crowded cities . . . or cornering the market in the necessities of life.[21]

Like his British predecessors, the Christian Socialists of the 1850's, Rauschenbusch had grave doubts as to whether Western civilization could be described as religious. "It is unjust to Christianity to call our civilization Christian: it is unjust to call it un-Christian. It is semi-Christian."[22]

Businessmen did not favour Christian principles that they considered "impractical." A practical idea that did appeal was that of the Community Chest for financing charities, which spread the cost throughout the community. Businessmen liked the publicity of leading charitable appeals in the community and supervising the budget. This concept grew in many cities into a "united fund" which incorporated national causes such as the American Red Cross, and in 1918 a national organization was formed. Growth of the Community Chest movement was slower in Canada. In 1917 a Federation of Jewish Philanthropists was established in both Montreal and Toronto. Canadian Protestants and Catholics were slower to join the movement than their American counterparts, and by 1938 only nine cities in Canada had Community Chests. Only when Protestant, Catholic and Jewish organizations united in a Central Committee which became a division of the Canadian Welfare Council in 1942, did growth of welfare agencies become rapid.

SOCIAL JUSTICE IN CANADA

Between the turn of the century and World War I, the social gospel movement had spread northwards into Canada. Concern began to shift beyond the advocacy of blue laws and prohibition to the larger question of social justice. This concern about society helped to consolidate religious opinion among North American denominations and was one of the earliest indicators that Protestant church union would follow. Canada led the way towards church union in 1907 by organizing a Protestant interdenominational group called The Moral and Social Reform Council. The following year the United States organized the Federal Council of the Churches of Christ to promote the social gospel and further the cause of co-operative Christianity. At the first meeting of this Council a report was adopted which called for a "social creed." Fear of the rising competition of Roman Catholicism undoubtedly inspired some of these social gospellers to advocate Protestant unity. From this American pattern was to emerge the idea that a social gospel and church union were complementary facets of the same Christian concern.

One of the major dilemmas confronting ministers embracing the social gospel was whether to accept money from tycoons who said they wanted to help mankind. A classic example occurred in 1905, when John D. Rockefeller gave a gift of $100,000 for use in overseas missions. Washington Gladden, Moderator of the Congregational Church, refused to accept such "tainted money." Gladden's stand was opposed by some ministers who were less squeamish as to the source of money and claimed that it was right to accept legal tender from its legitimate owner. Canada possessed a unique social gospeller who later reconciled these difficulties that worried thoughtful Americans. William Lyon Mackenzie King publicized his liberal philosophy in *Industry and Humanity;* unlike Washington Gladden, though, King had no difficulty reconciling his social concern with a "birthday gift" of $100,000 from John D. Rockefeller, Jr.[23]

The Methodists were the most active promoters of the social gospel in Canada. As usual, a radical minority showed concern about redeeming the whole social structure, while the main conservative body thought in terms of individual salvation. Prominent in the Canadian version of social gospelling were J.S. Woodsworth, an American named Salem Bland, and two Britons, William Irvine and William Ivens. The movement was born in the West where massive immigration during the Laurier boom had created social problems. A radical climate existed there; Keir Hardie, the pioneering socialist in Britain, received an enthusiastic response in Winnipeg in 1908 and 1912. J.S. Woodsworth gained his insight into the problems of the Canadian city by working in a settlement house in North Winnipeg, among immigrants attracted to the Golden West. The undenominational approach of the social gospellers seemed to suit the freedom of Western Canada.

In the more conservative East, urban settlement houses were opened under Presbyterian auspices: Christopher House in Toronto, and Chalmers House in Montreal. It was becoming increasingly apparent to all Protestant denominations that the churches were not reaching immigrants settling in the cities. Another illustration of this concern was shown in 1914, when the Methodists changed the name of the Board of Temperance, Prohibition and Moral Reform to the Department of Social Service and Evangelism.

Protestant Ontario was clashing with Catholic Quebec over language rights. Intolerance of the language of the French Canadian caused Ontario and Quebec to have very different attitudes towards the War that started in 1914. History books have rarely given much prominence to the role of discrimination against the use of the French language in Ontario schools, as a major factor in the conscription crisis of World War One. In 1910 a clash had occurred between the English-speaking and French-speaking wings of the Roman Catholic church in Ontario, with Bishop Michael Fallon of London leading the resistance of Catholics of Irish descent to the idea of bilingual schools. Tension increased in 1912 when the Ontario Department of Education issued Regulation 17 which was intended to curb the growth of schools in the Ottawa Valley that used French as the language of instruction. In this border region between Quebec and Ontario, an influx of French Canadians had resulted in teachers entering Ontario to instruct children in a language they understood. Regulation 17 was designed to reduce the French language to the status of a subject on the curriculum, with English to be used for purposes of instruction. A reaction in Quebec followed and, after the outbreak of the Great War, the

261

bitterness of the French Canadians was voiced by Henri Bourassa, who stated on December 21, 1914 that:

> In the name of religion, liberty and faithfulness to the British flag, the French Canadians are enjoined to ... fight the Prussians of Europe. Shall we let the Prussians of Ontario impose their domination like masters, in the very heart of the Canadian Confederation, under the shelter of the British flag and British institutions?[24]

This tragic situation reflected the basic deficiency of the British North America Act which distinguishes citizens on the basis of religious affiliation and not language rights. But this new cleavage concerning language rights was particularly unfortunate, as it widened the area of misunderstanding at a time when national unity was a paramount issue.

During World War One the campaign for the social gospel intensified in English-speaking Canada; war frequently blends the causes of patriotism and social justice. Protestant clergymen urged youths to enlist in the armed forces and this, in turn, intensified the clergy's commitment to a great cause. The conspicuous war profiteering made ministers determined to seek social justice for "our boys overseas." A few apostles of the social gospel who were also pacifists, such as Salem Bland and William Ivens, were assailed on patriotic grounds. It would be misleading, however, to depict the Protestant churches in World War One as being primarily interested in reforming society. Many churchmen in Canada were more concerned that Canadian soldiers were being defiled by the sophisticated temptations of Europe. One historian has concluded that, "many Canadian Methodists came to believe that sex and liquor in England were worse threats to Canadian manhood than the guns of France."[25] This view seems particularly surprising when considering that at least one in three of the members of the Canadian Army was British-born.

During the war the working man was living better than he ever had, and social gospellers felt that this trend should continue in peacetime. In 1918, the Methodist Committee on Evangelism produced a blueprint for implementing the social gospel. This was a radical document which advocated profit-sharing by labour, as well as legislation to regulate wages and profits. Capitalist exploitation of labour and resources was condemned in ringing terms. The company-owned town was seen as a menace to democracy. Businessmen were naturally perturbed by this denunciation, and their general reaction was expressed in 1919 by a prominent Methodist layman named S.R. Parsons. Parsons reflected the view of the Canadian Manufacturers' Association, a group which acted as a strong political lobby: addressing the Toronto Conference of the Methodist Church, Parsons solemnly announced that he "was one of a class of employers who were trying to earnestly apply the teachings of Christ." A year later, this speaker demonstrated his Christian attitude in a letter to the Prime Minister deploring the Business Profits Tax and suggesting that the government should raise the required revenue by taxing the public.

The Anglican Church had rather lagged behind in agitation for social reform, for its clergy's vigorous support of Canada's war effort distracted from social concerns. Yet in September of 1918, inspired by social concern voiced within the mother church, the General Synod of Canada condemned individualistic ideas, rejected the competition of economic life, and established a Council of Social Service.

As World War I ended general disillusionment was setting in. In the United States an Interchurch World Movement which required millions of dollars quickly collapsed. So did the efforts of workers to obtain social justice in Winnipeg during the General Strike of 1919, where Methodist ministers and social gospellers received considerable publicity. The hollowness of the social gospel was dramatically revealed in 1921, when a printers' strike occurred at the Methodist Book and Publishing Company, the largest church publisher. The strikers were protesting the existence of an open shop and they lost. Methodism was swinging away from the social gospel, whose remaining supporters were taking a more political path of reform in the West and in the cities.

In all countries the returned soldier looked sceptically at the righteousness of clergymen. In the mud and slaughter of 1914 to 1918, many soldiers lost belief in Victorian ideas of progress and God's mercy became suspect. The martial ardour of 1914, when German youths had "God With Us" embossed on their belt buckles, and British troops saw "Angels at Mons," was conspicuously absent in 1918. During the War heated nationalist statements had been made by academics who claimed to follow the Prince of Peace. For example, Archdeacon William Cunningham, an economic historian, actually attacked pacifists in England for quoting the Sermon on the Mount, and considered that it was the highest moral duty of English soldiers to kill as many Germans as possible.[26] The larger issue raised by such behaviour is whether any scholar can claim to be truly objective when he professes a specific religious creed.[27] Returning soldiers, however, were not inclined to discuss this issue on a lofty metaphysical plane.

THE 1920'S

In the postwar period of the 1920's, a frenzy of youthful activity upset the generation who recalled the good old days. As usual, youth was seen as going to the dogs. The president of Florida University proclaimed that "The low-cut gowns, the rolled hose and short skirts are born of the Devil and are carrying the present and future generations to chaos and destruction." In addition to a national prohibition on liquor, there was an effort by legislators in Utah, Virginia and Ohio to control the hemline.

In the Canadian Parliament of the 1920's, J.S. Woodsworth pursued the principles of the social gospel, throughout his career as an M.P. for Winnipeg. His biographer, Kenneth McNaught, describes Woodsworth as an "untypical Canadian" because he loved morality more than the dollar.[28] Woodsworth's contribution to promotion of socialism with a Methodist flavour, paralleled the similar contribution of some British Labour party leaders like Philip Snowden. What was different about Britain, however, was the secularistic strand of socialist development; Ernest Bevin symbolized a powerful, secularly-inclined type of Labour intellectual who had no counterpart in Canada. In Ottawa, secular social justice had to be sought by religious means, through such men as Woodsworth.

While the passion for social reform had somewhat abated since the 1918 Methodist Manifesto, it remained a factor in promoting the cause of church union. From 1918 to 1924 the Social Service Council of Canada had conducted research into social issues and tried to get legislative reforms through parliament. A united church would obviously speak with more authority on social problems, an argument for union used by Dr. S.D. Chown, General Superintendent of the Methodist Church. Furthermore, a strong Protestant union would enable Roman Catholicism to be watched. In 1925, the Congregationalists, Methodists and some Presbyterians joined in creating a United Church of Canada.

A major problem with church union was that it did not appeal to all Scots or Ulstermen. The author of *Church Union in Canada* notes that Canadians of Scottish origin had particular pride in their place in Canadian society and cites evidence of this in our literature:

> The author of *The Romance of the C.P.R.* and *Policing the Plains* and many other books dealing with the development of Canada never failed to state explicitly the shire whence came the Highland laddie, but usually forgets to mention that the Sassenachs [non-Scots] were born at all. There was, in short, a Scottish superiority complex.[29]

And the Presbyterian segment naturally kept out of the new United Church of Canada: regardless of theology, it was unlikely that the Scots élite would join hands with a Methodist movement inspired by three Englishmen. The Anglicans in Canada are still only contemplating union.

During the 1920's progress was also made on the controversial issue of bilingual instruction in the schools of Ontario. Heated exchanges had continued during World War One but, in the less emotionally charged postwar period, the issue was resolved by that unique court of appeal in Canada —the need for national unity. Professor C.B. Sissons sponsored a Unity League of Ontario in 1922 and, by 1927, a retreat of the politicians was underway when provisions were made for the training of bilingual teachers at the University of Ottawa. In the election of 1929 the Conservative party's flexibility on this issue, wavering between the anti-Catholic stand of Orangemen and the desire to retain the French Canadian vote in Ontario, was rewarded by another electoral victory.[30] But even as the Government of Ontario appeared to resolve the question of language rights, another controversial issue concerning Roman Catholic schools was being debated.

The Separate Schools of Ontario asked for permission to extend separate education to the end of the secondary period. But the then highest court of Canadian appeal, the Privy Council at Westminster, ruled in 1928 that Section 93 of the British North America Act could not be interpreted as permitting the development of education beyond the primary or elementary level. While Orangemen in Ontario rejoiced at the wisdom of such a legal decision, it illustrated clearly that there were pitfalls in trying to use the guarantee of one age for another. The British North America Act was a straitjacket at a time when educational tolerance was needed. Ontario could hardly expect to resolve such a religious and educational matter by legalistic argument, particularly when it was to be ultimately decided in a Britain not yet convinced of the imperative need for secondary education. Roman Catholic authorities were aware that the Protestant minority in Quebec had ensured at the time of Confederation that their interests would be safeguarded under the British North America Act. It seemed in Canada that the conservative East spent a great deal of energy in refighting old battles, for the topic of Catholic schools had already been hotly debated in Manitoba.

THE 1930'S

A close link continued in the 1930's between the Western agrarian movement and the politics born of the social gospel. In Alberta, William Aberhart, a Baptist, started the political movement known as Social Credit and passed on the leadership to his former pupil, E.C. Manning. Similarly Tommy

Douglas, a Baptist minister, and Stanley Knowles of the United Church campaigned in the ranks of the Co-operative Commonwealth Federation.

In the depression of the 1930's, radicalism reappeared. During this period a neo-Marxist group under Reinhold Neibuhr, an American Evangelical, attacked the "liberal" social gospel. In 1931, a Canadian Anglican denounced both capitalism and atheistic communism and advocated a new creed called "Christian Communism," reminiscent of the Reverend Charles Kingsley's attempt, in 1848, to Christianize the Communist Manifesto. During the Depression of the 1930's many men flirted with Communism. Britain produced a Red Dean of Canterbury, Dr. Hewlett Johnson, who saw Christ as a revolutionary socialist; William Temple, Archbishop of York, supported the Labour Party and chaired a committee investigating industrial conditions. The influential Temple report was entitled *Men Without Work* and advocated state planning in the location of industry.

SOME MODERN EXPRESSIONS OF FAITH

World War II witnessed some dramatic social developments in Britain. An Anglican Conference at Malvern in 1941 expressed radical ideas with William Temple advocating public control of land and money. Temple became Archbishop of Canterbury in 1942 and later wrote a best-seller named *Christianity and the Social Order*. A Council of Clergy and Ministers for Common Ownership began to take shape. Yet possibly a more representative attitude of most Englishmen towards the role of religion was expressed by Britain's wartime leader Winston Churchill in describing his boyhood:

> I always had to go to Church once a week. All of this was very good. I accumulated in those years so fine a surplus in the Bank of Observance that I have been drawing confidently upon it ever since.[31]

The unique flavour of religious influence in England was well explained by Bishop E.R. Wickham, who recorded in the 1950's:

Sharp lines of fidelity and infidelity cannot be drawn in English society, and another way of saying this is that the secular minded outside the churches have a Christian colouration, and that practising Christians have marked secular characteristics.[32]

An example of how the secular and religious blend could be seen in British and Canadian pubs in wartime, where a girl from the Salvation Army distributing her *War Cry* was treated with a respect rarely accorded to a sermon from the pulpit. Religion also moved into the schools when the Educational Act of 1944 was passed in Britain, decreeing that schools must teach non-denominational religion. The Archbishop of Canterbury declared that the Act "wrote religion into education in a way never done before," for religious instruction was now the only subject which could not be omitted from a school curriculum.

MODERN STRESS AND STRAIN

Members of the Roman Catholic Church, as well as the more vocal Protestants, have shown an increasing worldwide concern about social injustice. The broad and charitable vision of Pope John XXIII appealed to men of many faiths and backgrounds, and the encyclical *Mater et Magistra* of 1961 displays sympathy for the poor nations and seeks aid from rich countries, while simultaneously expressing concern for the little man at an individual level. In Canada, a Canadian Catholic Conference of 1961 discussed the question of land ownership, often a reason for condemnation of the wealthy Church.

In North America, Protestant pride in separating state from church has become a rather synthetic issue in the age of national concern with social welfare. Even those Protestant denominations who have insisted on their independence of civil government, have not hesitated to accept subsidies provided by the general taxpayer. In the United States, federal funds are supplied to denominational welfare agencies. One of the most common types of subsidy is that termed "purchase of service." Rather than expand public welfare services, the United States government authorizes public agencies to purchase specialized services from voluntary agencies. Hospitals, old people's homes, children's agencies are thus largely financed by public taxation in spite of the fact that they are nominally under the auspices of a religious group. It has been estimated that "many Protestant children's agencies receive from 30 per cent to 100 per cent of their operating budget in this fashion."[33] In 1961, the United States Grant in Aid Program, which had a budget exceeding $5 billion, helped to finance many church-related agencies.

One writer has recorded the dilemma of many Protestant agencies in the United States, which supposedly espouse the concept of voluntaryism, or the divorce of church and state. Is it ethical for a religious sect to use public funds? Or to be more specific, "Is it ethical for the church to pretend that it is offering services when the government is paying the bill? . . . Are Protestants just grabbing money because money is available?"[34] It is just possible that the church is aiding the development of that dreadful "socialism," which is not yet a respectable word for some Americans.

In Canada the position seems to be similar. The welfare field is covered by hundreds of federal, provincial, municipal and private agencies with both secular and religious backgrounds. The Canadian Welfare Council acts as a national co-ordinating body for over 500 agencies, by supplying research data and literature. There is no clear-cut answer as to who finances all of this activity. The Canadian Welfare Council gets its funds from community chest operations, from the government, and from private subscribers. A labour leader recently examining the idea of voluntary welfare in the Canada of 1969 concluded that there is a "grey area in this whole field. . . .those agencies which are neither wholly private nor wholly public but seem to have their feet in both camps."[35] The amounts of money involved in social and welfare causes are very large. A spokesman of the Canadian Chamber of Commerce noted that "in addition to the provincial, municipal and private agencies" the Federal Government spends over 5 billion dollars a year on over 200 programmes in human development.[36] The intricate ramifications of

Canadian organizations make it difficult to see exactly to what degree the taxpayer subsidizes denominational charities.

The issue of the separation of church and state in North America is a complex one. Some citizens have been urging that social action should be undertaken by the urban churches and by the churches alone: such a view would seem to be advocated in an editorial in *Christianity Today* of January 18, 1960.

> The socialist state subtly transforms human wants into human rights . . . Instead of hailing state welfare programs as an extension of Christian social ethics, it is high time Christian clergy and laymen consider the premise that state welfare programs are inherently anti-Christian.

On the other hand, the participation of the church in the field of social welfare may unwittingly prevent adequate remedial action. A well-documented study entitled *Your City* by E.L. Thorndike investigated leading American cities during the 1930's. The conclusion reached was that where church membership was high in a community, there was less provision for social welfare. In contrast, where less attention was paid to religion, concern over community welfare was greater. It may thus be argued that the church should concentrate upon spiritual matters.

As North America entered the 1960's there was concern shown by Roman Catholic leaders about the increasing problems associated with maintaining their own schools. Roman Catholic bishops in Ontario presented a brief to the Ontario government in 1962 requesting the right to organize schools for Roman Catholics up to the twelfth or thirteenth grade, as this was the contemporary accepted level of general education: the brief also advocated that a share of the federal grants provided for technical and vocational training should be used to assist Catholic students to benefit from this training. Similarly, in the United States there was a great deal of discussion at this time about supplying funds to Roman Catholic parochial schools. President John F. Kennedy had taken office determined to help public education at all levels but met resistance from the Roman Catholic hierarchy for some of his efforts and, furthermore, Supreme Court decisions prohibited public support for parochial schools. The age-old problem of church and state in educational matters is certainly not dead in the twentieth century. On the other hand, the assumption of many Americans that their country was based on Christian principles, was dashed by a Supreme Court decision of 1962 that ruled that a non-denominational prayer composed by New York State for use in public schools was unconstitutional. The pluralistic society of the 1960's was a long way from its Puritan foundation of three hundred years earlier.

A limited survey of religious and secular influences upon social action can cover only broad trends. Both religion and secularism have influenced our approach to social problems, and concern for social action is not new. The question as to whether or not I am my brother's keeper has been answered in different ways, but the collective efforts of many men and movements have left a legacy of concern for the underdog, and an increasing sense of responsibility felt by the world's "haves" for the world's "have-nots." Another way to view social action is from the perspective that education provides the only real solution to problems and, in the next chapter, this allied point of view will be considered.

1. *Toronto Star*, 20 June 1970, p. 45.
2. E.R. Wickham, *Church and People in an Industrial City* (London: Lutterworth Press, 1957), p. 118.
3. K.S. Inglis, "Patterns of Religious Worship in 1851," *Journal of Ecclesiastical History*, vol. 2, April 1960, p. 86.
4. K.S. Inglis, *Churches and the Working Classes in Victorian England* (Toronto: University of Toronto Press, 1963), p. 41.
5. Ibid., p. 117.
6. Ibid., p. 20.
7. "Why Skilled Workmen Don't Go To Church," *Fraser's Magazine*, 1869.
8. C.E. Silcox, *Church Union in Canada* (New York: Institute of Social and Religious Research, 1933), p. 15.
9. A.R.M. Lower, "Two Ways of Life," *C.H.A. Report* 1943, p. 16.
10. Thomas Paine, *The Rights of Man* (London: J.M. Dent and Sons, 1958), p. 281.
11. Bradlaugh Centennial Committee, *Champion of Liberty: Charles Bradlaugh* (London: C.A. Watts and the Pioneer Press, 1933), p. 6.
12. E.R. Wickham, *Church and People in an Industrial City*, p. 151.

13. G. Kitson Clark, *The English Inheritance*" (London: S.C.M. Press, 1950), p. 156.

14. C.R. Stewart Crysdale, *The Industrial Struggle and Protestant Ethics in Canada* (Toronto: Ryerson Press, 1961), p. 17.

15. W.L. Arnstein, *The Bradlaugh Case* (London: Oxford University Press, 1965), p. 166.

16. S.D. Clark, *Church and Sect in Canada* (Toronto: University of Toronto Press, 1948), p. 382.

17. Ibid., p. 393.

18. Robert T. Handy, ed., *The Social Gospel in America, 1870-1920* (New York: Oxford University Press, 1966), p. 205.

19. Ibid., p. 207.

20. Ibid., p. 259.

21. Ibid., p. 327.

22. Ibid., p. 339.

23. H.S. Ferns and B. Ostry, *The Age of Mackenzie King* (London: William Heinemann, 1955), p. 215.

24. Mason Wade, *French Canadians*, rev. ed. 2 vols. (New York: St. Martin's Press, 1968), 1:600.

25. J.M. Bliss, "The Methodist Church and World War I," *Canadian Historical Review* 49:3 (September, 1968), p. 225.

26. Harry E. Barnes, *A History of Historical Writing* (New York: Dover Publications Inc., 1962) p. 279.

27. Individuals who are ministers of religion sometimes appear on the faculties of Canadian colleges that are publicly supported institutions. Disciplines such as philosophy, history and more recently sociology particularly attract such teacher-ministers. The author has had the experience of apologizing to a politician who, as guest speaker, was challenged in the name of non-denominational Christianity by a teacher of Religions of the World. This makes one speculate if the perennial issue of the separation of church and state needs redefining for an age when mass higher education is becoming a reality.

28. Kenneth McNaught, *A Prophet in Politics* (Toronto: University of Toronto Press, 1967), p. 37.

29. C.E. Silcox, *Church Union in Canada*, p. 198.

30. Joseph Schwarz, "A Documentary Survey of the Bilingual School Controversy in Ontario: 1910-1927" (M.A. essay, Ontario Institute for Studies in Education, 1970).

31. New York Times, *Churchill* (New York: Bantam Press, 1965), p. 154.

32. E.R. Wickham, *Church and People in an Industrial City*, p. 188.

33. Haskell M. Miller, *Compassion and Community* (New York: Association Press, 1961), p. 128.

34. Ibid., p. 129.

35. Joe Morris, Executive Vice-President, Canadian Labour Congress, "Labour Looks at Voluntary Welfare," p. 4, *Proceedings of the 1969 Biennial Conference, Community Funds and Councils of Canada,* Ottawa.

36. Ibid, J. Allyn Taylor, Vice-President, Canadian Chamber of Commerce, "Business Looks at Community Welfare," p. 9.

272

7

Education

Human history becomes more and more a race between education and catastrophe.

H.G. Wells

In order to bring into focus the origins of modern Canadian education, this chapter will start with a brief survey of the background of early education in Britain, New England and New France.

EDUCATIONAL FOUNDATIONS

The Renaissance can be regarded as the starting point for modern education, with the invention of the printing press making possible the mass production of books and the spreading of knowledge. Pupils in the local grammar schools of Elizabethan England learned Latin and Greek, frequently starting at the age of three or four, and in such a school at Stratford-On-Avon, was educated William Shakespeare. For the children of the wealthy, there were boarding schools provided at Eton and Winchester. The fact that such schools were described by the term "public schools" was not completely inappropriate at this time because some free places had to be provided for King's Scholars, the children of poor parents.

In Scotland the Calvinistic zeal introduced by John Knox produced its own renaissance and it is worth noting that after the creation of Edinburgh University in 1583, Scotland possessed four universities, twice the number of universities in England. Scotland also established provisions for widespread elementary education, as a Scottish Education Act of 1696 ordained that there should be a "commodious house for a school settled and established, and a school master appointed in every parish." Similarly, those Calvinists known as Puritans who emigrated to the New World were active in furthering the education of their children. The Massachusetts legislature provided for an elementary school in every town of fifty householders, with towns of one hundred families to have a teacher of Latin grammar. To top off this educational framework of Massachusetts, Harvard College was established in 1636. A distinctive feature of Scotland and New England was that co-education of girls and boys was accepted as a normal pattern. It is interesting to note that the Roman Catholic tradition of the wisdom of separating boys and girls was one of the ideas that tended to carry over into the newly founded Anglican Church, as well as to New France. In the French-Canadian educational pattern the religious orders of Brothers taught the boys, while the Sisters of the Congregation had several schools for girls. Apparently, one of the most significant school regulations in New France stated that unmarried teachers were forbidden to teach children of the opposite sex.

After the American Revolution the political climate of English-speaking Canada, in the newly-formed province of Upper Canada, was ultraconservative. Lieutenant Governor John Graves Simcoe, appointed in 1791, encouraged the Legislature of Upper Canada to seek an endowment in land to sustain such traditional institutions as "a respectable grammar school in each District and also a College or University." The British government responded by setting aside 450,000 acres of crown land for educational purposes. Yet the problem of how to organize such schools in a wilderness remained and led Simcoe to plead for an educator capable of establishing the right kind of conservative school system. A young Scot, John Strachan, was attracted by Simcoe's enthusiastic vision of higher education in Upper Canada, but when he arrived in Upper Canada in 1799 he found that the project of establishing college education had vanished with the departure of Simcoe.

A similar pattern was emerging in Lower Canada where in 1801 a public corporation was established to be called The Royal Institution for the Advancement of Learning. Quebec's Anglican Bishop, Jacob Mountain, actively supported the proposals for public education which the French Canadians viewed, rightly or wrongly, as a plot to Anglicanize them. Despite official efforts to reassure the Roman Catholic hierarchy of the sincerity of the desire to promote public education, the project failed.

Greater success was attained in Upper Canada where pressure by clerics upon the Legislature produced the District Public School Act of 1807. This Act authorized a grammar school to be established in each of the eight districts of the Province and stipulated that the Legislature was to pay an annual grant of £100 towards the payment of each schoolmaster. Other expenses were to be met by fees and this provision illustrated the intention to make the schools "public" in the British sense. When the first of these schools opened at Cornwall, it was directed by John Strachan who accepted the premise that the Church of England should be the state church of the new colony and encourage loyalty to the Crown. A few years later, Dr. Strachan moved to York to become headmaster of the grammar school and started on his long career as the provincial leader of education. The crucial role of Strachan in expanding educational opportunities to include poor children was linked to related events in Britain.

METHODS OF INSTRUCTION

An English Quaker named Joseph Lancaster had invented a monitorial system to teach the 3 R's to large numbers of children. Under this system older pupils called "monitors" were instructed by the schoolmaster and in turn, passed on this learning to the rest of the class. The economical nature of this system of education appealed to an age that had seen heavy taxation to pay for the Napoleonic Wars. It also had the approval of the Archbishop of Canterbury until he discovered that the catechism was not taught and religion was deliberately made undenominational. Anglicans then promoted a rival to Lancaster named Dr. Andrew Bell who, as superintendent of an orphanage in Madras, India, had also discovered the monitorial principle. When Nonconformists founded the British and Foreign School Society in 1808, on Lancastrian principles, the Anglicans saw virtue in the Madras methods of Dr. Bell. In 1811 was formed the National Society for the Education of the Poor in the Principles of the Established Church, a title that was soon, mercifully, reduced to the abbreviation National Society. Hundreds of elementary schools, termed common schools, were established in England and Wales by the Anglicans, who appointed Dr. Bell as national superintendent.

The Madras system crossed the Atlantic and soon gained support in the Maritimes, where the endorsement of the Anglican establishment gave the common schools a degree of status. In Upper Canada Dr. Strachan imported an Englishman to introduce the Bell method to a school at York, a move that his critics chose to interpret as an effort to introduce more Anglicanism. Because of the sensitive nature of the religious rivalry in the British North American colonies, there was a tendency to copy the less sectarian approach of American solutions to educational problems. Nova Scotia and New Brunswick, for example, adopted in 1811 the New England precedent of having local school districts controlled by an elected board of trustees. John Strachan also incorporated the American concept of a three-man school board elected by parents in the Common School Act of 1816. A common school was to provide elementary education wherever a minimum attendance of twenty was assured, with a school board appointing the teacher and framing its own local regulations. In 1824, a Board of Education was created to supervise the colony's schools and John Strachan became its chairman. Strachan disliked American textbooks, with their pro-republican and anti-British bias, and compiled a list of books that he considered suitable. To his credit, Strachan insisted upon the need for well-trained teachers such as he had known in his native Scotland, and emphasized the need for quality rather than quantity.

John Strachan also aspired to found a college to crown his provincial system of education. In 1827 Strachan persuaded the British government to grant a charter for King's College and an endowment of 225,944 acres of Crown Reserve land. For that era, when Anglicanism dominated all aspects of life at both of England's universities, the charter was surprisingly liberal because religion was confined to a divinity school. But reformers such as William Lyon Mackenzie and Jesse Ketchum raised a public outcry against the foundation of a college under any kind of Anglican auspices and, to further compound Strachan's problems, a select committee of the Legislature condemned all grammar schools of Upper Canada as failures. At this point the Lieutenant Governor came through with a supposed compromise. A public school in the Anglican and English tradition would replace the grammar school at York and provide "a temporary university." Under these circumstances, Upper Canada College was founded as a state institution on the authority of Sir John Colborne, and opened in 1831.

DEVELOPMENTS OF THE 1830's

To the East, in Lower Canada, one of the best known of Canada's present universities was chartered at this time, financed by a bequest in the will of a Scots emigrant named James McGill who had prospered in the fur trade. A fellow Scot from Aberdeen started the Normal School at Montreal for training teachers in 1836. This development was three years ahead of the founding of the better-known first State Normal School in Massachusetts by Horace Mann, the great educational reformer.

Educational reform in New England had been sparked by fears that the private academies that had proliferated might become too selective. A democratic solution was the idea of public high schools, the first of which appeared in Boston in 1821. A broader objective was to secure the introduction of a complete system of free public schools run by the state, which were to be non-sectarian and tax-supported. Horace

Mann led the campaign to sell legislators on this idea and his home state of Massachusetts accepted it in 1827. To overcome the religious scruples of a variety of Christian sects, Horace Mann promoted the secular character of the public school system. One by one the New England states were forced into line and created state Boards of Education.

Americans were also attuned to educational developments in a rapidly industrializing Britain, where vocational training was being introduced for adults. The idea of Mechanics Institutes started in Glasgow, Scotland, where George Birkbeck inspired factory workers to study "mechanical and chemical philosophy." From such a humble beginning the Glasgow Mechanics Institute, founded in 1823, emerged much later as the University of Strathclyde. During the early nineteenth century, the idea of Mechanics Institutes supported by voluntary effort swept through Britain and North America. Reflecting the first genuine adult educational movement, a Mechanics Institute was aimed at helping the worker to understand the applications of science that were transforming his life. Some of these Institutes developed into technical colleges, while in England the London Institute later became Birkbeck College, a part of the University of London devoted to adult education. But after this bright start in the early nineteenth century, technical education lagged badly in Britain.

Edwin Chadwick and Dr. Southwood Smith, the Benthamites we have already met in connection with the Poor Law Act of 1834, were the instigators of the effort to get the state involved in education. These conspirators avoided a frontal attack on the religious factions by refraining from emphasizing a need for education, and quietly introducing provision for education in the guise of reform of factories and the poor law. By the terms of the Factory Act of 1833, a child could not work more than forty-eight hours a week, and had to attend school for two hours each working day. Parliament did not make any provision for financing the schools, as it assumed that manufacturers would set them up and recover the cost out of the wages of the children in their employ. Such an attitude towards financing education was hardly likely to be popular among the students. But free education gained a start when the New Poor Law Act of 1834 made the state responsible for the education of pauper children.

A very influential politician at this time was Lord Brougham who promoted the need for education at all levels. By 1828 Brougham had pushed through a new development in the organization of higher education, by the creation in London of a University College, open to students excluded from Oxford or Cambridge either because of religious tests or lack of funds. In 1836 the University of London was created to examine students from University College and grant degrees to them, as well as to those students of a rival Kings College established by Anglicans. The University of London was not allowed to teach, but the concept of external degrees granted to students of affiliated religious colleges and a non-denominational University College would profoundly affect the future organization of higher education in Canada.

EDUCATION IN BRITISH NORTH AMERICA

One indicator of the religious factor in the field of higher education within British North America is the large number of universities and colleges founded at this time under denominational auspices. Presbyterians founded Queens University at Kingston in 1841, while in the same year Baptists founded Acadia University in Nova Scotia. The Maritime provinces suddenly flowered, like Old Scotland, as a leading educational centre. Methodists created Mount Allison University, while Dalhousie University's cornerstone was laid by Lord Dalhousie, the Scottish Governor of Nova Scotia, who dedicated the college "in imitation of the University of Edinburgh."

In Upper Canada, Egerton Ryerson was appointed Assistant Superintendent of Education in 1844 and was given permission to spend a year abroad to study school systems in other countries. Ryerson's investigations were most significant because from the recommendations in his report was derived the basis of present-day Ontario's system of education. Ryerson admired the efficient Prussian system of centralized control and used this concept as a model in establishing the dominance of a provincial Department of

Education. But it was in Ireland that Ryerson felt that he had discovered the key to resolving religious strife in education. At that time the Catholics and Protestants in an undivided island had devised a national program whereby they had one mainly secular system of schools, but allowed visits from priests and ministers on specific occasions to handle religious instruction. To supervise this system a Board of National Education had been formed in Dublin in 1832, mainly upon the initiative of a Catholic named Thomas Wyse. Grants were supplied to those schools who conformed to the Board's requirements that extracts from a King James Version of the Bible, chosen so as not to give offence to Catholics, were read without comment twice a week. Textbooks called the Irish National Series purported to handle the religious issue in such a delicate manner that no religious group need feel offended, and these books appealed to the visitor from Upper Canada.

Egerton Ryerson was appointed Chief Superintendent of Education in 1846 and that year his recommendations were legislated into the Common School Act by the United Legislature of the Canadas. From the New England States, Ryerson adapted the general framework of elected school boards, taxation of property and government grants dependent on conforming to regulation. Irish National textbooks were to be used and Thomas Robertson, a Chief Inspector of Schools in Ireland, was persuaded to become a principal of the new Toronto Normal School. At the same time, however, to the chagrin of Ryerson, who wanted one educational system for the Canadas, the 1846 Act made a separate provision for Canada East (Quebec) by establishing parallel arrangements for Catholics and Protestants. Furthermore, the stipulated compulsory payment of taxes to sustain this new educational system was not too well received by the influential farmers. Riots and burning of schools took place in Canada East. In Upper Canada a district issued a statement which, after alluding to the average salary of £29 per annum paid in the previous year to Common School teachers, a sum which seemed exorbitant to them, concluded that the old inexpensive system was preferable:

... your Memorialists hope to secure qualified teachers ... by securing as heretofore the services of those whose Physical Disabilities from age render this mode of securing a livelihood the only one suited to their Decaying Energies.[1]

This statement is certainly a memorial both to the attitudes towards education of disgruntled famers and to the new calibre of teacher hired to staff the common schools.

EDUCATIONAL DIFFICULTIES

It was not only in the United Province of Canada that problems existed in the 1840's concerning the recruitment of poorly paid teachers from the rejects of other occupations. In England Dr. James Kay, the secretary to the Committee on Education, was an eloquent critic of a situation where most children received their education from Sunday School; on the other hand, Kay's examples of teaching incompetence in existing charity day schools indicated that these children may have been saved from a worse fate. One teacher in such a school ordered two globes, one for each hemisphere; another had refused to take the class attendance because King David had encountered trouble when counting the children of Israel. Yet the rivalry between the established Church and Nonconformism prevented much progress, despite praiseworthy attempts to sneak education through the back door by provisions in the Factory Acts of the 1840's. The bitterness of the tussle between the main religious groups can be judged from their slogans: "The watchword of the Church of England was 'a Church system or nothing'; that of the Nonconformists 'rather none than a Church system'."[2] But all was not lost as Lord Shaftesbury, the crusader for factory reform, also had an interest in promoting what were termed Ragged Schools. This movement began as a humanitarian effort to aid the ragged children of London. Shaftesbury learned from an appeal in *The Times* in February of 1843 that help was needed for a Field Lane Ragged School. Within three years, Shaftesbury had become President of a Ragged

School Union. Shaftesbury represented the paternalistic tradition at its best, and had a realistic approach to the problems of his age:

> You must keep your Ragged Schools down to one mark ... in the mire and the gutter; so long as the mire and the gutter exist. So long as this class exists you must keep the schools adapted to their wants, their feelings, their tastes and their level. I feel that my business lies in the gutter and I have not the least intention to get out of it.[3]

Upper Canada's educational system at this time showed influences from both Britain and the United States; while the Common School Act of 1850 sought free common schools in the British fashion, it also permitted the creation of individual separate schools. It is not widely known that the Act reflected the racial prejudice shown against slaves escaping through the "underground railway" from the United States. Negro children in the Chatham area of Upper Canada were refused admission to white schools, and this led to provision for separate Negro schools. Under the terms of this Act of 1850, funds for the common schools were to be raised by municipal assessments on property but not for the separate schools, who, while sharing in a provincial grant, were left to make their own arrangements for financing. What compounded the problem was that with heavy Irish immigration, the friction between Irish Protestant and Irish Catholic tended to make a mockery of Ryerson's belief in the tranquility created by the Irish national system. While the Irish textbooks were acceptable, and would remain so for the next twenty years, the same could not be said for the mixing of Catholics and Protestants: an independence of character of the Upper Canadian made him, it would seem, more like the stereotype of the argumentative Irishman than the Irish. Education became a political football, particularly as the equal representation in the Legislature from both Canadas permitted Lower Canada to exert considerable influence on provisions made for Upper Canada. French Canadians sought to ensure that Roman Catholics in Upper Canada had the same opportunity to organize their own school system, as they did in the parallel systems of education established in Lower Canada by the original Act of 1841. A bitter controversy began in the 1850's that saw the Roman Catholic Bishop, A.F.M. de Charbonnel, seeking to establish a separate school system in Upper Canada. Dr. Egerton Ryerson, the Chief Superintendent of Education, was assailed also by Protestants like the fire-eating George Brown, editor of the *Globe,* who accused him of being a tool of the Catholic Church. John Strachan entered the fray as the spokesman for the Anglicans, by proposing to form a coalition with the Catholics to exert pressure for separate schools. The embattled Ryerson had to lure the Catholics away from such a political union with his arch-enemy John Strachan, so he agreed to Catholic demands for a separate school system. Ryerson rationalized this decision in his *Annual Report of 1852:*

The existence of this provision for separate schools . . . prevents opposition and combinations which would otherwise be formed against one Common School system . . . it furnishes a safety valve for the explorations and evaporation of those feelings which would be arrayed against the Common School system.

This tendency towards denominational control was also apparent in the shaping of the University of Toronto. In 1849 the charter for Bishop Strachan's King's College had been revoked and a non-sectarian provincial university established, the University of Toronto. This had led Strachan to secure a new royal charter for Trinity College which was intended as an Anglican reproach to the "Godless University," while Bishop Charbonnel began St. Michael's College and the Free Presbyterians organized Knox College. Francis Hincks' University Act of 1853 was intended to get these religious colleges into the university fold and, to do so, he copied the framework employed at the University of London. A University College was established as a non-sectarian teaching institution, while the University of Toronto became an examining body to which the religious colleges might affiliate. As the University held all endowments, it was considered possible that the colleges might overcome their religious scruples to get the money they needed.

But in the short term there was little evidence that religious conviction could be undermined by financial considerations. This was made apparent in 1855 when the French Canadian Roman Catholic bloc in the Legislature secured the Taché Act, applicable only in Upper Canada, which officially established a full-scale separate school system with taxing power similar to that of the common school system. Egerton Ryerson was not even consulted when this change was made and, at one point, was so exasperated that he suggested the solution might be the abolition of separate schools. Yet from the French-Canadian point of view, the Roman Catholic faith had to be preserved intact in an increasingly secular age and the foundation of Laval University in 1854, a French-speaking institution in the city of Quebec, illustrated this determination.

And apart from the religious struggle that took the headlines then, there was the even more fundamental issue of how to finance education, a problem that continues to plague us to this day. The Common School Act of 1850 permitted school districts to tax all property to pay for free schools. Resistance then, as now, was based on the objection that a property owner should not be asked to contribute to the cost of educating children other than his own. One irate Toronto clergyman also took the position in the *Globe* of January 31, 1852 that free schools represented "communism in action." This resistance to paying taxes for education was even noticeable in the admired system of Massachusetts where Horace Mann had accomplished so much.

A recent study of this formative period in public education in Massachusetts has contradicted the view, popularized by progressive historians, that the worker was securing more education for his children. Michael Katz in *The Irony of Early School Reform* has pointed out that the introduction of the public high school did not benefit the working-class children for whom it was ostensibly intended. It was the middle class of Massachusetts that took advantage of Horace Mann's free public education, which was enforced by a law of

1852 requiring compulsory attendance. A by-product of the desire to keep the cost to a minimum was that teaching became a predominantly female occupation as women would work for lower wages than a man demanded: as Katz notes in his study of Massachusetts, the percentage of male teachers in the state declined in the quarter-century after 1840 from 61% to 14% of the total.

PROGRESS OF THE 1860'S

A contemporary of Horace Mann, William Holmes McGuffy, had a national impact upon the development of public education. For McGuffy's *Eclectic Readers,* a set of five graded textbooks developed over a twenty-year period, came to be regarded as the major tool in educating the masses. After the Civil War, the New England idea of a public educational system spread to the South and West and resulted eventually in the sale of 122 million copies of McGuffy's readers. There was a definite need for such a standard textbook, one which parents too would have studied, in view of the student-teacher ratio which in the 1860's reached the level of 80 to 1. A pattern also developed whereby a woman was expected, in the "easy" early grades of the elementary school, to cope with about one hundred and fifty little dynamos. Under such circumstances, corporal punishment to ward off incipient chaos was probably unavoidable.

A most important development in public education began in the United States with the passage of the Thirteenth Amendment. This constitutional change emancipated the slaves and presented the enormous challenge to public education of making the Negro literate. Initially Freedmen's Associations arranged for schools which by 1870 had 247,000 students, and higher education got underway with Fisk University, Howard University and Atlanta University. And as long as the Republican party maintained its policy of Reconstruction in the South, the process of integrating the new citizens into the Republic continued.

Social reconstruction was also in vogue in the British North American colonies during the 1860's. In preparation for the proposed union of the colonies, the Roman Catholics in Upper Canada took the precaution of ensuring the survival of their parochial school system. The Separate School Act of 1863 basically confirmed the status of the established Catholic school system and is important because this legislation was embedded, four years later, in the British North America Act. With the formation of the Dominion of Canada, education was entrusted to the Provinces and the rights of religious minorities were set out in section 93(1) of the B.N.A. Act as follows:

> Nothing in . . . law shall prejudicially affect any right or privilege with respect to denominational schools which any class of persons have by law at Union.

Considerable diversity existed in the various provinces concerning provision for education, although the method of financing education through municipal assessment of property was generally followed. In Nova Scotia, Charles Tupper had carried an Act for the Encouragement of Education in 1864 but when it became necessary to make a property tax compulsory, the Government fell in the following year. Further east, in Newfoundland, the fear of a property tax to sustain public education—on property where there was little arable land anyway—constituted a major reason for rejecting Confederation.

On the opposite side of the continent along the Pacific coast, a familiar drama involving religious controversy was being enacted. An Anglican minister, Robert Staines, launched the first school on Vancouver Island. Amor de Cosmos played a similar role to Egerton Ryerson in attacking Anglican dominance in his newspaper. Consequently a non-denominational system was established by the Free School Act of 1865, with the Roman Catholics then rejecting this philosophy and establishing their own parochial system.

As Canada was cutting her apron strings, the mother country was finally becoming vitally concerned about her own inadequate educational system. It was becoming apparent that Britain's lead in the process of industrialization was being reduced by competition from Germany and the United States, where public education was efficiently organized. The widespread illiteracy in Britain, estimated at one in five of the male population, made it difficult to expand technical training of the labour force. After the Reform Act of 1867 which enfranchised many illiterate workers, the anti-democratic politician Robert Lowe made his famous disparaging comment about this new electorate, that "we must educate our masters." Lowe, a cabinet minister, had already initiated a somewhat critical approach to the State's aiding voluntary schools to improve their performance. When a Royal Commission reported on the state of education in 1861, it revealed glaring inefficiencies in teaching and proposed that, in order to improve the level of instruction, an inspector check the classrooms before grants were issued. Parliament had seen the annual cost of grants rise from £39,000 to £831,400 and eagerly embraced the idea, with Robert Lowe evolving the details of a system of "payment by results." An examination of the pupils of voluntary schools was to be conducted by one of Her Majesty's Inspectors of Schools and the results were to be used for purposes of calculating the grant. Lowe explained to Parliament that, "If the new system will not be cheap it will be efficient, and if it will not be efficient, it will be cheap." Cheapness prevailed, and the grant fell to £656,000 by 1865. Furthermore, the emphasis on school attendance and examinations promoted by this system was to last for the next thirty years, an emphasis which made teachers feel that they were engaged in some kind of factory piece-work. Not until the Education Act of 1870 was passed, did England finally accept the idea that elementary school education should be provided for all children.

THE INFLUENCE OF ONTARIO

The early 1870's saw some drastic changes in the orientation of Ontario's school system. The 1871 Act to Improve the Common and Grammar Schools introduced the word "public" to describe elementary schools, and "high" to describe secondary schools. The new American terms reflected a more egalitarian approach to schooling, and one more suited to the new American-style capitalism which emphasized pragmatism rather than academic training in education. Efficiency now became a key word in educational circles. A revamping of the curriculum saw the classical subjects of Latin and Greek demoted to options, while the English language was emphasized and history and geography were added. Because of the fear that the classics might disappear, a special status of school was introduced, that of the collegiate institute. If sixty students in a school were enrolled to study the classics, which were still very important in terms of preparation for university entrance, that school would be classified as a collegiate, and a special grant given.

Dr. MacMurchy, headmaster of Toronto's Collegiate Institute between 1872 and 1900, was Ontario's equivalent to England's famed educational reformers Thomas and Matthew Arnold. MacMurchy, a stern Presbyterian disciplinarian, believed in building character by stressing integrity and self-discipline among both his students and teachers. These standards set by Ontario's leading secondary school widely influenced other schools. Gradually the distinction between the collegiate and the high school tended to disappear as the latter began to offer classics in order to qualify for the extra grant. After four years' attendance at High School, with Junior Matriculation at the end of the third year, a student could enter second year university.

Further changes developed in Ontario after the retirement of Egerton Ryerson as Chief Superintendent of Education in 1876. Ryerson had spent over thirty years establishing Ontario as a leader in the field of Canadian education. As recommended by Ryerson on his retirement, the cabinet-level post of Minister of Education was introduced. Another British idea transplanted in Canada in 1876 was that of "payment by results." Government grants to high schools were made dependent on the Intermediate (second form) examination written on a province-wide basis. As had happened in England, the results tended to discourage the giving of grant money because over half the high schools in the province failed to pass one student in the first examination. This result confirmed a suspicion that most high schools were operating at an unsatisfactory level. While the payment by results scheme was abandoned after seven years because it had produced an overemphasis on examinations, it left a feeling that a provincial examination was a good way of keeping schools up to the mark.

Education in Canada developed a pattern in which each province had its own examination to determine entrance to its high schools. To appreciate the harshness of the examination grind, it is necessary to recall that between 1873 and 1896, the country was in the grip of an economic depression. During this time parents were naturally inclined to support examinations as an accepted way to ensure that educational standards were high because they knew that in the harsh competition of the outside world, a child who had done well at a reputable school stood a better chance of employment. A less desirable feature of the high school admission examination was the use that principals made of it to exclude the poor student in order to recruit children of wealthier parents who were more likely to maintain a high academic standard, for the academic courses of the high schools were geared to prepare students for university entrance. Ontario's collegiate institute idea spread to the west where Manitoba, in 1877, had established a University. The University of Manitoba was established on the pattern of London and Toronto, as an institution that examined and granted degrees to students enrolled in affiliated colleges. While Canada still pursued the traditional classical studies, as there was not yet any widespread industrialism requiring technically trained graduates, new developments were taking place in Britain.

TECHNICAL AND ADULT EDUCATION

During the 1880's, great concern was shown over the deficiencies of technical education in Britain. A Royal Commission was established "to inquire into the instruction of the industrial classes of certain foreign countries in technical and other subjects for the purpose of comparison with that of corresponding classes in this country; and into the influence of such instruction on manufacturing and other industries at home and abroad." Two reports of this Commission issued between 1882 and 1884 deplored the deficiencies of technical training. It was customary at this time for a business executive and a technician to be trained within the firm, and this system was often inequitable, as the worker's son and the boss's son were not regarded as equal. While this system of on-the-job training tended to make the class structure more rigid, an even worse aspect was that it did not fully utilize the potential talent of the nation.

One man, however, attempted to encourage technical instruction in London: Quintin Hogg acquired a building known as the Polytechnic on Regent Street and, during the 1880's, financed it himself until public funds became available. These public funds came on the scene when Westminster passed the Excise and Customs Act of 1890 which diverted funds obtained from customs and excise duties on spirits and beer, commonly called "whisky money," to encourage technical education. "Whisky money" very soon made an impact on the educational scene. More Polytechnics were built in London, while science was encouraged on the curriculum of the public (independent) and grammar schools. Students were encouraged, for example, to study such subjects as chemistry, colloquially known as "stinks." Whisky money was a neat political way of financing technical education, since it tended to spread the cost between the working class who drank beer and their "betters" who drank spirits, while the drys could hardly complain about such an arrangement for educating the nation.

The 1890's saw a concern about adult education that was similar to the surge of interest in technical education in the previous decade. Considering that Oxford and Cambridge Universities were still mainly geared to turning out clergymen and theologians, or imparting a veneer of culture to gentlemen, the development of the Extension movement reflects great credit on those engaged in the work. Lecturers went forth with a zeal similar to that of John Wesley's Methodist revival, except that these missionaries were imbued with a secular faith. It has been estimated that over 50,000 students became involved with the University Extension movement in Britain. Essentially, the object was to cover the normal school syllabus in three years and encourage qualified students to go on to the final years of a university course. The term "extramural" was born to describe this activity, which

290

proved to be popular with members of the middle class but failed to reach the workers. The movement crossed the Atlantic when Herbert Adams, a historian at Johns Hopkins, started to give lectures away from the campus but, alas, they were not too popular with mature students. A new approach was then tried by the University of Chicago where their extension division encouraged group discussions, correspondence courses, production of films and concerts. Because of the diverse nature of this activity, incapable of clear definition, the term "continuing education" replaced "university extension." Possibly the different pattern of the development of adult education at the university level reflected different social attitudes in the United States from those in Britain.

For one thing, higher education in America was not regarded as a male preserve. Since the Civil War, there had been a number of new colleges founded for women: Vassar, Wellesley College, Smith College, Hunter College in New York City, with the latter becoming one of the largest women's colleges in the world. Meanwhile, Englishmen were anxiously debating the wisdom and propriety of establishing their first college to provide higher education for women, Cambridge's Girton College. Another reason for higher education spreading faster in the United States was the Morrill Land Grant Act of 1862 which had provided each state with 30,000 acres of public land for each Congressman, to be used for the support of agricultural and mechanical arts or the endowment of a college. Eastern states like New York benefitted from the original grants, with the newer Western states being recompensed with additional grants and compensation. The Morrill Act was the most important piece of educational legislation passed in the United States during the nineteenth century, for land grant colleges were founded in every state of the Union, and aid supplied to many existing universities and colleges.

HIGHER EDUCATION IN AMERICA

The rise of the United States to industrial prominence led to some sweeping changes in the curricula offered at the university level. Natural sciences were encouraged at the expense of classical and humanistic studies, while numerous professional and vocational schools turned out graduates trained to fit into the demands of the new economy. Older studies of law and medicine were rivalled by the newer ones of engineering, architecture, journalism and business management. Professionalism became a key word even for academics engaged in the more traditional classical studies. Graduates of American universities went to German universities in large numbers to acquire a Ph.D. and a love of the seminar. While the first American Ph.D. had been awarded at Yale in 1861, it was not until Johns Hopkins University was opened in 1876 that the German model was firmly transplanted to the New World. It is worth noting that the importation of the Germanic tradition of scientific scholarship produced a sharp distinction between "popular history" written by mere amateurs and "professional works" by university scholars.[4]

While much progress was being made in improving American higher education, there was a backsliding in the provision of elementary education for all American citizens. By the Supreme Court decision of *Plessy* v. *Ferguson* of 1896, the doctrine of "separate but equal" facilities for Negroes was given legal sanction. For over fifty years from that date, segregation by the colour of one's skin became an officially sanctioned feature of educational life in the Southern states.

CANADA STARTS TECHNICAL TRAINING

At this time Ontario was determined to keep abreast of educational trends and started to diversify its high schools by introducing commercial studies in 1891, and technical schools in 1897. It will be recalled that technical education in Britain had been helped along by whisky money: the Canadian equivalent for this was tobacco money. The "Macdonald Movement" sponsored by Sir William Macdonald, the tobacco millionaire of Montreal, encouraged manual training in such subjects as woodwork and drafting for boys and domestic science for girls. Macdonald financed the setting up of training centres in each province for three years, with English-trained teachers imported to get the programme going. The total cost to Macdonald was over four million dollars, with local authorities taking over at the end of the introductory three-year period.

COLLEGES AND HIGH SCHOOLS

On both sides of the Atlantic the word "college" traditionally referred to post-secondary institutions granting a Bachelor's Degree. In the United States, four-year liberal arts colleges stressed general education instead of the professional studies associated with the university. Because of the democratic desire to permit every citizen who could qualify for admission to attend college, the United States was beginning to develop a new form of two-year institution known as the "junior college." The first move in this direction came when the University of Chicago decided in 1896 to set up a separate division for the freshman and sophomore years. Based on this idea of separating the early years from the remainder of a degree programme, and to offer more general studies, separate institutions were established in Illinois for this purpose; these became known as junior colleges. This new type of college, a unique American contribution, slowly spread to many of the other states of the Union. In Canada, the idea of a junior college linked to a university had become established from 1899 in British Columbia, where Victoria and Vancouver had two-year colleges which were linked with McGill University.

Secondary education was also expanding rapidly in Canada at the turn of the century. British Columbia had only four high schools in 1900—at Victoria, New Westminster, Nanaimo and Vancouver—but plans were already afoot for the rapid expansion that followed in the next decade. Saskatchewan adopted the Ontario idea of four-year collegiate institutes in her Secondary Education Act of 1907. In Eastern Canada the familiar religious issue made expansion of the secondary school system somewhat more difficult.

Accommodating Roman Catholic students in ostensibly "non-denominational" schools led to some strange gentlemen's agreements. In New Brunswick, Roman Catholic schools functioned within publicly supported systems. Similarly, in Prince Edward Island convent schools were part of the public school system, while Halifax set aside certain schools for Roman Catholic students. A new dimension to this religious question developed as the Jewish population in Quebec increased through immigration and, rather than add a third system in that Province, the decision was made in 1903 to have Jewish children attend Protestant schools. Religious affiliations produced a need for flexibility in trying to adjust to the wishes of parents, but this had long been a feature of the Canadian educational scene. What was new around the turn of the century was the steady development of technical education in Canada.

EXPANSION OF EDUCATION TO THE 1920's

There were a number of factors that led towards the development of technical training. The Dominion was beginning to industrialize and consequently there was a need for skilled tradesmen. National attention in Canada was focused upon the need to provide technical training by the pressure that the Dominion Trades and Labour Council brought upon Sir Wilfrid Laurier for a Royal Commission. The then Minister of Labour, W.L. Mackenzie King, supported the creation of the Royal Commission of 1910 to enquire into Canada's needs "respecting industrial training and technical education and into the systems and methods of technical instruction obtaining in other countries." When the Commission's report was issued in 1913, its recommendations were soon legislated into law by the federal government. A sum of twenty million dollars was to be provided to the provinces, to be divided equally between students covered by the Agricultural Instruction Act of 1913 and the Technical Education Act. Due to the outbreak of war in the following year, the operation of this technical assistance act was postponed. But Ontario was forging ahead independently of the federal plans and had, in 1911, passed an Industrial Education Act to establish a provincial organization of vocational classes. To group together the vocational activities in the schools of Toronto a great project was planned and, in 1915, the attractive Central Technical School was formally opened.

Britain was only slowly coming to recognize the need for more education in the years before 1914. In 1901 Scotland raised her school-leaving age to fourteen. Parliament was also persuaded to provide secondary school education for a larger number of students under the Education Act of 1902. The duties of school boards were taken over by the councils of urban and county boroughs, so that "board schools" became "council schools." As council secondary schools could not be constructed quickly enough, the Board of Education paid grants to existing grammar schools to accept "free place" scholarship winners, and between 1902 and 1914 the number of children enrolled in secondary schools increased sixfold.

During the First World War there were a number of plans made on both sides of the Atlantic in anticipation of a need for training men in the postwar world. In 1915, the college at Vancouver which had been affiliated with McGill University was reconstituted as the independent University of British Columbia. A special Ministry of Soldiers' Civil Re-establishment aided thousands of Canadian veterans with federal assistance for free vocational and academic training. Technical education expanded rapidly in Canada due to the implementation of the federal Technical Assistance Act of 1919, which carried out the plans which had been postponed due to the outbreak of war in 1914. A sum of ten million dollars was provided to the provinces to introduce vocational training at the high school level. A system of equally shared costs between the provincial and federal governments encouraged this establishment of vocational schools and, in Ontario alone, sixteen day vocational schools existed by 1922.

Britain lagged behind in spreading the benefits of education despite Prime Minister David Lloyd George's plan to improve total educational opportunities. Lloyd George invited H.A.L. Fisher, vice-chancellor of Sheffield University, to become the president of the Board of Education during the war. Fisher planned for national growth which would eliminate the "halftimer" in the schools, raise the school-leaving age to 14 for everyone by removing exemptions, and provide compulsory continuation schools for young people between the ages of 14 and 18. Unfortunately, although the school-leaving age in England was raised to 14 in 1918, in the harsh postwar world Britain came to realize the economic cost of the war and the educational plans for continuation schools were soon scrapped in favour of trying to balance the national budget.

Canadian technical education developed quite rapidly in the 1920's, as the taxpayer was receptive to the idea that training students in trade or industrial courses would prepare them for employment. Federal funds were supplied for provincial programmes, providing these met the stipulation that half of the student's time was spent in an industrial area, which could include related subjects such as mathematics and science. Ontario tried to ensure that there would be jobs for these graduates by entrusting the course work of apprentice programmes to the technical schools under the Apprenticeship Act of 1928, intended to encourage students to enter such programmes and enlist the support of potential employers. Furthermore, vocational training was ideally suited to fit into the new educational philosophy of progressive education which was entering Canada from the United States.

THE IMPACT OF PROGRESSIVISM

John Dewey, a philosopher and educator, became a spokesman for Progressivism, a theory which stressed education for adult life rather than absorbing theoretical book-knowledge, and emphasized that the old learning-by-rote system should be replaced by a wider and more informal kind of education which developed a child's physical and social nature as well as his mind. Dewey's own books, *School and Society* (1900) and *Democracy and Education* (1916), combined with his prominence at Columbia University Teachers' College, spread the gospel on a nation-wide basis after World War I. As Progressivism or Deweyism was to profoundly affect the educational methods of North America, it is worthwhile examining the basic tenets of this faith. Essentially, Dewey accepted the view of Rousseau, the French philosopher, that a child's nature was fundamentally good, a view which denied the religious concept of original sin. It followed that discipline was a matter of encouraging self-control rather than having rules enforced by an autocratic teacher. Dewey adapted the European idea of a kindergarten, or garden of children, with its active little students who "learned by doing." The essential premise that schooling must be child-oriented was summarized in the dictum of "teach the child and not the subject." Under Progressive educators, the emphasis for teacher training was on how to teach. Subject content was reclassified into four major areas: those of health, fundamental processes, civic and social relations, and recreation. Disciples of Dewey agreed with his statement that there was no room "for any individual who wishes to lead his own life in reflective self-consciousness. Privacy is to be regarded as a sinful luxury." Education was not to be regarded as preparation for life but as life itself. It followed then that the key word was activity, as children were encouraged to participate in the educational process, whether as athlete, musician, student government leader or in numerous other activities provided by the school.

Americans welcomed this new professional approach to education during the 1920's; Progressivism brought a utilitarian approach that seemed to be consistent with their country's history and in tune with her contemporary needs. Democracy in the classroom would prepare citizens to take their role in society. Furthermore, Deweyism could be viewed in the context of the contemporary influence of the Frontier Thesis of Frederick J. Turner concerning the moulding of a national identity through frontiersmen, who had mastered the environment without reliance on book-learning. American inventiveness in industry and science had frequently come from such pragmatic pioneers as Henry Ford, then placing the nation on wheels with his mass-produced Model T. (This American hero of the automobile industry once outlined his attitude towards an academic discipline by his concise statement that "History is bunk.")

Academic content in the curricula of public schools was regarded by Progressivists as possibly inhibiting self-development and self-expression in a pupil. Another reason for the wide acceptance of Progressivism in the 1920's was that it seemed to offer a degree of tolerance in a very intolerant decade. Such organizations as the Ku Klux Klan and the American Legion were concerned about "Un-American" influences. This ostensibly patriotic belligerence was unleashed against textbooks or teachers that were alleged to adulterate or question the patriotic lessons of history. Nationalistic groups pressured almost every state legislature to pass laws banning the use of textbooks held to be disrespectful of American traditions. Typical of this trend was the New Jersey law forbidding in the public schools any book that "belittles, falsifies, misrepresents, distorts, doubts or denies the events leading to the Declaration of Independence or in any other war in which this country has participated." The American Legion undertook a programme of encouraging the writing of a truly patriotic history and everywhere during the 1920's history teachers were harassed by patriotic parents complaining about the textbooks. Few argued that history books should seek to tell the truth about the past. It was a flamboyant age when politicians sought votes by appealing to prejudice; Mayor Big Bill Thompson of Chicago denounced favourable references to Great Britain in textbooks, and announced that he was going to "bust King George in the snoot." There was never any question of punching the nose of the real King of Chicago, Al Capone.

The business community, and in particular the public utilities, sought to ensure that school textbooks on economics or economic history were influenced in the *right* direction. Science teachers also laboured under the threat of being called UnAmerican, for Fundamentalist sects resisted the teaching of such scientific theories as Darwinian evolution. An Anti-Evolution League kept its eye on teachers and led to the celebrated trial of a science teacher named James Scopes in Tennessee in 1925. One of the leading criminal lawyers of that age, Clarence Darrow, defended the teacher and held fundamentalist beliefs up to ridicule, but this did not prevent Scopes from being found guilty of teaching unsuitable material in his science classes, and this verdict could hardly inspire other teachers to pursue scientific knowledge.

University education tended to ignore the diminution of academic content in the schools and clung to the older curriculum involving separate disciplines of study. However, the faculty members of the universities could hardly disassociate themselves completely from Progressivism as the college student population doubled during the 1920's, to reach nearly a million at the end of the decade. Possibly the growth of the junior college owed something to Progressivism. By 1922, there were 207 junior colleges providing the lower years of a degree programme, plus numerous other programmes of activity. Going to college thus became a feature of the democratic process permitting students of widely varying abilities to develop their talents. On the other hand, the universities saw junior colleges as a bulwark against a flood of students who could not cope with their standards. Junior colleges provided a screening-out service for the State universities and thus their growth met little resistance. In any event, university authorities paid some lip service to the god of Progressivism by introducing physical education, home economics, and business administration: the University hero in some colleges was the man who scored the touchdowns on the football team, not the palefaced bookworm.

Progressive education came to affect public schooling in Canada as well, though to a lesser degree. Generally speaking, Western Canada was more willing to experiment with the new approach, although the impact was also felt in the East. Throughout Canada, there was less drill in the fundamental subjects and the importance of phonics in the teaching of reading was virtually ignored. Possibly the impact of Progressivism on Eastern Canada was diminished because of two major factors. First, the Eastern provinces of Ontario, Quebec, and the Maritimes had well-established programmes. Secondly, the provincial Departments of Education acted as centralized bodies that prescribed courses of study from above in a manner which tended to restrict permissiveness. Moreover, Canadian educators were quite different from Mayor Thompson of Chicago as, having no desire to bust King George in the snoot, they were watching British developments in the field of education.

SCHOOLS IN ENGLAND AND WALES

Plans for extending schooling beyond the age of 14 in England and Wales,[5] which had been proposed by the Fisher Act, perished under postwar retrenchment. There was a slight improvement in the relative position of working-class children, for a small number of local scholarships aided children to enter grammar schools, while State scholarships helped a few on to university. But only one in eight of those children who attended elementary schools in England and Wales ever reached a grammar school and only four in a thousand attended university. Not surprisingly there was frequent criticism of the educational discrimination that condemned a worker's child to finish school at 14. A committee was therefore set up, under the chairmanship of Sir Henry Hadow, to investigate the educational structure. When the Hadow Committee reported in 1926 on the Education of the Adolescent, it recommended that there should be primary education to the age of 11, and every student should then receive secondary education to the age of 15. But the British Conservative government that was grappling with such national issues as political prestige and economic difficulties was not interested in educating the working classes. Opposition was also voiced by Roman Catholics who did not want to finance secondary education.

While the Hadow Report was ahead of its time in recommending a secondary school education for all students, the ideals of the Hadow Report did make an impression in two areas of education. Selection of the age of eleven as the dividing point between primary and secondary education was prompted by the assurance of psychologists that intelligence tests could fairly accurately assess a child's mental capacity at that age. From then on, an "eleven plus" test assumed a major role in Britain's educational establishment. Furthermore, the Hadow Committee established a Consulting Committee of the Board of Education as a continuing body for making changes in the curriculum. These subsequent Hadow curriculum recommendations were used by educators in Canada to counter the Progressive pull to the South: for example, the influential province of Ontario based its curriculum on the Hadow recommendations and not on the dominant American philosophy.

CANADA AND AMERICA IN THE THIRTIES

Certainly there was a need for Canada to be concerned about the cultural influences flowing over the undefended border, if a Canadian national identity was to be preserved. W.L. Mackenzie King established a Royal Commission under Sir John Aird to investigate the impact of the new medium of radio and when after a year's study the Committee reported in 1929, it declared "Canadian radio listeners want Canadian broadcasting." In the eyes of the Aird Commission, Canadian radio should be concerned first with education, secondly to entertain and thirdly to foster Canadian nationalism. The first objective had already been attempted by the Nova Scotia Department of Education's regular broadcasting of school programmes in 1928. Whether the second objective has ever been attained is a matter of some dispute among Canadians, but the third aim did reinforce Canadian school books. History textbooks which extolled the Dominion's peaceful progression from colony to nation fostered nationalism during this decade and students were encouraged to appreciate the importance of Canada's new status, symbolized by the passage of the Statute of Westminster of 1931.

Decentralization of power in the British Empire had its counterpart within the educational framework of individual Canadian provinces. During the 1930's, departmental examinations for entrance to high school or matriculation examinations were played down, as Departments of Education gradually conceded to the schools the right to make decisions regarding admission and promotions. Alberta abolished Grade 8 examinations for high school admission in 1930, as did British Columbia in 1938.

Considerable attention was also given to equalizing educational opportunities between rural and urban communities, and this was facilitated by the introduction of bus transportation that enabled consolidation of larger school districts. A newly elected Social Credit government in Alberta led by a former teacher, William Aberhart, introduced in 1936 educational planning that had a large unit concept whereby, in the next five years, fifty large divisions absorbed 774 small districts. This consolidating process was encouraged by the economic depression as it provided more efficient units in Canadian rural areas and a larger tax basis from which to pay the teacher. For by the 1930's, even secondary school education was free to all pupils, with the exception of those in Quebec. One by-product of these grey depression years was that the perennial problem of absenteeism was virtually solved. Attendance was at an all-time high, as in the lean years of the "hungry thirties" it was better to stay within a warmly heated school than to be out in the cold, unemployed. Vocational training became increasingly important. By 1938, there were sixty-two daytime vocational schools in Ontario enrolling over 36,000 students.

In the United States during the depression, there was a sustained effort to try to reduce the pools of unemployment by adult educational classes. At one time over two million adult students were being taught by teachers drawn from various professions. Junior Colleges continued to expand, particularly where they were financed by public funds. These "opportunity colleges" were particularly prominent in densely populated states such as California and New York, and in 1938, over 575 such colleges existed. Economic depression also gave a boost to provision for education at the public school level. In view of the lack of jobs available, reformers seized the chance to push through federal legislation establishing conditions throughout the nation whereby children could obtain an adequate education. By the Fair Labor Standards Act of 1938 a national minimum age of 14 was set for employment outside of school hours in non-manufacturing occupations.

While Progessivism was well entrenched in the public school system of the 1930's, there was a new reform wind blowing at the university level. Economic depression left its mark on intellectuals as it became popular to rediscover the writings of Karl Marx; this in turn produced a strong reaction against the intolerance of the Red-baiting of the 1920's. Possibly a symbolic gesture at this time was the diplomatic recognition of the U.S.S.R. in 1933. Student radicalism was widespread and the high point came in 1936 when thousands of students publicly took the Oxford pledge never to bear arms in defence of their country. A total of 350,000 high school and university students went on strike on April 22, 1936 as part of an anti-war strike, including 3,500 at City College in New York and 5,000 on the University of California campus at Berkeley. Radicalism was worldwide, and in all the industrialized nations doubts were expressed about the future of capitalism.

BRITAIN BEFORE WORLD WAR II

Britain's economy showed few signs of revival before the introduction of a rearmament programme in the late 1930's. Consequently, there was not much effort expended to make national improvements in the much-criticized educational system, after the short-lived Second Labour government of 1931 had been unable to implement the Hadow plan to raise the school-leaving age to 15. In addition, many workers were now showing a negative attitude towards the value of academic education. There had been widespread unemployment since the end of the Great War, particularly in the declining staple industries of mining, ship-building and textiles, and parents showed a keen interest in preparing their children for other trades. As a result technical schools and colleges were generally filled to capacity, while many working-class parents refused to let their children accept free places they had won at grammar schools through scholarship examinations. The same attitude was reflected by those practical people who believed that a "utilitarian" university training available, for example, at the University of Birmingham, would better serve the needs of an industrial society than training at Oxford. In short, in Britain as in North America, the importance of practical or technical education was steadily gaining upon traditional humanistic studies. The university student population of Britain during the thirties remained at a stable figure of around 50,000: the woefully inadequate system of State scholarships, established in 1920 to provide 200 places, had only increased to providing 360

303

places by 1938. This static position was certainly not due to lack of desire on the part of potential university students in England and Wales for higher education, as was indicated by the approximately 12,000 degree candidates enrolled in University Extension tutorial classes.

The brightest spot in England's educational picture was the steady increase in the number of children attending secondary school. Over a fifteen-year period the grammar schools expanded their enrolment by over 40 per cent, with an attendance of about 545,000 students by the outbreak of World War II. Measured by the yardstick of attendance at American high schools this achievement was relatively modest, since up to five million students were attending secondary schools in the U.S.A. But plans were again afoot in Britain to give secondary schooling to all children. In 1936 Parliament took the plunge to introduce on September 1, 1939 the raising of the school-leaving age to 15. But an educator of a different breed named Adolf Hitler postponed the introduction of this educational advance for the next six years.[6]

EDUCATIONAL CHANGES PRODUCED BY WARTIME MEASURES

G.M. Trevelyan, the Cambridge historian, once suggested that the Battle of Britain in 1940 was won not on the playing fields of Eton but in the grammar schools of the thirties. Certainly the standards of scholarship in the prewar grammar schools had generally been high and this quality stood Britain in good stead during the 1939-1945 war. While education was naturally overshadowed by larger events of the early war years, a significant appointment was made when R.A. Butler became President of the Board of Education in 1941. For the next three years Butler probed and discussed all aspects of educational policy with various interested authorities. Butler discovered that the influential London Educational Authority favoured what was termed a comprehensive school where, as in the American high school, there was a mixture of students of varying abilities. Such a view conflicted with that of educational psychologists who were convinced that

304

intelligence tests around the age of eleven permitted separating children, so that they could attend different types of schools. Children were to be separated on the basis of ability and aptitude so that they would attend a school that concentrated either upon academic, general or technical education. Such a system of streaming, as it was termed, was also favoured by the Norwood Committee of 1943 which proposed a tripartite system of grammar, modern and technical schools. The increasing importance of educational reform was recognized in political circles. On August 10, 1944 Britain made a significant change in the title of Mr. Butler who became Minister of Education charged with "promoting" education: he had previously been President of the Board of Education authorized merely to "superintend" the system.

Meanwhile Canada was moving in the direction of the American model which favoured a high school organized on comprehensive lines. To encourage the introduction of vocational training in regular secondary schools, the federal government shared the cost with the provinces under the Vocational Training Co-ordination Act of 1942. Yet while the American method of organizing secondary education had many admirers, the weaknesses of the curriculum introduced by Progessivism were being severely criticized within the United States.

Before World War II, all subjects rated equally in terms of points and units, with the result that not enough time was spent on any one subject to gain mastery of it. Wartime Selective Service Boards found alarming deficiencies among potential recruits; they discovered many cases of illiteracy, and more generally, there was a dearth of men trained for positions requiring mastery of mathematics, science or foreign languages. To their credit, the American Armed Forces launched a widespread educational programme for off-duty servicemen who could take advantage of correspondence courses and study groups. The scale of this educational crusade can be gauged from the fact that, after the University of Chicago had prepared the necessary examinations, more than two million persons received advanced credit when they returned to high school and college after the war.

But while the general advance of the national level of education was a commendable objective, the prewar democratic tendency to rate all subjects as equally important was still prevalent. One would have thought that the danger of ignoring academic content, highlighted by wartime experiences, would have produced a change in Progressive attitudes, but so long as America appeared to be ahead there did not seem any need to panic. Therefore, as a Harvard report entitled *General Education in a Free Society* stated in 1945, "the tendency is always to strike a somewhat colorless mean."

Under the stress of wartime conditions, a determination developed in England not to continue with prewar non-democratic methods of permitting the wealth of parents rather than the talent of a child to determine the quality of his education. For up to 1944 secondary schools, whether grammar schools of old foundation or new schools run by local authorities, accepted only about 14 per cent of their enrolment from working-class children who had won free places through scholarships. In effect, three types of schools existed, each corresponding to a social class. Elementary schools trained members of the working class to the age of 14; secondary schools were a bastion of the middle class and continued schooling up to the age of 16; "public" schools or independent schools catered to the upper class.

In 1944, the Education Act was passed, embodying the careful planning of R.A. Butler. Essentially this historic piece of legislation carried out the proposal of the Hadow Committee of 1926 to provide "secondary education for all." "Secondary education" meant education between the ages of 11 and 15, with a raising of the age to 16 as soon as possible. Furthermore it was proposed that an adolescent worker between 15 and 18 should receive "post-secondary training" in an institution called a county college to be established by a local authority. The intention was to provide physical, practical and vocational education in the county college to students attending one day a week; unfortunately, like the similar proposal of H.A.L. Fisher after World War One, this aspect has never really materialized.

The feature of the Butler Act that aroused increasing controversy was that it allowed children to be streamed on the basis of an eleven-plus test. This idea was really not new as it had been used in prewar days in grammar school entrance examinations. Now, however, in 1944, the eleven-plus test was used by local authorities to determine whether a child joined one of three streams: the academic, the technical, or the practical. This classification embodied a belief that education should be suited to "age, ability and aptitude." Yet even before the new "secondary modern" schools were ready to receive those pupils classified as practically minded, a process that did not really get underway until about 1948, Scots educators condemned the whole pattern of education of England and Wales. For the Scottish Advisory Board report entitled *Secondary Education* (1947) flatly rejected the tripartite system of schools, coming firmly to this conclusion:

> We find the tripartite organization unsuitable for Scotland, because (1) it is wholly unrelated to the existing system; (2) grammar, technical and modern types cannot be distinguished at the age of twelve; (3) there is no evidence that the "modern" school will have adequate status; and (4) the conception of school as a community condemns the segregation of types at 12, even if it be possible.[7]

This report accurately predicted, in point three, the main difficulty of renaming senior elementary schools as "secondary modern": they would have no status.

In the late 1940's, secondary schools in Canada were changing from the traditional liberal arts institution to the composite or comprehensive school that provided secondary education for all. By 1948 approximately 30,000 Canadian veterans were taking secondary school training, and an additional 35,000 were enrolled at university. Some idea of the strain imposed on existing facilities can be gauged from the fact that the student enrolment at the University of British Columbia tripled to 9,000 between 1944 and 1947. Vocational training was also given a tremendous boost by the retraining of veterans under the rehabilitation programme which, between April 1944 and October 1948, helped 55,000 veterans to take vocational courses. The term "trade school" was considered demeaning in Canada, so was replaced by the more prestigious term Vocational or Technical Institute. One of the real accomplishments of this period was the establishment, on September 1, 1948, of the Ryerson Institute of Technology in Toronto, where the gradual raising of admission standards helped to build faith in this type of institution for post-secondary training.

CANADIANISM AND PROGRESSIVISM IN THE FIFTIES

Canada opened the Fabulous Fifties with the report of a Royal Commission on the National Development in Arts, Letters and Sciences. Popularly known as the Massey Report, after the chairman the Right Honourable Vincent Massey, this report of 1951 had as its purpose the encouragement of institutions which "express national feeling, promote common understanding and add to the richness and variety of Canadian letters." The major recommendation proposed that a Canada Council be established to give encouragement to the Arts, Letters, Social Sciences and Humanities. Ottawa responded by providing a meagre grant of $8 million to the universities in 1951-1952, to be subdivided on the safe political basis of counting heads in each province. Canadian universities eagerly accepted this chance to raise their standards of research, if not of teaching. However, there soon developed political opposition to this intrusion of the federal government into a provincial area of responsibility. Premier Maurice Duplessis withdrew Quebec from this attempt, as he saw it, of Ottawa to gain a foothold in influencing the educational bastion of French Canada.

In the United States at this time, education was linked to political considerations of defending a way of life; these became of great concern to the United States in August of 1953 when Russia exploded her first hydrogen bomb, and the Cold War threatened to become hotter. Congress responded by recognizing the vital role of education in the total political struggle, to the extent of authorizing federal aid to those schools where the establishment of defence industries had led to an abnormal growth of population. Yet this aspect of growth was not really abnormal in terms of the national postwar population boom, which completely confounded the predictions and plans of the experts of the 1930's, and threw a tremendous strain on the financial resources of municipalities and states. President Eisenhower tried to respond to the pleas of the mushrooming cities for federal aid for public school construction and programmes, but was defeated in his proposal of 1955 to give direct grants of $200 million and have the federal government purchase up to $750 million in local school bonds. Republican senators objected to government interference in local education, while southern Democrats feared it might undermine their resistance to racial segregation in the schools. To the political opposition towards expanding educational facilities at the public school level was added mounting criticism within educational circles about the effects of the "progressive philosophy" that had long dominated American thought. Following the death of John Dewey in 1952, this opposition became very vocal. The universities led the assault. In 1953 appeared Arthur Bestor's *Educational Wastelands* which criticized the mediocrity of American standards while, in Canada, a fellow historian named Hilda Neatby published *So Little For the Mind.*

These attacks on the "anti-intellectualism" of much of American education reflected a wider concern that something was drastically wrong. In spite of the fact that everyone was going to high school and unprecedented numbers were going to college and university, the national tastes were deplorably low in the eyes of the critics. Television programmes seemed fit only for imbeciles, politics were conducted in the manner of a circus extravaganza and, worst of all, "Johnny couldn't read." Teachers were seen as glorified babysitters. Such old-fashioned disciplines as spelling and arithmetic were neglected and student work habits were deplorable. Critics deplored the effects of a Progressivism that encouraged children to be critical of the school authorities, although these critics might have remembered that the right to criticize was a democratic sword that could be used to cut in many directions. The cry of back to McGuffy's readers seemed to be implicit in this searching reappraisal of whether "education for life" had failed. While attention to his social development made the American high school student a more gregarious creature than his British counterpart, fierce criticism was directed at his academic level of development. The crucial subject in the attack was reading, for in a textbook-oriented system reading was the key that enabled an individual to gain mastery of other subjects. British educators differed from most American experts in their belief that children should learn to read and write as early as possible, even before formal instruction began around the age of six.

DESEGREGATION AND THE SHOCK OF 1957

Education in the United States at this time was further complicated by the racial factor. The Supreme Court decision of *Brown* v. *the Board of Education for Topeka*, rendered in May 1954, spelled the end of segregation in the public schools of the South. Southern states now resorted to defiance of the law of the land in order to prevent integration, a defiance which reached a high point at Little Rock, Arkansas in 1957. Governor Orval Faubus used state militia to prevent integration: President Eisenhower reacted by assigning federal troops to keep order. Eisenhower had repeatedly stated that "there must be no second class citizens in this country" and in support of this statement, provided troops with steel helmets and fixed bayonets to ensure that Negro children could be escorted to school. Such incidents severely damaged the prestige of the United States in Africa and Asia where Communist propaganda capitalized on the apparent disregard for democratic principles.

Soon afterwards on October 4, 1957, came the traumatic shock to Americans of Russia launching the first Sputnik. All of the emotional feeling that had been building up from why Johnny can't read to wider doubts about progressive education burst forth in a torrent. Groups of educators hurriedly departed to Russia to investigate where the United States had gone wrong. These visiting educational experts were impressed by the emphasis placed on such subjects as mathematics, science and engineering. It was pointed out, for example, that in 1955 over 65,000 engineers had been graduated from the Russian universities against only 23,000 from American universities. The United States was convinced that Russia had a dangerous lead in scientific and technological personnel and, fearing to be second-best in anything, set off on a crusade to remake the characteristics of the nation. Back in the twenties, the craze had been to dry up all citizens from intemperate habits: now in the fifties there was a mission to create the largest possible number of qualified scientists and engineers. A crash programme was launched to catch up in the area of space research and, in July 1958, the National Aeronautics and Space Administration was created and supplied with immense sums of money. In the following month, the President had little difficulty in passing a National Educational Defence Act which provided $300 million for grants to public schools for providing laboratory facilities and textbooks and improving the teaching of mathematics, science and modern languages. Another $80 million was appropriated for ensuring enough college teachers, $300 million for a fund from which students could borrow on easy terms, and lesser sums for research into techniques to aid in the teaching of science and modern languages.

HIGHER EDUCATION EXPANDS IN CANADA

Canada's Parliament reacted to this new desire for the promotion of learning by finally implementing in 1957 the six-year-old recommendations of the Massey Report. The Canada Council was created with a capital sum of one hundred million dollars, divided equally between a capital fund for aiding university construction and an endowment fund for scholarships and loans. This endowment which yielded an interest of 6% annually could provide three million dollars for encouraging writers, painters, musicians and other citizens contributing to the intellectual life of Canada. The impact of Ottawa's new role of fairy godmother can be judged from the speed with which universities in Ontario began to be founded. Within three years, five new universities were established and the following decade would see another seven added. Not all of these universities started from scratch, as did Carleton and York Universities, for many were an outgrowth of existing institutions. Similar expansion was taking place in the west where, in addition, Alberta introduced the Junior College system. Meanwhile the public school system was undergoing a highly critical reappraisal as a result of the indictment of Canadian Progressivism voiced by Hilda Neatby's book *So Little For the Mind* (1953). As an historian, Neatby dismissed the mishmash known as social studies as worthless. Ruffled professional educators, who had built their careers on the sanctity of Progressivism, particularly in the educational establishments of Alberta and British Columbia, rather naturally fought back against those "academic intellectuals" who were so undemocratic as to want to train an elite which would be separated from the rest of the people. Such politically oriented words as elitism and segregation provided a powerful arsenal to mount a counterattack. But in a larger sense, all parties to this dispute of the 1950's had a common interest in improving educational facilities, and therefore supported the rash of Royal Commissions that investigated education in Ontario, Nova Scotia, Manitoba and Alberta. To those "old-fashioned" teachers who had clung throughout the heyday of Progressivism to the idea that academic subjects were as important as the style of teaching, it must have been balm to read the general conclusion that there was a need to upgrade the qualifications of teachers.

BRITAIN'S STATUS PROBLEM

Britain during the 1950's was again under a Conservative government who valued the traditional, segregated pattern of education. Yet there was mounting criticism of the eleven-plus test that determined which quarter of the twelve-year-olds of England and Wales attended grammar schools and thus, ultimately, who was admitted to university. Three out of every four students went into the terminal courses at secondary modern schools and a wave of applications for admission to private ("public") schools developed as middle-class parents sought an alternative for their children who had

Courtesy of the Salvation Army

The Salvation Army in Canada: (left) Jack Addie and Joe Ludgate, founders of the Canadian Army, 1882; (below) visiting a hospital patient in Winnipeg

Courtesy of the Foote collection, Manitoba archives

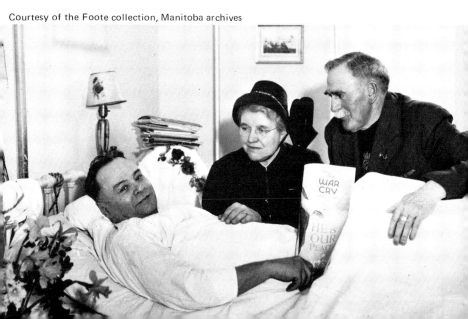

Courtesy of the City of Liverpool

Liverpool, home of the Beatles, has another claim to fame in its cathedrals. In the foreground is the circular Roman

Courtesy of the Public Archives of Canada

Upper Canada College, 1835

One-room school, Manitoulin Island, c. 1900

Courtesy of the Ontario Archives

FAITH HOPE and PARIT

Courtesy of *The Varsity*, Errol You

Student protest at the University of Toronto

Manual Training Room, O.A.A.C., Ottawa, 1901

Courtesy of the Public Archives of Cana

Courtesy of Jarrold and Sons Limited, City of Norwich Museum

Governor and Warders of the Norwich County Gaol, c. 1880

Messenger boys pose with policeman, City Hall Park, New York, 1903

Courtesy of Culver Pictures, Inc.

The Mountie Gets His Man: Fort Providence, N.W.T., 1921

Courtesy of the Public Archives of Canada

Courtesy of Karsh

The CCF Caucus, 1937. From left to right: T.C. Douglas, Angus MacInnis, A.A. Heaps, J.S. Woodsworth, M.J. Coldwell, Grace MacInnis, Grant MacNeil

Courtesy of Prime Minister Pierre Trudeau and Star Photo Studio

Pelé, the soccer star, with Prime Minister Pierre Trudeau

Courtesy of the Public Archives of Canada

Benjamin Disraeli, Earl of Beaconsfield (1804-1881): founder of the modern political creed of Tory democracy either disgraced the family by failing the eleven-plus, or were felt to be in need of removal from the influence of so-called common children. Such a process did not disturb the cabinet of Prime Minister Anthony Eden because a majority of the members had been educated at Eton. Successive Ministers of Education in Conservative governments displayed a tender regard for maintaining the existing educational framework.

Ideological arguments also raged in Britain over where to train the much-needed technologists. Everybody agreed that Britain needed more but the crucial issue was whether they should have the prestige of attending universities or should be trained in technical colleges. Academic argument was suddenly ended when Parliament decided to cut the Gordian knot by authorizing seven new degree-granting universities and converting ten leading technical schools into Colleges of Advanced Technology (C.A.T.s) where Diplomas in Technology were to be given for advanced work in applied science. These diplomas were intended to be the equivalent of an honours degree at a university. But the reforms did not go deep enough to ensure that advanced research would take place under the direction of leading scientists and engineers, for the staff at the C.A.T.s were paid on the same pay scale as faculty of the long-established technical colleges. By the 1960's there were over 300 local technical colleges with an additional 25 regional and 160 area colleges, so that it is not surprising that the general public failed to grasp the significance of the new C.A.T.s. It seemed that the problem of how to attract staff against the competition of the universities had to be solved if the C.A.T.s were to fulfill their intended role. The problem was one that had long plagued a Britain that valued both tradition and industrialization and it concerned prestige; it was hard to sell the idea of a diploma symbolizing a high professional status to the traditionally minded universities. But the issue was speedily resolved when a Prime Minister's Committee on Higher Education, led by Lord Robbins, recommended a much faster rate of university expansion to "help the nation meet the competitive pressures of the modern world."

The Robbins Committee published their report on October 23, 1963 and proposed that degree-granting should be widely expanded with the ten C.A.T.s to become technological universities. Furthermore, the number of students receiving higher education was to be increased from the existing level of 216,000 to 390,000 by 1973, with university places increasing from the existing 118,000 to 219,000 by 1973 and then to 350,000 by 1980. With a general election on the horizon, the government at once accepted this accelerated expansion of higher education, although it should be pointed out that this "educational crisis" was not seen as a party affair. Both the Labour and Liberal parties were consulted and supported the national aims of catching up in facilities for higher education, which involved a whopping capital outlay of £1,420 million in seventeen years, and an annual outlay of £742 million by 1980. Probably the real significance of the Robbins Report was the emphasis on status for those institutions concentrating on technological studies and, to implement these recommendations, a Council for National Academic Awards was founded in 1964 to grant degrees to students in technical colleges.

Thus culminated a long struggle over emphasis in curriculum between the older universities (Oxbridge) who concentrated on studies in the humanities and those newer utilitarian universities of the twentieth century (Redbricks) that were more oriented towards technology. As the political and ideological arguments had centred around the key concept of status, it is interesting to note the surge of interest in the field of sociology at these new technological universities, such as Aston and Bath. Did this mean that England was seeking to become a more democratic society in the 1960's?

The school system still displayed a strong aristocratic tradition. Of the nation's youth, only about 6 per cent went to preparatory school from age eight to eleven, then to "public" or independent school to the age of eighteen, and then, if the advanced levels of the General Certificate of Education (C.G.E.) were passed, to Oxford or Cambridge. These institutions were the bedrock of the aristocratically inclined upper class. In contrast, the newer provincial or Redbrick universities drew the bulk of their students from the 20 per cent of the youth going to grammar, comprehensive or technical schools that provided a General Certificate of Education. Of course, there were always exceptions to this pattern, such as those grammar school boys who went up to Oxford or Cambridge. The balance of the nation's youth, two out of three students, attended secondary modern schools that trained them to be the hewers of wood and drawers of water of society. To try to enhance the prestige of the educational training received at these secondary modern schools, a new diploma termed a Certificate of Secondary School Education was introduced in 1965.

Conservative Ministers of Education were generally in favour of preserving the existing grammar school structure, but also of widening opportunities by adding technical courses, and building up the university entrance level of instruction known as sixth form, which could also be used as terminal education at the level of the American Junior College. But Conservatives drew the line at the comprehensive secondary school, as it seemed another of those dreadful American ideas, and therefore tended to support this idea only in rural areas, on the grounds of economy. Certain industrial cities such as London, Coventry and Bristol did, however, adopt the comprehensive plan. So, for a combination of reasons, when Labour leader Harold Wilson announced his intention to remake the secondary school structure along comprehensive lines, a howl of protest was aroused. Conservatives saw this educational reform as an attack on their cherished grammar schools and as a dastardly Labour plot to tighten the "old school tie" until it really hurt. Education in the late 1960's had finally emerged as the major item in the national spotlight.

CANADA REVAMPS HER HIGH SCHOOL CURRICULUM

While the political struggle raged in England over revamping the system, Canada had been actively revising its provincial systems of education. As John Porter pointed out in his book *The Vertical Mosaic,* there is such a thing as class in Canada, although unlike in Britain, the existence of class structure is rarely discussed. An interesting North American phenomenon exists in that while it is undemocratic to discuss the concept of class, there is nothing wrong with discussing the topic of money, which provides the basis for a functional class structure. For those parents able to pay for private schooling, there exist in Canada a number of independent schools, usually modelled after the grammar schools of England, which provide the same service of ensuring that students sent to the university have been given a good education in basic subjects.

By the early 1960's, the postwar baby crop had become an adolescent boom that necessitated a good deal of adaptation in the traditional academic high school. There had always been a high proportion of dropouts by Grade 10, but now that secondary school training was a guaranteed right for everyone, there had to be a reappraisal of the academic needs of this booming student population. Canadian educators recognized that the traditional high school course geared to university admission was not suitable for more than 20 per cent of the population, for only these would derive some real benefit from such a strictly academic programme. On the other hand, there were indications that not more than 20 per cent of the students trained in specific vocational skills at high schools would actually take jobs that demanded these skills. This left around 60 per cent of the student population to be provided for, which was roughly equivalent, in percentage terms, to the group attending secondary modern schools in Britain. In order to cope with these conditions, most Canadian provincial authorities devised high school programmes with a vocational orientation where approximately half the pupil's time was spent on academic subjects such as Mathematics, English, History and Geography. Departments of Education offered four- and five-year programmes as well as terminal courses ending after two or three years which were intended for those students considered to have a more limited capacity.

Ontario was in the forefront of the new reorganization of curricula at the high school level. At the opening of the 1962 school year the Robarts Plan, named after the Minister of Education who had devised it, was introduced into Ontario secondary schools. A wide assortment of courses was provided under the three main divisions of Arts and Sciences; Business and Commerce; and Science, Technology and

Trades. The last two categories were described by the terms "commercial" and "industrial" in British Columbia, where the pattern of education was essentially the same as that in Ontario. In both provinces the students in regular four-year high school programmes graduate at Grade 12, while other students are enrolled in a five year programme that enables them to continue an extra year to qualify for admission to university. This extra year at high school is equivalent to the freshman year at an American four-year liberal arts college, or to Britain's sixth form.

Because of traditional attitudes which regard academic programmes as superior to training in trades or technical studies, there has been a tendency to use the blanket term Vocational Training. Changing the name of technical courses did not change the view of many Canadian parents that their children were getting an inferior education when they were not enrolled in the strictly academic stream. But for many children the academic stream was not suitable, and a high drop-out rate existed in academic programmes in the 1950's. This was a serious problem for the nation, for many of these young people could not find a place in a labour market that required skills or, at the very least, a graduating diploma of some type. In a Canada that continued to become more urbanized and industrialized, there was undoubtedly a need for skilled manpower but, so long as the stream of skilled immigrants continued to arrive, there had been no critical shortage. But there were signs that the peak of immigration by skilled workers had been passed. Faced with this dual situation of a diminishing flow of skilled immigrants, combined with a lack of Canadian facilities for training technical workers, the federal government decided to support the introduction of many new vocational schools which would contribute towards solving a future shortage of skilled workers and help to dry up pockets of unemployment. Up to 75 per cent of the cost of building and equipping such schools was provided to provincial governments under the terms of the federal Technical and Vocational Assistance Act that was passed on December 1, 1960. By the end of 1965, the Federal-Provincial arrangements had provided a total of 819 new technical, vocational and trade schools and

317

institutes of technology with a capacity of over 300,000 students. Over a billion dollars had been invested between 1961 and 1965 in creating this new wave of educational institutions and this financial drain aroused concern in political circles, particularly in view of the unrest that was evident in Quebec.

The "quiet revolution" in Quebec in the early 60's had an educational facet. A Royal Commission on Education under Monsignor A.M. Parent, Vice-Chancellor of Laval University, reported its first findings in 1963. The Parent Commission made an exhaustive study of the needs of Quebec in the modern urban and industrial setting and proposed a complete change in the traditional pattern of education which, while retaining distinctive French-Canadian features, would provide the citizens of the province with an education similar to that available in other provinces. The overall intention of the Parent recommendations was to ensure that Quebec produced enough technicians, skilled labourers, commercial and clerical workers. Stress was placed on the need for vocational and technical courses within regional comprehensive secondary schools, with the object of ensuring that French-Canadian workers would be able to find employment within their own province.

The essential proposal was that the private institutions operated by the church should be integrated into a more centralized administrative structure run by the province. Quebec had a unique church-operated, municipally maintained system of colleges classiques which provided a classical training that led at the end of the seventh year to a baccalauréat degree, a prerequisite for university training. These colleges had provided an elite class of broadly cultured leaders, much as the distinctive grammar and independent schools have done for Britain. But in the fast-changing scene of the 1960's, a widening of educational opportunities had to take place if Quebec was to adapt to the complexities of Western urbanized industrial society.

URBAN PRESSURES IN THE 1960'S

A number of factors contributed to the impression that the foundations of society were being shaken. A new vocabulary had sprung up to describe the character of the continuous bands of urban settlement that characterized North America. Such expressions as "megalopolis," "ecumenopolis," "polynucleated urbs," "the symbiosis of urban and rural" were enough to frighten anyone. But, in the language of laymen, the problem of overcrowding within cities and the growth of suburbia created severe urban problems that had an important impact on education, particularly in the downtown core of many large cities. In the United States, many Negroes migrated north into the larger cities and millions of whites fled to the suburbs. Teachers left with the exodus and whereas only a couple of decades previously new graduates from teachers' colleges had wanted to teach in the big city, the preference now was for suburbia. The result of these trends was that the downtown schools were hard-pressed to cope with a rapidly changing neighbourhood. In New York City, over three-quarters of the public school children of Manhattan were Negro or Puerto Rican while, by the end of the 60's, over 93 per cent of the school population of Washington D.C. was black. These new arrivals were often described as culturally deprived and federal aid was sought to finance special programmes to assist the parents to combat poverty and the children to raise their educational level.

President L.B. Johnson in January 1965 asked Congress to pass a budget of $1.4 billion for aid to elementary and secondary schools. In urging this step, Johnson declared that "Poverty has many roots but the taproot is ignorance." Furthermore, he noted that about a million young people quit high school each year in a society where higher education was "no longer a luxury but a necessity." Congress rapidly approved his Elementary and Secondary Education Act of 1965, covering a five-year programme, with President Johnson commenting that it would provide "hope for more than five million educationally deprived children." The federal government would provide up to 90 per cent of the cost of any community venture that would help to solve their problems. The educational programme that attracted particularly widespread publicity was the Headstart Programme of summer courses designed to prepare preschool children of low-income families for regular school or kindergarten.

REVOLT AT BERKELEY

A more complex situation existed in higher education at this time in the U.S. In the fall of 1964, the University of California felt the impact of the "Berkeley Revolt" which began with a wave of introspective pondering about the purpose of higher education. Students started from the basic premise of free speech in a liberal institution and proceeded rapidly to become active in a number of causes. There was support for the peace movement and civil rights, and, naturally, debate about the role of the university in modern society. As the 60's continued, mounting resentment was shown against big business and a power elite. Black students displayed pride in the increasing prestige of new African nations, which was reflected in their African style of dress and a desire to have courses that studied the accomplishments of black people. The type of student who was in the forefront of this crusade for change was one who majored in the humanities or social sciences, possibly because, unlike other students planning for professional careers such as lawyers or engineers, he lacked a specific career goal, with his interests centred more generally on social service, research and perhaps teaching. A further factor contributing to the unrest among the arts students, no doubt, was the high failure rate due to the open policy of admission to the state universities; for example, about fifty per cent of the freshmen entering Berkeley did not graduate.

Statistics on the size of the national student body convey an idea of the ease with which it was possible to be lost in a crowd. By the mid-1960's, there were over six million students attending college, and over forty-five million Americans attending a course of some type in college or high school, particularly in the evening. In other words, nearly a quarter of the adult nation was going to school. At the apex of this army of scholars were over 500,000 graduate students studying for higher degrees, who comprised an important subculture that deserves examination because it is directly related to events at Berkeley. It is hard to deny that the possibility of being drafted to go to Vietnam played a major role in stimulating the growth of this body of graduate students, with a resultant fear of the possible consequences of a drop in grades. At Berkeley, many of the professors used their graduate students as lowly paid teaching assistants and thus left themselves free to pursue the demands of prestige-conscious administrators that they should "publish or perish."

There are probably many explanations for the under-graduate's feeling that he is being short-changed, particularly at the state universities, but one of the most interesting involves the idea of differences in social class which, theoretically, do not exist in a truly liberal democratic society. Dr. Martin Meyerson, former Acting Chancellor at Berkeley, and a scholar who had taught at Harvard for many years, summed up the attitude of many of his colleagues:

> At Oxford and Cambridge, Harvard, Yale and Princeton, the rewards of teaching included the faculty's sense—even if not articulated—that their students were the sons of the famous or were themselves apt to be famous in the future. It is more attractive for teachers to spend time with the well-prepared and potentially powerful, than with the mediocre student of humble origins. The professor's frequent preference is to devote intellectual and leisure energies to colleagues or in some cases to men of affairs; he can be motivated to attention toward his students by a sense of duty, but this sense functions best when duty is reinforced by pleasure. And the pleasure the teacher gets seems to increase with the intellectual and social standing of his pupils.[8]

Large state universities, such as the University of California, may have attracted leading scholars but these were unlikely to be interested in the average student. Furthermore, the demand for places allowed private institutions to be more selective in their admission policy and recruit a higher pro-portion of talented students.

Students found it difficult to reconcile the liberal approach of colleges, based on Christian idealism, optimism and inevitable progress, with a world that displayed other tendencies. Inevitable progress had become suspect after Adolf Hitler massacred Jews and Americans atom-bombed Asians. Later, in the 1960's, many students began to suspect that the United States had an imperialistic attitude towards such countries as Vietnam. But the reaction was a different one to those students of the 1930's who had glimpsed Utopia in reading the Communist Manifesto, which had seemed like an extension of the Sermon on the Mount. In an age of instant communication, students knew the practice of Communism was frequently different from its theory. Therefore, to effect change, the students themselves had to become the revolutionaries, most of them rejecting any political dogma, except perhaps the slogan "Don't trust anyone over thirty."

CANADA EXPANDS EDUCATIONAL OPPORTUNITIES

The furor in educational circles visible in the United States did not extend on any equivalent scale to Canada. British Columbia could hardly fail to be influenced to some extent by events in California due to its geographic proximity, as exhibited by unrest at the new university of Simon Fraser. Quebec, on the other hand, was experiencing a new nationalistic pride that was basically home-grown. In general, Canada had fared quite well in her attempt to build new universities quickly enough to meet her student needs, with the number of students increasing, in a ten-year period ending in 1964-65, from 68,300 to 178,200. This represented an increase in enrolment of one hundred and sixty per cent. Capital expenditures on education in Canada had risen in this period from twelve million dollars to two hundred million.

Yet even university expansion was exceeded by the efforts that had been made to provide vocational training centres under the Technical and Vocational Act. By the end of 1966, under this Act the Federal Government had provided the provinces with assistance for 899 capital projects, such as new schools or additions to schools offering technical-vocational courses. This programme was also extended to cover the retraining of older persons and preparation of technical-vocational teachers. With the federal contribution amounting to as much as 75 per cent of the cost, it was not surprising to find the provincial premiers seeking control of this money without any strings attached. In 1966, Prime Minister Lester B. Pearson admitted that the technical-vocational agreements had made for a distorting effect on the educational structure, by giving a province a stronger incentive to build technical schools than to expand universities. Therefore, Pearson committed the federal government to paying half the operating costs of all post-secondary education. In the fall of 1967 the Minister of Finance, Mitchell Sharp, announced that the federal government would cease its grants to universities and would henceforth leave the provinces to control the general direction of educational financing. This placed control firmly in the hands of the provinces, although Ottawa insisted that it play its traditional role as an equalizer of opportunities in the provinces by acting as a benevolent Robin Hood.

Free to organize the educational scene, the provincial governments decided to introduce a new type of post-secondary institution, the community college. This was to some extent a version of the American two-year college, but was geared mainly to the needs of the high school graduate who was not destined for university training. Such "opportunity colleges" concentrating on vocational and technical programmes were established in a variety of forms.

British Columbia set out to secure local financial support for regional colleges by means of plebiscites but this did not secure widespread support. By 1971 the provincial government had decided to amalgamate their provincially operated vocational schools with adjacent regional colleges. This trend towards a comprehensive approach, that included an academic transfer stream in the style of the American Junior College, has also been a noticeable feature of Alberta's approach. Ontario, on the other hand, has tried to keep its community colleges known as Colleges of Applied Arts and Technology (C.A.A.T.s) separate from the university structure. The twenty C.A.A.T.s created by the end of 1967 were intended to be a distinctive creation, offering an assortment of vocationally oriented programmes. Political pressure to create colleges suitable to graduates of Ontario's Grade 12, combined with an effort to meet local economic needs, has provided a situation where considerable experimentation is taking place to help define the role of the C.A.A.T.s. Courses are divided into three divisions: technology, business, and applied arts. The curricula for the first two divisions tend to follow the outlines of the vocational programmes of the high schools: this is probably an inevitable trend as the students, and many of the staff, come from this background. The Applied Arts division is seeking to fulfill the service needs of modern society, for example by training women to work in the child-care centres in the cities or provide personnel to the restaurant industry. It might seem that the provincial politician has given a free hand to the administrators of the C.A.A.T.s but this is not really true. At a cost of a million dollars, a computer model simulation has been created of the C.A.A.T. system with the intention of helping to assess efficiency in future years. Ontario has sought to avoid the problems associated with transfer of marginal students to university, which have developed in the Junior Colleges in the United States; Junior Colleges there have become a screening ground for a multitude of students who have been encouraged to think that not to try to secure a university degree is virtually an unAmerican activity. On the other hand, the C.A.A.T. is not intended to be solely a vocational-technical institution. But faced with the political pressure from parents and students in the next twenty years, it is likely that considerable adaptions will be made to the system. In 1970, the C.A.A.T. system in Ontario was already roughly one-third the size of the university structure, having 40,000 students compared to 114,000 at the universities. During the winter of 1970-1971 a Royal Commission on Post-Secondary Education, under the chairmanship of Dr. Douglas Wright, studied the whole spectrum of education in Ontario. Manitoba has, in general, patterned its community colleges on those of Ontario and will no doubt watch further developments with interest.

Quebec has made the most drastic changes in her provision for higher education. Collèges d'enseignement général et professionnel (C.E.G.E.P.s) or Colleges of General and Vocational Training, have been introduced on a large scale since 1967. Over half the collèges classiques have become C.E.G.E.P.s, which are supported by the state rather than financed by the church. The impact of changing from a classically based system to a technologically oriented system has been a traumatic experience. Unlike Ontario and Manitoba, Quebec has instituted a comprehensive college system that includes a transfer stream to the University level. In fact, students can now progress to the university only by first attending a C.E.G.E.P. and, therefore, the introduction of these new colleges has had a profound effect upon all education in the province.

PREDICTIONS OF FUTURE GROWTH

Canadian universities have watched the sudden boom in community colleges since 1967 with a somewhat ambivalent attitude. Universities have been complaining that their growth has been inhibited by the fact that provincial politicians control the purse strings and considerable lobbying has been going on to secure more money. A brief submitted to the federal government in November 1970 by the Association of Universities and Colleges of Canada made the following predictions:

> Projections are that between 1968/69 and 1975/76 full-time enrolment at universities will have grown by 91% (from 293,600 to 560,000), and that part-time enrolment will have risen 107% (from 104,100 to 215,700). By 1980/81 full-time enrolment will have grown to 750,000, with part-time enrolment reaching 298,000—the total full-time equivalent would be 849,300.[9]

This submission states that, "We sense a growing demand for continuing university education on a full-time and part-time basis for retraining, upgrading and for general educational advancement." The brief continues, "It is our conviction that universities must prepare for a much deeper involvement in continuing higher education than they have in the past." And the brief cites a growing demand by women for further education, whether it be to enable them to take a greater part in professional life or for personal satisfaction. It argues that women are determined to break down the present barriers to their advancement and "while financial assistance alone cannot remove these barriers to education, the extension of facilities for continuing education would be a strong encouragement."[10]

Undoubtedly some of these predictions reflect the deep concern felt about what Dr. J.J. Deutsch, principal of Queen's University, called a "frightening picture." Yet one cannot take some of the statements too seriously when they imply a traditional concern about the general education of adults. For one suspects that, in view of the long disdain felt by many University faculty members for their Extension Division, that this is a case of special pleading, A new government policy in Ontario for the academic year 1971-1972 allowed part-time students to be included for grant purposes: conversely, the small army of students engaged in postgraduate study was to be diminished. Administrators now saw the need to study their part-time undergraduates in a new light. Similarly, university administrators show a great concern for community colleges partly because they feel these new institutions have drawn away funds they would have otherwise obtained.

NEW HORIZONS AND THE PERSPECTIVE OF TIME

The traditional university lecture hall or seminar room may not be the answer to modern educational needs for a mass audience. In an age of electronic marvels, a strong case can be made for bringing the course to the students and not the other way around. The most imaginative approach so far in this direction has been Britain's University of the Air, which has enrolled 25,000 students who take basic instruction from television. This system has several virtues: it is economical and can fully utilize top-flight lecturers, and furthermore, the taxpayer can readily see what he is getting for his money. And, in political terms, it is a good idea in an age when images are important.

Rapid social and technological change is also causing citizens to take a fresh look at education. Education must be a continuous process which combines "on the job" training, or life itself, with the learning acquired in a formal institution. Professional educators may not be the best judges of what is needed in a time of rapid change. Furthermore, there is a problem of communication. For Arthur P. Crabtree, a leader in adult education in the United States, has admitted that, had he met the jargon known as educationalese or professorialitis forty years ago, he would not have had the courage to tackle education.[11] To illustrate his point, this veteran of adult education cites the following definition of his own field.

Adult education is the action of an external agent in purposefully ordering behavior into planned systematic experiences that can result in learning for those for whom such activity is supplemental to their primary role in society, and which involves some continuity in an exchange relationship between the agent and the learner so that the educational process is under constant supervision and direction.[12]

In the 1970's education has become a major element in developing new life styles. It may be worth recalling that educational institutions have frequently reflected the forces of change. Prestigious colleges at Oxford and Cambridge have had periods of riot as well as periods of slumber; troops have been called out to disperse unruly students at Harrow and Eton, while at Winchester the red flag was flown defiantly on at least one occasion. History is basically a study of the process of change, and in education there can be seen the continuous interaction of cause and effect. Education is a facet of society that is apt to mirror the hope and the despair of each generation.

1   J.C. Hodgins, *Documentary History of Education in Upper Canada from the Passing of the Constitutional Act of 1791 to the close of Reverend Dr. Ryerson's Administration of the Education Department in 1876* (Toronto: Warwick Brothers and Rutter, 1894), vol. 2, p. 115.
2. A.D.C. Peterson, *A Hundred Years of Education* (London: Gerald Duckworth and Company Limited, 1952), p. 35.

3. Lord Beveridge, *Voluntary Action: A Report on Methods of Social Advance* (London: George Allen and Unwin Limited, 1948), p. 160.

4. The distinction between the two branches of historical writing suggests that the professional version is usually unpopular. A leading American scholar has made the following comment that helps to explain a major reason: "I have learned that the result of the historian's efforts to be detached . . . has been bloodless history, with no clear focus, arising from antiquarian curiosity rather than deep personal concern . . . ." H.S. Hughes, *History as Art and as Science: Twin Vistas on the Past* (New York: Harper and Row, 1964), p. 96.

   The concept of scientific history has made less progress in England's seats of learning. A Cambridge historian has remarked, "History as an academic discipline in this university is sometimes thought of as a catch-all for all those who find classics too difficult and science too serious." E.H. Carr, *What is History?* (New York: Alfred A. Knopf, 1969), p. 110. This is the twelfth printing of a series of lectures that provide illuminating discussion.

   Canada has drawn upon the literary tradition of Britain with D.G. Creighton setting a high standard of historical writing. In recent years some "popular" historians such as Barbara Tuchman and Pierre Berton have written some admirable historical literature for our enjoyment.

5. According to the *Canada Year Book, 1969,* p. 179, people of Welsh extraction are classified in an odd category known as "others." This is unfair to Wales which I prefer to treat as a country that is a part of the United Kingdom. One wonders how David Lloyd George, Nye Bevan or Richard Burton would respond to the term "other."

6. It is not generally known that the Fuhrer's Minister of Propaganda, Dr. Josef Goebbels, designed a uniform for German professors. See Henry E. Barnes, *A History of Historical Writing* (New York: Dover Publications Inc., 1962), p. 290. In view of this trend it is hardly surprising that academic support was rapidly mustered for an amateur historian named Winston Churchill.

7. W.O. Lester Smith, *Education in Great Britain* (London: Oxford University Press, 1967), p. 68.

8. Martin Meyerson, "The Ethos of the American College Student: Beyond the Protests," in Robert Morison, ed., *The Contemporary University: U.S.A.* (Boston: Houghton Mifflin, 1966), p. 274.

9. D.W. Judge, "Universities Seek Federal Policy on Higher Education," *Canadian University and College,* November 1970, p. 4.

10. Ibid.

11. Arthur P. Crabtree, "Quo Vadis, AEA?" *Adult Leadership,* vol. 20, no. 3, September 1971, p. 118.

12. Ibid.

8

Law and Order

When constabulary duty's to be done
The Policeman's lot is not a happy one.

W.S. Gilbert

Most people see the need for a leader who can enforce laws so that the strong will not prey on the weak. The development of an established authority to maintain customs and laws began with the rule of one man. Tribal loyalty towards a chief gradually gave way to allegiance to a national king whose power had to be built up to overcome the earlier tribal affinities. Thus the idea of the King's peace developed, in which one set of laws applied to the whole kingdom. To enforce the King's peace at the village level, a crude but effective system had matured for providing law and order by Saxon times. Every male over twelve years of age had to belong to a group of ten men, called a tithing, and the whole group was responsible for the good behaviour of each member. If an offence was committed and the offender fled, then the "hue and cry" was given for the group to pursue him. Each district, known as a shire, had an official called a reeve who was responsible for supervising this arrangement for law and order. The shire reeve became known as a sheriff and made visits to villages to collect taxes for the king. If the sheriff then discovered that any villager was living "outside tithing," he could fine the whole village; everyone thus was interested in seeing that his neighbour behaved himself.

When the Norman Conquest took place in 1066 the invaders retained the office of sheriff. But the Normans changed the basis upon which this appointment was made from the Saxon idea of using people of high birth, to whom recognition of status was owed, to the use of knights, members of a specialized military caste, who could enforce the discipline implied by the feudal system. English feudalism after 1066 was based on the division of land among about 180 tenants-in-chief who each held a fief in exchange for loyalty vouched to William I and who, in turn, demanded loyalty from the five thousand knights among whom they subdivided their holdings. Fear of assassination by a hostile Saxon population made the Norman rule harsh. When an assassination took place it was immediately assumed that the victim was a Norman, unless it could be clearly proven that he was a Saxon, and a heavy tax known as murdrum was imposed on a community, a procedure that provided the origin of the word "murder." The Saxons' resentment of their Norman overlords has been symbolized by the story of Robin Hood resisting the tyrannical sheriff of Nottingham.

The authority of the king was sometimes challenged by local lords who emerged as ambitious contenders for power. Henry II therefore established a system of travelling justices to keep an eye on local lords and shire reeves, while seizing the opportunity to build up respect for royal justice by trying offenders under the royal law at what were called the Assizes, a form of royal court. By the reign of King John many barons were chafing under the tight royal control and they included in the Magna Carta a request for the reduction of the power of the office of sheriff. In 1215, therefore, the sheriff was deprived of much of his judicial power as the principal law enforcement officer of the king.

By the early 1300's, a sheriff had become more independent of the king, because he was usually the local lord. Now the idea of an impartial royal justice became very difficult to sustain when lords created private armies and in effect made their own local law. Yet the rule of law was taking root because the King's Council began to emerge as a place of discussion, thereby laying the foundations of a parliamentary system that would replace the use of physical force as a means of settling disputes. This habit of discussion helped to provide the basis of the future House of Commons. This is not to imply that violence had been eliminated from medieval England, for civil battle—disarmingly known as the Wars of the Roses—raged for a hundred years. Medieval towns tried to ensure security from mass attack, and also from individual strangers, by surrounding each town with a wall, of which the entrance gates were locked at sundown. Inside the wall, an official known as a common sergeant, paid by householders, exercised police duties by organizing patrols that kept "watch and ward" after dusk. Finally, in this turbulent period, Henry Tudor emerged from the political chaos, married the lady who represented the other Rose, and began in 1485 to usher in an era of reform.

Henry VII took steps to ensure that the nobles behaved themselves by making them swear an oath that they would not cause riots, hold unlawful meetings, or keep private armies arrayed in their livery, and by imposition of crippling fines. Henry VII now developed the idea of using county gentlemen as Justices of the Peace who, as unpaid civil servants, took over many of the functions previously performed by the sheriff. During the reigns of the subsequent Tudors there was a great deal of discussion on how to deal effectively with what were termed "rogues," which term included those whom we would call burglars, cardsharps and con artists. By the time of Elizabeth I, the Englishman was developing a patriotic pride in his provisions for ensuring law and order, while appreciating that the Tudor opposition to a professional standing army helped to ensure his freedom.

This detestation of professional soldiers was reinforced by the era of Oliver Cromwell, whose authority ultimately depended upon the troops he stationed throughout Britain. Then, from the Puritan discipline imposed by Cromwell, England descended into the very difficult social climate of the eighteenth century. Nepotism and bribery now became commonplace and resulted in a greatly diminished respect for the impartiality of the law.

LAW ENFORCEMENT IN THE EIGHTEENTH CENTURY

The laws of the eighteenth century were brutal: there were over 160 crimes punishable by death, including stealing and sending threatening letters. Enforcement of these laws could hardly be impartial, however, in an age when unscrupulous magistrates known as "trading justices" could be easily bribed. Highwaymen who openly defied the authorities often became folk heroes, as did the legendary Dick Turpin. It was not safe to travel the King's highway even though the authorities gave highwaymen short shrift by hanging them from a gallows. Public executions in London took place at Tyburn and were regarded as entertaining spectacles. The final speech of the condemned man to his audience had the entertainment value, on somewhat less refined principles, of Prince Hamlet's soliloquy in Shakespeare's tragedy.

The brutality of the law did not encourage respect for it. A revival of respect for the impartiality of the law, however, was encouraged by the appointments in 1749 and 1750 of Henry Fielding, the author, and his blind brother, Sir John Fielding, as magistrates at Bow Street Court in London. The national capital abounded in footpads, or thugs, who did not hesitate to attack citizens on the street. There were men called watchmen who patrolled the streets at night but they confined their activity to the safe practice of merely calling out the hour and the state of the weather. The Fielding brothers began their attempts to make the city streets safe by repudiating the tradition of the "trading justices," for they themselves could not be bribed. Sir John Fielding became known as the "blind Beak" and is reputed to have been able to recognize over three thousand thieves by their voices. The Fieldings next organized a group of reliable men to arrest footpads. These officers in their red waistcoats became known as "Robin Redbreasts" and, later, as Bow Street Runners.

A similar development took place in the growing American ports on the Atlantic coast where the traditional night watchman was replaced by police patrols, financed by wealthy men who paid into a common fund to ensure the protection of life and property. Americans had good reason to be concerned with law enforcement, particularly because when British criminals were removed from prison, they were sent either to the gallows or to the convict ships that sailed regularly to the American or West Indian colonies. Prisons in Britain were not viewed as places of punishment but as temporary lodgings, particularly by debtors who could free themselves by paying their debts. Jailers charged for room and board and made such fat profits that the post of warden of a prison was highly prized. Many of the prisons were run as private capitalist ventures and little attempt was made to separate the inmates on the basis of the nature of their offence. Moreover, on both sides of the Atlantic the belief was held that the less the government interfered the better, and that government forces should only be called in to solve a crisis. So when the British Treasury financed, in 1783, a Police Horse Patrol to safeguard the roads into London, the patrol soon reduced the rate of highway robbery, and was therefore abolished as unnecessary because the crisis had been solved. Naturally, the highwaymen reappeared.

The War of Independence that culminated in the birth of the United States gave rise to two different traditions in English-speaking North America. The first was that established in the new republic under the American Constitution, where article two of the First Amendment reads, "A well regulated Militia being necessary to the security of a free State, the right of the people to keep and bear Arms, shall not be infringed." The intention seems to have been to ensure that public order could be maintained by an armed militia composed of ordinary citizens. But in practice, the right to bear arms was interpreted to mean that a citizen could defend himself by the use of weapons. The significance of this step can be seen in hindsight by the situation that was triggered by the assassination of President John F. Kennedy in 1963 and was heightened by the subsequent murders of his brother Robert and Martin Luther King in 1968. A wave of public protest led to efforts to effectively restrict and control the increasing number of firearms, but these were frustrated by powerful lobby groups, such as the National Rifle Association, that based their opposition on constitutional grounds.

A different tradition grew from the migration of United Empire Loyalists to the British North American colonies. These refugees had a strong dislike for violence, and their conservative attitude reinforced the innate conservatism of the French-Canadian community. As the British North American colonies were garrisoned by British troops, supplemented by local militia units, there was always a relatively large law enforcement body available for the use of the civil authorities. Furthermore, as this law enforcement body was principally composed of professional troops, it was relatively immune from the influence of local politics. This situation contrasted to that of the United States where the sheriff's office was elective, which meant that the principal law enforcement officer of the country was subject to partisan political pressure. Yet, at the same time, troops were not the best agents for enforcement of the law.

BRITAIN ORGANIZES CIVILIAN POLICE

Britain was discovering that more effective law enforcement could take place if civilians were employed as a police force. This discovery grew out of the turbulence of the early nineteenth century when Britain was struggling to cope with the social and political upheavals that stemmed from the industrial revolution. In 1819 an incident occurred that led to a change of attitude concerning law enforcement. At St. Peter's Fields, near Manchester, an orderly protest meeting held by 50,000 workers and their families was dispersed by a charge of the local militia, ordered by panic-stricken magistrates. Eleven people were killed by the sword-wielding cavalrymen.

Mockingly called the Massacre of Peterloo, in ironic reference to the recent national victory at the Battle of Waterloo, this event led to demands for reform in police methods. So, in 1829, the first disciplined civilian police force of one thousand men was established for the metropolitan area of London, with headquarters at Scotland Yard. The new force was received with hostility, despite the efforts made to give it a non-military appearance by dressing the members in top hats and belted blue coats. This hostility was intensified by the indignation of citizens who were financing the venture by paying a police tax. However, the force gradually earned the respect of the population by the co-operative way in which they served the public, and the nickname of Bobbies or Peelers was used as a popular tribute to the founder of the force, Secretary Robert Peel. Peel's reforms went much further than establishing this force; they included drastic revision of the barbaric criminal code abolishing capital punishment for a large number of crimes, scaling down lesser punishments and improving legal procedures and conditions of imprisonment. The wave of reform continued with the Prisons Act and Municipal Reform Act, both of 1835. The Prisons Act established inspectors of prisons while the Municipal Reform Act instituted city councils, elected by ratepayers, who exercised control over the police. This burst of activity in Britain influenced Upper Canada where, in 1835, the first chief constable of civil police and five constables were engaged at Toronto, with this force being organized along the lines of the Bobbies. There was now an emphasis upon the certainty rather than the savagery of punishment. It would be some time before this humanitarian approach would show results in substantially reducing the level of crime, but England was to benefit immensely from the change of attitude on the part of the authorities.

The British attitude towards the need to ensure the King's Peace was reinforced by the action of Parliament in 1856 when, under the terms of the Obligatory Act, the national treasury was to provide a quarter of the cost of maintaining local police forces. In the same year two men were appointed Her Majesty's Inspectors of Constabulary to enforce minimum standards required to ensure the government grant, which was increased in 1888 under the Local Government Act to cover half the cost of police maintenance.

ATTITUDES IN NORTH AMERICA

The general trend in Britain and in Canada towards national control of the police contrasted to the very different approach taken in the United States. Crime was increasing in the United States in the early nineteenth century, and in the crowded eastern cities, the native American tended to blame Irish immigrants for the higher crime rate. Certainly the ready availability of alcohol created a situation where most of the persons arrested were recorded as being "intemperate." By the 1840's criminal gangs had appeared on the streets of large cities and were making war on each other as well as terrorizing the neighbourhood. Philadelphia had its Blood Tubs and Copper Heads; Baltimore its Stringers; New York its Bowery Boys, Plug Uglies and Swipers. This gang warfare had its roots in religious, racial, ethnic and economic conflicts, and as a result of it, riots and street disorders were commonplace events. It is true that large cities provided policemen, but they were usually recruited from the ranks of the unemployed, and little effort was expended on training them. Furthermore, it was difficult to identify them: the wearing of uniforms was seen as a badge of European servitude, so plainclothes American policemen mingled with the population and could thus easily flee the scene of a serious disturbance. New York City finally took the problem in hand in May of 1844 and established a body of 800 policemen, but not until 1853 did uniforms become a feature of the force. The police uniform at that time comprised a blue swallow-tailed coat with large buttons, gray pants, and a blue cap labelled with the officer's number. After the subsequent creation of the metropolitan police district of New York in 1857, other large city police forces were established through the creation of state police boards. Such large cities as Philadelphia, Boston and Baltimore organized their police forces in the 1850's. The word "constable" was used to describe an ordinary policeman, who signed his report as a "Constable on Patrol": this identification was soon abbreviated to the familiar term "cop."

A serious flaw in initiating police work in cities in the United States was to place appointments directly under the control of municipal politicians. Under the New York law of 1844, policemen were appointed for one year only after nomination by aldermen of the wards to which they belonged. Therefore, "The chief of police was largely a figurehead with little, if any, authority over his force, a situation that has prevailed in many cities until modern times."[1] The real significance of this is that municipal politicians have been, to a considerable extent, above the law.

Establishment of law and order in Western Canada became important when a gold rush into the Cariboo country in 1858 drew many American miners. The crown colony government of Vancouver Island was hastily expanded to include the mainland, an action which the British government legalized by creating the Crown Colony of British Columbia. British Royal Engineers were employed to police the gold fields as well as to construct a road that permitted easy entry. When the Dominion of Canada was created in 1867, the new nation moved quickly to expand law and order into the Western prairies, both to establish sovereignty and to eliminate the American whisky-pedlars. To provide protection in the area between the newly established provinces of Manitoba and British Columbia, a quasi-military force was formed in 1873. Initially Prime Minister John A. Macdonald intended to call the force the North West Mounted Rifles but, to placate concern in the United States over such a military force, the name was changed to the more civilian-sounding North West Mounted Police. The new force of 274 men, dressed in the jackets associated with the British redcoat, trekked westwards in 1874 from the Red River to patrol 750,000 square miles. Forts were built at strategic points so that the motto "Maintiens le droit" ("Uphold the right") could be made a reality. Whisky-pedlars were soon routed and the Indians gained a respect for the Mounties' integrity and concern for fair play. Unlike in the American West, the pattern of police control was established well in advance of large-scale settlement.

In the eastern cities of Canada, the formation of local police forces under municipal authorities established a rule of law having no connection to the military. A most revealing summary of the experience of the Toronto police was given by their Chief in the *Globe* of January 26, 1869. During the previous five years the leading offence, by far, had been that of being drunk and disorderly. There was a tendency on the part of the public to blame the Irish for crime, a view which was substantiated by the official figures that listed the native countries of offenders charged in 1868, as follows:

Ireland	2,151
Scotland	1,258
England	927
Canada	298
U.S.A.	92

The Chief Constable of Toronto, W.S. Prince, pointed out in his annual message the difficulty of securing suitable recruits who were "in the prime of manhood . . . shrewd, intelligent, and possessed of a good English education, trustful, truthful and of a general good character." There was a steady loss of the best men who sought more remunerative employment, bemoaned the Chief, with a steady drain towards the U.S.A. because of the high wages offered there. It augured well for the future of his force, however, that the Chief Constable strongly pressed for higher salaries for his men in order to maintain a high calibre of policeman.

PROBLEMS OF LAW ENFORCEMENT

The Great Depression between 1873 and 1896 probably aided the cause of law enforcement in Canada, for the scarcity of jobs in general made the police force more attractive to recruits and made it wise for a policeman to weigh his prospects carefully before leaving the force. Furthermore, the lure of the United States may have diminished for a conscientious policeman aware of newspaper reports about lawlessness and corruption. For a torrent of immigration from Europe was crossing the Atlantic and, in view of the fact that many native Americans saw nothing particularly wrong with Social Darwinism, there was bound to be much criminal exploitation. No Canadian city had yet produced municipal corruption on the scale of Boss Tweed of New York City, whose "Tweed ring" plundered the city of a sum estimated somewhere between $100 million and $200 million by 1873. Whereas Canada had a pronounced British-French flavour, the United States had a heterogeneous citizenry which tended to complicate the problem of law enforcement. To please one ethnic group in the slums might antagonize another, while political corruption was rarely absent for any length of time at any level of government.

If a policeman turned his gaze from the cities to the wide open spaces of the American West the picture would hardly be reassuring. President Hayes provided this indictment of relations with the Indians of the plains in his annual message of 1877:

> The Indians were the original occupants of the land we now possess. They have been driven from place to place . . . . Many, if not most, of the Indian wars have their origin in broken promises and acts of injustice on our part.

It would be hard to equate this Presidential assessment with the popular mythology of the romantic Wild West. The cowboys-and-Indians myth has lasted much longer than the actual Western frontier which, within a remarkably short period of twenty-odd years, saw successive stages of mining, ranching, and farming. These waves of settlement that populated the American West produced their own unique forms of frontier justice. Mining towns that sprang up almost overnight framed local laws concerning property rights, with many of them being eventually incorporated into the legal code of the Western states. In the ranching country, the local sheriff sought to ensure that bad men were brought to justice, usually at the end of his Colt repeating revolver. The Saxon idea of giving a "hue and cry" to follow escaping offenders took a new form, with a posse riding after a fleeing bandit, and most of us have learned the basic vocabulary involved, "He went thataway" and "Head him off at the pass." Where law enforcement was absent or appeared to be breaking down, vigilante committees of citizens sought to ensure law and order. The image of a law enforcement officer complete with badge and gun took deep root in the American subconscious, and has continued to provide a vicarious pleasure for countless numbers of children involved in playing both cowboys and Indians, and cops and robbers.

An even more serious problem concerning the law than the primitive frontier justice was the deliberate attempt made in the United States to frustrate the dreams of the Negro slaves emancipated by Abraham Lincoln. Because the aftermath of the Civil War has had a tremendous impact upon the maintenance of law and order in America, the sequence of events needs to be examined. A triumphant Republican party passed three vital amendments to the American Constitution. The Thirteenth Amendment prohibited slavery, the Fourteenth implied that a Negro was now a citizen entitled to all a citizen's privileges, and the Fifteenth Amendment prohibited discrimination on the basis of colour. It was the Fourteenth Amendment which was the keystone of this constitutional attempt to ensure equality of the races. But the subsequent interpretation of this amendment by the Supreme Court in the 1870's complicated the issue of Negro rights. The Slaughterhouse decision of 1873 stated that the most important form of citizenship was the one provided by an individual state, and that it had never been intended to extend federal protection to ensure the full rights of citizenship. Thus the Negro had to look to his state legislature to ensure his rights as a citizen. Meanwhile white supremacy was being enforced by such underground organizations as the Ku Klux Klan and the Knights of the White Rose who intimidated potential Negro voters, while the Cruikshank decision of 1875 ignored an outright attack on Negroes who dared to vote at a polling booth. Then, in 1877, the Negro in the South lost the protection of federal troops when an arrangement was made for their withdrawal as part of a political deal: some Southern Congressmen had agreed to permit the election of President Hayes, the Republican candidate, if these troops were removed. Deserted by the Republican party that had championed his cause, the Negro had yet to experience the final act of betrayal. This final blow to Negro aspirations was delivered by the Supreme Court decision of *Plessy* v. *Ferguson* of 1896 which accepted, or invented, the idea of "separate but equal accommodations" and provided legal sanction to the pernicious doctrine of segregation. While the legal point at issue was over the right of a Louisiana railway company to provide "separate but equal" accommodations in railway cars, the effect of this decision was to remove the protection of the Fourteenth Amendment from the Negro. White Southerners hastened to apply Jim Crow laws to all aspects of life under the blanket protection of this Supreme Court decision. The bitterness of many black "citizens" made it difficult to accept the impartiality of the law. Furthermore, white policemen could with impunity apply the law that in practice allowed second-class citizenship.

It was easy to enforce discrimination: the colour of a skin was readily seen, as was also the colour of a uniform. Now began the tragic humiliation of a group of Americans by denying them simple courtesies, such as refusing to address them as Mr., Mrs. or Miss. A policeman might say, "Hey, boy!" to a Negro much older than himself, but would hesitate to address a white person in the same fashion.

Mob violence was widely prevalent in both the South and the new Western Frontier in the late nineteenth century. Lynch law was the result of a tradition of executing an offender without waiting to ensure a fair trial to determine if he was really guilty. From 1882 to 1959, 2,595 Negroes were lynched in nine Southern states, a total which indicates that this phenomenon was not a mere temporary phase. While in the South the Negro was the usual victim of mob violence, in the West the victim was usually one of the predominant white population. The usual crimes alleged to have been done by these victims were murder, rape or robbery. Bigotry could flourish in a social environment that permitted mobs to carry out their threat to "string him up."

THE POLICEMAN'S IMAGE

In the last decades of the nineteenth century the police of major industrial cities in the U.S.A. were often employed in a role that further diminished their prestige in the eyes of the poorer segment of the community. The era that saw the rise of industrial tycoons such as John D. Rockefeller and Andrew Carnegie, created a need for the protection of corporate property. Ironically, the Fourteenth Amendment was interpreted to protect the rights of corporations and corporation executives demanded, and got, police protection. The right of a corporation to conduct business free of interference, a right backed by conservative-minded law courts, implied that strikes by groups of workers were not permitted. Picket lines could be forced open to admit a fresh group of labourers, which the strikers called "scab labour." A by-product of this era was the increased activity of private detective agencies, such as the Pinkerton National Detective Agency, specializing in "labour problems": this helped to foster the workers' resentment of uniformed guards and policemen.

The image of the police in Canada at the turn of the century was best represented by the admired North West Mounted. The abbreviation Mountie, like the term Bobby in England, was a term of popular respect. Furthermore, the judiciary in both Canada and Britain were generally respected for being incorruptible and for trying to administer the legal code impartially. A good example of the part that established tradition can play in law enforcement came in 1898, when a handful of Mounties upheld law and order in the Klondike during the last great gold rush that drew men from all over the world. In recognition of the great service rendered to Canada by the Mounties, and of their deserved reputation for impartiality and effectiveness in getting their man, the prefix "Royal" was added to their title in 1904. In the following year the new provinces of Saskatchewan and Alberta were formed and they retained the services of the Royal North West Mounted Police (R.N.W.M.P.) as custodians of law and order. Canada still had a predominantly rural economy at this time and law enforcement in the greater part of Canada was not as complex as it was becoming in the densely populated cities to the south.

In Canadian cities, the conservative French-British outlook was still dominant, whereas a very different attitude prevailed towards enforcing laws in such leading American cities as New York and Chicago. One of the major reasons for a changing American attitude was the assimilation of European peasants into one of the world's most industrialized areas located in the Eastern United States. The "new" immigration after 1890 was composed of millions of peasants who were arriving not from the earlier main sources of Northwest Europe, but from Eastern and Southern Europe. Russians, Austro-Hungarians, Italians and Greeks were now much more numerous among arriving immigrants than the familiar Britons, Germans and Scandinavians. A language problem existed for this human wave of Europeans who crossed the Atlantic as steerage passengers after being told by shipping agents that a land of opportunity awaited them at the port of disembarkation. The opportunity may have been harder to find than the immigrants expected, but there were certainly opportunists waiting in the United States, as industrialists and ward politicians alike saw opportunities to exploit these new Americans. In turn, the new citizens learned that the item which commanded universal respect in the New World was the power represented by the dollar bill. Social Darwinism reinforced the Puritan idea of the deserving few, while the concept of public service in the European tradition had not taken widespread root. From the counting-house mentality, which believed mainly in heaping up money, it was but a step to the idea that everything had its price, including the law. Officials who enforced the law could be fixed or bribed, as had happened in eighteenth-century England. This situation confirmed the suspicion of the poor that, despite all statements about the impartiality of the law, there existed one form for them and another for the wealthy.

The problem was not merely one of ensuring honest policemen, but of seeing that the laws were reasonable and relevant enough to be enforceable. Pressure groups insisted that saloons should not open on Sundays and that gambling should be forbidden. This type of Protestant response to misery in the slums was hardly likely to impress Roman Catholic or Jewish immigrants, who had not expected a "holier than thou" attitude in democratic America, where they were sweated six days of the week and not trusted to behave on their one day of leisure. Unenforceable laws made possible a systematic pattern of graft and corruption. Repeated scandals rocked the political scene, and city government in leading American cities such as New York and Chicago was constantly being reformed. Most of these reform movements in the United States served the same purpose as some critics feel that Royal Commissions do in Canada: the disturbing situation was whitewashed, while the temperature of public indignation was allowed to cool. The United States copied a Canadian institution to some extent by establishing a federal police force in 1908, termed the Bureau of Investigation, but as political patronage was not discouraged this force could not hope to attain the prestige associated with Canada's Royal North West Mounted.

Another important police force took shape in Canada at this time when the province of Ontario decided that law enforcement had to be increased in the new mining towns in the north of the province. An order-in-council dated October 13, 1909 established the Ontario Provincial Police Force which was then stationed throughout the northland to enforce the Criminal Code.

The image of the Mountie sagged badly after World War One when, amid social unrest, some members of the force were cast in the roles of strike-breakers and of spies on a restless labour movement. Because the Mountie's image was tarnished in the larger urban centres of Western Canada, in the eyes of "intellectuals" and lunch-pail workers although not to rural residents and the white-collar middle class, the circumstances need to be examined. When the economic life of Winnipeg was paralyzed by the General Strike of 1919, the regular city police were dismissed by the Winnipeg municipal authorities since the police had shown sympathy for the strikers' objective, the right of collective bargaining. A private force of "specials" was hastily recruited by the municipal authorities, and with the fear of Bolshevist insurrection in the air a squadron of the R.N.W.M.P. was used to back them up. Accounts vary concerning the methods used by the Mounties to break the strike, but it is agreed that their reputation was not enhanced in the eyes of workers and returned veterans who saw them as enforcing the repressive policy of the federal government.

THE FEAR OF REVOLUTION

Allowance should be made for the panic among politicians on both sides of the Atlantic who feared that the Bolshevik virus would spread from Russia and produce local revolutions. The overreaction of Canada's federal government was due to their fear that workers and soldiers would form soviets. The inflamed mood of the time can be judged from the remarkable action of Acting Prime Minister White when he cabled Sir Robert Borden on April 16, 1919: Borden was attending the Versailles Peace Conference and, while grappling with large European issues, received White's message that in view of incipient Bolshevism in Western Canada, he should request that a British battleship be brought into Vancouver harbour. Borden replied nearly two weeks later that "it would be most unfortunate to have . . . a British ship called upon to suppress purely local Canadian riots or insurrection."[2] Borden was in close contact with Britain's Prime Minister, David Lloyd George, who had established a "Special Branch" at Scotland Yard to keep an eye on labour agitators in Britain's war factories and, undoubtedly, neither of these war leaders wanted to lose the peace by precipitate action against their own countrymen. Strikes for better conditions were widespread and included those by London and Liverpool city policemen in 1919, and by the city police of Boston, Massachusetts. What was to be called a "return to normalcy" produced widespread labour unrest as the national economies of Britain, the United States and Canada returned to peacetime conditions. Undercover activity by the R.N.W.M.P., Scotland Yard and the Bureau of Investigation was the political solution of the various governments to the unknown extent of Communist activity.

In the frenzy of the Red Scare of 1919-1920 the city police of Boston, Massachusetts, who had gone on strike for better working conditions, were accused of being Communists. Attorney General A. Mitchell Palmer launched a roundup of thousands of radicals, or suspected radicals, in thirty-three cities from coast to coast. Palmer brought in for questioning several thousand people without trial or even formal arrest, formally arrested more than five thousand persons and deported 556 individuals. Palmer later explained that the American way of life was in danger, because:

Like a prairie fire, the blaze of revolution was sweeping over every American institution of law and order . . . . It was eating its way into the homes of the American workman, its sharp tongues of revolutionary heat were licking the altars of the churches, leaping into the belfry of the school bell, crawling into the sacred corners of American homes, seeking to replace marriage vows with libertine laws, burning up the foundations of society.[3]

INTOLERANCE OF THE TWENTIES

A similar point of view to that of Palmer was taken by the Ku Klux Klan organization which gained a new lease on life by espousing militant patriotism and intolerant nationalism. The activities of the Klan spread well beyond the Southern states: as the Klan hated all un-American people, which category included Negroes, Jews, Roman Catholics, immigrants and aliens, their potential victims comprised a considerable segment of the total American population. A membership of five million was claimed by Klan spokesmen by 1925, and their red-blooded American policy included such practices as branding, tarring and feathering, mutilation and murder. The public parades of these white-robed "penitents" through the nation's capital seemed evidence that American concepts of law and order were more honoured in the breach than in the observance.

The Roaring Twenties saw a breakdown in another area of American law and order because of Prohibition. As discussed in the chapter on wets and drys, the Eighteenth Amendment proved to be unenforceable in the large cities. Speakeasies developed, bootlegging flourished, and the bribe or "fix" was used by the lawless to flout the law. Respect for the cop declined as he was placed in the unenviable position of trying to enforce a law, made by legislators who themselves were often offenders, which was bitterly resented by a large section of the public. The epitome of success in the organization of vice appears to have been the rule of Al Capone in Chicago. Capone's word was law: he once ordered his own completely bullet-proof automobile, equipped with a removable back window to enable the rear gunner to use his sub-machine gun; the executives of the automobile industry co-operated in building this custom-designed model, thereby exhibiting their faith in the virtues of free enterprise. Eventually President Herbert Hoover made a decision to regain control of Chicago and J. Edgar Hoover's Bureau of Investigation took up the challenge. There was plenty to investigate as, between 1927 and 1930, there were 227 killings in Chicago alone and only two convictions: among the most celebrated of the slaughters was the St. Valentine's Day massacre of 1929, when a group of gangsters dressed as policemen induced seven rival gangsters to raise their hands and machine-gunned them. In 1931, Al Capone was finally convicted, not of numerous murders or acts of terrorism but simply of not paying his income tax, which exhibits the truth of the old adage that crime does not pay. This adage, however, was often disproven: in 1930, the U.S. Bureau of Internal Revenue estimated the profits of the enterprises in which Capone was engaged to be ten million dollars each from prostitution and narcotics, twenty-five million dollars from gambling and fifty million dollars from the illegal liquor trade. Even allowing for the fact that these are estimates, and a historian would have to give or take a few million to arrive at an accurate figure, it was indisputably a sizeable income which, consequently, drew the interest of the tax collector. The moral lesson which other gangsters drew from the example of Al Capone was to recruit competent accountants. National statistics on crime in the United States date only from 1930 and therefore it is difficult to establish just how violent America became in the Roaring Twenties. Even statistics available for the post-1930 period are often un-reliable, as the local reports on which they are based are frequently incomplete. As the Presidential Wickersham Commission, the first body to investigate crime on a national scale, noted in 1931, some cities "use these reports in order to advertise their freedom from crime as compared to other municipalities."[4] Both politicians and the police wanted to appear to be doing a good job of keeping the crime rate down, while using the statistics to get larger forces and

347

better equipment. The Wickersham Commission took note of this tendency to obscure the facts when it noted that:

> Police statistics of offences are lacking in accuracy. The police are often afraid to publish reports stating accurately the number of crimes committed, especially if that means showing a material increase in crime, because such action may bring down upon them the wrath of the public.[5]

A contemporary historian has summarized the conclusions of the Commission as follows:

> The underlying causes for general police ineffectiveness were the politician's control of the chief . . . . The commission cited instances where underworld elements such as gamblers, through their political alliances, had named the chiefs of police in several large cities . . . . The average tenure of office for police heads of cities of 500,000 population was only a fraction over 2 years.[6]

It was inevitable that respect for policemen in the United States diminished. There were lots of honest cops, but they did not make the headlines as did ones who joined the robbers.

It was difficult to change the public impression that "anyone can be a cop," or to live down the political patronage frequently associated with appointments in the city police forces of the United States, and with lawyers and judges as well. In terms of social status, the American policeman was held in low esteem. There was no equivalent to the prestige attached to the British policeman because of his identification with the Crown, which engendered a respect and a loyalty from the public; the status of the Bobby was also high because of his selection and training and because of the standards maintained by a form of centralized control.

During the 1920's in Canada, respect for the laws and the people who enforced them remained higher than in the U.S.A., for Canadians never became such completely convinced drys that they made it legally necessary to cease manufacturing or trans-shipping vast quantities of alcoholic beverages. Consumption of alcohol did not increase particularly in Canada, but their self-proclaimed respect for resisting unjust laws gave many Canadians particular pleasure in aiding Americans to resist the tyranny imposed by the Eighteenth Amendment, and the Dominion became a giant liquor warehouse.

While Britons watched with interest North Americans proclaiming the virtues of prohibition, Britain was having her own problems with maintaining law and order. Britain's postwar economic problems intensified the social unrest and led to a General Strike in 1926. As had happened at Winnipeg seven years earlier, the local authorities enrolled "special" constables, but unlike the authorities in Winnipeg, the British did not dismiss their regular police. Possibly the role of the Bobby became crucial at this stage and, fortunately, he did not gain the reputation of being a strikebreaker. Reports were heard of soccer games being played between the strikers and policemen, which reflected a more sensible way to pass the time while waiting out the political power struggle than crushing skulls or shooting strikers. An unarmed Bobby engendered respect because he symbolized the majesty of the law: the American cop bearing a gun and ammunition reflected the failure of the law to secure public co-operation. There was one major exception in the U.S., though, to the generally low prestige of law enforcement agencies. When J. Edgar Hoover took charge of the Bureau of Investigation in 1924, he resolutely set out to eliminate political patronage. Recruits to the federal force had to have a college background in law or accounting and a start was made in setting an example of American law enforcement that might eventually compare with the prestige of Scotland Yard or the Mounties.

PROBLEMS DURING THE DEPRESSION YEARS

By the amalgamation in 1920 of the Royal North West Mounted Police and a federal organization known as the Dominion Police, a new force emerged known as the Royal

Canadian Mounted Police. The Mounties now became responsible not only for enforcing Dominion laws, but also for provincial statutes in Saskatchewan after 1928, in Manitoba, Alberta, New Brunswick, Nova Scotia and Prince Edward Island in 1932, and in British Columbia and Newfoundland in 1950. The era of the 1930's and the Great Depression proved to be a difficult one for the Mounties as the national custodians of law and order.

At Estevan, Saskatchewan on September 8, 1931, over five hundred members of the Mine Workers Union of Canada went on strike to try to force the mine owners to negotiate. The Royal Canadian Mounted Police reinforced the local force and the combined police force opened fire on a parade of strikers, killing three, wounding many more and arresting fifty workers. Meanwhile action was being taken to imprison Communist leaders in Kingston Penitentiary under the notorious Section 98 of the Criminal Code, which had been rushed through Parliament at the time of the Winnipeg General Strike. Section 98 was a remarkable piece of legislation which made it clear that the government would decide what was seditious, and it reversed the usual British assumption that a man was innocent until he was found guilty. But while J.S. Woodsworth continued his personal crusade to eliminate this repressive legislation from the statute book, the police had the unenviable responsibility for enforcing it. In 1935, the unemployed organized an "On to Ottawa" trek to publicize their plight to get the attention of the federal government, and about one thousand unemployed workers left Vancouver on June 3. This unemployed army gathered size as it approached Regina, with further large contingents waiting to join at such centres as Winnipeg, Toronto and Montreal. Faced with this situation, the cabinet of Prime Minister R.B. Bennett decided to try to stem the trek at Regina. Mounties armed with everything from baseball bats to Vickers machine guns were used to coerce the wave of unemployed men, while two federal cabinet ministers negotiated for a settlement that would reduce the size of the marching group to the leaders only. In the final analysis, the bitter resentment of many workers at the failure of Prime Minister Bennett to provide jobs was reflected in the federal election of 1935, when Bennett was soundly defeated at the polls.

Ontario did not use the R.C.M.P. for enforcing provincial statutes, as the province had its own Ontario Provincial Police. In 1937 the Premier of Ontario, Mitchell Hepburn, decided to use his police force to break the strike of workers at the General Motors plant in Oshawa who wanted the United Automobile Workers to represent them. Branding the U.A.W. a Communist organization, the Premier sent in squads of Provincial Police aided by a contingent of Mounties. A wave of indignation swept across Ontario and the police were removed. But the power of a provincial premier who controlled his own police force was exhibited again that year in Quebec. Premier Maurice Duplessis passed his "Padlock Act" which claimed to be an act to protect the province against communist propaganda, but could conveniently be used to eliminate opponents "tending to propagate" a creed not acceptable to Duplessis.

During the Depression, enforcement of the law by municipal police was a hard task. Policemen came from the same general working-class background as the unemployed, yet sympathy for the workers' plight did not absolve the officers of responsibility for upholding the existing laws. There were bound to be clashes between workers protesting their condition and the police protecting property rights. Furthermore, with the increasing use of the automobile the enforcement of the Highway Code brought the police into contact with a larger segment of the population; law enforcement ceased to be an abstract issue when every motorist was convinced that it was not he who deserved a ticket. While the total municipal police force of large cities comprised many organizational divisions, such as criminal investigation and morality, the public impressions of the force were largely formed from the behaviour of the uniformed branch.

CHANGING ATTITUDES TO VIOLENCE

The impact of the Second World War created many new problems for law enforcement agencies. The concepts of law, order, and justice that had been upheld by Western civilization were hard to justify in the light of the Nazi atrocities against the Jews, or the Allied extermination of civilians through air assault on Dresden, Hiroshima and Nagasaki. It is hard to escape the conclusion that in the War Crimes trials after 1945 not all the criminals were placed in the dock. Yet while the wartime Allied propaganda about the monopoly of iniquity held by the enemy now sounds rather hollow, the hope expressed for a bright new world was taken seriously by the working classes, who supplied most of the fighting men. In the postwar world there was to be an increased expectation by the poor regarding the services to which they felt entitled, which included that of adequate police protection.

The general prewar pattern of allowing the occupants of the slums, including minority groups, to solve their own problems now changed. Policemen were now expected to provide protection to all citizens, and this helped to account for an increase in crime statistics on both sides of the Atlantic. As the University of Cambridge Institute of Criminology stated after an exhaustive study of the sharp increase in crimes of violence,

> One of the main causes for an increase in the recording of violent crime appears to be a decrease in the toleration of aggressive and violent behaviour, even in those slum and tenement areas where violence has always been regarded as a normal and accepted way of settling quarrels, jealousies or even trivial arguments.[7]

Another reason for the increase in crime statistics was the method of reporting them. In 1949 the Federal Bureau of Investigation (the prefix "Federal" was added in 1935) refused to publish the statistics on robbery collected from New York City, as it no longer believed them. New York soon afterwards switched from a system whereby complaints were collected by precincts to a central reporting system: the result was that the statistics on robberies rose by 400 per cent and on burglaries by 1,300 per cent.[8] This increase supports the results of door-to-door surveys conducted in Chicago, Washington and Boston which indicated that the rate of crime was at least three times higher than that shown in the national Uniform Crime Reports issued by the Federal Bureau of Investigation.[9] This view is confirmed by a recent book entitled *Crime in the City* in which the editor states:

> It is difficult to know the dimensions of criminal violence in American cities because statistics on crime are collected primarily by the police, yet most violence is not reported to the police.[10]

CULTURAL CONFLICT AND URBAN PRESSURES

It has long been a truism that crime flourishes in the slums. During the 1950's the difficulties of policing the slums of the northern cities of the United States were compounded by many factors. Racial and ethnic minorities began to grow into majorities, like the Negro and Puerto Rican populations in the heart of New York City. Yet inhabitants of the ghettos were not usually policed by people of the same cultural background as themselves, for while the educational standards were low for recruits to the city police force, these standards were usually high in relation to the background of most of the new arrivals in the large cities. Moreover, police departments in these large cities were usually short-staffed, for most white Americans could obtain better-paid employment in their affluent society.

Every large American city seems to have its Skid Row area. The police spend a disproportionate amount of their time trying to cope with such illegal activities as prostitution, drug trafficking, robbery and other criminal activities. Furthermore, as the Presidential Commission on Civil Disorders pointed out in 1967, American urban society is becoming polarized into two groups, one white and one black. This trend has continued in spite of the 1954 Supreme Court decision that outlawed segregation. Drastic changes in social attitudes have also been encouraged by the new technology. Television makes all viewers feel they should be partaking of the good life; the human and accessible cop on the beat is replaced by the impersonal sound of a wailing siren; new methods of merchandising like the self-serve store provide increased opportunities for pilferage.

Urban redevelopment housing schemes have often had an unfortunate impact on the keeping of law and order, for slum dwellers are often crowded even closer together when high-rise luxury apartments replace their former homes. Jane Jacobs, a critic of the American urban scene, has pointed out that such urban redevelopment destroys a sense of community spirit, and that public peace is mainly established by the people themselves, rather than by policemen. The classic example of what can happen when no community sense of responsibility exists occurred in the case of Catherine Genovese, who was murdered in New York City in 1964. Sociologists have pondered the significance of the fact that thirty-eight persons heard the victim's screams or knew of the attack, yet failed, over a prolonged period of time, to call the police. The phrase "don't get involved" reflects a lack of community spirit in the large city and has led to attempts by some residents to isolate themselves. Some residents of upper-income areas in densely populated regions have recruited security guards to keep out outsiders. One of the first protective fences with "Keep Out, No Trespassing" signs was placed around the Johns Hopkins Hospital in Baltimore, Maryland; the idea quickly spread to New York City and California. One of the disturbing features of the large American city has been the way that some of the wealthy have tried to insulate themselves against possible violence by the use of private guards, a technique which seems like a throwback to the medieval days when walls were built around cities and private watchmen were recruited.

POLICE ORGANIZATION

Unfortunately for the writer about modern crime, there are few really reliable sources of information. A criminal in the forefront of illegal activity does not generally write an autobiography or turn over his personal papers to a sociologist or historian to write an official study. Some idea of the scale of activity, however, can be gauged from the size of the army of policemen, which numbers approximately 400,000 in the United States alone. While this total number is very impressive, the organization of this army, equivalent to about forty infantry divisions, is much less so. For these policemen operate within approximately 40,000 separate and largely autonomous jurisdictions that range from federal to state, county and municipal levels. The total force is thus highly decentralized with the exception of a few relatively small federal bodies such as the F.B.I. that can handle only certain types of crime. At the state level there are large bodies of well-trained highway troopers, particularly in densely populated areas such as New York State and California. These state patrols are fully occupied because, for example, it has been estimated that in California there is a motor accident every three minutes. Other well-trained police forces exist in large cities but, even though they are well-organized, their efficiency is diminished by increasing urban populations.

The quality of American law enforcement varies tremendously as there are no national standards as there are in Britain, and at the village level there may be only one untrained policeman acting in this capacity on a part-time basis. The organization of the police in the U.S.A. reflects American distrust of centralized control. Every state is divided into counties, with each county electing a sheriff for a period of from two to four years. A county jail is often supervised by a warden who is a political appointee, as are many of the judges at the municipal level. In addition, there is a prestige factor involved in the appointment of judges, with those who handle civil cases involving the wealthy being rated higher than those who deal mainly with the poor in criminal courts. Not only are the best men generally not recruited as judges in city or county criminal courts, but the question of patronage has ethnic overtones as there is felt to be a need to appoint judges suited to the ethnic character of districts, such as an Italian, Irish or Jewish candidate. In New York City, it has been estimated that the "going rate" in the 1960's for a judgeship was the equivalent of two years' salary contributed to a political party. This situation has not helped to create an image of impartial law enforcement.

Not only is it difficult to attract a recruit of high calibre to police duty, but the poor pay and lack of prestige tend to reinforce the attitude of the American public that a man with a badge and a gun is apt to be a bully. It is unfortunately true that hatred for policemen in general can stem from one well-publicized incident involving unprofessional conduct. Public opinion polls rate policemen low on the status scale. Sociologists have generally condemned the attitude of the police towards the poor, while left-wing radicals view the police as a tool of the rich whose main purpose is to crush revolutionary activity. Police chiefs are naturally concerned about the image of their men and one interesting experiment is underway at Lakewood, California. Police uniforms have been discarded in favour of flannel trousers and dark blazers, whose embroidered crest over the breast pocket serves as a badge. The root of the problem of law enforcement, however, is probably too deep to be solved by a change in the policeman's appearance.

The military nature of the R.C.M.P. organization in Canada has been criticized as inappropriate for the modern age. With a strength of approximately 4,500 men, the force has had to cope in an increasingly complex society with a diverse array of laws, ranging from surveillance of suspected radicals to suppression of narcotics traffic. The well-publicized spread of American culture to Canada has been noticeable in police work, both in the problems that police confront and in the police forces themselves. Symbolic of the latter type of American influence was the discarding of the Bobby-style helmet by the Toronto Police in 1946, although the helmet was discarded for practical reasons as well, and the change of the British term "Chief Constable" to the American title "Chief of Police" when the Toronto Metropolitan force was organized in 1957. Furthermore, the American term had the virtue of being readily translated into "Chef de Police" and therefore was appropriate to the constant Canadian concern for national unity. Fortunately, however, the organization of the twelve thousand municipal police in Canada does not follow American lines, but still tends to follow the British pattern of immunity from political pressure.

PUBLIC RELATIONS

Even the home of the Bobby has recently seen widespread changes in the nature of police work. Faced with a growing crime rate and increasing public complaints, the government established a Royal Commission to review the role of the police, which presented its report in 1963. It is noteworthy that, unlike their counterparts in North America, the British police are ultimately under centralized direction by the Home Secretary and that, within this framework, the local police are completely responsible for their own area, with no overlap of jurisdiction. Based on the findings of the commission a new Police Act was introduced in 1964, which envisaged securing more efficiency by phasing out police forces with less than five hundred members. As the 125 Chief Constables of Britain secure the bulk of their funds from Parliament, it is obvious that this power of the purse can secure compliance with the provisions of the Act. Furthermore, in what some policemen view as a restrictive measure that inhibits the investigation of crime, new rules were established concerning the issue of warnings to people being investigated. A cautionary warning about his rights must be given not only to a person about to be arrested, but even to a person who is interrogated and is merely "suspected" of committing a crime. The idea of an ombudsman, or neutral party, to investigate disputes between the police and citizens was examined but rejected.

The cities of Rochester N.Y. and Philadelphia have created review boards staffed by civilians unconnected with the police. In view of the poor image of the American police and wide distrust of their impartiality, such review boards were probably necessary in order to maintain public confidence. One of the most damning indictments of the American policeman appeared in a book called *Kids, Crime and Chaos*, where it is stated that foreign visitors are "unimpressed with the caliber of policemen who deal with children."[11] This type of judgment does not inspire confidence that impressionable children will mature into adults with a respect for the police.

LAW AND ORDER IN THE STREETS

During the Presidential election campaign of 1964, the Republican candidate Barry Goldwater made "law and order" a national political issue. By 1965, there was so much discussion about crime in America that President Lyndon B. Johnson created a National Crime Commission. At the same time, a new Office of Law Enforcement Assistance was established with a budget of several million dollars in federal funds to promote the further training of police officers and to encourage innovative programmes. In 1967 the President's Commission on Law Enforcement and Administration (the National Crime Commission) reported and its report makes disturbing reading. Teenagers in the fifteen- to sixteen-year-old category had the highest arrest rate of any age group in the United States; the long-range significance of this trend is revealed by the fact that 23 per cent of the total American population is ten years old or younger. A commission study of high crime areas in two large cities found that 43 per cent of the respondents stated they stay off the streets at night because of fear of crime, while 35 per cent would not speak to strangers for the same reason. The recommendations of the Commission included improving the environment of slum schools and creating employment opportunities for young people. To enable the police to take quick action against criminals, it was proposed to unlock the existing police call boxes and mark them clearly as "public emergency call boxes"; it was also proposed that the telephone company should create a single police number for each metropolitan area, and eventually have one number for the whole United States.

The ineffectiveness of courtroom procedures for dealing with offenders was criticized. As the Report of the Commission summarized,

> It [the Commission] has seen cramped and noisy courtrooms, undignified and perfunctory procedures, and badly trained personnel. It has seen dedicated people who are frustrated by huge caseloads, by the lack of opportunity to examine cases carefully, and by the

impossibility of devising constructive solutions to the problems of offenders. It has seen assembly line justice.[12]

In Washington, D.C. it was found that the courtroom time for a defendant who pleaded guilty usually totalled less than one hour, but the average time from his initial appearance to disposal of his case was four months. To aid crime prevention and unclog the courts, it was proposed to establish Youth Service Bureaus, to which juveniles could be referred for counselling and for help in being integrated into society. Furthermore, to bridge the gap between the police and the urban poor, the Commission recommended community relations programmes, with police departments making special efforts to recruit officers with the same background as the minority groups they would serve. A community service officer was to be a uniformed but unarmed member of the police department, with an educational background of at least two years college work in the liberal arts or social sciences. Probably most important were the recommendations that the selection of judges should be taken out of partisan politics, and that efforts should be made to develop a greatly enlarged competent pool of defense attorneys.

THE LAW

The complexity of the legal system in North America can only be explained by the right of each province in Canada and each state in the U.S.A. to organize its own Bar Association. In turn, this means that lawyers are licenced by autonomous law societies. As early as 1876 a group of German immigrants in New York City felt a need to organize an ethnic organization to protect the rights of its members, and to aid poor citizens of German origin. The subsequent development of legal aid for poorer citizens developed on a voluntary basis and by the mid-1960's legal aid offices in the United States were co-ordinated by a National Legal Aid and Defender Association. Canada has followed the general American pattern with provincial bodies taking care of legal aid. In contrast to this North American method, Britain since

1949 has made legal aid available at government expense to all citizens. The national Law Societies of England and Scotland administer their separate schemes. A traditional separation exists between solicitors who handle most of the civil law and pleading in the lower courts and barristers who specialize in pleading in the higher courts. Solicitors pass cases to a barrister who has a professional duty to take a case, which is a great contrast to the right of a lawyer in North America to select his own cases.

While Canada inherited the British legal code, it has not always updated this inheritance. The majesty of Canadian law is essentially a nineteenth-century magnificence reflecting an age of laissez faire; for example, there is still not an adequate programme of legal aid to an accused person of limited income. Lawyers who take the cases of poor people have often been accused of being more concerned with a fast turnover of clients, than with adequate preparation of cases which might not prove remunerative. In the richest province of Canada, the idea of assisting the poor with legal aid seems to have become mixed with the idea that the legal profession should also be assisted. In *The Poverty Wall*, Ian Adams summarized the situation in this way:

> The legal aid program in Ontario began March 13, 1967. It uses public funds to pay the legal fees of people who can't afford to hire their own lawyers. The lawyers charge 75 per cent of the regular fee. It seems fairly safe to assume that justice for the poor hardly existed before 1967 . . . . The public money for legal aid is administered by the Law Society of Upper Canada, which in fact means the legal profession has a new multi-million dollar pie to slice up among its members.[13]

Another area of concern which is receiving increased attention involves compulsory automobile insurance. The idea of a person being allowed to drive a car without adequate insurance is somewhat outmoded, as a victim of an accident must then rely on winning his case in court, and will probably find himself waiting for a long time to receive damages from a fund such as that called Unsatisfied

360

Judgments. Insistence on compulsory car insurance would seem to be a basic consideration in framing laws to cover damage to life and limb of another motorist or to his automobile.

Protection of the ordinary citizen has become a critical and hotly debated issue in our complex society. Policemen are under pressure from all sides, from those who call them pigs to those who feel they should perform miracles. The degree of skill with which the individual policeman and police forces as a whole walk the fine line between repression and permissiveness, will determine to a large degree how successfully we meet the challenges of the urban frontier.

1. V.W. Peterson, "Development of Local and State Law Enforcement," *Current History*, June, 1971, p. 329.
2. R.C. Brown and M.E. Prang, eds., *Canadian Historical Documents* (Scarborough: Prentice Hall of Canada, 1966), vol. 3, pp. 183-184.
3. Hugh W. Peart and John Schaffter, *The Winds of Change* (Toronto: Ryerson Press, 1961), p. 236.
4. Nicholas de B. Katzenbach, Chairman, *A Report by the President's Commission on Law Enforcement and the Administration of Justice* (New York: Avon Books, 1968), p. 112.
5. *National Commission on Law Enforcement* (Washington: U.S. Government Printing Office), vol. 1, p. 43.
6. V.W. Peterson, *Current History*, p. 330.
7. F.H. McClintock, *Crimes of Violence: An Enquiry by the Cambridge Institute of Criminology into Crimes of Violence against the Person in London* (London: Macmillan and Co. Ltd., 1963), p. 74.
8. Thompson S. Crockett and James Kelly, eds., "Crime in America," *Police Reference Notebook*, (Washington: International Association of Police Incorporated, 1970), 2B-10.
9. Ibid, 2B4-5.
10. D. Glaser, *Crime in the City* (New York: Harper and Row, 1970), p. 200.
11. Roul Tunley, *Kids, Crime, and Chaos* (New York: Harper and Bros., 1962), p. 188.
12. United States President's Commission on Law Enforcement and Administration of Justice, *The Challenge of Crime in a Free Society* (Washington, D.C.: U.S. Government Printing Office, 1967), p. 128.
13. Ian Adams, *The Poverty Wall* (Toronto: McClelland and Stewart Ltd., 1970), p. 120.

9

The Politics of Reform

New York politics were always dishonest . . . there was never a time when you couldn't buy the Board of Aldermen. A politician in coming forward takes these things as they are. This population is too hopelessly split up into races and factions to govern it under universal suffrage, except by the bribery of patronage.

Boss William Tweed of New York, 1871

This chapter will consider political leaders and movements that have made significant contributions to social reform. The emphasis is upon why reform movements were launched, rather than upon what was actually accomplished, as detailed discussion of particular legislation is contained in earlier chapters. The main emphasis is on the nineteenth and twentieth centuries when many modern social problems developed as a result of the industrialization that began in Britain in the eighteenth century. As the British political structure has proved so durable despite many economic and social upheavals, the basic features of parliamentary-style politics will be examined.

PARLIAMENTARY POLITICS

The right to be elected to an eighteenth-century Parliament was a privilege jealously guarded by the wealthy. Political parties in the modern sense evolved during the long parliamentary dominance of Sir Robert Walpole, who developed the art of using patronage as political cement so as to ensure loyalty to his Whig party, or rather to the leader who controlled jobbery. The opportunities for patronage were rather restricted and, therefore, Walpole kept tight control over such appointments as clerks, customs and excise officers, commissions in the Army or livings in the Church of England. In an age of political amateurs Walpole was a professional who foreshadowed the later development of the powerful American political boss. But, more importantly, Walpole developed the idea of the King's government sharing collective responsibility for any planning.

The much-praised idea of cabinet solidarity that hinged upon loyalty to a first or prime minister did not develop because of a political theory. Rather, Walpole was a pragmatist who wanted to ensure that Queen Caroline, who exercised the real monarchical power by controlling her husband, could not control Parliament by beating Walpole at his own game of dividing and ruling Parliament. So when Walpole as prime minister (a term, incidentally, he wisely disavowed so as not to flaunt his power) visited the Palace, he made sure that he had the support of his Whig colleagues.

The Whig faction in Parliament reflected the power of the large landowner. Prominent families such as the Russells proudly recalled that in the seventeenth century they had ensured that the monarchy was kept Protestant by importing William of Orange. In short, the leading Whigs felt themselves somewhat superior to the monarch and were apt to have a casual attitude towards the Palace. As that acute observer of British political life, Benjamin Disraeli, later observed, one if necessary could become a Tory, but one had to be born a Whig. The Tory group tended to reflect the squirearchy, or smaller landowners, who generally staunchly upheld loyalty to the monarchy as an article of faith.

The bulk of the population had no say in the way Britain was governed, for the privileged minority that sat in Parliament ruled in the name of "the people," a term which in fact included only the wealthy classes. Yet there was one tradition that was to prove tremendously significant to future events and this concerned the concept of noblesse oblige, or the social responsibility of the rich for those who were less fortunate. This concept had evolved in feudal times, and the tradition still held in the basically rural England of the late eighteenth century.

But under the hammer blows of succeeding revolutions—Industrial, American, French and Napoleonic—some political readjustments had to be made. For the Industrial Revolution broke down the dominance of the village world controlled by the squire, and taught masses of the labouring poor the new harsh daily discipline of the factory bell in industrial cities of the North. To these exploited labourers the French democratic ideals of freedom, equality and brotherhood might prove to be heady wine, a possibility that disturbed the *nouveau riche* of industry. Under these circumstances, what was subsequently termed the Great Victorian Compromise was effected: the established landed wealthy joined forces with the new industrially wealthy to exclude the labourer from political power.

EARLY NINETEENTH-CENTURY REFORM

An illusion of widespread political reform was provided by the Great Reform Bill of 1832 which did marginally increase the size of the total electorate relative to the total population. About one in thirty of the population now held the voting franchise. When the more politically conscious elements among the working classes finally woke up to what was happening, they organized the Chartist movement which between 1838 and 1848 tried to secure political change. The Chartist movement took its name from the five demands listed on its charter: namely, payment of M.P.s, equal electoral districts, no property qualifications, the use of the secret ballot and annual parliaments. Ultimately all of these demands except the last would be conceded, but not until the twentieth century. The militancy of the Chartist movement petered out in 1848, due principally to internal weaknesses concerning aims and leadership. The skilled artisans then decided to strive for immediate economic gains through trade union activity, rather than to support political activity to secure the franchise.

Yet the idea of reform was not dead. Parliament passed laws in an effort to exert controls over conditions in factories and coal mines. Most importantly, the Municipal Corporations Act of 1835 provided for the election of city councils by householders; this Act rapidly changed the membership of the former closed corporations that had reeked of nepotism as they controlled many cities. Municipal politics became important, and such basic matters as sanitation and street lighting were tackled by elected representatives who exhibited great pride in their cities. A basic uniformity of administration was provided for England and Wales with one-third of a council being required to stand for re-election annually, thus ensuring new blood along with continuity of experience. These elected municipal councils could levy local taxes and were zealous in reforming the living conditions within industrial cities that had grown too quickly.

The spirit of reform also existed in North America, although the New World had yet to become as industrialized as the Old. A fiery Scots radical named William Lyon Mackenzie denounced privilege in Upper Canada and praised the Jacksonian democracy operating in the United States. In that country, President Andrew Jackson appealed to the pioneering rural element of the population that distrusted the commercial interests of the city and, therefore, welcomed the idea that the holders of government office should be changed frequently to prevent corruption. Furthermore, Jackson felt that jobs in the public service were, in his words, "so simple that men of intelligence may readily qualify themselves for their performance."[1] Unfortunately, "rotation in office" was often a synonym for a spoils system whereby the victor in an election distributed the fruits of patronage. In his praise of Jacksonian democracy, however, it seems that William Lyon Mackenzie felt that American politicians were inclined to be altruistic individuals. But the real reform movement in the

Canadas was formed on the different basis of biculturalism, when Robert Baldwin and Louis Lafontaine joined forces with the object of minimizing direct political control by Britain. The fact that this appeal to freedom and independence also implied that future patronage would be dispensed by Canadians, gave it a widespread appeal. In short, the grease of patronage oiled political wheels in both North America and Britain. But the more important issue was the degree of corruption involved in political life and whether the interests of the population were being served.

Only in a national crisis such as war, it seemed, could private gain be temporarily subordinated to higher interests. Abraham Lincoln in his Gettysburg Address made the acute diagnosis that government should exist of the people, by the people, and for the people. But in practice politicians often prefer to limit government *by the people* to recording a vote every few years, and ignore altogether the other two aspects.

THE SECOND HALF OF THE VICTORIAN AGE

The American belief in local autonomy provided a setting where "bosses" controlled patronage. Elections were seen as the means of providing a victor with the opportunity of dividing up the spoils with his supporters. Boss Tweed of New York City claimed, in the quotation that heads this chapter, that bribery was the only way to rule large cities. As Tweed is usually credited with milking over 100 million dollars from the treasury of New York City, we can assume that he knew his business. Bosses in the large cities possessed considerable business expertise in gaining the electoral support of the large immigrant groups by promoting their own ability and willingness to dispense favours. Corruption produced reactions that led to spasmodic attempts at reform and kicking rascals out of office, but American politics suffered from such low prestige that reformers were unable to maintain public interest. The concept that politics was a dirty business was possibly a natural attitude in an age that generally accepted the idea of Social Darwinism. An astute observer of the political scene wrote that "The desperate race for wealth has absorbed the citizen, and has not left him time to attend to the public welfare; it even encouraged his want of public spirit and converted it almost into a virtue."[2] America did not believe in aristocratic notions such as noblesse oblige or paternalism and the political climate lacked the British tradition of deference for men in authority.

There was a marked improvement in the level of political morality in Britain at this time, due principally to the influence of William Gladstone whose parliamentary career covered most of the nineteenth century. Gladstone has been described as a man who would have made a good Archbishop of Canterbury and his influence on the morality of British politics was widespread. By 1865 Gladstone's enthusiasm for reform was being restrained only by the innate conservatism of Lord Palmerston, the Whig Prime Minister. Pam, as he was affectionately known, had been involved in parliamentary politics for over 60 years and his particular specialty was foreign affairs—Palmerstonian tactics included despatching gunboats to intimidate "foreigners." National interests during Palmerston's later years were centred on issues abroad rather than domestic reforms. But in 1865 Pam proved to be mortal and his successor as Prime Minister revamped his heterogeneous following into what was termed a Liberal party. The road now seemed clear for widespread reform by extending the democratic right to the franchise and limiting the sort of patronage that had traditionally been thought the prerogative of the upper classes.

But now appeared the great rival to Gladstone, Benjamin Disraeli, who led the Tory faction that was rebuilding its image by the use of the party label Conservative. Disraeli held office briefly in 1866 and, by some skilful parliamentary manoeuvring, managed to get the credit for passing the Second Reform Act of 1867 that enfranchised many workers. Disraeli was a self-made man who had an objective view of British political life: on becoming Prime Minister, he wrote that he had climbed to the top of the greasy pole. This was hardly a traditional view of the position he occupied, although it was corroborated by his slide back down in the election of 1868.

Back into office came the virtuous Gladstone whose Christian outlook did not extend to his political rival:

Courtesy of the National Portrait Gallery, London

William Gladstone (1809-1898):
the giant of liberalism

Gladstone once remarked that while Disraeli's doctrine was false the man was more false than his doctrine. Paradoxically, although Gladstone received his educational training at establishments such as Eton and Oxford, he did not defend privilege in England, but instead set about dynamiting some of the social foundations of the establishment. Between 1868 and 1874 many of the bastions of privilege virtually reserved for the so-called upper classes, such as posts in the Civil

Service, the Army and the Church, were opened by competitive examination to the sons of a rising middle class. Furthermore, the passage of the Ballot Act authorized the secret ballot at elections and enabled the electorate to vote for the candidates of their choice, rather than be subjected to physical intimidation by bully boys who had been paid to attend the "open voting" meeting where a count was taken of raised hands.

Electoral behaviour often tends to be perverse, to the chagrin of politicians: the electorate of 1874 used Gladstone's secret ballot to vote into office his rival. Relations between these two leaders can be gauged from Disraeli's statement that "Posterity will do justice to that unprincipled maniac [Gladstone] . . . with one commanding characteristic whether praying, speechifying, or scribbling . . . never a gentleman."[3] The opposing idea that Disraeli had raised himself to the status of a Tory gentleman was hotly disputed by Gladstonians, as well as by many Tories who were suspicious of a Jewish adventurer leading their party, but had reluctantly accepted Disraeli as a leader with ideas that could appeal to the electorate. In the years between 1874 and 1876, Disraeli succeeded in carrying out an intensive programme of social reform, as described in the chapters concerning housing, health and labour.

One of the beneficiaries of this drive to improve living standards was the mayor of Birmingham, Joseph Chamberlain, who took advantage of the Parliamentary offer to finance what is now termed urban renewal. Chamberlain was an able man drawn into municipal politics who would advance to becoming a leading M.P. urging national reform. British politics offered a prestigious career to such men who were devoted to public service and, of course, who were able to finance their political ambitions.

Disraeli, who had twice ascended the greasy pole to become Prime Minister, was old and ailing by 1878. The Conservative leader naturally aspired to gain a more permanent position of prestige. So his friend, Queen Victoria, whom Disraeli privately called "the faerie," elevated him to the peerage as Lord Beaconsfield. This was fitting recognition for a loyal political servant who had revived the public prestige of the monarchy, and the image that the world held of Britain's power. But once Gladstone decided that Beaconsfieldism stood for immorality in the conduct of foreign affairs, the greasy pole came into sight again. Gladstone appealed to "the people," a term which he expanded to include anyone who would listen at giant public rallies, and was subsequently returned to office in the election of 1880.

An interested observer of the Gladstone-Disraeli duel was the Prime Minister of the recently created Dominion of Canada. John A. Macdonald was of Scottish background like Gladstone, but shared many personal characteristics with Disraeli. Macdonald's physical appearance was similar to that of Disraeli, as was his whimsical manner that masked a hardworking professional politician who was concerned about fostering national unity. Macdonald was possibly more cautious in his approach to problems but possessed the same courage and tenacity of purpose that characterized both Disraeli and Gladstone. On the other hand, the influence of American politics was seen in the methods Macdonald employed to buy harmony in the newly created state of Canada through the financial arrangements completed with the new provinces of Nova Scotia, Prince Edward Island and British Columbia.

Politics in Canada were dominated by businessmen who were interested in the possibilities for profit in their developing country. The National Policy of Macdonald was supported by railway promoters who encouraged the lavish expenditure of public funds to complete the C.P.R. Businessmen also welcomed tariffs as a way of excluding foreign competition. Yet so long as a National Policy existed the population was basically content: the dire alternative then, as now, was to accept complete control by the United States. The nearby presence of Uncle Sam ensured a definite decision on political issues; as a leading commentator has written, "there should be erected a monument to this American ogre who has so often performed the function of saving us from drift and indecision."[4]

370

CORRUPTION AND POLITICS

Canada is certainly not an easy country to govern. The only successful way to ensure federal leadership has been to have leaders willing to unite on a bicultural base. George Cartier was indispensable to the success of John A. Macdonald in forging Confederation. National unity continued to provide the main theme of Canadian political life and it is noteworthy that Sir Wilfrid Laurier did not tamper with the National Plan when he continued in Macdonald's role as the architect of unity. Social reform was not a crucial issue in the Laurier years from 1897 to 1911, as Canada had yet to experience heavy industrialization or urbanization. The price of nation-building was heavy, however, in terms of lowering the tone of public life for as Sir John Willison, an able Liberal journalist, recorded, "all that distinguished Liberals from Conservatives in nation-building was their 'voluble virtue'."[5] The moralistic outpouring of Liberalism was doubtless connected with the fact that many of the leading members of the party were intellectuals—such as journalists, professors and lawyers—who pictured themselves as crusaders. Furthermore, this moralistic fervour was consistent with the view that a distinguishing mark of Canadian life was freedom from the deplorable corruption publicly visible in the United States.

This was the American era of the Robber Baron and the Muckraker, with "political machines" available to aid the needs of businessmen. A good example of the way in which politics operated, occurred when an industrial tycoon named Mark Hanna, national chairman of the Republican party, claimed he "made" President William McKinley. But in 1900 Boss Hanna over-reached himself when he approved the idea of Boss Tom Platt of New York that Governor Theodore Roosevelt should be kicked upstairs to rest on the obscurity of the Vice-Presidential shelf. For on September 6, 1901, President McKinley was assassinated and Roosevelt was elevated to the Presidency, and the new President revealed himself as a new breed of rich reformer not easily corrupted by party bosses.

Roosevelt emerged as the champion of the Progressive movement that was crusading on both the municipal and state levels. Such cities as New York and Cleveland had Progressive movements that were concerned with trying to overthrow the boss rule that had resulted in

> inefficient, inadequate and costly city utilities, organized prostitution, a lawless liquor trade, and general corruption and venality . . . an even more comprehensive aim of the [Progressive] municipal movement was to make the twentieth-century American city a decent, healthy and enjoyable place in which to live. This meant the abolition of slums and tenements, the abatement of crime, juvenile delinquency and disease, the creation of parks, playgrounds and efficient social services.[6]

This type of thinking appealed to the belief of many rural communities that the city was the source of evil and, also, to progressive thinkers who felt all urban problems would disappear if only the environment were changed. Reforming mayors such as Samuel "Golden Rule" Jones of Toledo, Ohio and Thomas L. Johnson in Cleveland campaigned as "a friend of the people." In other words there was an attempt to project a personal image in order to break the grip of the regular Republican and Democratic machines.

On the higher level of state government, reforming governors like Robert LaFollete of Wisconsin and Woodrow Wilson of New Jersey fought economic privilege. Efforts were made to regulate trusts, monopolies and railroads and, in particular, to ensure that corporations could not evade paying a fair share of taxes.

Roosevelt called for a Square Deal for Americans and initiated such reforms as Pure Food and Drug legislation and conservation policies to save land for national parks. Predatory economic interests were rather taken aback by this notion that natural resources should be preserved for the enjoyment of the nation, rather than available for the exploitation of the few. Theodore Roosevelt raised the prestige of the Presidency to the highest point since the days of Abraham Lincoln. In fact so high did Roosevelt's stock rise that the leading financier of that age, J.P. Morgan, began to be concerned about a big rival operator, and scheduled a visit to the White House. No higher praise could have been bestowed upon the President than a personal visit by the Dean of the Robber Barons.

THE MECHANICS OF AMERICAN POLITICS

Theodore Roosevelt found, however, that power in Washington had to be shared with the Senate. For until 1913 it was the state legislatures, or rather the state bosses, who selected senators rather than the electorate. In turn, businessmen dealt with the "boss" to ensure that all proposals considered detrimental to his interests, such as regulation of wages or maximum hours, were opposed as interference with economic laws. The political climate of New York State was described by Elihu Root, Secretary of State in the Roosevelt Administration, in this way:

> They call the system—I do not coin the phrase, I adopt it because it carries its own meaning—the system they call "invisible government." For I do not remember how many years, Mr. Conkling was the supreme ruler in this state; the governor did not count; the legislators did not count; comptrollers and secretaries of state and what not, did not count . . . . Then Mr. Platt ruled the state; for nigh upon twenty years he ruled it. It was not the governor; it was not the legislature; it was not any elected officers; it was Mr. Platt . . . . The ruler of the state during the greater part of the forty years of my acquaintance with state government has not been any man authorized by the constitution or by the law.[7]

At the federal level the most powerful President-Maker was J.P. Morgan, who issued his instructions through a Colonel Harvey, sometimes called his errand boy. Harvey selected Dr. Woodrow Wilson, President of Princeton University, as a potential office-holder who held the right type of conservative views. As the first step on his way to the White House, Wilson was assisted to become Governor of New Jersey. But Wilson then displayed real character by denouncing the party bosses, beating the New Jersey machine of Senator Smith, and popularizing his programme under the slogan of the "New Freedom." Furthermore, because the Republican party was split between two warring factions in 1912, Wilson became a minority President and launched a new wave of Progressive reforms on a federal level that touched on such issues as the abuse of child labour and better conditions for seamen of the merchant marine.

LIBERALISM AND SOCIAL REFORM

On the other side of the Atlantic, rich men were also having difficulty coping with reformers. David Lloyd George, the Welsh Wizard, led this reform movement on behalf of a new Liberalism. Essentially the Liberal party had turned its back on its Gladstonian heritage of tight budgets, free trade and laissez faire; the concern now was to take action on the domestic front in order to head off the threat of socialism. Lloyd George decided that a popular programme would be to attack the wealthy landowners sitting in the House of Lords; this approach would gain the support of workers, but not antagonize the wealthy manufacturers supporting the Liberal party. The budget of 1909 deliberately antagonized the landed aristocracy by applying a tax on unused land. The House of Lords, which was the bastion of the Conservative party, rose to the bait by condemning the efforts of a Robin Hood named Lloyd George to make them finance Liberal reforms. Lloyd George now whipped up public enthusiasm by attacking rich landlords. In a speech at Newcastle on October 9, 1909, he baited the House of Lords with, "Should 500 men, ordinary men, chosen accidentally from among the unemployed override the judgment . . . of millions of people?"[8] Demagogue Lloyd George thus adroitly focused public attention on a constitutional crisis involving the House of Lords, while simultaneously carrying a wave of social reform through Parliament.

The famous National Health Insurance Act was passed in 1911. A fellow conspirator of Lloyd George named Winston Churchill, despite the aristocratic hue of his Marlborough background, carried many useful Acts to their completion, such as those providing Labour Exchanges for unemployed workers seeking employment and a minimum wage structure in certain sweated industries. Churchill shared Lloyd George's views about the threat of socialism and was an eloquent opponent. For example, in a speech in Glasgow on October 11, 1906, he pointed out that it is hard to draw a line between individualism and collectivism. Churchill told his working-class audience that, "The nature of man is a dual nature . . . . Collectively we light our streets and supply ourselves with water . . . . But we do not make love collectively, and the ladies do not marry us collectively."[9] In the face of such invincible logic, it would be hard for a worker to explain the socialist point of view to his wife.

But Winston Churchill and David Lloyd George were fighting a losing battle in their efforts to stem the tide of socialism. A parliamentary Labour party was active in 1902 and proceeded to gain strength, with such able Fabian propagandists as George Bernard Shaw and Beatrice and Stanley Webb providing the intellectual artillery for the socialist campaign. To the disgust of Marxists, the popular British brand of socialism sought peaceful change by constitutional methods. Once the Liberal government had reluctantly agreed to pay M.P.s in 1911, thereby fulfilling another of the Chartist aims, the way was open for a larger number of working men to sit in Parliament and make the voice of Labour heard.

IMPLEMENTATION BY THE CIVIL SERVICE

Political reform can only be effective when an efficient and respected civil service implements legislation. In the United States there had long been lack of respect for the federal civil service, where vacancies were filled by political patronage and there was frequently an accompanying kickback system that contributed to party funds. In 1883 a clean-up campaign started with the passage of the Pendleton Act, named after a senator called "Gentleman" George Pendleton of Ohio. This Act created a Civil Service Commission to ensure that approximately 14,000 key jobs at the federal level were filled by open competitive examination. This initial classified list of jobs covered only about twelve per cent of the total employees in the federal service, but it represented the thin end of a wedge, as the President was empowered to extend it to other parts of the civil service. By the end of the century, the number of civil servants covered by this legislation had increased to approximately 100,000, and public confidence was developing in the idea of a non-partisan federal civil service. It should be noted that establishing new standards in a federal structure was far more difficult than the Gladstonian reform of the relatively centralized bureaucracy of England and Wales. For where power is fragmented, as it is in a federal system, then the lower levels of government can remain relatively immune from national standards applicable to a federal service. On the other hand, federal reform tends to awaken public opinion to the need for further reform and thereby establish a trend which, in the long run, will be significant.

Canada's civil service was affected by the reform current that was flowing in North America. Patronage had been rampant in the federal service where a candidate for employment had to have a recommendation from a cabinet minister. After half-hearted attempts to remove patronage by the Civil Service Acts of 1882 and 1908, really widespread reform of the federal service took place during the period of the Unionist government in World War One. The coalition government of 1918 supported the right of an independent Civil Service Commission to control competitive examinations for entrance and promotions by merit. This wartime measure, which passed with a minimum of partisan controversy, meant that there would be no return to pre-1914 days, when reformers lamented the nepotism and patronage that were within the power of the wealthy.

VARIOUS APPROACHES IN THE EARLY TWENTIETH CENTURY

The first independent working-class representative to sit in the British House of Commons, Keir Hardie, made several trips to Canada before World War I to address meetings in Winnipeg. Socialism was carried to Canada in the baggage of the many British immigrants who crossed the Atlantic. But the idea of collective responsibility remained anathema to the American belief in the virtues of rugged individualism.

The political climate in the United States has been well described by Richard Hofstadter, a leading historian, who has written about the

> rootlessness and heterogeneity of American life . . . its peculiar scramble for status and its peculiar search for secure identity give rise to status politics: in search for scapegoats rather than positive action.[10]

The concept of a need for collective action or responsibility could not take root in such a situation, so that a true left could not develop. The reputation of socialism as a devious foreign philosophy was given a considerable boost by the Russian Revolution in 1917, and the implication that it might subvert the American way of life was given widespread publicity.

Canada could not fail to be influenced to some extent by her neighbour, but at least in Canada socialism was not regarded as something completely alien or foreign, possibly because an embryonic socialist movement had evolved from British precedents. The Winnipeg General Strike of 1919 did see some hysteria about Bolshevism taking over Canada, but with the arrival of Prime Minister W.L. Mackenzie King these fears soon subsided. King had been closely associated with capitalism through services rendered to John D. Rockefeller that had helped to curb American trade unionism. King did have constructive ideas on social reform but was also a politician who clearly understood that Canadian unity required a minimum of action on the part of the federal government. Therefore Mackenzie King emphasized Ottawa's administrative role, which did not envisage sweeping reform but rather a piecemeal advance. A visitor to Canada, Ben Tillett, the British labour leader, appraised the political situation and summed up his reaction in these words:

> There is something lacking, it appears to me, in the statesmanship and political leadership of Canada. The ineptitude which prevents a rational and practical use of

Canada's immense territory can be variously explained. It can be attributed to indolence, it can be attributed to a lack of political understanding, but undoubtedly it exists.[11]

The creative role of the federal government had passed with the nation-building efforts of John A. Macdonald and Wilfrid Laurier, and now political apathy was fairly widespread. Furthermore, the Prime Minister of Canada was not free to select the best talent available to serve as his colleagues in the cabinet. As one of the biographers of W.L. Mackenzie King has recorded, a Prime Minister "is not free to choose Ministers at his personal wish or will. Considerations of geography, of the size and total population of the Provinces, as well as the economic, racial and religious considerations . . . are all among the factors of which full account must be made."[12] The need to placate interest groups in forming a cabinet naturally weakened any inclination to make drastic reforms that would weaken the status quo.

The English-French rift over conscription in 1917 provided Mackenzie King with his basic appeal to Quebec: he was the only English-speaking politician who opposed conscription. Using Quebec as his base of power, Mackenzie King set out to promote French-English harmony. This involved neutralizing any political philosophy that threatened to disturb the status quo. Any ideas proposed by the Progressive party from the West were listened to very attentively until the movement was undermined, lost momentum and disappeared. The main heir to the political agitation for social reform symbolized by the Winnipeg General Strike was J.S. Woodsworth, and one of his great services in Parliament for the next twenty years was to crusade as the conscience of Canadian Prime Ministers. The passage of a moderate Old Age Pensions Act in 1927 by Mackenzie King was inspired by Woodsworth.

THE IMPACT OF THE DEPRESSION

In the political terminology of the late 1920's, the left was symbolized by the U.S.S.R. and the right by American

378

capitalism. When the Wall Street Crash occurred in 1929 the relationship of politics to social reform became an urgent issue for the right. The American dream that words like "democracy" and "capitalism" were interchangeable became suspect when many workers discovered that their dribbles of capital known as wages had dried up. As unemployment mounted, and President Herbert Hoover seemed unable to restore confidence and prosperity, the role of reformers became urgent. By 1932, the Great Depression had produced an electorate willing to try anything to secure a return to economic prosperity. It has been said of Franklin D. Roosevelt, who was elected President in 1932, that he provided American capitalism with a breathing spell to put its house in order. The New Deal spawned many collective efforts sponsored by federal funds that would have been unthinkable before 1929. Social reform took a great leap forward culminating in the Social Security Act of 1935. As might be expected, Franklin D. Roosevelt was seen as a socialist by some staunch right-wing elements but, in retrospect, the New Deal seems to have been a conservative effort to restore faith in capitalism. The American economy did revive after 1935, but this improvement probably owed as much to the increasing need for the munitions of war, as to any specific legislation outlined in the New Deal. Yet it is important to acknowledge that Franklin Delano Roosevelt was the only national leader in Canada, the U.S. and Great Britain to try a variety of new programmes at this time in an attempt to get the economy moving.

Britain's Stanley Baldwin had no constructive ideas to contribute to alleviating the Great Depression. The one great contribution towards a solution of the economic problem was John Maynard Keynes' treatise *The General Theory of Employment, Interest and Money* (1936). But the prophet of the idea of deficit spending in times of underemployment was heeded not in his own country but in the United States. Many intellectuals flirted with the idea of abandoning capitalism, and such prominent socialist figures as George Bernard Shaw and the Webbs visited Russia to view the alternative system.

Socialist thinking in Canada tended to be a product of university intellectuals such as Frank Underhill or ministers of the gospel like J.S. Woodsworth. Behind these former students of sophisticated Oxford University stood the farmer of the Canadian West who voiced traditional rural discontent with the Eastern capitalist. From such elements was formed the Co-operative Commonwealth Federation which, in its manifesto of 1932, envisaged the end of capitalism. The item which was most commendable in this Manifesto was the proposal for socialized medicine which, thirty years later, was implemented by T.C. Douglas when he formed the first C.C.F. government in Saskatchewan. Another reform group that took shape in the politically active West was the Social Credit Party, which settled in to rule as the establishment of Alberta. Social Credit claimed to have solved the consumer's problem of a lack of purchasing power but its ideas were declared *ultra vires* of the constitution and therefore the party retreated from "funny money" to traditional finance.

R.B. Bennett could not find a solution to unemployment and, in 1935, was succeeded as Prime Minister by W.L. Mackenzie King. Mr. King solved the problems of the Depression by appointment of a Royal Commission, whose excellently documented report on the health of Canada, known as the Rowell-Sirois Report, was not presented until 1940. By then, Canada was at war and unemployment difficulties had virtually ceased. It is noteworthy that Canada has usually been prosperous in wartime, whether one considers 1812, the Crimean War of 1853, the American Civil War, the Boer War, both World Wars, or the Korean War. The experience of the Second World War clearly displayed how unemployment problems vanished when a shortage of labour resulted from the service of men in the Armed Forces, and increased productivity became a major goal. There was no need to talk about discrimination when virtually every able-bodied person regardless of age, skill, colour or sex was needed to fill the insatiable demand for more workers. Fighting for freedom was meaningful when opportunity on the home front was unrestricted.

WORLD WAR II AND THE AFTERMATH

After Britain had been chased out of Europe by Hitler in 1940, the embattled British had time to reflect on why they were fighting. Men dreamed of a postwar world in which want and poverty would be eliminated. Thus when the Beveridge Report of 1942 appeared proposing social care of every citizen from cradle to grave, it received a hearty reception. As outlined in the chapter on poverty, the acceptance of the Beveridge blueprint by the Labour party, coupled with Winston Churchill's failure to read the mood of the people on this particular issue, led to the first sweeping victory of the Labour Party in Britain's history.

The Conservative party was shrunk to 189 seats and a massive bloc of 393 seats was captured by the Labour party. But the envisaged socialist millenium of sharing the wealth had arrived too late, for after the war Britain was financially bankrupt. An austerity drive by the spartan Sir Stafford Cripps was more notable for trying to restrict the level of one's bath water to six inches, than for success in persuading American capitalists to finance Britain's socialist experiment. Anglo-American accord which had been a feature of Prime Minister Winston Churchill's wartime eminence diminished rapidly with the takeover of Clement Attlee. Yet in spite of Britain's desperate economic plight, the period after World War II witnessed a productive series of reforms, of which the highlight was the National Health Scheme of 1948.

By 1948 in Canada, the remarkable political career of Prime Minister W.L. Mackenzie King drew to an end. To his credit, Mackenzie King had led a united Canada to war at a time when, because of the interpretation of the B.N.A. Act, the power of the central government was acknowledged as paramount. But once World War II was over, the alternative peacetime interpretation of the constitution became operative, and the individual Provinces demanded restoration of their right to be the main instrument of social change. To his successors in the Liberal party, King bequeathed a policy which was basically unconstitutional: most of the issues that touched the daily welfare of Canadians had been deemed, by successive interpretations of the British North America Act, to fall in the area of provincial jurisdiction.

Nevertheless, after 1945 the federal government insisted that it had a role to play in ensuring that opportunities for Canadians were equalized in the emerging welfare state, even if such a view could not be justified by the constitution. As Canadian politics have always been noteworthy for the high percentage of lawyers who practise as politicians,[13] one of the more fascinating aspects of political activity is the way constitutional hurdles rarely inhibit "practical" politics. But a case can be made that the political difficulty of applying a rigid federal constitution requires language that can be made to fit. An American writer has remarked that "The question is not 'Does federalism condone this or dictate that?' but rather 'How can I make the language of federalism fit what it is I want to do?' "[14] However, Quebec's Maurice Duplessis fought the intrusion of Ottawa into the provincial area of responsibility, while the "have" provinces of Ontario, British Columbia and Alberta resisted the idea of Ottawa providing their tax money to the "have-not" provinces. Canadian reform politics in the quarter-century since 1945 have tended to be dominated by a succession of federal-provincial conferences, held at the expense of the taxpayer, to decide how to share the funds provided by the same taxpayer.

An issue which proved to be contentious at the federal-provincial conference of 1971 had been opened twenty years before when the British government authorized the federal government of Canada to handle Old Age Pensions. This wedge in the provisions of the B.N.A. Act was widened in 1964 by the federal government with the passage of Section 94A, which empowered the federal government to make laws regarding supplementary benefits. But these amendments requested by Ottawa categorically state that no such federal law should affect the operation of any present or future provincial law in the same area. In other words the prevailing power is still with the provinces: therefore at Victoria in 1971 a clash occurred as Quebec again resisted these encroachments of Ottawa.

FEDERALISM

This emphasis on administering Canada is understandable once it is realized that the primary goal of Canadian politics is to promote national unity. Creative politics that have specified major social goals are disruptive to national unity, and therefore emphasis is placed on the difficulties of governing Canada. Any attempt to polarize political thought in terms of the right or left is regarded as a disruptive force. For this reason the New Democratic Party that emerged in 1961 was viewed with deep suspicion by the traditional Liberal-Conservative supporters. There seemed a challenge to tri-party consensus politics where the C.C.F. supplied ideas, the Liberals held the necessary conferences, and a variety of provincial parties implemented the reforms. The fact that the civil service frequently launches a scheme on April 1 probably concerns administrative practice rather than a sense of humour. The Conservative party under the leadership of John G. Diefenbaker had displayed concern after 1958 about the social Condition of Canada, by championing the cause of the little man and increasing the old age pension. But the greatest electoral landslide in Canadian history was followed by disenchantment. The illusion that Canada had found a David Lloyd George was rapidly dissipated. Diefenbaker concentrated on usurping the Liberal stock-in-trade of being the champion of national unity. Ironically, this caused an internationalist named Lester B. Pearson to become a type of Canadian flag-waver.

Lester B. Pearson in his role as peacemaker pursuing the goal of national unity revived a concept called co-operative federalism, which had been popular in Roosevelt's administration during the depression years. This concept envisaged the two levels of government, federal and provincial (state), supporting and augmenting each other in developing public policy, rather than being at odds with one another.

In a federal system political power is fragmented, but as urban problems intensify and cities grow to unmanageable size, a new need arises for strong central leadership. Thus, while Americans have continued their tradition of local autonomy wherever possible, there is also a belief in the need for strong executive action from Washington. This means that if a state legislature ignores the problems of the cities, then the ordinary citizen turns towards the President. The vigorous response of Lyndon B. Johnson in supplying aid directly to cities was obscured by the war in Vietnam, but the initiation of a War on Poverty displayed the leadership potential of the occupant of the White House. An American city mayor is also a strong executive who tends to be closely identified with his city, as are Richard Daly of Chicago, and John V. Lindsay of New York. In the densely populated metropolitan areas of New York City, the difficulty of governing over eight million people, and trying to please the majority, presents a challenge that boggles the imagination. The Mayor of New York has responsibilities that rival those of the President himself and indicate that, increasingly, the political problems of urban areas demand political ability of the highest calibre.

Canada has produced a mayor who has been regarded as one of the leading municipal leaders in North America. Jean Drapeau's administration of Montreal since 1954 has earned widespread admiration. Originally drafted for the mayoralty by the reform-minded Civil Action League, Drapeau vigorously tackled the problem of ensuring adequate law enforcement, then placed his city in the forefront of change by completing a subway, promoting urban renewal and staging EXPO '67.

Another French-Canadian revitalized interest in politics, this time at the federal level, when Trudeaumania caught the imagination of many voters in 1968. The charisma that is needed by a leader in a television age was apparent in the Canada of 1968, as it had been some years earlier in the United States with the election campaign of President John F. Kennedy. One of the interesting trends that seems to be evident is that Pierre E. Trudeau appears more like a President than a traditional Prime Minister, in that he has depended more on personal popularity than a parliamentary majority. In fact, some critics say that he views Members of Parliament with some disdain, as when he commented that, "When they are 50 yards from Parliament Hill, they are no longer hon. members—they are just nobodys, Mr.

Speaker."[15] But there is one issue which is important in Canada, and upon which all Prime Ministers have been judged. That issue is simply whether economic prosperity existed during their period of office. For while many different versions have been advanced as to the nature of Canadian nationalism(s), there is possibly general agreement that the critical issue on which the Prime Minister will be judged by public opinion is the Canadian standard of living relative to that of the U.S.A.

MUNICIPAL POLITICS

It is precisely this question of an adequate standard of living that is stirring new political elements within Canada. For unlike Britain and the U.S.A., Canada has not had a two-party structure that extended down to the municipal level. Apathy at municipal elections may be partially attributable to the fact that the electors in Canada have not known what a candidate represents, other than the traditional public relations talk that he is a good guy. Reform elements in the city that want social action are now beginning to show a determination to fight City Hall, as related in the chapter on housing. Whether traditional consensus politics can contain this grass-roots swell, or whether the new movements will change the nature of municipal politics, is not yet clear. One is reminded in the Canada of 1972 of Disraeli's characterization of the two Englands—one rich and one poor. What seems evident is that the politics of reform in Canada are undergoing a change of direction as politicians try to determine and adopt new trends.

One of the disturbing features of our federal system of government has been the way in which deadlocks develop in the carrying out of social policy. For political power in the last analysis means control of the public purse and the three levels of government tend to be jealous of each other, and to try to operate independently. In the United States the Office of Economic Opportunity has become hopelessly entangled with government bureaucracies, with the sad result that the goal of helping the poor has not been attained to any significant degree. Similarly, in Canada on June 15, 1969, Health and Welfare Minister John Munro admitted that the provinces and the federal government had to get together to work out a better system than the present complicated cost-sharing programmes.[16] Possibly President Richard Nixon was right in telling Congress that funds had to be turned over to municipalities to permit them to deal with social problems at the local level.

The extremely rapid growth of metropolitan areas, through the steady expansion of suburbia, has created many difficulties for local government conducted through the traditional municipal council that supervises a local area. Problems associated with health, sanitation, protection by fire and police forces or transportation do not, unfortunately, confine themselves within the boundary lines established in an earlier age. Toronto recognized in 1953 the need for a federal form of municipal government and created a Metropolitan Council that supervises major issues such as planning, housing, roads and parks. This Metropolitan Council comprised representatives of thirteen otherwise autonomous local municipalities and thereby reduced the rivalry between local councils that can impede the provision of vital public services. It could be argued, also, that the autonomous local unit of government is not really adapted to the television age. Television has posed a psychological problem by giving the ordinary citizen the impression that he is more familiar with the daily routine of the Prime Minister than with the political actions of his alderman. From the point of view of the taxpayer, undoubtedly economics of scale are possible by having a centralized body, but this has to be balanced against the loss of contact with local councils that form grass-roots democracy in action.

NEW POLITICAL FORCES

The complexity of modern government and the difficulty of changing traditional attitudes to the political structure are well illustrated in this summary:

> But what is modern American federalism? For one thing, it is the heritage of an old, but deeply rooted controversy between those who view America as a single union of 200

million people with basically common attitudes and common goals and those who view her as a voluntary association of separate and unique states, the people of each state having the right to basically determine their own future. It is over 10 million people administering over 170 aid programs through over 400 separated appropriations. It is over 75 planning assistance programs entangled in a maze of 50 states, 3000 counties, 18,000 municipalities, 17,000 townships, 35,000 school districts, 1000 housing and urban renewal districts, 2200 drainage districts, 2400 soil conservation districts, 3200 fire districts and 700 health and hospital districts. It is spending over 100 billion dollars. It is coordinating the lives of people in over 92,000 local governmental units. It is, by any definition of the word, a problem. The question is, "Whose problem?"[17]

Added to the myriad of official voices now are those of many groups outside the formal framework of government bodies. The key word now is "power" and a great deal of stress has been placed on how to acquire it. In the past few years we have heard about Student power, Black power, Woman power and People power. These groups together comprise a very large segment of society demanding faster reform.

The strongest potential political group that has appeared recently in Canada is that of women who are poor. According to Ian Adams in *The Poverty Wall*, "The majority of the poor in this country are women; it is as simple as that. By conservative standards there are some three million of them."[18] Working women bear the brunt of the reluctance of many employers to pay females a living wage, and there are social welfare payments made to 350,000 non-working women who are the heads of families. When the Royal Commission on the Status of Women set out it did not realize this problem of many women seeking some degree of independence through adequate provision for the raising of their families. As Chairman Anne Francis admitted, poverty was one aspect of the status of women that "all the women's groups who pushed for a Commission hadn't spent much time thinking about."[19] Furthermore, articulate spokesmen for female heads of families made it clear that these women wanted no longer to be restricted to low-paid, part-time jobs or inadequate welfare allowances. For these women to secure full-time employment and thereby raise the standard of living of their families, opportunities have to be provided for day-care centres for small children and homemaker services. It should be noted that apart from the inherent injustice of employers exploiting the cheaper labour of females, a constant theme since the nineteenth-century rise of industrialism, there is a most important political consideration. Social justice would seem to suggest that as women comprise approximately half the human race, it would be democratic to aim at fifty per cent of the M.P.s in Ottawa being women. Grace MacInnis in the present House of Commons must feel very lonely in this setting. The emancipation of women is not really a question of merely guaranteeing equal rights, so much as of harnessing the talent of citizens who have a unique contribution to make as social reformers.

Progress through reform, often arising from the dissatisfaction of citizens themselves, has long been a main feature of our liberal-style democracy, regardless of the party labels that are used. The right to dissent has long been accepted in Britain, Canada and the United States. But whether deliberate militant dissent can be permitted in a democracy that prides itself on tolerance is one of the main problems that has not yet been resolved. John Stuart Mill in *On Liberty* expressed the view that freedom has a limit, specifically where the action of one individual violates the freedom of another individual. Unfortunately, it is hard to use this sound philosophical view as a firm practical guide amid the complexity of modern urban life. The only really constant element in reform politics is the need to change peacefully an aspect of what exists. The issue now is not really what to do, but rather how quickly it can be accomplished.

1. Charles N. Glaab and A. Theodore Brown, *A History of Urban America* (Toronto: Collier-Macmillan Canada, 1967), p. 192.
2. Ibid., p. 221.
3. D.C. Somervell, *Disraeli and Gladstone* (New York: Garden City, 1926) p. 196.
4. Frank H. Underhill, *The Image of Confederation* (Toronto: Canadian Broadcasting Corporation, 1967), p. 4.
5. Ibid., p. 26.
6. George E. Mowry, *The Progressive Movement 1900-1920: Recent Ideas and New Literature*, Service Centre for Teachers Publication No. 10 (New York: The Macmillan Co., 1958), p. 2.
7. Oscar Theodore Barck Jr. and Nelson Manfred Blake, *Since 1900: A History of the United States in our Times* (Toronto: Collier-Macmillan Canada, 1965), p. 23.
8. Philip Guedalla, ed., *Slings and Arrows: Sayings Chosen from the Speeches of the Right Honourable David Lloyd George* (London: Cassell and Co. Ltd., 1929), p. 128.
9. Martin Gilbert, ed., *Churchill* (Englewood Cliffs, New Jersey: Prentice Hall, 1967), p. 31.
10. T.E. Bottomore, *Critics of Society: Radical Thought in North America* (London: George Allen and Unwin, 1967), p. 53.
11. Ben Tillett, *Memories and Reflections* (London: John Long Ltd., 1931), p. 232.
12. H. Blair Neatby, *William Lyon Mackenzie King* (Toronto: University of Toronto Press, 1963), vol. 2, p. 172.
13. Canadian prime ministers have frequently been lawyers, from John A. Macdonald to Pierre Trudeau. In 1970, the number of M.P.s in the Canadian House of Commons who were listed as lawyers comprised twenty-five per cent of the total membership, and for the Ontario federal contingent the proportion was thirty per cent. (*Canadian Almanac and Directory, 1971*, p. 549). The premiers of Quebec and Ontario are lawyers, as are many provincial representatives sitting in the legislatures. If as was once suggested diplomatic history comprises what one clerk said to another clerk, Canadian history tends to be what one lawyer said to another lawyer.
14. James A. Riedel, ed., *New Perspectives in State and Local Politics* (Walkham, Mass.: Xerox College Publishing, 1971), p. 99.
15. Paul W. Fox, *Politics Canada* (Toronto: McGraw-Hill of Canada, 1970), p. 369.
16. Ian Adams, *The Poverty Wall* (Toronto: McClelland and Stewart Ltd., 1970), p. 66.
17. James A. Riedel, *New Perspectives in State and Local Politics*, p. 78.
18. Ian Adams, *The Poverty Wall*, p. 62.
19. Ibid., p. 73.

389

Suggestions for Further Reading

There are many general history textbooks available in libraries which sometimes touch upon the social scene. A review of the index will usually determine the amount of information available in a specific textbook.

The following source material has been selected so that topics discussed in this book can be explored in more depth. The bibliography contained in each of the listed books can be used as a guide for further research into the topic. The title and place of publication of a book usually indicate the content but where this is not clear, a short descriptive note has been added.

GENERAL SOURCES

Government publications and the news media provide a running commentary upon the social scene and are, therefore, a major source of information about contemporary social issues. Periodicals such as *Current History* (United States) and *Social History* (Canada), along with Britain's *History of the Twentieth Century* (Editor-in-Chief A.J.P. Taylor), frequently contain pertinent articles tracing historical background; professional organizations specializing in one particular subject often have their own periodicals. There follows a selected list of books providing some social background for each country.

CANADA

Brebner, J.B., *North Atlantic Triangle: the Interplay of Canada, the United States and Great Britain*, New Haven, 1945. *Canadian Historical Documents*, 3 vols., Scarborough, Prentice Hall of Canada Ltd.; source material from New France to 1949. Careless, J.M.S. and Brown, R.C. (eds.), *The Canadians 1867-1967*, Toronto, 1967. Lower, A.R.M., *Canadians in the Making*, Toronto, 1958. Morton, W.L. (ed.), *The Canadian Centennial Series*, Toronto, McClelland & Stewart Ltd.; a projected seventeen-volume history of Canada's past with excellent bibliographies in the volumes published so far. Porter, J., *The Vertical Mosaic*, Toronto, 1965; an incisive analysis of Canada's social structure. Wade, M., *The French Canadians 1760-1945*, Toronto, 1955.

BRITAIN

Bruce, M., *The Coming of the Welfare State*, London, 1966; a good survey of social legislation. Cole, G.D.H., *A Short History of the British Working Class Movement*, London, New Edition, 1948. Gilbert, B.B., *British Social Policy 1914-1939*, London, 1970. Graves, R. and Hodge, A., *The Long Week End: A Social History of Great Britain, 1918-1939*, New York, 1941. de Sweinitz, K., *England's Road to Social Security 1349-1947*, Philadelphia, 1943. Quennell, Marjorie and C.B., *A History of Everyday Things in England*, 4 vols., London, 1968. Taylor, A.J.P., *English History 1914-1945*, London, 1965; readable and clear account of recent social conditions. Traill, H.D. and Mann, J.S., *Social England*, 4 vols., London, 1897. Trevelyan, G., *Illustrated Social History*, 4 vols., London, 1949-1952; Chaucer to Victoria.

UNITED STATES

Beard, Charles and Mary, *The Rise of American Civilization*, New York, New Edition 1934. Handlin, O., *The Uprooted: The Epic of the Great Migrations that made the American People*, New York, 1957. Hofstadter, R., *Social Darwinism in American Thought*, Philadelphia, 1944. Morison, S.E. and Commager, H.S., *The Growth of The American Republic*, 2 vols., New York, 1962. Pumphreys, Ralph and Muriel (eds.), *The Heritage of American Social Work*, New York, 1964; readings in philosophical and institutional development, 1601-1937. Woodroofe, K., *From Charity to Social Work in England and the United States*, London, 1962.

SPECIFIC THEMES

CHAPTER 1: POVERTY

Adams, I., *The Poverty Wall*, Toronto, 1970; a view of contemporary Canada. Addams, J., *Forty Years at Hull House*, New York, 1935; an account of a famed settlement house in Chicago. Armstrong, L.V., *We Too Are The People*, Boston: Little, Brown & Co., 1938; administration of relief during the Great Depression. Bremner, R., *From the Depths: the Discovery of Poverty in the United States*, New York, 1964. Harrington, M., *The Other America*, New York, 1962. Lorimer, J. and Manfanwy Phillips, *Working People: Life in a Downtown City Neighbourhood*, Toronto, 1971. Marshall, D., *The English Poor in the Eighteenth Century*, New York, 1969; reprint of 1926 edition. Splane,

R.S., *Social Welfare in Ontario 1791-1893*, Toronto, 1959. Tawnay, R.H., *Poverty as an Industrial Problem*, London, 1913.

CHAPTER 2: TRADE UNIONS AND UNEMPLOYMENT

Bullock, A., *The Life and Times of Ernest Bevin*, 2 vols., London, 1960-1967. J. Commons (ed.), *History of Labor in the United States*, New York, 1918-1935. Forsey, E., "History of the Labour Movement in Canada," *Canada Year Book*, 1967. Josephson, M., *The Robber Barons*, New York, 1934. Lipton, C., *The Trade Union Movement of Canada 1827-1959*, Montreal, 1968. Logan, H.A., *Trade Unions in Canada*, Toronto, 1948. Masters, D., *The Winnipeg General Strike*, Toronto, 1950. Millis, H. and Brown, E., *From The Wagner Act to Taft-Hartley*, Chicago, 1950. Pelling, H., *A History of British Trade Unionism*, London, 1963. Thompson, E.P., *The Making of the English Working Class*, London, 1963. Spargo, J., *The Bitter Cry of The Children*, New York, 1969; re-issue of original 1904 edition. Webb, Sidney and Beatrice, *The History of Trade Unionism*, New Edition, 1920.

CHAPTER 3: MEDICINE, HEALTH AND INSURANCE

Abel-Smith, B., *History of the Nursing Profession*, London, 1960. Abel-Smith, B., *The Hospitals 1800-1948*, London, 1964. American Public Health Association, *Medical Care in Transition*, 2 vols., Washington, D.C., 1964; reprints from *American Journal of Public Health* 1949-1962. Beveridge, W.H., *Voluntary Action: A Report on the Methods of Social Advance*, London, 1948. Brockington, C.F., *A Short History of Public Health*, Second Edition, London, 1966. Finer, S.E., *The Life and Times of Sir Edwin Chadwick*, London, 1952. Flinn, M.W., *Public Health Reform in Britain*, London, 1968. Frazer, W.M., *A History of English Public Health 1834-1939*, London, 1950. Gibbon, J.M., *Three Centuries of Canadian Nursing*, Toronto, 1947. Lindsey, A., *Socialized Medicine in England and Wales: The National Health Service, 1948-1961*, University of North Carolina, 1962. Lewis, R.A., *Edwin Chadwick and the Public Health Movement, 1830-1856*, London, 1952. MacDermot, H.E., *History of the Canadian Medical Association*, 2 vols., Toronto, 1935-1938. Newman, G., *The Building of A Nation's Health*, London, 1939. Roberts, M.M., *American Nursing: History and Interpretation*, New York, 1955. Simon, J., *English Sanitary Institutions*, London, 1897. Titmuss, R.M., *Essays on the Welfare State*, New Haven, 1959.

CHAPTER 4: HOUSING AND THE DEVELOPMENT OF CITIES

Abercrombie, P., *Town and Country Planning*, London, 1967. Bellan, Ruben C., *The Evolving City*, Toronto, 1971. Bellush, J. and Hausknecht, M., *Urban Renewal: People, Politics and Planning*, New York, 1967; a reader about the current American scene. Cramond, R.D., *Housing Policy in Scotland, 1919-1964*, Glasgow, 1966. Dewsnup, E.R., *The Housing Problem in England*, Manchester, 1907. George, H., *Progress and Poverty*, New York, 1911; a classic that outlines the single tax idea of Henry George for financing civic improvements. Glaab, C.N., *The American City, A Documentary History*, Homewood, 1963. Glaab, C.N. and Brown, A.T., *A History of Urban America*, Toronto, 1967. Hill, O., *Homes of the London Poor*, London, 1875; a revealing study by a leading pioneer in housing reform. Howard, E., *Garden City of Tomorrow*, London, 1965; a reissue of the classic suggesting green belt towns. Lowe, J.R., *Cities in a Race With Time*, New York, 1967; examines American renewal programmes. Mumford, L., *The City in History*, New York, 1967; a cultural approach. Norwich Union Insurance Group, *The Norwich Plan*; booklet available from Toronto Head Office. Queen's Printer, *Report of the Federal Task Force on Housing and Urban Development*, Ottawa, 1969. Riis, J.A., *How the Other Half Lives*, New York, 1890; a graphic description of New York. Wendt, P.F., *Housing Policy: The Search for Solutions*, Berkeley, 1963; useful statistics.

CHAPTER 5: WETS AND DRYS AND THE DEMON RUM

Two indispensable works are: Sinclair, A., *Era of Excess: A Social History of the Prohibition Movement*, New York, 1962; Alcoholism Research Foundation, *Statistics of Alcohol Use and Alcoholism in Canada: 1871-1956*, Toronto, 1958.

Other sources include: Alford, S.E., *Habitual Drunkards Act of 1879*, London; a paper read before the Social Science Association, February 2, 1880. Carter, H., *Control of the Drink Trade in Britain*, London, 1919. Fisher, I., *The Noble Experiment*, New York, 1930. Harrison, B. and Trinder, B., "Drink and Sobriety in an Early Victorian Town: Banbury 1830-1860," *The English Historical Review*, Supplement 4, 1969. Hose, R.E., *Prohibition or Control? Canada's Experience with the Liquor Problem*, Toronto, 1928. Shadwell, A., *Drink In 1914-1922*, London, 1923. Spence, R.E., *Prohibition in Canada*, Toronto, 1919; a useful outline of the activity of the Dominion Alliance. Stephenson, J.A., *Before the Bar*, Toronto, 1919; an attempt to balance the pros and cons of prohibition.

CHAPTER 6: RELIGION, SECULARISM AND SOCIAL POLICY

Allen, Richard, *The Social Passion: Religion and Social Reform in Canada, 1914-1928*, Toronto, 1971. Bradlaugh, Charles, *Humanity's Gain From Unbelief and Other Selections from the Works of Charles Bradlaugh*, London, 1930. Clark, S.D., *Church and Sect in Canada*, Toronto, 1948. Crysdale, R.C. Stewart, *The Industrial Struggle and Protestant Ethics in Canada*, Toronto, 1961. Commons, J.R., *Social Reform and the Church*, New York, 1894. Handy, R.T., *The Social Gospel in America 1870-1920*, New York, 1966. Holyoake, G.J., *Hostile and Generous Toleration*, London, 1886. Inglis, K.S., *Churches and the Working Classes in Victorian England*, Toronto, 1963. May, H., *Protestant Churches and Industrial America*, New York, 1949. Moir, J., *Church and State in Canada West*, Toronto, 1959. McNaught, K. *A Prophet in Politics* (J.S. Woodsworth), Toronto, 1967. Silcox, E., *Church Union in Canada*, New York, 1933; describes the 1925 union. Warner, W.J., *The Wesley Movement in the Industrial Revolution*, London, 1930. Wearmouth, R.E., *Methodism and the Working Class Movements, 1800-1850*, London, 1937. Wickham, E.R., *Church and People in an Industrial City*, London, 1957; an account of an industrial parish in Sheffield, England.

CHAPTER 7: EDUCATION

Armytage, W.H.G., *Civic Universities: Aspects of a British Tradition*, London, 1955. Burgess, T., *A Guide to English Schools,* Pelican Book A690. Conant, J., *The American High School Today*, New York, 1959. Cotgrove, S.T., *Technical Education and Social Change*, London, 1958. Curtis, S.J. and Boltwood, M.E., *A Short History of Educational Ideas*, London, 1966. Dewey, J., *The Child and the Curriculum* and *The School and Society*, Chicago, 1956; a reissue of the fundamental teachings of the main proponent of Progressivism. Ferguson, E., *Newcomers and New Learning*, Toronto, 1966; a study of immigrant groups in Toronto under the auspices of The International Institute of Metropolitan Toronto. Hodgins, J.C., *Documentary History of Education in Upper Canada from the Passing of the Constitutional Act of 1791 to the close of Reverend Dr. Ryerson's Administration of the Education Department in 1876*, 28 vols., Toronto, 1894-1910. Johnson, F.H., *A Brief History of Canadian Education*, Toronto, 1968; covers the full range from New France to the current scene. Katz, M., *The Irony of Early School Reform*, Cambridge, Massachusetts, 1968; describes the orientation of Massachusett's system towards the middle class. Kelly, T., *A History of Adult Education in Great Britain*, Liverpool, 1962. Medsker, L.L., *The Junior College*, New York, 1960. Neatby, H., *So*

Little for the Mind, Toronto, 1967; a reissue of an incisive analysis of the school curriculum in Canada by a university historian. Ontario Department of Education, *Colleges of Applied Arts and Technology: Basic Documents*, Toronto, 1967; the political framework for the colleges serving economic and social needs. Ontario Institute for Studies in Education, *What Culture? What Heritage?*, Toronto, 1969; a summary of a nationwide survey of the teaching of Canadian history. Smith, W.O. Lester, *Education in Great Britain*, London, 1967.

Histories of individual universities or colleges are often available, and can be discovered by an enquiry to the librarian of the institution concerned.

CHAPTER 8: LAW AND ORDER

Chapman, S.G. (ed.), *The Police Heritage in England and America*, East Lansing, 1962; a useful survey. Glaser, D. (ed.), *Crime in the City*, New York, 1970; a reader on aspects of urban crime. Howard, D.L., *The English Prisons: Their Past and Their Future*, London, 1960. Katzenbach, Nicholas deB., *A Report of the President's Commission on Law Enforcement and The Administration of Justice*, Washington, 1968. Klein, H.T., *The Police: Damned if they Do—Damned if they Don't*, New York, 1968; reminiscences of a former police lieutenant in New York City. Marshall, A., *Police and Government*, London, 1967. McClintock, F.H., *Crimes of Violence: An Enquiry by the Cambridge Institute of Criminology into Crimes of Violence Against the Person*, London, 1963. Mill, J.S., *On Liberty*; a classic nineteenth-century philosophical treatise on the meaning of liberty. Reith, C., *A New Study of Police History*, Edinburgh, 1956. Robson, R., *The Attorney in Eighteenth Century England*, Cambridge, 1959. Tobias, J.J., *Crime and Industrial Society in the 19th Century*, London, 1967. Tunley, R., *Kids, Crime and Chaos*, New York, 1962.

CHAPTER 9: THE POLITICS OF REFORM

Creighton, D.G., *John A. Macdonald*, 2 vols., Toronto, 1955-1956; an outstanding biography of Canada's first prime minister who formulated many of the political rules. Ferns, H.S. and Ostry, B., *The Age of Mackenzie King: The Rise of the Leader*, London, 1955; a well-documented critical account of the rise to power of Canada's longest serving prime minister. Gilbert, M. (ed.), *Churchill*, Englewood Cliffs, New Jersey, 1967; a popular reader by the official biographer of Sir Winston Churchill. Gilbert, M. (ed.), *Lloyd George*, Englewood Cliffs, New Jersey, 1968. Hovell, M., *The Chartist Movement*, Manchester, 1925. Jackman, S.W. (ed.), *The English Reform Tradition 1790-1910*,

Englewood Cliffs, New Jersey, 1965. Josephson, M., *The President Makers 1896-1917*, New York, 1940. King, Martin Luther, *Why We Can't Wait*, New York, 1964. Link, A., *Road to the White House*, Princeton, 1947; the rise of Woodrow Wilson. Lorimer, J., *The Real World of City Politics*, Toronto, 1969. Magnus, P., *Gladstone*, London, 1954. McGinnis, J., *The Selling of the President*, New York, 1970; a revealing account of the campaign of Richard Nixon. Morrison, H., *An Autobiography*, London, 1960; political life of a Labour politician who went from municipal politics to the Cabinet. Mowry, G.E., *The Era of Theodore Roosevelt*, 1900-1912, New York, 1958. McNaught, K., *A Prophet in Politics* (J.S. Woodsworth), Toronto, 1967. Namier, L.B., *Monarchy and the Party System*, Oxford, 1952. Newman, P., *Renegade in Power–The Diefenbaker Years*, Toronto, 1964. Plumb, J.H., *Sir Robert Walpole*, 2 vols., 1956-1961. Rozwenc, E., *The New Deal: Revolution or Evolution*, Boston, revised ed. 1959. Reidel, J.A. (ed.), *New Perspectives in State and Local Politics*, Waltham, 1971; a reader on recent political trends in the United States. Smith, P. *Disraelian Conservatism and Social Reform*, London, 1967. Steffens, L., *The Shame of the Cities*, New York, 1948; a reissue of a classic indictment of corruption in American municipalities.

Index

Drapeau, Jean (mayor), 384
Drew, George, 239
Dunkin, Christopher, 204
Duplessis, Maurice, 77-78, 79, 308, 351, 382

Ecclesiastical Corporations Act of 1853, 18
Economic Opportunity, U.S. Office of, 33-34, 35, 385
Education, elementary, in Britain, Act of 1870, 287; Act of 1944, 268; under poor law, 278-279; for secondary *see* schools; technical, in Britain, 278, 289-290, 305, 307; in Canada, 270, 294-295, 296, 302, 307-308, 316-317, 318, 322-323. *See also* schools, colleges and universities
Educationalese, 327
Eighteenth Amendment, U.S.A., 225-226, 234, 346, 349
Eisenhower, Dwight D., 118, 171, 309, 310
Eleven Plus test, England, 300, 304-305, 307, 312, 313
Elizabeth I (queen of England), 9, 88, 130, 331
Employers and Workmens Act of 1875, 48
Engels, Friedrich, 137, 245, 252
Episcopalians. *See* Anglicans
Evangelicals, 246, 247

Fabians, 111. *See also* G.B. Shaw, Beatrice and Sidney Webb, H.G. Wells
Factory Acts, of 1833, 43, 91, 278-279; of 1840's, 43, 281; of 1874 (U.S.A.), 43; of 1878, 246; of 1880's, Canada, 53
Fair Deal, 169
Fair Labor Standards Act (U.S.A.), 72, 302
Family Allowances, 83
Federal Bureau of Investigation (FBI), 344, 345, 347, 349, 352, 353, 355
Federal Emergency Relief Act of 1933 (U.S.A.), 29

Federal Family Allowances Act of 1944, 32
Federal Housing Administration (FHA), U.S.A., 161-162, 173, 186
Federal Task Force on Housing (Hellyer Report), 186-187, 189
Fielding, Henry and John, 332
Fisher, H.A.L., 295-296, 300, 306
Ford, Henry, 82, 227, 297
Fourteenth Amendment, U.S.A., 50, 340, 341
Fredericton, 310
Freedmen's Associations, 285
Friendly Societies, 103-104, 107, 116

Galbraith, John Kenneth, 33
Garden city, 152-154, 156, 163-164, 181
General strike, in Britain, planned for in 1914, 61; of 1926, 66-67, 349. *See also* Winnipeg General Strike
George, Henry, 152, 167, 189
Gin drinking, in England, 195-196
Gladden, Washington, 20, 255, 260
Gladstone, William E., 48, 207-208, 367-370, 374, 376
Gompers, Samuel, 49, 50, 59, 232

Habitual Drunkards Act of 1879, 212
Hadow, Henry, 300-301, 303, 306
Halifax, N.S., 42, 133, 294
Hamilton, Ont., 46, 148, 184
Hanna, "Boss" Mark, 371
Hardie, J. Keir, 261, 376
Harding, Warren G., 228
Harrington, Michael, 33, 34
Haymarket Incident, Chicago, 51
Headstart programme, 320
Health Insurance, Britain, Act of 1911, 107-109; Canada, 117; U.S.A., 118-119
Hellyer, Paul. *See* Federal Task Force on Housing
Henry VIII (king of England), 8, 86, 88, 102
Hepburn, Mitchell, 72, 236, 351
Hill, Octavia, 142-143
History, of Canada, dryness of, 203; made by lawyers, 389 n.13; and

status, 301; of U.S.A., chamber of commerce style, 147; in 1920's, 298; influence of Turner thesis, 189 n.3; teaching of, 1, 291, 292, 328 n.4

Hitler, Adolf, 30, 165, 304, 322, 328 n.6, 381

Hoffa, James, 78

Holyoake, George, 251, 252

Homeopaths, 97, 104

Homestead Act of 1862, U.S.A., 141

Homestead steel strike, 55

Hoover, Herbert, 161, 233, 234, 235, 347, 379

Hoover, J. Edgar, 347, 349. *Also see* FBI

Hospitals, in Britain, 86, 89, 98, 102, 115; in Canada, 90, 117; in New France, 8, 88; in U.S.A., 89, 114, 117

House of Correction, 10

House of Industry, 17

House of Refuge, Ontario, Act of 1890, 20

Housing Acts, in North America, of 1937 (U.S.), 162; of Canada, 162, 166, 169, 171, 175, 177. For Britain *see* Addison, Chamberlain, N. and Wheatley

Housing, Maritimes, 159; Ontario (1913), 150; public, in U.S.A., 161-164, 172-174; in Canada, 167, 175-178, 186, 187; in Scotland, 155-156, 158-159, 165, 168-169; Tudor meaning of, 144; zoning regulations, 151, 160, 161

Howard, Ebenezer, 152-154, 163, 180

Hughes, Sir Sam, 220, 221

Hull House, 21

Indians, of Canada, 34, 105, 195, 248, 337; of U.S.A., 242, 249, 339

Irish National Textbooks, 280, 282

Jacksonian Democracy, 365

Jacobs, Jane, 180, 354

Jews, in Canada, 259, 294; in U.S.A., 151, 256, 343; and Hitler, 322, 352; and Ku Klux Klan, 346

John XXIII (pope), 268

Johnson, Lyndon B., and crime, 358; and education, 319; and housing, 174; leadership of, 384; and medicare, 118; on poverty, 33-34

Judges, in U.S.A., 54, 355, 358-359

Justices of the Peace, 9, 87, 193

Kelso, J.J., 22-23

Kennedy, John F., 33, 178, 179, 270, 333

Kennedy, Robert, 78, 333

Kerner Report. *See* presidential advisory commission on civil disorders

Ketchum, Jesse, 200, 277

Keynes, John Maynard, 379

King, Mackenzie, W.L., Byng affair, 229, 231; and education, 294; friend of J.D. Rockefeller, Jr., 260, 377; labour expert, 59, 60; and liquor, 229, 231, 236-237; and national unity, 301, 377, 378; retirement and accomplishments, 381-382; and unemployment insurance, 76

King, Martin Luther, 258, 333

Kingsley, Charles, 252, 267

Kingston, city of, 244

Knights of Labour, 49, 50-51

Ku Klux Klan, 233, 298, 340, 346

Labour Management Relations Act (Taft-Hartley), 76-77

Labour Reform Act of 1959, U.S.A., 78

Labourers, Statute of (1351), 7, 82

Lafontaine, Sir Louis Hippolyte, 366

Land sales, grid pattern, Canada, 141; U.S.A., 132, 134; homesteading, Canada, 141-142; U.S.A. 141

Laurier, Sir Wilfrid, on arbitration, 60; boom years of, 61; and education, 257, 294; and Joseph Chamberlain, 143; and national unity, 371, 378; and prohibition, 217

Laval, Francois de Montmorency, (bishop), 195

Law of Settlement of 1662, 11

Lawyers, in Canadian politics, 382, 389 n.13

Leacock, Stephen, 227
Legal Aid, 359-361
L'Enfant, Pierre, 133
Leo XIII (pope), 57
Lewis, John L., 71
Lewis, Stephen, 80
Liberal party, in Britain, formation of, 316
Life insurance, Britain, 103-104, 116
Lincoln, Abraham, 205, 340, 366, 372
Liquor, attitudes towards, of Anglicans, 196, 197, 200, 202, 205, 208, 212, 214, 238; of Baptists, 199, 214; of Congregationalists, 199, 214; of Jews, 214; of Methodists, 196, 197, 199, 200, 202, 214, 217; of Presbyterians, 199, 214; of Nonconformists, 202, 204, 208; of Roman Catholics, 197, 214, 218, 238; of United Church of Canada, 239
Liquor Licencing Acts, in the Canadas (1845), 201; Canada Temperance Act, 210, 213, 215, 216, 222; in England, of 1552, 193; of 1872, 207; of 1891, 217; of 1904, 218; in New England, of 1647, 194; in New France, 195; in Nova Scotia, 203; in Ontario, of 1884, 213. *See also* prohibition
Liquor sales, under provincial control, 229, 235
Lister, Joseph, 101
Lloyd George, David, 66, 345, 383; reforms after 1906, 25-26, 30, 107, 109, 113, 374-375; on liquor, 220, 221-222, 225; reforms after 1918, 110, 157, 295
Local Government Act of 1929, 28
Local Government Board, 102
London, Ontario, 46, 134
Lowe, Robert, 287
Lundberg, Felix, 34
Lynch law, 341

McCoy, William, 234
Macdonald, Sir John A., 120; and liquor legislation, 213; on national policy, 51, 120, 370, 371, 378; starts North West Mounted Police, 337; passes trade union legislation, 49
Macdonald movement in Canadian education, 292-293
McGuffy readers, 211, 285, 310
MacInnis, Grace, 388
Mackenzie, Alexander, 210
Mackenzie, William Lyon, 182, 277, 365
MacMurchy, Archibald, 288
Madry, Jean, 88
Malthus, Thomas, 13
Mance, Jeanne, 88
Manchester, England, 91, 136, 137, 141, 245
Mann, Horace, 277-278, 284-285
Manpower training, 35
Marsh report, 32
Marxism, attempts to christianize, 252, 259, 267; and the Fabians, 375, 379; rediscovery during the depression, 69, 302-303, 322, 379. *See also* Bolshevism
Massey Commission Report, 308, 311
Meany, George, 78
Medical Acts, of Britain (1858), 101; of Canada, 90, 101, 104
Medicare, Canada, 117-118, 120 foll.; U.S.A., 118
Meighen, Arthur, 64, 229
Methodists, 43, 243-244, 245, 246; in the Canadas, 250; in Nova Scotia, 244. *See also* church union, liquor and social justice
Midwifery, 87, 105
Military medical services, 89-90, 98-99, 104, 109, 115; in the Canadas, 90. *See also* Royal Navy
Mill, John Stuart, 388
Mines Act of 1842, 44
Monitorial system of education, 275, 276
Montreal, 46, 132, 149
Morgan, J.P., 109, 372-373
Morley, John, 217
Morley, Samuel, 204
Morrill Land Grant Act, 291
Mothers Allowance, 27-28

Mountain, Jacob (bishop), 275
Mowat, Sir Oliver, 213, 215-217
Mumford, Lewis, 141
Municipal Corporations Act of 1835, Britain, 137, 365
Murder, origin of term, 330

Nation, Carry A., 214
National Crime Commission in U.S.A. (1967), 358-359
National Health Act of 1946, Britain, 114, 116, 124, 381
National Industrial Recovery Act (NRA), 70
National Insurance Act (1911), 26, 27, 107-109, 111, 125
Naval medicine, 90-91, 99
Neatby, Hilda, 309, 312
Negroes, in North America, 7, 33; and civil rights, 340-341; and education, in Canada, 282; in U.S.A., 285, 292, 319, 320; and housing, in U.S.A., 146, 150, 163, 171, 172, 173, 179-180; and police, 353; and temperance, 206, 233. *See also* Ku Klux Klan and Martin Luther King
New Brunswick, and temperance, 199-200
New Canadians, 182
New Deal, 29-30, 65, 161-164
New Democratic Party (NDP), 79-80, 125, 383
New France, social aspects of, 8
New Freedom, of Woodrow Wilson, 374
New Model craft unions, in Britain, 46 foll.
New York City, bustle in 1830's, 138; Central Park, 140; cultural assimilation, 145-146, 150, 353; Penn station, 151; planning, 134, 159; tenements, 145-147, 354. *See also* police
Nixon, Richard M., 239-240, 386
Nonconformists, 94, 245, 257, 276, 281
Norwood Committee (1943), 305
North West Mounted Police. *See* RCMP
Nova Scotia, anti-union (1816), 42;

temperance, 199
Nursing, 88-89, 98; and Florence Nightingale, 99, 105; organization of, 106

One Big Union (OBU), 63
Ontario Labour Relations Board, 75
Osteopaths, 104
Owen, Robert, 44, 250
Oxford. *See* universities

Padlock law in Quebec, 351
Palmer raids, 345-346
Parent Commission, 318
Parker Medical Act (1865), 101
Paternalism, 148, 243, 282, 367
Pearson, Lester Bowles, 120, 323, 383
Peel, Sir Robert, 335
Pendleton, Civil Service Reform, U.S.A., 375-376
Penn, William, 132, 133
Pensions, old age (1908), 25; Canada, 25, 32, 83, 382; veterans', 32
Peterloo, massacre of, 42, 334
Philadelphia, 42, 132, 133, 150, 172
Pilgrim Fathers, 88, 242
Pinkerton Detective Agency, 55, 342
Platt, "Boss" Tom, 371, 373
Plessy versus Ferguson, 292
Police, British, 334-335, 335, 348, 349, 357; Canadian, 72, 335, 337-338, 344, 351, 356; in U.S.A., 336-337, 348, 349, 354-355, 355-356, 359. *See also* FBI, RCMP and Scotland Yard
Political bosses in U.S.A., 371, 372, 373
Pollution, air, 126-128, 153, 251; water, 87, 102, 103, 126, 128
Polytechnic Institute, 290
Poor Law, of 1601, 4, 9, 38 n.2; adoption of in Maritimes, 10, 18; not adopted in Upper Canada, 16-17; of 1834, 14-16, 278, 279; absence of in Canadian West, 18; repeal in Britain, 31; repeal in Nova Scotia, 33. *See also* Speenhamland system
Poor Law, Royal Commissions, of

1832, 13-14; of 1905, 24-25
Poor, provision for in Upper Canada, 18
Poor, Statute for the relief of (1536), 8
Port Sunlight, 144, 153
Presbyterians, in Canada, 244, 245, 248, 249, 250, 265, 283. *See also* MacMurchy
Presidential Advisory Commission on Civil Disorders, 179, 353
Prisons, in Britain, 333, 335; Ontario Royal Commission on, in 1891, 19
Progressive movement, in U.S.A., 371-372, 374
Progressive party of 1920's, 229, 378
Progressivism, in education, 296-299, 300, 302; reaction against, 305-306, 309-310, 310-311, 312
Prohibition, in Alberta of 1916, 223; in Canada of 1917, 225-226; repeal by Canadian provinces, 229; in New Brunswick (1855), 203; party of, 206, 213, 214; in Saskatchewan of 1915, 222; in United States, 225-226, 233, 234, 236
Public Health Act of 1875, Britain, 102
Public houses, Britain, 207-208, 218, 222, 231, 237
Public housing. *See* housing
Pullman Strike, 54, 148
Pure Food and Drug Acts, in Britain, 102; in U.S.A., 106, 115, 372
Puritanism, 193-194, 205, 218, 245, 271, 274, 331, 343

Quebec City, 46, 132, 284
Quebec Revenue Act of 1774, 197-198

Rand formula, 77
Rauschenbusch, Walter, 258-259
Regulation 17, about teaching French in Ontario, 261-262
Report on the Sanitary Conditions of the Labouring Classes of Great Britain (1842), 92
Republic Steel, massacre at (1937), 47

Reuther, Walter, 72
Ricardo, David, 12
Riis, Jacob, 24, 145-146
Robber Barons, 147, 371, 373
Robbins Report, on higher education, 313-314
Robin Hood concept, 4-5, 35
Rockefeller, John D., 260, 341
Rockefeller, John D., Jr., 235, 260
Roman Catholics, in Britain, 245; in Canada, 248, 249, 257, 260, 265, 268, 270, 274. *See also* separate schools; in U.S.A., 247-248, 270, 343, 346. *See also* liquor
Roosevelt, Franklin Delano, and housing, 162-164, 166; promotes New Deal, 29, 56, 69, 379; repeals prohibition, 235-236; on unions, 40, 74
Roosevelt, Theodore, 106, 146, 371-372, 372-373
Rowell—Sirois Report, 380
Rowntree, Seebohm, 24
Royal Canadian Mounted Police (RCMP), and Bolshevism, 344; in Klondike, 342; and labour, 62-63, 64, 77, 345, 350, 351; organization of, 356; prestige of, 337, 342, 349-350
Royal College of Physicians and Surgeons, of Canada, 111
Royal Navy, medical facilities in, 90-91, 99, 109; revolts in, 41, 68
Rum row, 228
Ryerson, Egerton, 249, 279-280, 286, 288; on separate schools, 283, 284; and temperance, 200
Ryerson Institute of Technology, 308

St. John, N.B., 46, 200, 203, 210
Salvation Army, 253-255, 268
Saskatoon, 184
School, arrangements for medicine and feeding, Britain, 106, 111
Schools, common, 249, 276, 280-281, 282, 283, 284, 287. *See also* monitorial system; continuation, 296; council, 295; collegiate, 288, 289, 293; collèges classiques, 318; com-